Tagore in 1936, at the age of seventy-five

RABINDRANATH TAGORE

A BIOGRAPHY

KRISHNA KRIPALANI

LONDON
OXFORD UNIVERSITY PRESS
NEW YORK BOMBAY TORONTO

1962

Oxford University Press, Amen House, London, E.C.4

GLASGOW NEW YORK TORONTO MELBOURNE WELLINGTON
BOMBAY CALCUTTA MADRAS KARACHI LAHORE DACCA
CAPE TOWN SALISBURY NAIROBI IBADAN ACCRA
KUALA LUMPUR HONG KONG

*Printed in Great Britain by
Taylor Garnett Evans & Co. Ltd,
Watford, Herts*

TO

NANDITA

ACKNOWLEDGEMENTS

The Author's grateful acknowledgements are due to the late Rathindranath Tagore for his encouragement and permission to quote freely from his father's writings and from his own; to the authorities of Visva-Bharati and Rabindra Sadana, Santiniketan, for their courtesy and co-operation; to Victoria Ocampo and Leonard Elmhirst for sharing their reminiscences of Tagore; to Pulinbihari Sen for his learned co-operation in preparing the bibliography and to Kshitis Roy for many helpful suggestions; and to Balu Rao and D. S. Rao for their valued assistance in the preparation of the copy and Index as well as in proof-reading.

CONTENTS

ILLUSTRATIONS

INTRODUCTION

In the hundred years that have passed since Rabindranath Tagore was born, the face of India has undergone such radical changes as no optimist living in 1861 could have envisaged. But even more remarkable are the changes that have taken place in the mind and spirit of modern India of which the transformation in outward appearance is but a partial reflection. It is as though a tired and over-timid pony which needed a lash to move at all has turned into a spirited charger that has to be tightly reined in to hold it back from running too fast.

In 1861 when Tagore was born India lay prostrate at the feet of the British. The foreign traders had been firmly entrenched as rulers and the British Queen had been proclaimed the Empress of India. It seemed to be taken for granted that this bright jewel would continue to shed lustre on the imperial crown for ever. That the rulers should think so is understandable. What is of significance is the remarkable fact that many Indians shared this faith and welcomed it. The eighteenth century in India had been the dark age of misrule and internal wars, a jungle in which the beasts of prey, native and foreign, roamed and ravaged at will, so that when in the end some kind of law and order was established over the whole realm, the people in general were primarily conscious, not of the subtle tragedy that India had lost her freedom but of the simple and concrete fact that they could at last breathe in peace. After the menace of the jungle the peace of the desert seemed a blessing.

The great mutiny of 1857 had been ruthlessly quelled and the ancient ruling classes had been either wiped out or lay cringing in the dust. A new class, a mixed middle class, with new interests and new education was on the rise, sedulously fostered under the patronage of the new regime. It is unfair to dub this rising class as the Quislings, for not they but the previous rulers had betrayed the interests of the country. This new class was in fact to become the vanguard of India's new destiny. But this awareness of a new destiny was to come later.

The outstanding feature of the intellectual and spiritual climate of the period which preceded Tagore's birth is the fact that Indians were enjoying the peace of the desert. India had ceased to be creative. Politically she was hardly aware of the loss of national freedom, and culturally she hugged the trappings of the new servitude or blindly clung to the shackles of the old. A few solitary incongruities apart, it was an age of toadies and of reactionaries, those who aped the Western ways and those who sought consolation in the bondage of immemorial tradition and dogma.

Eighty years later, when Tagore died, the face of India had been transformed. Politically she was on the eve of an adventure un-paralleled in her history, culturally she had recovered her self-respect and spiritually she was discovering the hidden springs of creative life. It is not without significance that Mr. Nehru named his book in which he surveyed his country's heritage *The Discovery of India*. We have all had to discover India—to recover it. We are still doing so. This in itself was a revolution, perhaps the only true revolution— to discover oneself. The rest were mere concomitants.

A multitude of forces and factors were responsible for this trans-formation, not the least of which was what happened in the rest of the world and its impact on India. But forces, whether in nature or in the world of men, are in themselves blind and unless harnessed and directed by individuals might prove more destructive than creative. Among individuals who made these forces creative in shaping the destiny of India, two stand out as pre-eminent, Gandhi and Tagore. The contribution of Gandhi is too obvious to need telling; that of Tagore was subtler and deeper, for it released and fed the hidden fountains of creative activity in fields which the politician is powerless to exploit.

Though Tagore was essentially a poet, he was much more than a mere poet in the Western sense of the term, as Gandhi was more than a mere politician or patriot. He was a poet in the traditional Indian sense of the word, *kavi*, a seer, an intermediary between the human and the divine. His genius enriched whatever it touched. Like the sun after which he was named (*rabi* in Bengali, derived from Sanskrit *ravi*, means the sun), he shed light and warmth on his age, vitalized the mental and moral soil of his land, revealed unknown horizons of thought and spanned the arch that divides the east from the west. To those who have access to the language in which he wrote the vitality of his genius is truly amazing. No less amazing are the variety and beauty of the literary forms he created. He gave to his people in one lifetime what normally takes centuries to evolve—a language capable of expressing the finest modulations of thought and feeling, a literature worthy to be taught in any university in the world. There is hardly a field of literary activity which was not explored and made fruitful by his daring adventures, and many of these were virgin fields in Bengali which his hands were the first to stir into life. He is one of the world's few writers whose works—in his own language—withstand the severest tests of great literature, eastern or western, ancient or modern.

Among modern writers he is unique in that while the sophisticated Bengali intellectuals delight in his verse and prose and learned professors write volumes on them, the simple unlettered folk in the congested lanes of Calcutta or in the remote villages of Bengal sing his songs with rapture. Mr. Ernest Rhys has related[1] the experience of Mr. Edwin Montagu (who later became Secretary of State for India) during his travels in India. Once when riding through an Indian forest at night, Mr. Montagu came upon a clearing and found a few men sitting round a fire. He too dismounted and joined the group and sat listening to their songs. Soon after, a poor-looking boy came out of the forest and joined the group. When his turn came, the boy sang 'a song more beautiful in words and music than the rest.' When asked whose song it was, he replied that he did not know: 'They were singing these songs everywhere.' Later on Mr. Montagu heard the same song '. . . in a very different place, and when he asked for the name of the maker of the song he heard for the first time the name of Rabindranath Tagore.'

[1] *Rabindranath Tagore: A Biographical Study* by Ernest Rhys. Macmillan & Co. London, 1917.

This was many years ago, before Tagore received the Nobel Prize. Today this experience would be more common. And no wonder; for each change of the season, each aspect of his country's rich landscape, every undulation of the human heart, in sorrow or in joy, has found its voice in some song of his. They are sung in religious gatherings no less than in concert halls. Patriots have mounted the gallows with his song on their lips; and young lovers unable to express the depth of their feeling sing his songs and feel the weight of their dumbness relieved.

All this, however, is true mainly for those in whose language he wrote and composed. Those who read him in translations only can have little conception either of the scope or the quality of his genius.[2] Unfortunately, his own language Bengali is only one of the many in India, so that even in his own country the majority of the people have access to his writings in translation only. To them, apart from what they can so receive, Tagore's main significance lies in the impulse and direction he gave to the course of India's cultural and moral development, and in the example he presented of a genius passionately devoted to his art and no less passionately dedicated to the service of his people and of humanity in general. He gave them faith in their own language and in their cultural and intellectual heritage. The contemporary renaissance in Indian languages is due largely to his inspiration and example. Nor was the renaissance confined to the languages and their literatures. His many-sided genius and his almost missionary zeal for the development of the Indian arts, whether it be dancing or music or painting or the handicrafts, his appreciation of the indigenous folk arts and his fostering of both the classical and the folk traditions in his School at Santiniketan provided a stimulus and a prestige to these arts which has enabled them to survive and to flower.

What is even more remarkable is the fact that he who taught his people to cherish and take pride in their own heritage also gave them the courage and the example to break the fetters of tradition. Trying always to conform to a conventional type, he warned, is a sign of immaturity. Only in babies is individuality of physiognomy blurred, their babbling sounds similar everywhere. The adult must

[2] As Robert Frost has well put it, 'Poetry is what gets lost in translation.'

cultivate and assert his personality, must outgrow the fixed pattern and respond to the stimulus from outside, no matter from where it comes.

'When in the name of Indian art we cultivate with deliberate aggressiveness a certain bigotry born of the habit of a past generation, we smother our soul under idiosyncrasies unearthed from past centuries. These are like masks with exaggerated grimaces that fail to respond to the ever changing play of life. Art is not a gorgeous sepulchre, immovably brooding over a lonely eternity of vanished years. It belongs to the procession of life, making constant adjustment with surprises, exploring unknown shrines of reality along its path of pilgrimage to a future, which is as different from the past as the tree from the seed.'[3]

The basic and most robust characteristic of Tagore's philosophy of life was his emphasis on the development of the human personality and his deep-set conviction that there is no inherent contradiction between the claims of the so-called opposites—the flesh and the spirit, the human and the divine, love of life and love of God, joy in beauty and pursuit of truth, social obligation and individual rights, respect for tradition and the freedom to experiment, love of one's people and faith in the unity of mankind. These seeming opposites can and must be reconciled, not by tentative compromises and timid vacillation but by building a true harmony out of the apparent discordance. This faith runs through all his poetry in a thousand echoes. Take the following from the English *Gitanjali*:

Thou art the sky and thou art the nest as well.

The same stream of life that runs through my veins night and day runs through the world and dances in rhythmic measures.

When I go from hence let this be my parting word, that what I have seen is unsurpassable.

[3] *Art and Tradition* by Rabindranath Tagore, published in the *Visva-Bharati Quarterly*, May 1935.

> In this playhouse of infinite forms I have had my
> play and here have I caught sight of him that is
> formless.

The religious, moral, aesthetic and intellectual aspects of Tagore's own personality were so well developed and matched that of no one was it more true than of him that he saw life steadily and saw it whole.

There is a tendency to lopsidedness in our Indian character. We are inclined to overvalue certain aspects or ways of living at the expense of other aspects. In our religious zeal we are tempted to repudiate altogether the ties that bind us to the earth. In order to attain peace of mind we frown on the very joy of life. In their exaggerated regard for the purity of race and social stability, our forefathers so divided society in watertight compartments that the hierarchy of caste with its condemnation of large numbers as untouchables became the greatest curse of our society.

'O my unfortunate country,' wrote Tagore in one of his poems, 'those whom you have debased, they shall drag you down to their own level, till your shame shall equal theirs; those whom you have deprived of their human rights, who stand before you but find no room in your lap, they shall drag you down to their own level, till your humiliation has equalled theirs.'

This is precisely what happened in Indian history. Innumerable instances can be given of this tendency to lopsidedness in our character which makes us at once primitive and refined, ignorant and wise, inhibited and serene, compassionate and indifferent to cruelty. What we needed most was to learn to appreciate the beauty of a sane and balanced outlook, of a way of living that is manly without being brutal, sensitive without being sentimental, rational without being materialistic, religious without being fanatic and patriotic without being chauvinistic. This is indeed what Tagore taught and gave.

If Tagore had been nothing more than a poet and writer, the quality and output of his contribution to his people's language and literature would still entitle him to be remembered as one of the world's truly great immortals. But he was something much more. He was an artist in life. His personal life was as clean and noble as his verse is simple and beautiful. He lived as he wrote, not for pleasure or profit but out of joy, not as a brilliant egoist but as a dedicated spirit, conscious that his genius was a gift from the divine, to be used in the service of man.

> My poet's vanity dies in shame before thy sight.
> O master poet, I have sat down at thy feet.
> Only let me make my life simple and straight,
> like a flute of reed for thee to fill with music.[4]

This is not a mere religious attitude of feigned humility; it is an intuitive and profound awareness of the immanence of the divine which ran as an undercurrent in all that he wrote or did.

And yet he was in no sense a religious ascetic or a saint, as the word is commonly understood. He loved this earth too well to turn away from it. He was human and humane, a fully developed man who responded as keenly to the joy of life as he did to the cry of human distress. He was a lover of his people, a lover whose loyalty was pledged to all mankind. All his life he pleaded and strove for social justice, for the right of the lowly to dignity, of the poor to material well-being, of the citizen to self-government, of the ignorant to knowledge, of the child to unfettered development, of the woman to equal status with man. The religion he preached was the religion of man, the renunciation he extolled was not of this world but of the base passions of cupidity and hatred, the freedom he fought for was not of one people to exploit another but the freedom of the human personality from all that strangles it, whether it be the tyranny of an external organization or the worse tyranny of man's own blind passion for power.

He was a pioneer in the field of education. For the last forty years of his life he was content to be a schoolmaster in humble rural surroundings, even when he had achieved fame such as no Indian had known before. He was the first, in India, to think out for himself and put in practice principles of education which are now become commonplaces of educational theory, if not yet of practice. Today we all know that what the child imbibes at home and in school is far

[4] *Gitanjali.*

B

more important than what he studies at college, that the teaching is more easily and naturally communicated through the child's mother-tongue than through an alien medium, that learning through activity is more real than through the written word, that wholesome education consists in the training of all the senses along with the mind instead of cramming the brain with memorized knowledge, that culture is something much more than academic knowledge, etc., etc. But few of Tagore's countrymen took notice of him when he made his experiments in education in 1901 with no more than half a dozen pupils. A poet's whim, thought most of them, and many said so. For a long time the only children sent to his school at Santiniketan were problem children whom the parents found it inconvenient to keep at home. Even today few of his countrymen understand the significance of these principles in their national life. The schoolmaster is still the most neglected and ill-paid member of our community, despite the fact that Tagore attached more merit to what he taught to children in his school than to the Hibbert Lectures he delivered before the distinguished audience at Oxford.

Mahatma Gandhi adopted the scheme of teaching through crafts many years after Tagore had worked it out at Santiniketan. In fact the Mahatma imported the first teachers for his Basic School from Santiniketan. The earliest experiments in what is today known as Community Development were conducted by Tagore, first among the peasants of his own estates, later in the institute which he founded for this purpose and named Sriniketan. His writings on rural education and on the problems of community development are still the finest manual for all workers in the field. If Tagore had done nothing else, what he did at Santiniketan and Sriniketan would be sufficient to rank him as one of India's greatest nation-builders.

He had a very healthy contempt for mere agitational politics which he likened to an engine which continually whistles and throws out columns of smoke without ever moving. To the pilots of India's ship of destiny his advice was, 'Fear not the waves of the sea, but mind the leaks in your own vessel.' If we became a subject-people, it was not because the British were wicked but because we were weaklings. We had ceased to believe in ourselves. Instead of tapping the sources of our own power, we were content to pick rags from other peoples' dustbins. Unlike Mahatma Gandhi, Tagore believed in the power and resources of science, though he dreaded the prospect of man becoming the slave of machines instead of machines being the slaves of man. In fact, he dreaded every form of organized power, whether social, political or industrial, which ignored human values and tended to stifle the personality of man.

Though outside India Tagore upheld and interpreted the Indian philosophy of life, in his own country he was the severest critic of its social institutions and religious practices which encouraged superstition and inequality and tolerated injustice. He likened the social and educational structure of his country to a two-storeyed house without a staircase to connect the vast maze of ill-ventilated, germ-infested slums on the ground floor with the rickety, cheap and shabbily-modernized flats on the upper floor. No political miracles can be built, he warned time and again, on the quicksands of social slavery. The same inertia which leads us to the idolatry of dead forms in social institutions will create in our political life prison houses with impregnable walls. Blind loyalty to tradition which narrows men's sympathies and makes them tolerate discrimination of caste against caste, of class against class, of man against woman, may one day recoil on them and turn into a blind loyalty to State, turning men into mere cattle herded in a pen.

Tagore had no illusion about what is today glibly called progress and has come to be synonymous with multiplication of luxuries and worship of mechanized living. By progress he meant the increasing provision of facilities, material and moral, for the all-round development and free expression of the human personality, without discrimination. As he put it,

'I believe in life only when it is progressive, and in progress only when it is in harmony with life. I preach the freedom of man from the servitude of the fetish of hugeness, the non-human.'

The real crisis of civilization was due, according to him, not to the conflict between one class and another, between one group of States and another, between this ideology and that or between the East and the West, but between man and the machine, between personality and organization. Man needs both machine and organization for his welfare, but they must be mastered and humanized by him instead of his being mechanized and dehumanized by them.

Unlike many modern thinkers, he had no blue-print for the world's salvation. He believed in no 'isms'. He merely emphasized certain basic truths which men of wisdom have known in all ages and which men may ignore only at their peril. His thought will therefore never be out of date. We are obsessed with political issues. As a man whose liver is out of order can think of little else and believes every quack to be a miracle-man, so we hang on the words of every politician who has the brazenness to proclaim himself a saviour. Today it is not the priest or the monk who is the supreme parasite but the politician. The priest promised to take us to heaven, the politician promises to bring heaven to us. But in national as in individual life there are no watertight compartments. No sharp lines can be drawn to mark off the political from the moral, the social from the economic aspects of life. Politicians often talk as though one has only to introduce some institutional changes for the paradise to descend on earth, unmindful of the fact that the efficacy of an institution depends on the way it is worked, which itself is determined by the character and wisdom of men who work it. For example, it is not the parliamentary system that guarantees democracy in a State, but certain specific virtues in the citizen, namely, courage to stand up for one's rights while respecting the rights of others, tolerance of opposition, moderation in passion and a sense of humour which refuses to take a politician at his face value. No people who lack these virtues can ever be democratic, whatever their political institutions.

Today it is the fashion in politics to be an internationalist and to shout for peace. Even politicians who cannot see beyond their noses in their everyday activity talk loudly of one world. It was not always so. When Tagore talked of a world 'not broken up into fragments by narrow domestic walls' he was ignored as a lone visionary and was ridiculed for the very largeness of his sympathies. He went from country to country, of Asia, Europe and America, on a forlorn mission preaching the values which could make possible this One World, at a time when in the fever of inflamed nationalism in his own country his words fell like seeds in a desert. With his very limited resources he built up at Santiniketan a centre of international understanding and study which at that time roused the amused contempt of his nationalist contemporaries. But he never lost faith or judged others harshly. 'They call you mad,' so runs one of his early songs; 'wait for tomorrow and keep silent. They throw dust upon your head. Wait for tomorrow. They will bring their flowers.'

Tagore was not a politician. He was not interested in wielding power over the lives of others, for good or for evil. But he had a clear and steady vision of man's destiny and an unerring instinct for those first principles which if men and nations betray, they perish at the root. How well he summed up in an aphorism the tragedy of power politics! 'The clumsiness of power spoils the key and uses the pickaxe.' Mahatma Gandhi called him the Great Sentinel, the conscience of his people whose voice never failed to protest against any injustice or wrong. As a poet he will always delight and deepen our sensibilities, his songs will never cease to enchant his countrymen, as a teacher he will always enlighten. The world has reason to be grateful to one whose genius was so consistently dedicated to the good of humanity.

To the western world Tagore's chief significance lies in the new dimension he gave to its understanding of the East. The West had known the East for some centuries before but had known it primarily as a field of profit where investment of surplus capital fetched quick and fabulous returns, as a sphere of influence for rival imperial ambitions, as an almost inexhaustible market for export of factory products and of Christian religion, and incidentally a happy hunting ground for adventure and exotic thrills and occasionally for exercise of Christian charity. Now and again a western thinker or scholar drew attention to some old literary classic or religious teacher and tributes were generously offered to the ancient wisdom of the East. But the general attitude was one of superiority and the basic incentive of exploitation.

It is obvious that no true understanding can be built on the basis of such an abnormal relationship. Between nations as between individuals a relationship based on the motive to gain advantage over the other automatically shuts the door of true understanding. And yet never was such understanding between the eastern and the western hemispheres of more consequence to the peace and welfare of the world than it is in the twentieth century—understand or annihilate, pacify or perish! The need to understand and to accept for what they are values other than those which have come to be identified with one's own way of living is the greatest moral challenge with which the world is faced today. The conflict cannot be resolved by compromise, no good is done by diluting the differences to make them palatable, nothing is gained by clipping facts to fit one's fancies. The sharper and more clearly defined the differences, the more stimulating is the ultimate discovery that truth has many voices, beauty many forms and civilization many patterns.

Tagore startled the West into a recognition of the real India, not the mysterious India where once shone the Light of Asia, not the India of the antiquarians, nor the romantic India of the story books, of striped tigers and the Maharajas, of naked sadhus and snake charmers, of the benevolent white sahibs and their brown lackeys, but the living India that was soon to forge weapons of victory out of the very chains that bound her. Here was the authentic voice of a civilization that had seen many rises and falls, that had passed through and survived many vicissitudes of prosperity and poverty, of glory and abjection, but had never ceased to be itself, had never wholly ceased to be creative in the worst periods of defeat, had never abandoned its quest for the Eternal in periods of highest prosperity. This voice was as clear and true and unaffected as the utterances of the *Upanishads* three thousand years ago. Its beauty was of utter simplicity and its wisdom was unobscured by the dust of centuries. The values of a civilization that has seen many empires rise and fall, many religions flower and decay, many humans deified and many deities corrupted, are bound to be different from the values which the West considers its special discoveries and, because they have prospered for a few centuries, as everlasting verities. But the two sets of values are not antithetical, they do not contradict each other. They challenge only to stimulate each other. Where they do not overlap, they are supplementary. Each has to learn from the other and he who learns more is the wiser.

However we may seem to differ, we come of the same earth, are moulded of the same clay—the shade may vary somewhat—and are lit by the same spark which we call divine because it is beyond our manipulation and our comprehension. We grow by giving and taking and our destinies are intertwined. If this is not true, then all religions are a mockery and all our science a snare made by man for his self-destruction. This was the essence of Tagore's message, as it is the essence of all philosophy and wisdom, eastern or western.

I

FAMILY BACKGROUND

One would imagine that in a society where people have doted on their caste for untold centuries, where the accident of birth has determined man's status, obligations and opportunities more severely than in any other known civilization, the families—or at any rate such as owe their privileges to their birth —would preserve very carefully an authentic record of their genealogy. But strange as it may seem very few Hindus, including those whose traditional occupation has been learning, can actually furnish documentary evidence of their lineage for more than a few generations. And so when we trace the genealogical history of even such a remarkable family as the Tagores we are soon lost in the mists of popular tradition and family lore so vague as to be indistinguishable from myth and legend. 'We know' has to give way to 'It is said'.

And yet the oral tradition cannot be totally brushed aside, if for no other reason than the natural curiosity to know why, if a story is totally baseless, it has survived for so many centuries. Moreover, popular lore has its own interest and, apart from the fact that it is more picturesque than history, may even hide a core of truth which history had to ignore because it could not isolate the facts. The tradition current in Bengal about the ancestry of Tagore is not without such interest.

In the middle of the eighth century A.D., after a long period of political unrest and religious and social chaos, Bengal was consolidated as a powerful Hindu Kingdom. This much is history well corroborated by textbooks. To restore the purity of Hindu society corrupted by Buddhist anarchy and to rehabilitate it on the ancient foundations of caste hierarchy, five Brahmins were imported from the Western Kingdom of Kanauj which was a stronghold of Brahminic culture. The progeny of these five Brahmins whose names

are remembered to this day made the new racial aristocracy of
Bengal which has continued since then. History has little to say of
this interesting and colossal eugenic experiment which has made
Bengal what it is. However, the breed must have prospered, for in
Bengal the number of Brahmins is legion and they all trace their
descent from one or the other of these five Brahmins—sacred stud
bulls in human form, if ever there were any. One of them was named
Daksha and is reputed to be the ancestor of the Tagores.

History is full of ironies. The Hindus, so proud of their social
organization and caste hierarchy that they gloried in destroying the
democratic legacy of the greatest of their race, the Buddha, were
soon to suffer abject humiliation at the hands of an alien race with
an alien religion. At the end of the twelfth or the beginning of the
thirteenth century Bengal was overrun by Turko-Afghans from
the west and in course of time came to be ruled as a province of the
Muslim Emperor in Delhi. Many Hindus were converted to Islam,
some by force, some lured by greed to share the power of the new
masters. A Brahmin adventurer in love with a Muslim girl was
clever enough to kill two birds with one stone. By voluntarily
adopting the new religion he got the woman he loved and rose to
be an influential dignitary, the Dewan or right-hand man of the
Muslim Governor of Jessore, a district in South Bengal. His name
was Pir Ali Khan. Two of his trusted officers were the Brahmin
brothers Kamadev and Jayadev, descendants in direct line, after
many generations of vicissitudes unrecorded by history, of the
legendary ancestor Daksha.

One day—so the story goes—during the festival of Ramazan
when every devout Muslim fasts during the day, Kamadev found
Pir Ali Khan smelling a lemon and jestingly remarked,

'According to our religious code smelling is half-eating. You
have therefore violated your fast.'

Pir Ali Khan said nothing, but having been born a Hindu, the
words rankled in his mind. Some days later he invited the Brahmin
brothers, along with several other Hindus, to a music concert in the
Governor's palace. In a room adjoining the hall where the audience
was listening to the music, a feast of choice Muslim dishes which
included beef was laid on the table. When the smell penetrated the

concert hall the Hindus began to feel uneasy. Pir Ali Khan smilingly remarked:

'If smelling is half-eating, as your religious code enjoins, you have all tasted of the forbidden food and have lost your caste.'

A panic ensued and the Hindus fled, covering their noses. But the stigma remained. Since then the Tagore family is said to have fallen in the hierarchy of caste and is looked down upon by the orthodox Brahmins who refer to them derogatively as Pirali or Pirili Brahmins.

The Brahmin's position in Hindu society depends almost entirely on the assumed purity and holiness of his caste. Having lost that 'purity' the family must have found it difficult to live in a community which judged it harshly and gave it little quarter. The predicament must have been particularly galling when it came to finding suitable husbands for the daughters. To the orthodox Hindus of that age—to some extent even now—no disgrace was greater than to harbour an unmarried daughter beyond a certain age which then was fairly low. And so the family, hounded from their ancestral home, must have wandered from place to place, each member seeking fortune for himself and husbands for the daughters. He would be a bold Brahmin who accepted the daughter of such a family. Such a bold fellow was one Jagannath Kushari who married a niece of the ill-fated brothers Kamadev and Jayadev whose indiscreet jest had caused the family all the trouble. Jagannath Kushari had to pay a heavy price for his boldness, for he too was obliged to leave his home and settled down in a village called Uttarpara in what is today known as the Khulna district in South-East Pakistan. It was a descendant in the male line of this bold and rash man who may be said to have founded what is today known as the Tagore family.

His name was Panchanan Kushari. Exile, misfortune, and social persecution had made the descendants of the family defiant and adventurous. Having lost the pride of caste they lost their fear too, for not much else was left to lose. Since they could not be more holy they decided to be more human and seek the other good things that life and the times made possible. Adventure was in the air. Unheard-of things were happening in the country. White men from across the seas had opened a factory and trading centre on the banks of the holy river Ganges and, though 'unclean barbarians', such was their power and prestige that even the Muslim rulers thought it prudent to keep on good terms with them. So Panchanan and his uncle Sukhdev left home in the last decade of the seventeenth century, as their forefathers had done earlier, and settled down in a village called Govindpur on the bank of the Ganges not far from the British settlement. Govindpur (now part of the teeming city of Calcutta) was at that time a small fishing village whose inhabitants were all of the so-called low caste. Seeing a Brahmin family settle in their midst they felt elated and gave the uncle and his nephew all the honour due to their caste as Brahmins. Panchanan was always referred to or addressed by them as Panchanan Thakur— Thakur meaning Holy Lord, as the Brahmins are often addressed even to this day. Panchanan had found a lucrative occupation in supplying provisions to the foreign ships that sailed up the river. The British and other foreigners had thus ample opportunities of dealing with Panchanan and naturally assumed, as most foreigners would still do, that Thakur was Panchanan's surname or family name. So they referred to him as Mr. Thakur and unable to articulate the unfamiliar name pronounced it as Tagore or Tagoure. This is how the Tagores came to be known as such and are still known even in India.

The Muslims polluted the family's holy caste, the Christians its no less holy name. The change was more than nominal, it was symbolic, for the Tagores were soon to represent in their new destiny a fine fusion of the three great strands of culture—Hindu, Muslim, and Christian—which have made modern India what it is.

The family prospered. Its fortunes were from the beginning linked with the rise of the British power in India. In a way the family may be said to be the first in India to perceive, dimly but surely, the revolutionary significance of the new age that was dawning in the country, the age of international commerce and capitalism, of industry and science, of a long period of tutelage under a foreign power that by depriving India of its native rule was paradoxically to create conditions of a new and fuller freedom. As British power and commerce grew, what was originally a group of fishing villages became the rich and prosperous city of Calcutta, the commercial

metropolis of new India; and the fortune of the Tagore family grew
with it. The descendants of Panchanan Thakur became merchant-
princes and landed aristocrats. With wealth came jealousies and
quarrels and the family split into two branches. Both the branches
continued to prosper, owning vast estates in the country and huge
mansions in Calcutta.

The family fortune reached its peak in the life and career of
Dwarkanath Tagore, the grandfather of the subject of this biography.
Born in 1794, Dwarkanath was only thirteen years old when his
father died. Handsome, versatile, clever and enterprising, he was a
romantic figure who in an earlier age would probably have carved
out a kingdom for himself and become a prince. Prince, however,
he came to be called. In a commercial age, under the aegis of 'a
nation of shopkeepers' he grew to be a merchant-prince and came
to be popularly known as Prince Dwarkanath Tagore because of
his magnificent way of living and his large public charities. His
extensive business covered many fields, indigo factories, saltpetre,
sugar, tea, coal-mines, etc. He owned large agricultural estates in
Bengal and Orissa, a fleet of cargo boats that plied to the British
coast, and founded the first modern bank with Indian capital, known
as the Union Bank. All these multifarious concerns he controlled
through his firm, Carr, Tagore & Co.

He lived lavishly and entertained regally. The aristocrats of those
days lived a double life. At home in the joint family the orthodox
and traditional ways of life were maintained, the household deity
was scrupulously worshipped morning and evening, the women
went about the house bare-footed and worked with their own hands
in the kitchen, however large the number of servants; outside the
house they could only venture in covered palanquins, well guarded,
and many of them were so taken daily for a dip in the holy Ganges,
closed palanquin and all. Outside the family quarters proper, where
women and children lived, there were spacious reception rooms and
banquet halls hung with chandeliers where the master of the family
entertained his friends and visitors, where anybody (provided he was
a somebody) could come at any time and be fed, where the orna-
mented hookah was always ready with fragrant tobacco, where
whisky flowed freely, where famous musicians vied with one

another in displaying their virtuosity and the professional dancing girls their charms. In the heart of Calcutta in the quarter known as Jorasanko the family mansion of the Tagores still stands, dilapidated and shabby, a pathetic witness to a past glory.[1] What no longer stands is the stately edifice which Dwarkanath had built on the adjoining land where he entertained his friends and guests and all the leading lions of the then ruling hierarchy and society of Calcutta. He also owned a large garden-villa in the suburbs where the entertainment was even more extravagant.

No less lavish and extravagant were his public charities. There was no public institution or cause to which he did not give generously. Today as one ascends the steps of the National Library in Calcutta the first sight to greet the visitor is the bust of Prince Dwarkanath at the entrance, a graceful acknowledgement of the debt which this oldest and finest library in India owes to his generosity. He helped in the founding of the first centre of modern education in India, the Hindu College, established in 1816, which later grew into the now famous Presidency College of Calcutta. He was actively associated with the establishment in 1835 of the first medical college and hospital in Calcutta which is today a vast network of hospitals and a major centre of medical education in the country. He gave free scholarships to encourage students to take up the study of medicine and, in order to break down the Hindu prejudice against dissection of dead bodies, he used to be present in the room when the dissection took place. In 1844 when he was contemplating his second visit to England he wrote to the Council of Education offering to pay the expenses of two students willing to accompany him to England for higher medical education. His offer was not only accepted but was emulated by the Government which undertook to pay the expenses of two more students for the same purpose. Accordingly four students were taken to England who were in due course awarded the Diploma of the Royal College of Surgeons.

He was the first Indian member and patron of the Asiatic Society

[1] The Government of West Bengal, India, have announced their intention to acquire the entire ancestral property and preserve it as a national monument to mark the centenary of the birth of Dwarkanath's illustrious grandson, the poet Rabindranath Tagore.

of Bengal founded in 1784 by Sir William Jones 'for enquiring into the History, civil and natural, the Antiquities, Arts, Sciences and Literatures of Asia'. It was through the activities and publications of this Society that the western world came to know of the wealth of Sanskrit literature and Goethe rhapsodized over Kalidasa's *Sakuntala* and Schopenhauer over the *Upanishads*. Many of the leading scientific institutions of today, like the Archaeological Survey of India, the Zoological Survey of India, the Botanical and Geological Surveys of India as well as the Indian Museum in Calcutta, the oldest and biggest in India, owe their origin to this Society. The Agricultural and Horticultural Society of India founded in 1820, the Calcutta District Charitable Society founded in 1830, the Hindu Benevolent Institution established in 1831—there was hardly a public institution in Bengal of his time which did not owe its existence or its successful working to the active support of this remarkable man who did for his people, in his way and single-handed, what the Rockefellers and the Fords have done for theirs in the United States.

On the eve of his departure for England a contemporary English journal published in Calcutta, the *Friend of India*, which otherwise differed from him on many issues, wrote: 'To describe Dwarkanath's public charities would be to enumerate every charitable institution in Calcutta, for from which of them has he withheld his most liberal donations?'[2] Calcutta today has the reputation for the best and most lively modern stage and theatre in India. The early ventures in this field owed not a little of their success to Dwarkanath's active patronage.

It was not only that he gave of his wealth generously and wisely. He stood up bravely, in the teeth of popular opposition, for every social reform and progressive movement of his day, religious, social and political. He was a faithful friend and staunch supporter of Raja Rammohun Roy, that remarkable religious and social reformer and visionary whom Indian historians have unanimously described as the Father of modern India.[3] In his bold denunciation of the super-

---

[2] *Memoir of Dwarkanath Tagore* by Kissori Chand Mittra, Calcutta, 1870.

[3] *An Advanced History of India* by R. C. Majumdar, H. C. Raychaudhuri and Kalinkar Datta. Macmillan & Co., London, 1950.

stitious beliefs and practices of his countrymen as well as in his public controversies with the Christian missionaries in defence of the basic values of Hindu philosophy and religion, in his heroic crusade against the practice of Suttee (the Hindu widow burning herself on the funeral pyre of her husband) as well as in his passionate advocacy of the modern system of education with its emphasis on the teaching of the sciences, Raja Rammohun Roy had the powerful support of Prince Dwarkanath Tagore.

The Prince had a shrewd political sense and though he welcomed the establishment of the British rule in India and recognized in it a historical necessity for the consolidation of his country into a modern nation, he was the first to organize public opinion and bring the influence of the new rising interests to bear on the good government of the country. In 1838 he founded the Landholders' Society to represent the interests of the landed aristocracy which was at that time the most powerful class in the country. Later on this society was merged in and was superseded by a more broad-based political body called the British Indian Association, representing many classes and many interests. Nearly half a century was to elapse before the idea of organizing constitutional agitation on a national scale for the good government of the country was taken up seriously by his countrymen. By then good government had come to mean self-government.

To cross the seas in those days was for the Hindu much more than a mere adventure. It meant a revolutionary act of defiance against society, for there was a taboo against sea-voyage and severe penalties were prescribed against culprits.[4] Dwarkanath went to England twice, in 1842 and again in 1844. On his second visit he took with him a nephew and his youngest son Nagendranath. The diary kept

[4] How and why this taboo arose it is difficult to say. At one time the Hindus must have been adventurous voyagers, for testimonies of their enterprising spirit, their genius in building and sculpture, are scattered all over South-East Asia. But in course of time the genius of the race must have shrivelled up, its virility drained. Society became static and religion a set of taboos. It needed a shock therapy which the impact of western domination and education provided and the dynamic leadership of a succession of remarkable men and social reformers, from Raja Rammohun Roy to Mahatma Gandhi, to shake the moral and intellectual lethargy of the Hindus. The contribution of three generations of the Tagore family to this awakening is significant.

by Nagendranath and the letters written by him to his family in India are a valuable record of Dwarkanath's life in England and show the very high esteem and affection in which he was held by Queen Victoria and the nobility of England.[5] He was indeed a fabulous figure who would have attracted attention in any age, in any society.

The distinguished orientalist Friedrich Max Müller was then a young student in Paris, studying the *Rig-Veda* under Professor Burnouf. In his *Autobiography* Max Müller has described the vivid impression left on his mind by his chance encounter with the lively and versatile personality of Dwarkanath in Paris. This is how Professor Max Müller's wife later summed up this impression:

'One most interesting acquaintance Max Müller made in Paris, Dwarkanath Tagore, a rich Hindoo who, though no student of Sanskrit himself, took a lively interest in the young scholar presented to him by Burnouf at the Institut de France. He invited Max Müller to his house and they spent many an hour together talking or enjoying music, for the Hindoo was a good musician, had a fine voice, and had been fairly well taught. He liked Max Müller to accompany him when singing either Italian or French music. After a time he was persuaded to sing Persian and real Indian music, and when his hearer confessed that he saw no beauty in it, neither melody, rhythm nor harmony, his Indian friend lectured him on the prejudices of Western nations who turn away from all that is strange and unpleasing to them. Max pacified him by assuring him that he knew that India possessed a remarkable science of music founded on mathematics. He was present at the great party given by Dwarkanath Tagore to Louis Philippe, when the room was hung with Indian shawls, afterwards distributed among the most distinguished guests'.[6]

Dwarkanath did not return home from his second visit to Europe. Like his friend and senior contemporary Raja Rammohun Roy who had died in Bristol thirteen years earlier, Dwarkanath died, away

[5] *On the Edges of Time: Personal Memoirs of Rathindranath Tagore.* Orient Longmans, Calcutta, 1958.

[6] *The Life and Letters of the Right Honourable Friedrich Max Müller,* edited by his wife. Two Vols. Longmans, Green & Co., London, 1902.

from his home, in London on 1 August 1846 at the age of fifty-one. His death was sudden and took place 'under somewhat mysterious circumstances'.[7] There are stories current about his death but as the circumstances were never properly investigated and have failed to arouse the curiosity of any historian, they may be dismissed as gossip.

Dwarkanath left behind three sons of whom the eldest was Debendranath, father of the poet Rabindranath. In his own way Debendranath was even more remarkable than his fabulous father. As the father had come to be known popularly as Prince on account of his grand style of living and his generous charities, the son came to be known as the Maharshi, which means one who is both saint and sage, who lives in the presence of God and has attained the highest knowledge. Though born of Dwarkanath he was truly the moral heir and spiritual successor to Raja Rammohun Roy whose mission he continued and made fruitful. His personality left a deep impact on the intellectual development of Rabindranath, which makes it necessary to say a little more about him, though he is fully worth writing about in his own right.

Born in 1817 he was brought up in circumstances of increasing luxury and pomp which reached their peak when he attained his youth. The pampered darling of a wealthy father and a doting mother and a still more doting grandmother, he grew up as a wilful young man and for some time gave himself up to a life of luxury. But not for long. Sensitive and intelligent, an awareness of the unhappy contradiction between the life lived at home in the ladies' quarters and that lived outside its walls in the fairyland where his father entertained his guests must have worked early on his subconscious and made him prematurely brooding and introspective. He was deeply attached to his grandmother who lived a life of extreme simplicity and religious piety, eating nothing but boiled rice and vegetables cooked by her own hand, and fasting as often as eating, reciting sacred verses and weaving garlands for the household deity. No less pious and austere, and perhaps even more uncompromising was his mother, Digambari Devi, who refused to let her husband touch her because he had lost caste by dining with 'unholy barbarians'.

[7] *On the Edges of Time:* Rathindranath Tagore.

C

Torn between his loyalty to these two extreme ways of life, one of piety, self-abnegation and irrational fears, the other of worldly success and self-indulgence, young Debendranath must have brooded and wondered what was the true meaning of religion? Was Hinduism nothing but worship of images and a code of meaningless taboos? Did piety have any meaning divorced from a living morality and unguided by rational thinking? Unable to reconcile the contradiction he saw around him, he gave himself up to a life of pleasure and ease. Then suddenly the crisis came.

His grandmother to whom he was very attached was on her death-bed and had to be removed to a tiled shed on the bank of the Ganges, for to die near the holy river was what every pious Hindu desired. For three nights the grandmother lingered on, during which Debendranath was with her almost all the time, spending lonely, weird hours of the dark in the imminence of death. On the night before her death, as he was sitting alone by the river he was suddenly seized by an intense spiritual elation and he lost his normal consciousness. When he recovered it—

'I was as if no longer the same man. A strong aversion to wealth arose within me. The coarse bamboo-mat on which I sat seemed to be my fitting seat, carpets and costly spreadings seemed hateful, in my mind was awakened a joy unfelt before. I was then eighteen years old.'[8]

In his autobiography which he wrote many years later he has described vividly his spiritual hunger, his search for truth and the development of his faith. It is a remarkable document which Evelyn Underhill in her learned Introduction has described as '... one more amongst the small number of authentic histories of the soul. This book must rank with the few classic autobiographies bequeathed to us by certain of the mystics and saints: Suso, Madame Guyon, even the great St. Teresa herself. It is essentially of the same class as the *Testament* of Ignatius Loyola, the *Journal* of George Fox.'

On his return home he gave away many of his personal possessions to friends and others; but merely divesting himself of material possessions brought him neither joy nor understanding. He longed for a

---

[8] *Autobiography of Maharshi Debendranath Tagore*. Macmillan & Co., London, 1916. Translated into English by Satyendranath Tagore and Indira Devi.

recurrence of the ecstatic vision he had had on the river bank and waited and prayed for it, leading a life of austerity. He studied and read the sacred books of his religion as well as books of Western philosophy, but found no satisfaction. 'Great grief was in my heart. Darkness was all around me. The temptations of the world had ceased, but the sense of God was no nearer; earthly and heavenly happiness were alike withdrawn. Life was dreary, the world was like a graveyard.'

What he saw of the Hindu religion around him sickened him with its idolatrous practices and its unmeaning ritual. In this state of mind, '. . . one day all of a sudden I saw a page from some Sanskrit book flutter past me. Out of curiosity I picked it up but found I could understand nothing of what was written on it.' He sent for a well-known Sanskrit scholar, one of the devoted band of Hindu reformers inspired by Raja Rammohun Roy. The pundit identified the text as the first verse of the *Isopanishad* and explained its meaning:

'All this, whatever moves in this moving world, is enveloped by God. Therefore find your enjoyment in renunciation; do not covet what belongs to others.'[9]

This came as a revelation to the young devotee groping in the dark.[10] 'My faith in God took deep root; in lieu of worldly pleasures I tasted divine joy . . . When I had thoroughly entered into the *Upanishads*, and when my intellect began to be daily illumined by the gift of truth, I felt a strong desire to spread the true religion.' On the very day of the year in 1839 when the Hindus of Bengal celebrate with great *éclat* the annual festival of the worship of the

[9] Dr. Radhakrishnan's English translation. *The Principal Upanishads*, edited by S. Radhakrishnan. The Muirhead Library of Philosophy. George Allen & Unwin, London.

[10] It may seem strange that the *Upanishads* which are so well known today as containing the highest speculative wisdom of the Hindu religion and philosophy should have been unknown to the Hindus in general in the first half of the last century. The fact is that in course of centuries of foreign invasion Hinduism, exposed to repeated persecution, had been on the defensive and had clung in fear to the outward symbols of its traditional faith. This had given undue power to the priests who exploited it in the interest of a blind faith whose sole guardians they claimed to be. The position was somewhat like that in medieval Europe before the Christian Reformers discovered the Bible for themselves. In India this service was performed by Raja Rammohun Roy and Maharshi Debendranath, later supported by the researches of western Indologists.

goddess Durga, Debendranath called his friends and followers together and formally inaugurated a purely theistic association which he named *Tatvaranjani* (soon after renamed Tatvabodhini) *Sabha*, dedicated to the worship of the One Formless Divine and the propagation of the basic tenets of the Hindu faith as propounded in the *Upanishads*, before they were corrupted by idolatrous forms of worship and other superstitious practices. At that very time the gongs were sounding in his own house where the worship of the goddess was in full swing. He was powerless to prevent it.

Raja Rammohun Roy had already founded in 1825 the Brahma Sabha as a meeting place for all people, 'without distinction' for the worship of the One True God, without the use of any images or symbols or any sectarian ritual. But the movement had failed to win any popular support and the cause had languished until this young, passionate and intrepid mystic, with the sure instinct of a religious reformer, amalgamated his own new-born Sabha with the older organization in 1843 and renaming it Brahma Samaj turned the meeting place into a movement and what was little more than an intellectual club into a vigorous centre of a living and dynamic faith. This movement, religious in its inspiration, later developed into a revolutionary movement of social and moral reform working as a powerful ferment in the moribund Hindu society of the day. Its aggressive missionary zeal, having done its useful work, over-reached itself and by-passing its founder developed an anti-Hindu bias, thereby causing as a reaction a neo-Hindu fervour which sought, equally aggressively, to recover national pride in the past culture and heritage of the people.

The emotional and intellectual pattern of Indian nationalism can only be properly understood in the context of this psychological conflict in the racial mind. Pride gives strength. Without a certain amount of pride and faith in one's past a nation cannot grow strong. And yet a blind self-admiration can become a stumbling block in a people's progress resulting in self-destructive chauvinism. It is necessary to understand this emotional background of Indian nationalism for it alone can explain many of today's obvious contradictions. In any case, to understand the subject of this biography it is necessary to know the climate in which Tagore was born and grew up and the impact which his father's personality and faith left on his mind. When Tagore was born this conflict was at its height and religious and moral ideals (which the contemporary Victorian England accepted smugly and at which we today smile cynically) were very real to the people who had taken up the challenge of revaluing themselves. In their utterance we feel the glow of a heightened moral consciousness which one gets in the contemporary writings of such American idealists as Thoreau, Emerson and Walt Whitman. Much of what Tagore thought, felt and wrote was conditioned by this climate of his early upbringing. The influence of the Maharshi's personality is so intimately linked with the son's intellectual and spiritual development that it is necessary to tell a little more of the Maharshi's life.

While the son Debendranath, God-intoxicated, was laying the foundations of a reformed church, the father continued to dazzle his countrymen with his ostentatious ways. It was at this time that Prince Dwarkanath gave a grand ball in his Belgachia garden-house in honour of Miss Eden, the sister of the Governor-General, Lord Auckland. The extravagant splendour of the event was for long the talk of the town. Many of Dwarkanath's countrymen complained that the Prince entertained only the foreign notables. When this reached Dwarkanath's ear he gave another splendid party at the same place, with Indian music and dances, at which were invited all the Bengali gentry. His son Debendranath was given the charge of receiving and looking after the guests, but the son was too busy with his missionary activities to do more than put in a fleeting appearance. The father was naturally hurt and annoyed. 'As it is he has very little head for business,' he is said to have remarked at one time, 'now he neglects business altogether; it is nothing but Brahma, Brahma, the whole day!'

Apparently the feelings between the father and the son were not too estranged, for the son continued to work in his father's bank, while giving more and more of his time, resources, and zeal to what he felt was his life's mission. Though the zeal was solely his, the resources could not have been available but for the generous allowance his father gave him. The Prince was too full-blooded and practical to admire his heir's other-worldliness. On the other hand, he who had so warmly admired Raja Rammohun Roy and had so staunchly befriended his cause could not have been unaware that his son was but continuing the work which the Raja had begun. One shrewd precaution the father did take. Not knowing how his vast and fast-expanding business, delicately poised on credit, would fare in his son's hands after his death, he made a trust of some of his landed estates, making the sons beneficiaries to ensure that they would always have an assured income whatever ill-luck might overtake the business. A superb gambler, he knew that fortune was an uncertain mistress.

And so it proved to be. Soon after Dwarkanath's death in London in 1846 it was discovered that the firm's liabilities far exceeded its assets. There was a rush on the bank and the famous House of Carr, Tagore & Co. had to close its doors. This crisis showed the mettle the son was made of. He called the creditors together, placed all the cards before them and announced that though in law the creditors had no rights over the trust property (which was considerable), he and his brothers voluntarily renounced their claims to the benefit of the trust until the last penny of the liabilities had been paid. Having thus reduced himself and his family to penury, he felt the strange joy that comes of renunciation.

'What I had desired came to pass. I wanted to renounce the world and the world left me of its own accord. What a singular coincidence! I had prayed to my God, "I desire nothing but Thee," and the Lord in His mercy granted my prayer. He took away everything from me and revealed Himself unto me. My heart's desire was fulfilled to the letter.'

He was not, however, reduced to utter penury. The creditors were so impressed with his integrity that they allowed him and the brothers a fair monthly allowance and after some time handed over the management of the entire property to Debendranath's hands. It took him many years of judicious management and frugal living to pay off all the debts. Not only did he succeed in paying off all the debts with interest, but he even fulfilled all the moral obligations of his father and made good all the charities and donations which the Prince had hastily and generously offered or promised before he left for England. In one such case he not only paid a lakh of rupees (£6,666—the actual value of this amount must have been many times larger in those days) which his father had promised to a Charity Fund but he paid even the interest on this amount from the date of the promise.

Although still young (he was only twenty-eight when his father died) he was by now a highly respected figure among his people who later referred to him as the Maharshi, one great in wisdom and in righteous living, an enlightened man of God, in the tradition of the great sages who wrote the *Upanishads* more than 2,500 years ago. He was now the patriarch of a large joint family, active in the management of vast estates, scrupulous in his obligations, a passionate religious reformer and mystic whose feet were firmly planted on the earth. This aspect of the Maharshi's life left a profound impression on his son who was to sing later: 'Deliverance is not for me in renunciation. I feel the embrace of freedom in a thousand bonds of delight.'

The Maharshi drew his inspiration from the most robust and intellectual period of Indian history when profound speculations on the meaning of Truth and God were mixed with an innocent wonder at the beauty and mystery of Nature and with a joyous and full-blooded acceptance of life. He had little sympathy with the later phases or aberrations which drew strength from despair and built spiritual values on a denial of life, rejection of the senses and renunciation of the world. His aristocratic pride and intellectual masculinity recoiled from any form of spiritual exhibitionism, so popular in later Indian tradition, identifying God-consciousness with esoteric practices and hysteric manifestations of religious ecstasy.

The Maharshi travelled widely in India—in those days when travelling was full of hazards and was a real adventure. Almost each year he left his home in spring or in autumn and travelled over the western plains to the Himalayas. Like the Rishis of old he loved the lofty, snow-capped mountains. He was unafraid of risks and would climb to lonely spots where he would sit down and be lost in contemplation of nature's wild grandeur. He was also a keen observer of nature and men and his autobiography is full of vivid descriptions of

nature and shrewd observations on men and events. Here is a description of what is today known as Allahabad (the birth-place and home-
town of Jawaharlal Nehru) and of the sacred spot, a centre of
pilgrimage, where three holy rivers, two seen, one unseen, are
supposed to meet:

'This is the holy land of Prayag; this is the famous Beni-ghat. At
this spot on the riverside, people shave their heads, and give
offerings on land and water to their ancestors and distribute alms.
As soon as my boat touched the shore, there was a regular invasion
of *pandas* [professional priests who look after the pilgrims] who
boarded it. One of them laid hands on me saying, "Come and bathe
here and shave your head." I said, "I have not come as a pilgrim,
nor will I shave my head." "Pilgrim or not, give me some money,"
said another. "I shall give you nothing," I replied; "you are able to
work and earn your bread." He said in Hindi, "I won't let you go
without giving me money; you must give me something." I replied
in the same language, "I shan't give you money; let's see how you
take it from me." Upon this he jumped down from the boat on to
the land, and laying hold of the tow-rope, began to pull away hard
with the others; after pulling for some time he ran up to me
in the boat, and said, "Now I have done some work, give me
money." I laughed and gave him some money, saying, "That's
right." '

This was just before the fateful year 1857 when the famous Sepoy
Mutiny caused the first great convulsion to the British Empire. The
conflagration had not yet broken out and the Maharshi was slowly
and blissfully travelling up to the very region where the trouble was
brewing. A month after leaving Agra (nowadays it takes three
hours by car) his boat touched the sands of Delhi in early
January.

'I saw a great crowd collected up above. The Badshah [Moghul
Emperor] of Delhi was flying kites there. There was nothing else to
occupy him now; what was he to do?' After more than a year during
which he was marooned in Simla, not without danger to his life,
he was returning home and had neared Kanpur (some 273 miles
east of Delhi) when he saw many tents pitched there and an improvised bazaar set up. When he asked what it was about he was

informed that the British soldiers were taking away the Badshah of Delhi captive. 'On my way to Simla I had seen him happy, flying kites on the Jumna sands, and on my way back I found him a captive, being led to prison. Who can tell what fate will overtake anybody in this dissolving sorrowful world?'

Beyond this detached and philosophic pity for an individual, the Maharshi who spent the entire period of fighting on the edge of the battlefield, as it were, has almost no comments to offer on this historic event on which hung the future of his country. And yet the Maharshi was a person of considerable enlightenment whose pride in his country and concern for its welfare cannot be questioned. Nor was he a British stooge in any sense of the term. This would suggest that at any rate in Bengal, which had come to enjoy the benefits of orderly government and modern education after a long period of disorder and maladministration, the events of 1857 were looked upon more as the last desperate kick of a dying feudal order than as the people's first war of independence, as some patriotic historians choose to believe.

Before the Maharshi had left for the Himalayas at the end of 1856, he had for some time been overcome by a persistent and morbid sense of 'the world is too much with us' and had longed to retire for good to his beloved Himalayas. He had intended not to return to his family but to spend the remaining years in quiet contemplation. It is worth relating why he failed to keep to his resolve which, had he kept it, would have been unlike him. One day in September 1858 he was walking over the mountains, as was his wont, and stopped to enjoy the sight of a waterfall. He was led to muse on the blind destiny of the waters; so clear, cool and beautiful here—but as they enter the plains they will soon become muddy, dark and soiled. And yet muddied and bereft of their pride, they will fertilize the land and help mankind. Suddenly he heard a voice within say, 'Give up thy pride and be lowly like this river. The truth thou hast gained, the devotion and trustfulness that thou hast learnt here, go, make them known to the world!'

Escapism was alien to his nature and philosophy. He obeyed the command which was but the prompting of his own true self and returned to the world of his duties in Calcutta. Though he continued to travel and visit the Himalayas, he never again thought of escaping. He lived to a ripe old age,[11] lived to see the sunset of the last century and the sunrise of the new, lived to see the religious and social movement he had started gain such momentum that it left him far behind —a solitary peak on the frontier between the old and the new.

[11] He died in 1905, at the age of eighty-eight.

2

BIRTH AND UPBRINGING

It was fortunate that the Maharshi came down to earth from his lofty perch in the Himalayas where he at one time threatened to spend the rest of his life in divine contemplation. It was fortunate that his other-worldliness did not result in an aversion to this world, that he did not neglect his duties and functions as a householder nor disdain the natural claims of the flesh; for three years after the Himalayan interlude was born, on 7 May 1861, Rabindranath Tagore. The mother, Sarada Devi, had already borne the Maharshi thirteen children and two years later was to bear him one more son who did not survive. A United Nations sociologist, harassed by the spectre of increasing pressure of population on the earth's limited supply of food, may complain that the Maharshi overdid it. Nevertheless, posterity is grateful that he did not stop at the third or fourth child, whatever may be the number the sociologists permit, for great as were the Maharshi's many other gifts to his people, the greatest was his fourteenth child.

When the child was born, however, the event seemed of little significance. Perhaps in no family would the fourteenth child be particularly welcome and much less so in a family where all the elder brothers and sisters and their families lived together in one joint household. The huge and rambling mansion at Jorasanko in Calcutta which was the family residence swarmed with children and grandchildren and the birth of an additional member could not have been an event of any special importance. The child was named Rabindranath, or Rabi for short. He was a healthy and fair baby but perhaps not as fair as some of his elder brothers and sisters, for his eldest sister Saudamini (who in fact looked after the new-born baby —the mother was ailing and could not be bothered) used to remark playfully as she bathed the child, 'My Rabi may be dark and not so fair but he'll outshine all the others.' She herself was unusually fair-skinned for an Indian girl. It is said that once when she was going to school in her palanquin the police detained her, thinking her to be an English girl who was being kidnapped in a changed costume.

When the child grew up into a little boy he was relegated, along with nephews and nieces of more or less the same age, to the care of servants. The joint family was like a small community owing allegiance to a common head and sharing a common kitchen. Each married member had his or her separate quarters, the men occupying the outer apartments, the women the inner. The number of servants, male and female, was legion and children of the family who had outgrown infancy were looked after by them. The grand old head of the family, the Maharshi, lived aloof and was almost unapproach-able. When he was not away on his periodic visits to the Himalayas, he was wrapped up in his meditations or engaged in his reformist crusade, while keeping a shrewd and vigilant eye on the management of his landed estates and other property. The mother, Sarada Devi, whose health had broken down after the birth of the fifteenth child, had a vast household to supervise, with many daughters and daughters-in-law, sons and sons-in-law and their children. To the many normal complications of a joint Hindu family the Tagores had added some new ones by the practice of enlisting the sons-in-law as regular members of the household. Sarada Devi must have been a woman of considerable character, tact and patience to keep such a household together and in harmony. It is a pity that not more is known of this remarkable woman who made possible others' great-ness while leaving no trace of her own.

Her husband, the Maharshi, was a truly great man, but like most religious reformers possessed by a sense of mission and of their own righteousness, he could hardly have been an easy husband to live with. Herself the daughter of an orthodox Hindu family, brought up in the traditional forms of worship, she must have exercised considerable flexibility of mind to suffer his iconoclastic zeal. Her numerous progeny, robust, handsome and talented, overflowed with vitality and presented problems of their own. Some of them were geniuses or near-geniuses and some were mental cases. Her eldest son, Dwijendranath, was a man of gigantic intellect, poet, musician, philosopher and mathematician. If he did not achieve the fame of his youngest brother, it was largely due to his utter lack of ambition and perseverance. He was too versatile to stick to any one line and too philosophic (in the traditional Indian sense of being unattached) to take anything too seriously. But in whatever he did he showed a mind of great originality, a fertile and inventive imagination. His experiments in poetic composition, ingenious and daring, left a deep impress on the poetic development of his youngest brother. His long poem *Svapnaprayan* (Dream Journey) is an allegorical masterpiece comparable to Spenser's *Faerie Queene* or Bunyan's *Pilgrim's Progress* and has survived as a Bengali classic. Nor is he less distinguished as a thinker and writer of philosophic prose. He invented the shorthand in Bengali and wrote a manual on it in verse which has been described by a discerning critic as 'a monument of ingeniousness as well as a metrical wonder'.[1] He also composed music and is said to have been the first to introduce the use of the piano in Bengali music.

Her second son Satyendranath is remembered in history as the first Indian to break into the stronghold of the Indian Civil Service, the steel-frame of the British administration of India. But he has other and better claims to distinction. He was a fine scholar of Sanskrit and wielded an excellent pen in Bengali and in English. In the former he published verse-translations of the Sanskrit classics, *Gita* and Kalidasa's *Meghaduta*, a book on Buddhism, and his own reminiscences which are of considerable interest. He was also the first writer to introduce Marathi religious poetry to Bengali readers. In English he translated the Maharshi's *Autobiography* which was later published by Macmillan, London. His influence, direct and indirect, on the development of his youngest brother, Rabindranath, if not as a poet as a man, was deep, subtle and abiding. He acted as a gentle and healthy corrective to the overpowering moral and intellectual influence of the Maharshi on the young Rabindranath. The Maharshi was radical in his religious convictions but conservative in his social attitudes, though he was big enough to tolerate differences of outlook from members of his family. It was Satyendranath who first asserted his freedom to live as he chose, in accord-

[1] *History of Bengali Literature.* Sukumar Sen. Sahityc Akademi, New Delhi.

ance with the new values of women's education and their rights which he had imbibed during his education in England.

His young wife was a girl of extraordinary beauty and intelligence but like most Hindu women of that period more or less illiterate and in purdah. He insisted on educating her, not only in Bengali and English, but in all the accomplishments of her counterparts in Victorian England. It is said that when Satyendranath first took her out, unveiled, in an open horse-carriage through the streets of Calcutta the city was dumbfounded and the incident was long remembered as a major scandal. But Satyendranath was undaunted and even took her with him to England. He shifted from his ancestral house in Jorasanko and lived with his family in a separate bungalow where his charming and witty wife presided over many a distinguished *salon*. It was she who changed the orthodox women's costume and adapted the old-fashioned way of wearing the *sari* to the modern style which is now the fashion all over Bengal and it was she who designed the blouse which is today worn with it. Their son Surendranath and daughter Indira, both handsome and versatile, were favourite playmates (though several years younger) of their gifted uncle, when Rabindranath first went to England for his studies, and continued to be his warm admirers till the end. Indira Devi lived to be a grand old dame of Bengali letters and a recognized authority on her uncle's music—a beautiful and gracious figure who carried her years as lightly as she carried her many accomplishments until her death in August 1960, at the age of eighty-seven.

Sarada Devi's third son Hemendranath died comparatively young, at the age of forty. He is chiefly remembered for the tribute which his youngest brother paid him while recalling the education of his early years in his memoirs.[2] Hemendranath who was in charge of directing the studies of little Rabi and his companions had insisted that the children should be taught in their mother-tongue and not in English. Commenting on this little mercy the poet wrote many years later:

'Learning should as far as possible follow the process of eating. When the taste begins from the first bite, the stomach is awakened to its function before it is loaded, so that its digestive juices get full

[2] *My Reminiscences*. Rabindranath Tagore. Macmillan & Co., London, 1917.

play. Nothing like this happens, however, when the Bengali boy is taught in English . . . While one is choking and spluttering over the spelling and grammar, the inside remains starved, and when at length the taste is felt, the appetite has vanished . . . While all around was the cry for English teaching, my third brother was brave enough to keep us to our Bengali course. To him in heaven my grateful reverence.'

Her fourth son proved to be feeble-minded but his son Balendranath was a brilliant writer who, although he died in his twenties, has left a permanent place for himself in Bengali literature.

Her fifth son Jyotirindranath was, however, a genius of uncommon versatility and one of the most accomplished men of his age. Handsome, elegant and daring, he was a Prince Charming of the Indian renaissance and a pioneer in almost every field. Musician, composer, poet, dramatist and artist of remarkable sensibility, his overflowing energy and ardent nationalism led him into many adventures far beyond the range of the arts and letters. He strove to break the British monopoly of shipping and industry and nearly ruined himself financially in the process. His influence on the intellectual and poetic development of his younger and more famous brother, who was thirteen years his junior, was considerable and has been gratefully acknowledged by the latter. It would hardly be an exaggeration to say that evidence of Jyotirindranath's genius is to be seen only partly in his own individual achievements; in part it lies hidden in the great fulfilment of his brother's powers.

Of the other children of Sarada Devi, the most noteworthy, apart from the youngest son, were two of her daughters, the eldest, Saudamini, who looked after the infant poet and was later the devoted companion and caretaker of the aged Maharshi, and the fifth daughter, Swarnakumari, who was a distinguished musician and writer and is remembered as the first woman novelist of Bengal. Swarnakumari's two daughters also achieved considerable distinction, Hiranmayi Devi as a social worker, Sarala Devi as a writer, musician and an active participant in the political struggle for national freedom.

To keep such a progeny, brilliant, headstrong and wayward, together and in peace was no small achievement. If Sarada Devi had little time or inclination to look after her youngest-born, it is not surprising. Her motherliness had been taxed to the utmost and she had perhaps little surplus left to spare. But the hunger for a mother's affection, never appeased in childhood, was to survive in the son as a recurring longing for feminine affection and care. Its haunting echoes can be heard in the exquisite poems of childhood he wrote in maturity, some of which were later published in English translation as *The Crescent Moon*. In some of his short stories and novels the mother's love has been delineated with such wealth of tenderness as to make one wonder whether the author was not partially satisfying his own unappeased hunger.

And yet years later when he recalled his childhood in his memoirs[3] there is no trace of self-pity. Rather he congratulated himself on his good luck at having escaped the danger of being spoiled by parental solicitude. 'While the process of looking after,' he commented, 'may be an occasional treat for the guardians, to the children it is always an unmitigated nuisance.' Nor was the child pampered in any other respect. Though the family had the reputation of an aristocratic way of life and a tradition of luxury, the children were brought up more or less austerely.

'Our food had nothing to do with delicacies. A list of our articles of clothing would only invite the modern boy's scorn. On no pretext did we wear socks or shoes till we had passed our tenth year. In the cold weather a second cotton tunic sufficed. It never entered our heads to consider ourselves ill-off for that reason. It was only when old Niyamat, the tailor, would forget to put a pocket into our tunic that we complained, for no boy has yet been born so poor as not to have the wherewithal to stuff his pockets . . . Nothing ever came so easily to us. Many a trivial thing was for us a rarity, and we lived mostly in the hope of attaining, when we were old enough, the things which the distant future held in trust for us. The result was that what little we did get we enjoyed to the utmost; from skin to core nothing was thrown away. The modern child of a well-to-do

---

[3] He wrote two, one in middle age which was later translated into English and published by Macmillan in 1917 as *My Reminiscences*, the other when he was nearing eighty which was translated into English as *My Boyhood Days* and published by Visva-Bharati, Calcutta, in 1940.

family nibbles at only half the things he gets; the greater part of his world is wasted on him.'[4]

The period of childhood and early boyhood which was spent under the tutelage of family servants was later dubbed by him as 'servocracy'. The child was restless and, as ever after, 'athirst for the far-away'. To save himself the bother of chaperoning the child on his sprees, one of the servants hit upon an easy strategy. He would place Rabi in a convenient spot and tracing a chalk circle around him would warn him with a solemn face of the deadly peril of stepping outside the magic circle. The child had been told the story of *Ramayana* and knew of the fearful calamity which Sita had courted when she transgressed the ring which Lakshmana had drawn round her. So he remained rooted to the spot and dared not step out, even though the servant had disappeared. Fortunately the chalk circle was near a window which overlooked the outer grounds where shimmered a bathing pool with a large banyan tree on one side and a fringe of coconut palms on the other. Through the venetian shutters of the window the child would gaze below and be absorbed in watching the antics of the various bathers, each with his peculiar ritual. One would come down the steps sedately, muttering his morning prayers, another would cover his ears with his hands and take his regulation number of dips, a third would jump down from the bank and so on. When the noon fell and the pool was deserted save for the ducks paddling about after water snails the child's interest would shift to the giant banyan tree and the play of shadows round its base. Years later he was to recall this childhood companion:

> With tangled roots hanging down from your branches,
> O ancient banyan tree,
> You stand day and night like an ascetic wrapt in meditation.
> Do you recall the child whose fancy played with your shadows?

If Rabi submitted meekly to the rigours of servocracy it was not because he was unduly docile but because of his boundless curiosity in his surroundings which invested even the most trivial object with

[4] *My Reminiscences.* Rabindranath Tagore. Macmillan & Co.

D

interest and the liveliness of his fancy which took flight even when his limbs were immobilized within the chalk circle.

'Looking back on childhood's days the thing that recurs most often is the mystery which used to fill both life and world. This mystery lurked everywhere and the uppermost question every day was, when would we come across it? It was as if Nature shut her hands and laughingly asked, "What have I got inside?" and nothing seemed impossible.'[5]

This sense of wonder and this gift of finding delight in the seemingly commonplace experiences of life was to survive as a major spiritual asset of the poet and to save him from becoming blasé and cynical in an age when such affectation had won for itself the glamour of a literary and intellectual fashion.

The painful experience of a circumscribed and regimented child-hood was also to survive as a lasting impression and to mould his ideal of education in later years. The child's curiosity and longing for the big and mysterious world of men and nature beyond the confines of home and the school became for him symbolical of the soul's yearning for 'the great beyond'. In his little play *Dak Ghar* which he wrote in 1911 and which was three years later published in English as *The Post Office*, he dramatized this longing in the character of the little boy Amal. Amal is a delicate and sensitive child who is confined to his bed in a dark room because his over-solicitous guardian and the ignorant family physician fear that he will catch all kinds of ailments if exposed to 'the elements'. From his sick bed Amal watches the procession of life in the street outside and longs to participate in it. The village postman jokingly assures him that he will bring him a letter from the King. Amal dies in the hope and as he closes his eyes the Herald announces the coming of the King. Death brings deliverance and innocent faith its final reward.

But the child Rabi was more robust than Amal and survived the neglect of his parents and the tyranny of the servants. In fact, he was none the worse for it. Listening to the conversation in the servants' quarters and the stories he was told to keep him quiet, he must have early acquired an ear for folklore and the racy idiom of the colloquial

[5] *My Reminiscences.*

Bengali of which he became a great master and protagonist in later life. The first nursery rhyme he learnt sent a thrill of joy through his being. It was a common jingle in Bengali meaning 'The rain patters, the leaf quivers', but to the child it was a first revelation of the magic of poetry—the first poem of the 'Arch-Poet', as he described it later.

'Whenever the joy of that day comes back to me even now, I realize why rhyme is so needful in poetry. Because of it the words come to an end, and yet do not end; the utterance is over, but not its ring; and the ear and the mind can go on and on with their game of tossing the rhyme to each other. Thus did the rain patter and the leaves quiver again and again, the livelong day in my consciousness.'[6]

His school-going began earlier than it need have. A tutor had been engaged to teach him elementary reading and writing at home but the arrangement came to a premature end. When the child found that his elder brother and a nephew (his eldest sister's son) were going to school in a carriage, he started to howl for the same privilege. The exasperated tutor gave him 'a resounding slap' and said, 'You're crying to go to school now, you'll have to cry a lot more to be let off later.' The child had his way but it did not take him long to discover that no truer prophecy was ever uttered.

The first school he went to was known as the Oriental Seminary. What he learnt there he was never able to recall but the ingenious methods of punishment that the teachers in the school practised to drill learning into the children left a vivid impression both on his mind and on his limbs. Returning home he would work off his repressed rage and fear by beating with a cane the wooden railings of the veranda of his house and playing the teacher with his dumb pupils. 'I have since realized,' he philosophized later, 'how much easier it is to acquire the manner than the matter. Without an effort I had assimilated all the impatience, the short temper, the partiality and the injustice displayed by my teachers to the exclusion of the rest of their teaching. My only consolation is that I had not the power of venting these barbarities on any sentient creature.'

But the holidays were still his own and at midday when the

6 *Ibid.*

servant in charge of him retired for his own meals and rest, the child sought refuge in an old, discarded palanquin which belonged to the days of his grandmother and still bore traces of the family's past wealth. Between the neglected child and the discarded palanquin was a secret fellow-feeling and comradeship. Sprawling within its closed shutters, safe from all prying eyes, he gave full rein to his fancy.

'My palanquin, outwardly at rest, travels on its imaginary journeys. My bearers, sprung from "airy nothing" at my bidding, eating the salt of my imagination, carry me wherever my fancy leads. We pass through far, strange lands, and I give each country a name from the books I have read. My imagination has cut a road through a deep forest. Tigers' eyes blaze from the thickets, my flesh creeps and tingles. With me is Biswanath the hunter; his gun speaks—Crack! Crack!—and there, all is still. Sometimes my palanquin becomes a peacock-boat, floating far out on the ocean till the shore is out of sight. The oars fall into the water with a gentle splash, the waves swing and swell around us. The sailors cry to us to beware, a storm is coming. By the tiller stands Abdul the sailor, with his pointed beard, shaven moustache and close-cropped head. I know him, he brings *hilsa* fish and turtle eggs from the Padma for my elder brother.'[7]

Soon after, while he was still in his seventh year, Rabi was admitted into another school known as Normal School, which was supposed to be a model school fashioned on the British pattern. The only memories of this school which survived in his later life were the foul language of one of the teachers which shocked the child and the compulsory community singing of an English song before the lessons began—'evidently an attempt to introduce an element of cheerfulness into the daily routine'. The Bengali boys could neither follow the words which were in English nor the tune which was unfamiliar. The only line of it which Tagore could recall in his later life sounded somewhat like this: *Kallokee pullokee singill mellaling mellaling mellaling*. After much thought he was able to decipher a part of what were perhaps the original words . . . *full of*

---

[7] *My Boyhood Days.* Rabindranath Tagore. Visva-Bharati, Calcutta, 1940.

glee, singing merrily, merrily, merrily! What the original of the word *Kallokee* was continued to baffle him and he left the riddle unsolved to provide an additional subject for a doctorate thesis in philology.

He wrote his first verse in his eighth year. A young cousin, Jyoti, who was six years older took him to his room one day and insisted on his writing a verse, explaining that nothing could be easier. All one had to do was to pour words into a fourteen-syllable mould and they would condense into verse. Thus the child scribbled his first verses in the popular Bengali metre, *Payar*. 'The lotus of poetry blossomed in no time in this fourteen-syllabled form and even the bees found a foot-hold on it.' The child was, however, disillusioned. Was poetry no more than this amusing exercise? 'One day a thief had been caught in our house,' he related later in his *Reminiscences*. 'Overpowered by curiosity, yet in fear and trembling, I ventured to the spot to take a peep at him. I found he was just an ordinary man! And when he was somewhat roughly handled by our door-keeper I felt a great pity. I had a similar experience with poetry.'

Nevertheless the experience was intoxicating. He got hold of a blue copy-book in which he started scribbling his verses. 'Like a young deer which butts here, there and everywhere with its newly sprouting horns, I made myself a nuisance with my budding poetry.' His companions tried to show off the infant prodigy and would make him recite his verses on every conceivable occasion. When he recited the verse in which he lamented that as one swims forward to pluck the lotus it floats farther and farther away on the waves raised by one's own arms and thus remains always out of reach, the elders smiled and said the boy had no doubt a gift for writing. Fortunately or unfortunately the blue manuscript is lost and no thesis can be written on the infantile affectations of a great poet.

Though the child had less than enough of his parents' company and of maternal fondling, his education was by no means neglected. Much more than the lessons at school it was the private tutoring at home that laid the foundation in Rabi's mind of his wide range of interests as well as his life-long aversion to 'the mills of learning'. As he confessed later, the greater part of the cargo with which his mind was loaded by the tutors was tipped out of the boat and sent to the bottom. 'My learning at any rate was a profitless cargo. If one seeks to key an instrument to too high a pitch, the strings will snap beneath the strain.' The day's routine was well packed with lessons. The child was wakened up while it was still dark and made to practise wrestling with a celebrated one-eyed professional wrestler. Hardly was the wrestling bout over and the dust removed from the body when a student from the Medical College turned up to teach him 'the lore of bones'. A human skeleton hung on the wall of the room and the child had to learn by heart the jaw-breaking Latin names of the various bones. At seven in the morning the mathematics tutor came and, slate in hand, the boy had to work out the problems in arithmetic, algebra and geometry. Sometimes there would be a lesson in natural science illustrated with simple experiments, followed by lessons in Bengali and Sanskrit. At half past nine the servant brought the monotonous, unvarying meal of rice, *dal* and fish curry which the child found unvaryingly insipid. At ten he was packed off to school.

Returning from school at 4.30 in the afternoon, he found the gymnastics master waiting for him to give him an hour's practice on the parallel bars. No sooner was he gone than the drawing master arrived. After the evening repast came Aghor Babu, the English teacher, and as the lesson proceeded by the light of an oil lamp the child would nod, then jerk himself awake with a start, and then nod again, missing far more than he read. Recalling this ordeal later the poet recorded in his *Reminiscences*:

'Books tell us that the discovery of fire was one of the biggest discoveries of man. I do not wish to dispute this—but I cannot help feeling how fortunate the little birds are that their parents cannot light lamps in the evening. They have their language lessons early in the morning and how gleefully they learn them! But then they do not have to learn the English language.'

This rigid time-table was supplemented by lessons in music. Fortunately, unlike other lessons, these were not drilled into him at set hours. Music floated in the very air he breathed at home. Almost every member of the family was a musician of some sort and either sang or played on some instrument or another. The child was gifted with a fine voice and an uncommon aptitude for picking up whatever he heard—and he picked up indiscriminately from classical, folk, devotional and other music, in utter disregard of the very rigid caste barriers that separate one class from another, no less in music than in society. His young niece Pratibha was a gifted singer and excellent tutors, professional musicians known as *Ustads*, were engaged by her father for her training. Besides, the family fame and patronage attracted distinguished musicians from different parts who came and stayed as guest-musicians for months at a time. One of them was Jadu Bhatta, a celebrated musician of the time whose name is a legend in Bengal. From them all young Rabi picked up scraps of musical knowledge as and when he liked. It was difficult to make him learn except what he wanted to learn.

Recalling the days spent with Jadu Bhatta, he wrote later: 'He made one big mistake in being determined to teach me music, and consequently no teaching took place. Nevertheless, I did casually pick up from him a certain amount of stolen knowledge.' Half in humility, half in irony he confessed: 'It was no one's fault but my own that nothing could keep me for long in the beaten track of learning. I strayed at will, filling my wallet with whatever gleanings of knowledge I chanced upon.'[8]

Brajeswar was the name of the servant who was in charge of Rabi's meals. He had a way of appropriating part of the rations for himself. He would dangle each delicacy before the hungry child and ask in a stern voice, 'Do you want any more?' Knowing by the tone of his voice what answer he desired, the child invariably answered in the negative. The offer was never repeated. These short rations, however, suited the child's constitution, though not his appetite, well.

'I was, if anything, stronger, certainly not weaker, than boys who had unlimited food. My constitution was so abominably sound that even when the most urgent need arose for avoiding school, I could never make myself ill by fair means or foul. I would get wet through, shoes, stockings and all, but I could not catch cold. I would lie on the open roof in the heavy autumn dew; my hair and clothes would be soaked, but I never had the slightest suspicion of a cough. And as for that sign of bad digestion known as stomach-ache, my stomach

[8] *My Boyhood Days*. Rabindranath Tagore. Visva-Bharati, Calcutta, 1940.

was a complete stranger to it, though my tongue made use of its name with Mother in time of need. Mother would smile to herself and not feel the least anxiety, she would merely call the servant and tell him to go and tell my master that he should not teach me that evening. Our old-fashioned mothers used to think it no great harm if the boys occasionally took a holiday from study . . . Serious fever I do not remember and I never heard the name of malaria . . . I never knew the slightest scratch of a surgeon's knife; and to this day I do not know what measles and chicken-pox are. In short, my body remained obstinately healthy. If mothers want their children to be so healthy that they will be unable to escape from the school-master, I recommend them to find a servant like Brajeswar. He would save not only food bills but doctor's bills also.'[9]

In the meanwhile the blue exercise-book was filling with verses. The reputation reached the ear of the teacher in the Normal School who one day sent for little Rabi and ordered him to write a poem on some moral precept which he set down. When the child complied and brought the verses the next day he was made to recite them before the whole class. 'The only praiseworthy thing about this moral poem was that it soon got lost,' recalled the author. 'Its moral effect on the class was far from moral. It merely roused envy and unbelief. Stolen goods, they said. One pupil even volunteered to produce the book from which the verses were copied.' These early attempts have been compared by the author to the blossoms of the mango-tree's first flowering in late winter, destined like them to wither forgotten.

His reputation as a precocious author, however, spread and impressed even his mother who one day begged him to write a letter to his father who was on one of his periodic sojourns in the Himalayas, warning him of the impending danger of a Russian invasion and imploring him to come back soon. In those days the pet bogy of the British Government in India was the threat of a Czarist encroachment from across the Himalayas and rumours were periodically set afloat that a Russian horde was about to descend from one Himalayan pass or another. Rabi's mother was thus kept in a chronic state of anxiety concerning her husband's safety. Not

[9] *My Boyhood Days*. Rabindranath Tagore. Visva-Bharati, 1940.

satisfied with the assurances which she received from the astrologers whom she was always consulting, she coaxed the child to write a letter to his father begging him to return. This was the child's first epistolary effort. The Maharshi must have been amused, for he promptly replied assuring his son that there was no cause for anxiety. If the Russians descended, he would drive them back single-handed. This assurance was adequate for the child; the mother continued to worry.

But the Maharshi never failed to return. The home-coming of this august wanderer was always an event in the family. His presence in the house made itself felt in every way and the very atmosphere was charged with alertness and solemnity. Even his wife lost all interest in astrologers and personally supervised cooking. The children moved about on tiptoe and talked in whispers, eager to catch a glimpse of the legendary sage but afraid to peep inside his study. During one such visit in the winter of 1872-3 when Rabi was eleven years and nine months old, the Maharshi arranged and personally presided over the *upanayana* or the investiture with the sacred thread of his two young sons Somendra and Rabindra and his grandson Satya. The Tagores are Brahmins and the Brahmins are known as the twice-born, the second birth being the investiture with the sacred thread and initiation in the Vedic rites. Although the Maharshi had revolted against many orthodoxies of his religion and caste, there were certain forms and ceremonies which he meticulously observed and the sacred thread ceremony was one of them. Even Rabindranath, who was much more liberal and radical in his religious and social outlook, continued to honour some of these forms till very late in life.

The three boys, their heads shaved and gold rings dangling from their ears, were closeted in 'a three-day retreat' on the third storey of the house to meditate on the mystery of life and the universe. The budding Brahmins stared at each other's shaven head and giggled; they pulled at each other's ear-rings and scared the servants with their pranks. Recalling this episode the poet wondered in his middle age if the stories in the ancient texts of little boys seated in ascetic meditation could be relied upon, 'because the book of Boy Nature is even older and more authentic'. Nevertheless, the Vedic

chant known as the *Gayatri*[10] which the boys were made to recite and
to memorize left a deep and abiding impression on Rabi's mind.
The splendid cadence and intonation of this verse in Sanskrit must
have appealed strongly to his sense of rhythm. Although he was not
of an age when he could comprehend the meaning of the words,
something in them moved him deeply and made him experience an
expansion of consciousness. He continued to recite the verses and to
meditate on their significance whenever he felt an urge to withdraw
into himself and often when he did so his eyes would overflow with
tears. The *Gayatri* remained his life-long companion and he continued to find in it a source of strength and joy long after he had
discarded the sacred thread.

But the shaven head was for the time being a source of considerable embarrassment, the more so as shortly before the ceremony
he had changed his school and had been admitted to an English
school called the Bengal Academy run by one De Cruz. The shaven
head was sure to be a target of the jeers of the irreverent Anglo-
Indian classmates. While the ear-rings could be discarded the hair
could not be made to grow to order. Young Rabi was much worried
and did not know what to do when providence came to his rescue.
He was summoned by his father who asked him if he would like to
accompany him to the Himalayas. Rabi was overjoyed and would
have danced for joy if his father's presence had not restrained him.
The next few days were spent in excitement. For the first time a full
suit of clothes was ordered for him, the Maharshi himself selecting
all items of the outfit including a gold-embroidered velvet cap. And
so one day, thus handsomely attired, the boy accompanied his father
and set out on the first great adventure of his life.

Their first halt was Santiniketan, now famous as an international
seat of learning but at that time its very name was unknown. Little
did the boy know that the spot he was visiting would be intimately

---

[10] *Tat savitur varenyam bhargo devasya dhimahi, dhiyo yo nah prachodayat.* Let us accept
this magnificent light from the lord of light, and may he stimulate our thoughts.
A. S. MacDonell renders the verse as follows: 'May we attain that excellent glory of
Savitar the God that he may stimulate our thoughts.' *Hymns from the Rigveda*. Oxford
University Press, London. Dr V. Raghavan's rendering is: 'We meditate upon that
adorable effulgence of the resplendent vivifier Savitar; may He stimulate our
intellects.' *The Indian Heritage*. The Indian Institute of Culture, Bangalore.

linked with his life and would be known the world over as the scene
of his biggest creative experiment. The history of this spot which
began as a private retreat or family villa and is today a University
campus is almost co-eval with that of Rabindranath. Soon after
Rabi's birth the Maharshi happened to visit a friend whose country
estate was situated about a hundred miles west of Calcutta. Getting
down at Bolpur which was then, as it still is, the nearest railway
station he proceeded in a palanquin and as the sun was about to set
found himself in an open plain bereft of vegetation, stretching to the
western horizon with nothing to break the view of the setting sun
except a thin row of wild palms lining the horizon. Such open
stretches are not common in Bengal where the characteristic landscape is one of luxuriant vegetation. The Maharshi was enchanted
and sat down for his usual evening meditation under a pair of *chhatim*
trees.[11] When he rose from his meditation he had already made up his
mind that the place would be his. He lost no time in negotiating for
its purchase and later built a house and laid out a garden and named
the place Santiniketan, which literally means an abode of peace.

There the father and son spent the first few days of their journey.
This holiday in Santiniketan and the opportunity of close association
with his father were perhaps the most profound and formative
influence on the boy's mental and moral development. This was
also his first experience of freedom of physical movement in the
midst of open nature which he loved and he revelled in the luxury.
His own recollection of the experience is worth recalling:

'It was evening when we reached Bolpur. As I got into the
palanquin I closed my eyes. I wanted to preserve the whole of the
wonderful vision to be unfolded before my waking eyes in the
morning. The freshness of the experience would be spoilt, I feared,
by incomplete glimpses caught in the vagueness of the dark. When I
woke at dawn my heart was thrilling tremulously as I stepped outside . . . There was no servant rule here, and the only ring which

[11] A beautiful seven-leaf tree known in Sanskrit as *saptaparna*. These two ancient
trees still stand side by side, enclosed by a railing of red sandstone. Beneath them is
a stone tablet on which is inscribed in Bengali the quintessence of Maharshi's faith:

> He is the refuge of my life,
> The joy of my heart,
> The peace of my soul.

encircled me was the blue of the horizon which the presiding goddess of these solitudes had drawn round them. Within this I was free to move about as I chose. Though I was a mere child my father did not place any restrictions on my wanderings.'[12]

The father, however, did not leave him entirely to his own resources. He had brought his youngest son with him to mould his impressionable mind and he did so, directly and indirectly. He read with him select pieces from Sanskrit, Bengali and English literature, one of the books in the last category being a life of Benjamin Franklin. In the evening he made him sit by his side and sing his favourite hymns, and at night when the Indian sky revealed the undimmed splendour of the stars, he gave him lessons in astronomy. In order to give him confidence and a sense of responsibility, he gave him money to keep and asked him to maintain accounts of the daily expenses; he entrusted him with the duty of daily winding his expensive gold watch. The watch was wound with such zeal that it had to be sent to the watchmakers in Calcutta for repair. But the Maharshi did not blame or chide the boy. Among the Maharshi's books the child noticed the several volumes of Gibbon's *Decline and Fall of the Roman Empire*. He turned over the pages but found them too dry. Children read books because they have to, but why should the grown-ups who are free to do what they like waste their time over such dull books?—wondered the child.

It was here that sprawling under a young coconut palm he wrote his first verse-drama (or martial ballad as he chose to describe it later) on a historical theme dealing with the defeat of the great Hindu King, Prithviraj, at the hands of the Moslem invaders. The drama was never published and the manuscript is lost. 'In spite of the superabundance of its martial spirit,' recalled the amused author later, 'it could not escape an early death.'

Though nothing concrete survived of this visit to Santiniketan the memory of the place and its later associations were to become the most potent single influence on his intellectual and spiritual development. There is nothing very beautiful or enchanting about the landscape or climate of Santiniketan which would explain its extraordinary hold on the mind of Rabindranath and of the genera-

[12] *My Reminiscences.*

tions of students who were taught there. In fact, the soil is poor, the weather in summer rigorous, made more so by lack of an adequate supply of water. Its avenues of trees and groves of flowering bushes, which are so pleasant a feature of its landscape today, were not there in 1873 when young Rabi first went there. Its chief merit was its openness, its long stretches of barren fields broken by ravines of red earth, its bare and rugged simplicity—the earth and sky facing each other, naked and unashamed. Coming from the confines of the brick-and-mortar prison of the Calcutta mansion, this freedom of space must have seemed to the child a very heaven. Later in life he was to see and admire many beauty spots of this earth, both in the East and the West, but no other place ever moved him as deeply as this stretch of barren wasteland which he described as 'the darling of our hearts' in the song he wrote on it.

From Santiniketan the father and son left for the western Himalayas, visiting several places on the way. Their longest halt was at Amritsar, with its golden temple. The Sikhs are theists and worship no images of gods and goddesses; their religion is devotional and emphasizes the cardinal principles of oneness of God and the brotherhood of man. The Maharshi felt a strong kinship with their faith and regularly visited the temple accompanied by his son and often joined in the community singing of Sikh hymns. This early training in respect for other religions helped to broaden the child's sympathies which were later to attain such wide proportions.

An incident during the railway journey to Amritsar illustrates the Maharshi's high sense of dignity and aristocratic pride which left a marked impression on the son's memory. At a station on the way, the ticket examiner doubted the Maharshi's word that the boy accompanying him was under twelve years of age and therefore entitled to travel at half-ticket. He went and brought the station-master with him who looked the boy up and down and insisted that full fare be paid for him, as he was undoubtedly over twelve. (By Indian standards the Tagores are uncommonly tall and well-built.) The Maharshi, unused to his word being doubted, grew red in the face and without a word handed over a high currency note to the station-master. When the change was returned to him he flung it away disdainfully on the platform. The station-master was abashed.

How could the poor man have known that his passenger was the famous Maharshi who had voluntarily paid all the business debts of his father, even when not legally liable for them!

By the time the father and son reached the foot of the Himalayas it was April, the beginning of summer in the plains and early spring in the mountains. Their destination was Dalhousie, at that time a small cluster of bungalows over 7,000 ft. above the sea. The trek up the mountains had to be done by stages, either on foot, or on horseback or in *jhampans* carried on poles by professional bearers. The mountain-sides were covered with tall, graceful deodars and a riot of spring flowers which the boy had never seen before and of which the names were still unknown to him. High up were the snow peaks and beneath, as the road turned and wound upwards, the great gorges with thick clusters of giant trees, underneath whose shade a little rivulet trickled out, 'like a little daughter of the hermitage playing at the feet of hoary sages wrapt in meditation'. Already the spirit of Kalidasa was stirring in the eleven-year, wonder-eyed boy. 'My eyes had no rest the livelong day, so great was my fear lest anything should escape them . . . Why, oh why had we to leave such spots behind, cried my thirsting heart, why could we not stay on there for ever?'

At last they reached their cottage at Bakrota, perched on the top of a mountain. The boy was now free to wander about and feast his eyes on the loveliness and the grandeur of the Himalayas spread out before him. An iron-spiked stick in hand he roamed at will, wandering from peak to peak. The father kept no guard on him.

'To the end of his life,' testified the grateful son,[13] 'he never stood in the way of our independence. Many a time have I said or done things repugnant alike to his taste and his judgement; with a word he could have stopped me; but he preferred to wait till the prompting to refrain came from within. A passive acceptance by us of the correct and the proper did not satisfy him; he wanted us to love truth with our whole hearts; he knew that mere acquiescence without love is empty. He also knew that truth, if strayed from, can be found again, but a forced or blind acceptance of it from the outside effectually bars the way in.'

[13] *My Reminiscences.*

But it was not all fun and spree. The Maharshi, for all the tribute his son has paid to his liberalism, was a stern disciplinarian and task-master. Early in the morning, long before the sun rose, he woke up the boy and practised with him Sanskrit declensions. 'What an excruciatingly wintry awakening from the caressing warmth of my blankets!' The Maharshi himself was up much earlier and the son recalls seeing him sometimes in half-sleep, softly passing by his bed, wrapped in a red shawl, with a lamp in his hand, on his way to the veranda where he sat in his meditation, 'at what hour I could not make out'. Sanskrit lessons over, the father and son would have their morning glass of milk. The Maharshi would then chant verses from the *Upanishads*, the boy listening, spell-bound by the sonorous rhythm. By the time the sun rose above the eastern peak they would be on their morning walk. Returning home the father gave him an hour's lesson in English, after which 'came the bath in icy-cold water'. There would be lessons in the afternoon, too, and in the evening when the two of them sat in the veranda the son would sing to the father the devotional hymns so dear to the Maharshi, and the latter explained to him the rudiments of astronomy. What better class-room could the child have had for learning the science of the stars than beneath the clear Indian sky! No wonder that the study of astronomy remained the favourite hobby of Rabindranath till his death.

No less lasting was the fruit of the training in discipline he thus received from his father. Much as he might have grumbled and shivered then at leaving the warmth of his bed at an unearthly hour of the morning or at having to plunge in ice-cold water, he remained grateful to his father for having inculcated in him habits of healthy and clean living which remained with him till the end. To greet the rising sun and to catch the first twitter of the birds became for him not a mere ritual but a delight which he never missed during his long life except when he was bed-ridden. The four months he thus spent in his father's company away from the dull routine of home and school were not only the happiest days of his boyhood but became the richest experience and source of his early education. Their immediate effect was that when he returned to Calcutta he was no longer a child.

3

ADOLESCENCE

The return home was much more than the home-coming of a schoolboy. It was more like the return of a little hero from an adventure. The Himalayas then were not what the automobiles and airplanes have made them now. They were a far-away dream, a legendary abode of the gods, accessible only to heroes and sages of which one read in books. To have been in that fabled region and in the company of the fabulous Maharshi was an order of merit which immediately raised the boy's status in the family. The servants' régime was at an end. He was now welcome in the inner apartments where the proud mother was only too glad to show off her young prodigy to the other ladies who were all eager to listen to his adventures. Nor was young Rabi averse to strutting about like a young peacock displaying its newly-acquired feathers.

For one whose days had hitherto been spent between the servants' room and the class-room, who had never had his due share of mother's love, the inner apartments must have seemed an enchanted palace and access to it a rare privilege.

'In infancy the loving care of woman is to be had without the asking and, being as much a necessity as light and air, is as simply accepted without any conscious response; rather does the growing child often display an eagerness to free itself from the encircling web of woman's solicitude. But the unfortunate creature who is deprived of this in its proper season is beggared indeed. This had been my plight. So after being brought up in the servants' quarters, when I suddenly came in for a profusion of womanly affection, I could hardly remain unconscious of it . . . The Zenana, which from an outside view is a place of confinement, was for me the abode of all freedom.'

He had often envied his youngest sister whom the family tutor never punished for not doing her lessons well and who, while the boys were getting ready to go to school, walked unconcernedly away into the inner apartments, her pigtail dangling behind her.

The inner apartments had become the more alluring ever since a new bride had entered its portals, 'slender gold bracelets on her delicate brown hands'—his elder brother Jyotirindranath's wife, Kadambari. She was only a little older than Rabi and he longed to be her playmate. 'I encircled round her at a safe distance, but I did not dare to go near.' She who came from outside to become one of them, who was unknown and yet their own, attracted him strangely and he yearned to make friends with her. But as soon as he drew near, the youngest sister would snap at him, 'What d'you boys want here—off you go!' The humiliation made the disappointment more galling.

All this was now changed. The unwelcome intruder had suddenly become an interesting visitor. Everyone wanted to listen to the story of his travels and the little romancer had no scruples about making it more colourful by a deft touch here and there. 'I cannot say that my head was not turned.' He was now the centre of interest at his mother's open-air gatherings on the roof-terrace in the evening. There he told his tales, recited his poems and astounded the audience with the tit-bits of astronomical knowledge he had gleaned from his father. But the biggest feather in the tail of this young peacock was his recitation of *Ramayana* in the original Sanskrit of Valmiki. The ladies had known this epic in its Bengali version only; the original was a mystery to which none but the learned had access. 'Do read us the *Ramayana*, Rabi dear,' the proud mother would coax. No coaxing was needed. The prodigy was only too eager to astound the audience among whom was the youngest daughter-in-law of the family, whose admiration he craved most. He recited the verses his father had taught him and translated them into Bengali. He had forgotten the meaning of several difficult words, '. . . so that, in the reading I gave, a large divergence occurred between Valmiki's intention and my explanation. That tender-hearted sage, from his seat in heaven, must have forgiven the temerity of the boy

E

seeking the glory of his mother's approbation.' But no one was there to mark the divergence. The mother was all admiration. 'You must read this to Dwijendra,'[1] she said. The boy's heart sank. The young pretender would soon be caught by the learned brother. Summoned by the mother, Dwijendra arrived. 'Just hear Rabi read Valmiki's *Ramayana*, how splendidly he does it!' she said. Fortunately, the learned brother was in a hurry—perhaps his own composition had been interrupted—and after listening absent-mindedly to a few verses, he muttered, 'Very good,' and walked away, without waiting to hear the Bengali rendering. Far from being damaged, Rabi's reputation, thus accidentally confirmed by his brother's cryptic remark, rose higher in the ladies' esteem.

But if he imagined that his new status would earn him an exemption from attendance at school he was mistaken. The elders who directed his studies insisted on his going back to the Bengal Academy and also engaged two private tutors to coach him in Sanskrit and Bengali. But the tutors soon found to their cost that while it is easy to drag the horse to the water's edge it is not easy to make it drink. So giving up all attempts to teach the pupil the hard way of grammar, they started to read the classics with him, the Sanskrit tutor *Sakuntala*, the Bengali tutor *Macbeth* in English. The Bengali tutor, Gyan Babu, who came from a distinguished family of scholars, soon discovered an effective way of dealing with the refractory pupil. Having read a couple of scenes from *Macbeth* with him, he would lock him up in a room and set the prisoner free only after the latter had rendered in Bengali verse the scenes previously read with him. Thus the whole play was rendered into Bengali verse—the budding poet's first tribute to the great English dramatist. Unfortunately, the manuscript has not survived; only the first portion, the translation of the Witches Scene, was published seven years later, in 1880, in the literary journal *Bharati*. This specimen bears testimony to the young boy's amazing mastery of Bengali language and rhyme and, in particular, the folk idiom. Obviously, in translating this particular portion he had adopted a special metre and diction to support the weird character of the scene; the rest of the play was presumably in blank verse with the technique of which he was familiar, having earlier

[1] Her eldest son, the distinguished philosopher and scholar.

studied the great epic of Michael Madhusudan Dutt, then popularly known as the Milton of Bengal.

But the Bengal Academy with its Anglo-Indian atmosphere, the foul slang of the boys, the lessons being pelted at the dumb pupils, continued to be insufferable. It was probably during these dismal class hours that he wrote his first long poem, 'Abhilash' (Yearning). This was published in the following year (1874) in the family journal *Tattvabodhini Patrika*, without the author's name; the editor's note described it as the composition of 'a twelve-year boy'. This is the earliest record in print of the boy-poet's metrical exercises.

Soon after he changed the school once again and was admitted into St. Xavier's—with no better result. While the teaching here was as dull and mechanical as in the previous school, the atmosphere was rendered even more cheerless by the solemn observance of religious forms. The only pleasant memory that remained with him of this school was of Father De Peneranda, a Spaniard who could not speak English well and was therefore not taken seriously by the pupils. 'I know not why, but my heart went out to him in sympathy . . . Whenever I looked at him his spirit seemed to be in prayer, a deep peace to pervade him within and without.' One day a writing exercise had been set and Father De Peneranda was pacing up and down behind the benches keeping an eye on the boys. Rabi as usual was absent-minded and his pen was not moving. All of a sudden Father De Peneranda bent over him from behind and gently laying his hand on his shoulder asked anxiously, 'Are you not well, Tagore?' Such gentle treatment was so uncommon in the schools of that period that the boy was deeply moved. 'I cannot speak for the other boys but I felt in him the presence of a great soul, and even today the recollection of it seems to give me a passport into the silent seclusion of the temple of God.'[2]

Finally in 1875 at the age of fourteen he gave up going to school altogether. No amount of family pressure could bully or coax him any longer to 'the eternal grind of the school mill' which he described as a 'combination of hospital and gaol'. His guardians gave up all hopes of his career and even ceased to scold him. His eldest sister who had nursed him as a baby lamented, 'We had all hoped Rabi

[2] *My Reminiscences.*

would grow up to be a man, but he has disappointed us the worst.' By all academic standards he had proved himself a good-for-nothing. The St. Xavier's school register does not contain his name among the list of pupils promoted to the next higher class. 'He who escapes, lives.' He lived.[3]

But though he played truant from school, he did not idle away his time. He was a born devotee of Saraswati, the goddess of learning and the arts, but he refused to be led to her altar by any priest. He must woo her in his own fashion. Like a wild horse he would not be yoked; he must graze at will in what pasture he liked. The family atmosphere was congenial for such wayward pursuit of knowledge. The Jorasanko house was like a lively bee-hive where honey sucked from many flowers, wild and cultivated, was being gathered. Poets and scholars, musicians and philosophers, artists and social reformers, geniuses and cranks—they were all there in the family and more came in from outside. Dramas were written and acted inside the house and music was in the air. Bengal was in a ferment of early renaissance and new books and literary magazines carrying poems, serialized novels, and translations from foreign literatures were achieving a popular response hitherto unknown. Young Rabi read voraciously whatever fell into his hands and listened eagerly to the compositions and conversation of his elders. His cousin Gunendra[4] told him stories from Indian History and later in life he recalled how surprised he was to learn that Robert Clive, after laying the foundation of British rule in India, went back home and cut his own throat. 'How could there be such dismal failure within and such brilliant success outside? This weighed heavily on my mind the whole day.' The newly-awakened consciousness of the intelligentsia and its

[3] All his life he continued to joke about his lack of academic qualifications which his countrymen prized so highly—such qualification being almost the only passport for government service under the British rule in India, as it is largely so even today. In an amusing letter written on 13 April 1935 (Bengali New Year Day) to his granddaughter Nandita who had shortly before left for Europe he sent her his blessings and good wishes for the New Year and included among them a hope that she would fail in the University Entrance exam (for which she had sat shortly before), for how would he show his face to the world if his grandchild succeeded where he had failed!

[4] Father of the famous artist-brothers Abanindranath and Gaganendranath who led the modern movement in Indian art.

inevitable counterpart, the rising tide of nationalism, had found expression a few years earlier, in 1867, in the organization of an annual cultural-cum-political festival known as the Hindu Mela. Like other progressive movements of Bengal in that period, this too had been sponsored by the Tagore family. This Mela may be said to be the precursor by nearly two decades of the Indian National Congress, the political organization which fought for and won independence for India under Mahatma Gandhi's leadership. In February 1875 young Rabi recited his composition, a patriotic poem, at this annual festival.[5] The poem was published in the *Amrita Bazar Patrika*, then an Anglo-Bengali weekly. This was not only young Rabi's first public appearance but also the first occasion when his name appeared in print over his composition. (His earlier long poem 'Abhilash' had been published without his name appearing with it.) Encouraged by the success he repeated the triumph by reciting another poem, 'Prakritir Khed' (Nature's Lament), before a literary gathering.

On 8 March of the same year his mother, Sarada Devi, died. He was then thirteen years and ten months old. Though this was his first introduction to death and the loss of this remarkable lady must have been deeply mourned by the family, the bereavement did not leave any marked impression on Rabi's mind. For one thing there had never been that clinging affection between the mother and son which would leave a void; secondly, his elder brother Jyotirindra and his charming wife Kadambari, 'the new sister-in-law' referred to earlier, poured their affection on him and gave to this motherless boy a home in their little household such as he had never known before.

On the night his mother died Rabi was fast asleep in the children's room downstairs. 'At what hour I cannot tell, our old nurse came running in weeping and crying: "Oh my little ones, you have lost your all!" My sister-in-law rebuked her and led her away, to save us

---

[5] A local English journal, *Indian Daily News*, has the following news item in its issue of 15 February 1875: 'The Hindu Mela . . . Baboo Rabindranath Tagore, youngest son of Baboo Debendranath Tagore, a handsome lad of some 15, had composed a Bengali poem on Bharat (India) which he delivered from memory; the suavity of his tone much pleased his audience.'

the sudden shock at dead of night.'[6] When in the morning he was told of her death, he could not realize all it meant. He saw her laid out on a bedstead in the courtyard and there was nothing in her appearance to strike terror in the child's mind. She looked as though she were enjoying 'a calm and peaceful sleep'. Only when the body was carried away from the house and Rabi accompanied the elders to the cremation ground 'did a storm of grief pass through me at the thought that mother would never return by this door and take her accustomed place in the affairs of her household'. When he returned from the cremation ground and looked up at the house he saw his father in the front veranda of the third storey, still seated motionless in prayer. The picture was engraved on the child's mind and helped him later in life to face many bereavements.

It was Rabi's good luck—for which he never ceased to be grateful —that at this critical period of his adolescence he found in his brother a friend and guide who fostered and directed his budding, chaotic genius and in his sister-in-law a playmate and guardian angel who not only replaced his mother but more than replaced her and chastened and sustained his wild adolescent yearnings. The idealized picture of love, 'half-human, half-divine', which the Vaishnav religious poetry he loved to read had engraved on his mind found its concrete image in this gracious lady, half-mother, half-playmate.

Ever since the 'new bride' entered the house, a new vista of imagination had opened for the shy, lonely Rabi whose daily routine between the schoolroom and the servants' hall had been dull and drab in the extreme. Here was a new being from the outside world, more or less of his age and perhaps like him feeling shy and lonely in that vast household. She was young enough to play with dolls' weddings and on such occasions would invite her young brother-in-law to partake of the feast. She was, moreover, an excellent cook and regaled him with dishes which were unknown in Brajeswar's cuisine. 'The monsoon rain, rushing down suddenly from the distant mountains, undermines the ancient banks in a moment, and that is what happened now.'[7] The house, a prison before, had become

[6] *My Reminiscences.*   [7] *My Boyhood Days.*

a home where affection and tenderness so long denied were to be had in abundance. Sometimes when the sister-in-law went to stay with relatives and he did not find her in her accustomed place, he would be disconsolate and would fly into a temper and steal some valuable object from her room 'to teach her a lesson'. When she returned and asked for an explanation he retorted, 'Am I expected to guard your room when you go away? Am I a watchman?' She too would feign anger and snap, 'No need to guard the room. Watch your own hands.' Recalling the scene when he was eighty years old and near his death, Rabindranath comments, 'Modern women will smile at the naïveté of their predecessors who knew how to entertain only their own brothers-in-law, and I dare say they are right. People today are much more grown-up in every way than they were then. Then we were all children alike, both young and old.'

About this time the Maharshi shifted his Calcutta residence from the Jorasanko family house to a separate bungalow in the European quarter of the city where he could have more peace and quiet. His rooms in the old house were taken over by Jyotirindranath and his wife Kadambari. The rooms, which were on the second floor, opened on to a large roof-terrace which she turned into a garden. She loved flowers and she loved birds. While young Rabi admired the flowers and plants she grew in tubs on the roof, he hated the sight of lovely birds in cages and would quarrel with her for keeping them. Once she took a fancy for keeping pet squirrels in a cage and when he protested she asked him to mind his own business and not to set himself up as her teacher. Taking advantage of her absence he set the little creatures free and had to bear with her scolding which he no doubt enjoyed. She would make him assist her in household tasks, in cutting betel-nuts or in drying finely cut mango slices which make a delicious preserve. She poured affection on him and yet constantly teased and snubbed him for failings, real or imaginary, so as not to make the precocious boy too conscious of his attainments. When he read her his new compositions, she merely smiled and remarked, how much better other poets had written! She only praised his skill for cutting betel finely and 'would never admit that I had any other good quality, so much so that she even made me

angry with God for giving me such a faulty appearance'. Whenever
he was inclined to compliment himself on his own performance she
reminded him of a Sanskrit saying that 'the unworthy aspirant after
poetic fame departs in jeers'. Thus while she checked his conceit
from growing, she sedulously encouraged the best in him, for
at that time his most ardent ambition was to win her
admiration.

She herself was a genuine lover of literature and music and had a
keen and sharp sensibility. It was she who gave him a taste for the
lyrics of Biharilal Chakravarty, a contemporary whom young Rabi
grew to admire—an admiration which had some influence on his
own poetic development. She also shared with him her keen
appreciation of his eldest brother Dwijendranath's recently published
poetic composition, *The Dream Journey*, a superb allegory and a
masterpiece of metrical experiments whose 'beauties had become
intertwined with every fibre of my heart', to quote Rabindranath's
own words. That was the time when the novels of Bankim Chatterji
were being serialized in the literary journal *Bangadarshan*, 'taking the
Bengali heart by storm'. The excitement caused by this new phenomenon in the literary firmament of Bengal was even greater than
the eagerness with which the French reading public awaited the
next instalment of Balzac's novels.

'The whole country thought of nothing else but what had happened
and what was going to happen to the heroines. When *Bangadarshan*
came there was no midday nap for anyone in the neighbourhood.
It was my good fortune not to have to snatch for it, for I had the
gift of being an acceptable reader. My sister-in-law would rather
listen to my reading aloud than read for herself. There were no
electric fans then, but as I read I shared the benefits of her hand fan.'[8]
Thus there grew up between the motherless boy and this childless
lady a warm affection and friendship which satisfied and sublimated
the pent-up, chaotic yearnings of his adolescence and warmed his
wayward genius into fruitfulness.

While she supplied the emotional stimulus and the caressing
warmth and shade which he needed most at that age, it was her
husband Jyotirindranath who gave the first necessary discipline and

[8] *My Boyhood Days.*

direction to his nebulous and unformed talent. Himself at the peak of his creative powers, Jyotirindranath took the young brother under his wing and made him an apprentice in the workshop of his genius. He sat at the piano and made Rabi sing; he composed new melodies as his hands strayed over the keyboard and encouraged his young brother to improvise verses to fit the tune; he read to him the first drafts of his dramas and gave him confidence by incorporating in them Rabi's suggestions and even compositions; he staged these dramas and made his brother act in them. He did not allow the difference between their age to stand in the way of the younger brother's full freedom of expression, either in intellectual discussion or in literary creation.

This healthy and stimulating companionship enabled Rabi to shake off the diffidence which the repressed years of his infancy had given him.

'But for such snapping of my shackles I might have become crippled for life. Those in authority are never tired of holding forth the possibility of the abuse of freedom as a reason for withholding it, but without that possibility freedom would not be really free. And the only way of learning how to use properly a thing is through its misuse. For myself at least I can truly say that what little mischief resulted from my freedom always led the way to the means of curing mischief. I have never been able to make my own anything which they tried to compel me to swallow by getting hold of me, physically or mentally, by the ears. Nothing but sorrow have I ever gained except when left freely to myself.'[9]

The apprenticeship was not confined to literary exercises only. Jyotirindranath took the young brother with him on his tour of the family estates at Shelidah in north-east Bengal. Like the earlier visit to Santiniketan with his father, this visit too was a precursor of his intimate association with a spot which was later to become the scene of one of his most fertile periods of creative activity. At Shelidah Jyotirindranath taught him to ride and took him with him on his tiger-hunting expeditions.

'The jungle was dense, and in its lights and shadows the tiger refused to show himself. A rough kind of ladder was made by

[9] *My Reminiscences.*

cutting footholds in a stout bamboo, and Jyotidada climbed up with
his gun ready to hand. As for me, I was not even wearing slippers,
I had not even that poor instrument with which to beat and humiliate
the tiger. Biswanath (the accompanying *shikari*) signed to us to be
on the alert, but for some time Jyotidada could not even see the tiger.
After long straining of his bespectacled eyes he at last caught a
glimpse of one of its markings in the thicket. He fired. By a lucky
fluke the shot pierced the animal's backbone, and it was unable to
rise. It roared furiously, biting at all the sticks and twigs within
reach, and lashing its tail. Thinking it over, I know that it is not in
the nature of tigers to wait so long and patiently to be killed. I wonder if someone had had the forethought to mix a little opium with
its feed on the previous night! Otherwise, why such sound sleep?'[10]

He has recalled one more encounter with a tiger during
the same trip. A report was received that a tiger was lurking in the
jungle near by. 'My brother and I set out on elephants to look for
him. My elephant lurched majestically on, uprooting cane from the
sugar-cane fields and munching as he went, so that it was like riding
on an earthquake. The jungle lay ahead of us. He crushed the trees
with his knees, pulled them up with his trunk and cast them to the
ground. I had previously heard tales of terrible possibilities from
Biswanath's brother Chamru, how sometimes the tiger leaps on to
the elephant's back and clings there, digging in his claws. Then the
elephant, trumpeting with pain, rushes madly through the forest,
and whoever is on his back is dashed against the trees till arms, legs
and head are crushed out of all recognition. That day, as I sat my
elephant, the image of myself thus being pounded to a jelly filled
my imagination from first to last. For very shame I concealed my
fear, and glanced from side to side in nonchalant fashion, as though
to say, "Let me but catch a glimpse of the tiger and then! ..." The
elephant ... suddenly stood stock-still. The *mahout* made no attempt
to urge it forward. He had clearly more respect for the tiger's powers
as a *shikari* than for my brother's. His great anxiety was undoubtedly
that Jyotidada should so wound the tiger as to drive it to desperation.
Suddenly the tiger leaped from the jungle, swift as the thunder-
charged storm from the cloud. We are accustomed to the sight of a

[10] *My Boyhood Days.*

cat, dog, or jackal, but here were shoulders of terrific bulk and power, yet no sense of heaviness in that perfectly proportioned strength.'

While in Shelidah the budding poet was seized with the romantic notion of scribbling his verse, not in ordinary prosaic ink but appropriately in the perfumed extract of flowers. But the moisture he could extract by squeezing the petals was not sufficient even to wet the tip of his pen. He thought of designing a mechanism by which a pestle could be made to revolve in a big cup-shaped wooden sieve by means of strings and pulleys. He discussed the plan with his elder brother. It may be that Jyotirindranath smiled to himself, but he gave no sign of being amused. He merely said, 'Go ahead!' and sent for a mechanic to work under Rabi's instructions. The machine was ready and the sieve was filled with flowers, but turn the pestle as he would, the flowers merely turned to mud and not a drop of essence ran out. The young romantic realized to his discomfiture that he was no Leonardo da Vinci. 'This was the only occasion in my life on which I tried my hand at engineering.' But he never forgot his debt to his elder brother who not only did not discourage him in his futile experiment but allowed him full scope to learn from his failure. 'My brother Jyotirindra unreservedly let me go my own way to self-knowledge, and only since then could my nature prepare to put forth its thorns, it may be, but likewise, its flowers. This experience of mine has led me to dread, not so much evil itself, as tyrannical attempts to create goodness. Of punitive police, political or moral, I have a wholesome horror. The state of slavery which is thus brought on is the worst form of cancer to which humanity is subject.'[11]

Thus under the warmth of affection and encouragement he received from his talented brother Jyotirindra and his charming wife Kadambari, the fountain of young Rabi's poetic exuberance was released. He was now fourteen and his first long narrative poem in eight cantos, running to over 1,600 lines, was published in a literary magazine, *Gyanankur*. The poem was called *Banaphul* (The Wild Flower) and told the story of a young girl, Kamala, who was brought up by her father in a solitary retreat in the Himalayas. Like

[11] *My Reminiscences.*

Sakuntala her playmates were the wild plants and denizens of the forest and like Miranda she had not set her eyes on any other human being save her father. The father dies and she is left an orphan, disconsolate. A young traveller passes by and, struck by her loveliness and her plight, takes her home with him and marries her. But Kamala, unused to living among men, finds it hard to adjust herself to the conventions of society and pines for her beloved forest in the mountains. She is, however, greatly attracted by her husband's friend Nirad, a young, handsome poet and in her innocence confesses her love for him. Though Nirad is also secretly in love with her he is shocked by her frank avowal which he considers wrong and lectures to her on her duty and loyalty to her husband. But this child of nature does not understand such high-sounding terms and merely says, 'I know not what marriage means, nor what is husband and what is wife. All I know is that what I love I love.' Nirad spurns her in anger and goes away, only to be killed by his friend, Kamala's husband, who suspects him of seducing his wife. Kamala is heart-broken at this murder and leaving her husband and home keeps vigil by the dead body of Nirad. After cremating him she returns to her mountain retreat to seek solace in nature, her first great love. But having known human love she is unable to find peace in solitude and finally jumps from a snowy peak into the river below. The waves, like a mother's arms, take back the child to its bosom. The wild flower plucked from its stem has withered.

His first prose writing was also published in the same journal, an essay in literary criticism analysing the features of different kinds of poetry. The occasion was a book of poems published recently and anonymously which had caused something of a minor literary sensation, its authorship being popularly attributed to a lady. A young fan even came and showed to Rabi letters written and signed by the alleged authoress. But the poems were so lacking in reticence that young Rabi refused to share the popular belief and tried to prove in the article that they could not have been written by a woman. That his surmise was correct was later proved. Meanwhile the young fan came and reported to him that a B.A. was going to write a rejoinder to the article. A B.A. was in those days the high-water mark of erudition and Rabi had not even passed his middle school. He was scared and spent several days in fear and suspense. Fortunately no B.A. challenged him.

The range of his interests was widening. He joined a Secret Society called Sanjivani Sabha, founded by his elder brother Jyotirindranath and Rajnarayan Bose. Their aim was the political liberation of India and it was modelled after Mazzini's Carbonari. Its sittings were held ' . . . in a tumbledown building in an obscure Calcutta lane' and its proceedings were shrouded in mystery. 'This mystery was its only claim to be awe-inspiring, for as a matter of fact there was nothing in our deliberations or doings of which government or people need have been afraid. The rest of our family had no idea where we were spending our afternoons. Our front door would be locked, the meeting room in darkness, the watchword a Vedic mantra, our talk in whispers.' Jyotirindranath was incorrigibly romantic and his fertile imagination lured him to incredible adventures, sometimes with Quixotic consequences. His own rendezvous with destiny petered out but it helped considerably to stimulate his brother's many-sided interests, not the least of which was his passionate concern in his nation's freedom.

On the first day of the year 1877 the new Viceroy of India, Lord Lytton, held a Durbar in Delhi to emulate the splendour of the Moghul emperors and to impress on Indians the newly-acquired majesty of Queen Victoria as the Empress of India. At the same time a terrible famine raged over the land and numberless skeletons haunted the countryside. This ghastly contrast was the theme of a satirical poem written by Rabi and read on the occasion of the Hindu Mela of that year.[12]

About this time Jyotirindranath, the restless and prodigal innovator, started a literary monthly named *Bharati*, with his eldest brother Dwijendranath, the philosopher-poet, as editor. Like everything else he put his hand to, this magazine blazed a new trail in Bengali literature. Young Rabi had now a family forum at his disposal, though he needed little incentive to scribble. The fountain

---

[12] A leading poet of the day, Nabin Chandra Sen, has described in his memoirs how impressed he was at the sight of a handsome lad reciting the moving poem in his sonorous voice. When he inquired who he was, he was told that the lad was the youngest son of Maharshi Debendranath Tagore.

had been released and there was no holding back the gushing spray, with its bubble and froth. His first short story, *Bhikarini* (The Beggar Maid), an unfinished novel, *Karuna* (Pity), a historical drama in blank verse, *Rudra Chanda*, a long narrative poem in blank verse, *Kavi Kahini* (A Poet's Story), a sheaf of songs in archaic style and many poems, articles, studies in Western literature and translations, poured from his pen, as fast as he could scribble. About these out-pourings, most of which he ruthlessly discarded from his collected works in mature years, he has said: 'My mind had nothing in it but hot vapour, and vapour-filled bubbles frothed and eddied round a vortex of lazy fancy, aimless and unmeaning. No forms were evolved, there was only the distraction of movement, a bubbling up, a bursting back into froth. What little of matter there was in it was not mine, but borrowed from other poets. What was my own was the restlessness, the seething tension within me.'[13]

He wrote this harsh self-appraisal at a time when he had already achieved the mastery of word and form, so that these early attempts must have made him blush for their crude effusions. And yet some of them are not devoid of poetic merit and are of considerable interest as illustrating the nebulous state, not only of his genius but of that literary period in Bengal when the old forms and values were dead or dying and the new ones had yet to take shape with this new star. The boy-poet was feeling his way through a chaos and had to chase many shadows before he discovered his own form.

The *Kavi Kahini* is in fact the story of this young poet's spiritual bewilderment and groping. The poem begins with a highly idealized picture of a poet's childhood when he is brought up in the lap of Nature which is at once mother and playmate to him. As he grows up he discovers that Nature is more than a mere playground, it has its purpose and its laws which will yield their secrets only to objective, scientific study (Rabindranath's life-long interest in science is thus early evidenced). And so the days pass happily, shared between love of nature and study of its phenomena, until at the age of about fifteen or sixteen the poet feels a growing emptiness in his life and realizes the need of human love and companionship: *Manusher mon chaya manusheri mon*—a lovely line meaning 'the human heart longs

[13] *My Reminiscences.*

for human intimacy'. He wanders disconsolate in the forest and chances upon a maiden with whom he falls in love. Her name is Nalini—a name that was to remain a favourite with Rabindranath. They live together. The poet is happy at first but soon wearies of dalliance in love and mere happiness. A restlessness seizes him, he leaves her in search of what he himself does not know or understand and wanders in the big world of men. When he returns, still disconsolate, he finds that Nalini, pining away in his absence, is on her death-bed. Then he realizes that he had never ceased to love her and that it was this love that he was vainly seeking elsewhere. However, it is too late. Nalini dies and the poet is left to philosophize on universal love.

Recalling this early effusion in *My Reminiscences* Rabindranath commented: 'It was the product of an age when the writer had seen practically nothing of the world except an exaggerated image of his own nebulous self. So the hero of the story was naturally a poet, not the writer as he was, but as he imagined or desired himself to seem. . . In it was a great parade of universal love, that pet subject of the budding poet, which sounds as big as it is easy to talk about . . . When I blush to read these effusions of my boyhood I am also struck with the fear that very possibly in my later writings the same distortion wrought by straining after effect lurks in a less obvious form. The loudness of my voice, I doubt not, often drowns the thing I would say; and some day or other Time will find me out.'

While this long narrative outburst bears an unmistakable impress of the reading of the English romantic poets, particularly Shelley and Keats, the other major attempt of this period, the sheaf of songs entitled *Bhanusinher Padavali* (Songs of Bhanu Singh) bears an altogether different impress. The three major literary influences on the poetic development of Rabindranath may be said to be the influence of Sanskrit literature, of medieval Vaishnav or religious love poetry, and Western literature. As the confluence of three rivers makes the spot sacred in India, so these three diverse streams met and mingled and made Rabindranath's poetry what it became. *Bhanusinher Padavali* bears witness to the impact of Vaishnav religious poetry on this boy-poet. Vaishnav poetry sings mainly of the love of Radha and other milk-maids of Brindaban for Krishna the divine cowherd (and supposed author of *Bhagavad Gita*) and this love is deemed to symbolize the yearning of the soul for the Oversoul or God. For sheer lyricism and ecstasy of sentiment, ranging from the ethereal to the erotic, this form of poetry has not been surpassed in India. Its blend of the mystical and human, of the abstract and concrete, of extravagance and simplicity had made it a popular vehicle of religion and philosophy. In the nineteenth century, however, this form of poetry had gone out of vogue and had fallen into disrepute among the intelligentsia who had come under the spell of Western literature. Its poetic form had become too conventional, its sentimental effusions trite, and in the Tagore family in particular, its religious symbolism had come to be identified with superstition and idolatry.

When Rabi was about twelve or so these lyrics were being collected and published in Bengali and came into his hands. He was fascinated by their lyrical movement, their metrical boldness and the directness of their imagery.[14] How much of its religious philosophy he understood it is difficult to say; but despite the antipathy of his upbringing to its symbolism based on the worship of a human god, he had an intuitive appreciation of its underlying deep humanism. The poet understood the poet while the theologians wrangled. This fascination grew till when he was sixteen he was seized with a strong desire to pour his own vague yearnings in the same mould which would express the fervour of his feelings while screening their object. One day in the season of rains when thick clouds had gathered in the sky, he lay in his room alone and taking a slate in hand wrote the first of these lyrics in the archaic language of the medieval poets: *Gahana kusuma kunja majhe* . . .

> The thick groves of flowers vibrate with the melody of flute,
> Casting off all fear and shame, come, dear one, come.

In the manner of these poets he strung in the last line the name of the author which he transformed for the purpose into Bhanu Singh which means exactly what his own name Rabindranath means,

---

[14] He often talked of it in later life and would quote the following verse: 'Eyes starting like birds about to fly.'

A portion of the Tagore house at Jorasanko, Calcutta

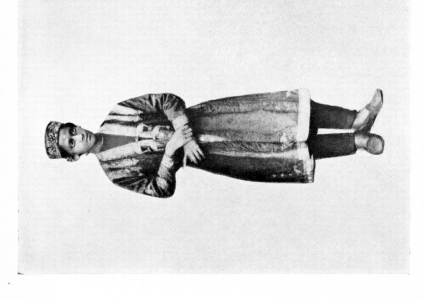

namely, the lord of sun. Pleased with the attempt he read out the poem to a friend saying that it was written by a fifteenth-century poet, Bhanu Singh. The friend was much impressed with the poem and swallowed the yarn about the authorship. And thus these poems came to be published in *Bharati*, young Rabi explaining in an introductory note that while rummaging in the archives of the Brahma Samaj Library he had come across the manuscript of this fifteenth-century poet.

Several readers were taken in by this hoax and Rabindranath has told us in his *Reminiscences* how a Bengali scholar, Dr. Nishikanta Chatterjee, who had studied in the universities of Edinburgh, St. Petersburg and Leipzig and was in Germany when the issues of *Bharati* in which these lyrics appeared reached him, was so impressed by them that in his book on the lyrical poetry of India published in German he gave a very high place to this fifteenth-century poet Bhanu Singh. Recalling this joke Tagore observed: 'Any attempt to test Bhanu Singh's poetry by its ring would have shown up the base metal. It had none of the ravishing melody of our ancient pipes, but only the tinkle of a modern, foreign barrel-organ.' But though Rabi could compliment himself on the partial success of this literary hoax, he could claim no credit for its originality, for he has himself told us that he got the idea from the story he had heard and read of the life of the eighteenth-century English boy-poet Thomas Chatterton who had successfully passed off his romance of Thomas Rowley, an imaginary monk of the fifteenth century as 'perhaps the oldest dramatic piece extant, wrote by one Rowley, a priest in Bristol, who lived in the reigns of Henry VI and Edward IV', which he claimed to have discovered in St. Mary Redcliffe.[15] Apart from this innocent literary fraud associated with these early lyrics, what is of chief significance is the fact that these were almost the only compositions of this period which the author in his mature years allowed to be included in his collected works. They are still so included and some of these lyrics, set by him to music, are commonly sung and loved to this day.

[15] *Encyclopaedia Britannica*, Vol. 5. Rabindranath also wrote an article on Chatterton which appeared in the same journal, *Bharati*, about two years after the publication of the lyrics.

F

The boy was growing fast and though he was by no means idling away his years, the Maharshi and the elders were worried about his future. A literary career by itself was no profession in those days and it was a matter of legitimate concern to the family, how to harness the impetuous talents of this precocious boy to some useful and respectable occupation. His elder brother, Satyendranath, who was the first native member of the Indian Civil Service, suggested to the Maharshi that he might take Rabindra to England with him (he himself was to proceed there shortly on leave, his wife and children having already preceded him) and give him a chance to become something, preferably a Civil Servant like himself or, at any rate, a barrister at one of the Inns of Court, a tribe held in high esteem in India in those days. The father agreed and Rabindra accompanied his brother to Ahmedabad[16] where the latter was the District Judge —the idea being that a few months' stay with his England-returned brother would give him the necessary preliminary training and polish in British social etiquette. Thus began his second sojourn outside Bengal, in western India.

The Judge's bungalow where he stayed with his brother was a seventeenth-century palace originally built by Prince Khusru (later Emperor Shah Jahan, the builder of Taj Mahal), its open terrace overlooking the river Sabarmati. Satyendranath was in Court the whole day and the young brother transplanted from the festive, overflowing gaiety of the family home in Calcutta must at first have felt lonely and dejected. A sense of his inadequacy weighed on him and he felt that life was bigger than literature, that he must face the world and play his part as a man among men—a feeling that was to recur again and again in his life. In one of the first poems he scribbled in Ahmedabad he invokes the presiding deity of his life and begs her to redeem the futility of his days, to infuse spirit and purpose in his life, 'useless, helpless, bereft of wisdom,' so that he may justify his manhood by his deeds and 'leave my unfading signature on the scroll of time'.

[16] Now the capital of the new State of Gujarat in the Indian Union; a famous centre of textile industry and for many years the scene of Mahatma Gandhi's activities. It was here that the Mahatma built his first Asrama or Colony in India, on the bank of the river Sabarmati.

His brother's study was well equipped with books, both English and Sanskrit, and the lonely boy read voraciously of English literature and through English of European literature. The articles he contributed to *Bharati* during this period bear ample evidence of the wide range of his reading, some of the titles being, 'The Saxons and Anglo-Saxon Literature', 'The Normans and Anglo-Norman Literature', 'Petrarch and Laura', 'Dante and his Poetry', 'Goethe', 'Chatterton', etc. Years later, writing in *Contemporary Indian Philosophy*,[17] he recalled:

'When I was young I tried to approach Dante, unfortunately through an English translation. I failed utterly, and felt it my pious duty to desist. Dante remained a closed book to me. I also wanted to know German literature and by reading Heine in translation, I thought I had caught a glimpse of the beauty there. Fortunately I met a missionary lady from Germany and asked her help. I worked hard for some months, but being rather quick-witted, which is not a good quality, I was not persevering. I had the dangerous facility which helps one to guess the meaning too easily. My teacher thought I had almost mastered the language, which was not true. I succeeded, however, in getting through Heine, like a man walking in sleep crossing unknown paths with ease, and I found immense pleasure. Then I tried Goethe. But that was too ambitious. With the help of the little German I had learnt, I did go through *Faust*. I believe I found my entrance to the palace, not like one who has keys for all the doors, but as a casual visitor who is tolerated in some general guest room, comfortable but not intimate. Properly speaking, I do not know my Goethe, and in the same way many other great luminaries are dusky to me.'

He also freely translated from these European poets and included these translations in his articles on them as illustrative specimens. Besides these literary studies which throw light on the range of his reading and curiosity, he had been writing and was to write a large number of light essays, playful and provocative, on a variety of themes. This early prose of his which, unfortunately, has been neglected because of his reputation as a poet, shows a firmer hold on form and a more concrete awareness of the world around him

[17] Edited by S. Radhakrishnan and Muirhead. Published by George Allen & Unwin, London.

than his more famous and nebulous poetic compositions. These essays are less verbose and repetitive and in penning them, the boy-author had not only a wink in his eye but was well aware that brevity is the soul of wit, for he quotes the French philosopher Pascal who, having written a lengthy letter wrote at the end apologizing for its inordinate length which was due to his being in a hurry and not having enough time to make the letter brief. Here are a few lines from these essays:

'Very few persons are so rich as to afford to seem poor. For myself I am poor enough to flaunt gilded buttons. The day I can expose their brass, I shall have become truly rich.'

'They say, love is blind. Does that mean that to see more is to be blind? For love sharpens the eye and enlarges the understanding.'

'The difference between friendship and love is that while the former means two persons *and* the world, the latter means that the two persons *are* the world. In friendship one plus one are three, in love one plus one are one.'

'Suffering is another word for obsession with self. That is why the sight of beauty brings joy by taking us away from ourselves.'

'Our mind is a bundle of hungers.'

'Some people say that woman is like the zero; when put on the right side of the numeral 1 (which is man) she gives him the strength of ten men; but alas for the poor fellow who has her on the wrong side, she breaks him into a fragment of himself ($\cdot$01). Needless to say, I do not agree with them who thus malign the fair sex.'

'Our ancients said that modesty is woman's best ornament. But women put on so many ornaments that there is little room left for this one.'[18]

Though he stayed in Ahmedabad for about four months[19] only, the period marks a stage in his mental development. It was here that he first composed his own music for his songs. In Calcutta he had watched his brother Jyotirindranath compose new melodies as his hands strayed over the piano and he himself had helped to extem-

[18] These English renderings are mine. Except where quotations refer to published English texts, the translations given throughout this volume are mine.

[19] The house known as Shahibag where he stayed is now the Governor's residence and is a protected monument under the Ancient Monuments Preservation Act.

porize words for the tunes. Now he composed his own tunes and words. This form of composition, at once literary and musical—sometimes the words came first and the tune followed, sometimes vice versa, sometimes both the words and tune came simultaneously—was to become a major creative delight which lasted till the end of his life. In all he composed over two thousand songs, words and music, which are sung in Bengal on almost every conceivable occasion and have a popular appeal that surpasses even that of his poetry. He himself said on more than one occasion that while his poetry might be forgotten, his songs never. Which is both true and not true. His songs will assuredly never be forgotten—not in Bengal; but neither will his poetry be, as long as the Bengali language survives. Indeed, not a little of his prose too will remain as an imperishable legacy to his language.

It was in Ahmedabad too that he conceived the plot of one of his loveliest short stories, *Kshudhita Pashan* (The Hungry Stones), which he wrote later. Staying in the house where the stones had been mute witnesses of scenes of revelry and intrigue redolent of the Arabian Nights, his fancy, free to wander, conjured up pictures of those days. 'In Ahmedabad I felt for the first time that history had paused, and was standing with her face turned towards the aristocratic past . . . How many hundred years have passed since those times! In the *Nahabat-Khana*, the minstrels' gallery, an orchestra played day and night, choosing tunes appropriate to the eight periods of the day. The rhythmic beat of the horses' hoofs echoed on the streets, and great parades were held of the mounted Turkish cavalry, the sun glittering on the points of their spears. In the court of the Padshah whispered conspiracies were ominously rife. Abyssinian eunuchs, with drawn swords, kept guard in the inner apartments. Rose-water fountains played in the hamams of the Begums, the bangles tinkled on their arms. Today Shahibag stands silent, like a forgotten tale; all its colour has faded, and its varied sounds have died away; the splendours of the day are withered and the nights have lost their savour.'[20]

After a few months' stay in Ahmedabad, his elder brother Satyendranath felt that it would do Rabi more good and prepare

[20] *My Boyhood Days.*

him better for his visit to England if he stayed with a family where
he would have more practice in conversational English and where he
might learn to feel easy in the company of ladies used to the western
way of living. So he sent Rabi to Bombay to stay with the family of
a Marathi friend, Dr Atmaram Pandurang Turkhud, an eminent
physician and one of the most progressive men of his time. The
burden of 'educating' Rabi fell on the young daughter of the family,
very lovely to look at, England-returned and highly sophisticated by
the standards of those days. Anna (her full name was Annapurna) was
only slightly older than Rabi. The teacher enjoyed her burden and
the pupil was entranced with so lovely a teacher. How much he
learnt during the two months he stayed there we do not know, but
there grew up between the teacher and pupil a tender and innocent
intimacy which left a permanent impress on his memory. Recalling
the episode at the age of eighty Rabindranath wrote:

'My own attainments were only ordinary, and she could not have
been blamed if she had ignored me. But she did not do so. Not
having any store of book-learning to offer her, I took the first
opportunity to tell her that I could write poetry. This was the only
capital I had with which to gain attention. When I told her of my
poetical gift, she did not receive it in any carping or dubious spirit,
but accepted it without question. She asked the poet to give her a
special name, and I chose one for her which she thought very
beautiful. I wanted that name to be entwined with the music of my
verse, and I enshrined it in a poem which I made for her. She listened
as I sang it in the *Bhairavi* mode of early dawn, and then said, "Poet,
I think that even if I were on my death-bed your songs would call
me back to life." There is an example of how well girls know how
to show their appreciation by some pleasant exaggeration. They
simply do it for the pleasure of pleasing. I remember that it was from
her that I first heard praise of my personal appearance—praise that
was often very delicately given. For example, she asked me once
very particularly to remember one thing: "You must never wear a
beard. Don't let anything hide the outline of your face." Everyone
knows that I have not followed that advice. But she herself did not
live to see my disobedience proclaimed upon my face.'[21]

[21] *My Boyhood Days.*

The name he gave her was Nalini, the name of the imaginary sweetheart in his long narrative poem *Kavi Kahini* (The Poet's Story) published earlier. He used to read this poem to her and to translate it into English for her. When the poem was later published in book-form and Jyotirindranath sent her a copy from Calcutta (no doubt, at the request of his younger brother, then in England) she wrote back thanking him for it and added that Rabi had 'read and translated [it] to me till I know the poem by heart'. She inspired not one but several poems of his in which he lingers lovingly on the name Nalini.

This brief romantic interlude, though little more than an innocent intimacy, left a permanent impress on Rabindranath's memory. Anna was strongly drawn to the young and handsome poet, and being more mature and experienced (she is said to have married a Scotsman whom she left soon after), she no doubt exercised her charms to the full. She would play all kinds of pranks to tease and provoke him, tiptoeing from behind and clapping her hands over his eyes; she would pull him by his hands pretending to measure strength in a fake tug-of-war and then suddenly yield and fall on his chest. One day she told him, by way of initiating him in the mysteries of English etiquette, that a man who succeeded in stealing a lady's gloves while she was asleep had a right to kiss her. 'She was reclining in an easy chair. Suddenly I found her in deep sleep. When she opened her eyes, she cast a furtive glance at her gloves which lay just where she had placed them. No one had had the sense to steal them.'[22] The young man who no doubt enjoyed all this flirtation and probably felt a flutter in his heart was too innocent or inhibited to understand the full significance of the game being played. But the memory remained and the poet never forgot the image of this charmer or ever ceased to be grateful for her love.

His references to her in his later life, whether in conversation or private correspondence, are instinct with tenderness and respect. Take this tribute to her in *My Boyhood Days* (in old age he was less reticent than when he wrote his first autobiography in middle age):

'In some years, birds strange to Calcutta used to come and build in that banyan tree of ours. They would be off again almost before I

[22] *Among the Great*: Dilip Kumar Roy. Jaico Publishing House, Bombay.

had learnt to recognize the dance of their wings, but they brought
with them a strangely lovely music from their distant jungle homes.
So, in the course of our life's journey some angel from a strange and
unexpected quarter may cross our path, speaking the language of
our own soul, and enlarging the boundaries of the heart's possessions.
She comes unbidden, and when at last we call for her she is no
longer there. But as she goes, she leaves on the drab web of our lives
a border of embroidered flowers, and for ever and ever the night
and day are for us enriched.'

4

YOUTH

On 20 September 1878 Rabindra sailed for England on s.s. *Poona*, escorted by his elder brother Satyendranath. His heart was heavy as the ship moved, for he was leaving behind on the shore his charming Anna. Back at home in Calcutta was his sister-in-law Kadambari who had been to him mother and friend both, for whom his love was too deep and sacred to be categorized in terms of normal human relationship. He was leaving behind all that had enriched his life so far. Ahead lay the prospect, not so much of fresh woods and pastures new as of being once again yoked to the mills of academic studies.

Fortunately he has left behind a fair record of his sojourn abroad, first in the letters he wrote home which were published serially in *Bharati* and again much later in his autobiography. The letters are interesting as the authentic record of the first, fresh impressions of his youthful mind, with all the swagger of immature sophistication characteristic of that age. The recollection as recorded partly in *My Reminiscences* written more than thirty years later and partly in *My Boyhood Days* written at the age of eighty, is sober and modest and recaptures only such impressions as had retained a lasting significance for him. Indeed, he regrets in his *Reminiscences* that he ever wrote the letters as he did. 'In an unlucky moment I began to write letters to my relatives and to the *Bharati*. Now it is beyond my power to call them back. These were nothing but the outcome of youthful bravado. At that age the mind refuses to admit that its greatest pride is in its power to understand, to accept, to respect; and that modesty is the best means of enlarging its domain. Admiration and praise is looked upon as a sign of weakness or surrender, and the desire to cry down and hurt and demolish with argument gives rise to this kind of intellectual fireworks.'

This is harsh judgement; for the letters[1] describe faithfully and intelligently what he saw and understood of English life in the seventies of the last century and are full of shrewd observation and comments and have some fine passages on the beauty of the English countryside. They have considerable literary merit and are historically significant as an early specimen of Bengali prose written in the colloquial style. If they seemed impudent to the author in his mature age, it was because he had outgrown the temper of youth which makes impudence so delightful and disarming. He was, however, aware of their literary merit and knew that even in his flippancy he had created a new way in the literature of his language.

This was Rabindra's first voyage and he was not a good sailor— not then, at any rate, for he has described in the first letter how desperately he clung to his bed in the dingy cabin for the first six days, unable to face the tossing of the Arabian sea still turbulent with the Indian monsoon. He regretted that he could not share the 'rapture which the great poets of the world, from Valmiki to Byron, have felt at the sight of the sea'. It was only when the ship reached Aden that he breathed a sigh of thanksgiving and was able to move about and mix with the other passengers, of some of whom he has given amusing portraits. 'There was no dearth of ladies on the board, but the gentlemen grumbled that not one was young or pretty.' At Suez the two brothers left the boat and travelled overland to Alexandria where they caught another boat, which took them to Brindisi on the Italian coast. He was impressed with the town and harbour of Alexandria and noted with shame that ships of all countries were visible in that harbour except his own country's. The only things he liked in Brindisi were a fine garden full of luscious fruits and the beauty of dark-eyed Italian girls which reminded him of the girls at home. From Brindisi they went by train to Paris, drinking in eagerly the beauty of the rich landscape on the way. He found Paris 'too gorgeous' for his taste, but he enjoyed his first Turkish bath there. After the accumulation of dust and sand in Egypt, the brothers needed a thorough scrubbing which they got

---

[1] *Yurop-Pravasir Patra* (Letters of a Visitor to Europe). Still available in the collected Bengali edition of Tagore's works, *Rabindra Rachanavali*. Recently issued in a separate volume as centenary edition. No full English translation has been published.

now. 'A Turkish bath is like having one's body laundered by a *dhobi*.' At last they reached London. 'Such a dismal city I had never seen before—smoky, foggy, and wet, and everyone jostling and in a hurry.' (He grew to admire it later.) On this occasion he only had a glimpse of it in bad weather, on his way to Brighton where his sister-in-law (Satyendranath's wife) was expecting them.

In Brighton he was happy and felt at home. The sister-in-law was kind and the two children, Suren and Indira, aged six and five respectively, doted on their young and handsome uncle. It is worth quoting what the little niece, who grew to be a gracious and venerable lady highly respected by her people, recalled of her uncle more than eighty years later. 'After all these years I still remember how my uncle used to entertain us with his comic style of singing a particular Hindi song. He would start singing in common time. Then gradually the tempo would get faster and faster until his lips became a mere trembling line, and we would rock with laughter. . . He possessed a fine tenor voice which was much admired when he began to learn and sing English songs then in vogue, such as "Won't you tell me, Mollie darling", "Good-bye sweetheart, good-bye", etc. I was not old enough then to appreciate these songs, but after coming back home and learning English music in the Loreto Convent, I used to accompany him very often on the piano and his repertoire of European music was also gradually enlarged.'

But he had not been brought to England to exchange a home in Brighton for the one in Calcutta. So he was soon put into a public school. 'The first thing the Headmaster said after scanning my features was: "What a splendid head you have!"' Unlike the popular conception of public school 'ragging', the newcomer was well treated by the other boys. He could not, however, stay long in the school. A friend[2] of his elder brother who happened to be on a visit to England persuaded Satyendranath that if Rabindra was to derive any benefit from his education abroad, he should be made to live alone on his own. So Rabindra was brought to London and put in a lodging-house facing Regent's Park. It was winter and there

[2] A distinguished Indian lawyer, Tarak Palit, who was later knighted. He had brought his own son, Loken Palit, to be admitted to the London University. He and Rabindra became good friends later.

was not a leaf on the trees in the Park. More than the actual cold, it was this bleakness which chilled him to his bones. It seemed as if Nature wore a perpetual frown, the sky was turbid and the light of day lacked lustre 'like a dead man's eye'. In Brighton he had seen the romantic aspect of Nature in winter when it snowed. 'It was bitingly cold, the sky filled with white moonlight, the earth covered with white snow. It was not the face of Nature familiar to me, but something quite different—like a dream. Everything near seemed to have receded far away, leaving the still white figure of an ascetic steeped in deep meditation. The sudden revelation, on the mere stepping outside a door, of such wonderful, such immense beauty had never before come upon me.'

In Brighton he had not only children to play with at home—and he loved children all his life—but he had interesting social life in the evenings, for his brother and his wife had many friends and received many invitations to dinners and balls. The boy had an eye for observation and described what he saw in his letters home. Here are a few tit-bits translated at random:

'Here there is a pub in every street corner, but bookshops are rare.' 'The girls play on the piano and sing, they sit by the fire and read novels, are expected to entertain visitors and enjoy flirting for its own sake.' 'The people here imagine that I knew nothing of civilization until my arrival here. The other day Dr. —'s brother tried to explain to me at length what a camera was and at an evening party Miss — asked me if I had ever seen a piano before.' 'I get up at six in the morning and have a cold shower, which seems to amuse all those who hear of it.' 'Here the houses are well-kept and very clean, the floor well-scrubbed and the furniture shining. Their idea of cleanliness is, however, different from ours. While we would not mind having a spittoon in the room, here where people seem to suffer much more from cold and cough, they prefer to spit in their handkerchiefs which they put back in their pockets. Some men wear detachable cuffs and shirt-fronts which alone are regularly laundered. Ladies are very particular about their appearance but all they need wash regularly are the face, arms and hands. In many houses there are no bathrooms at all. Nor is frequent washing as necessary in this country as in ours due to the difference in climate. On the other hand, if we bathe more often, we keep our surroundings much less clean.' 'One day we were invited to an evening party at Dr. M—'s. There were many other guests, among them two very pretty girls. Needless to say, they were very conscious of their looks. In this country it is practically impossible for an attractive woman not to be made conscious of her charm. She is so ardently sought after . . . After some time I was asked to sing an Indian song. I was most reluctant to do so, knowing how unfamiliar our music would sound to their ears. But I had to obey. Politeness is a virtue even when it makes one ridiculous. I sang. It was an ordeal, for I could not help noticing how difficult it was for the audience to suppress their smiles and giggles. I heaved a sigh of relief when the song came to an end, but in the meanwhile my face and ears had become red.' 'Despite the many differences between the ways of women here and in our own country, there is one thing in common between them. Society trains and equips them, each in its fashion, to win the highest bidder.' 'Spinsters in this country do a lot of social work. They run temperance societies, organize workmen's clubs, etc.'

In London he felt lonely. He knew no one. A tutor had been engaged to teach him Latin—a good soul but rather a crank. He was obsessed with a theory that in each age one dominant idea is manifested in every human society all over the world, irrespective of there being any outward channel of communication between these different societies. He was so absorbed in this research that he had little time to spare for his livelihood. He was ill-clad and ill-fed and it was obvious that his family at home despised him. When he had discovered a fresh proof or argument for his theory he would talk of nothing else and forget to proceed with the Latin lesson; on other days he would be preoccupied and gloomy. This pretence of learning Latin lasted for some time until Rabindra changed his lodgings. When he offered to settle his dues, the honest tutor would not accept any payment, saying, 'I have done nothing and only wasted your time.' It was with great difficulty that he was persuaded to accept the fee. Recalling this incident, Rabindranath comments in his *Reminiscences*: 'Though my Latin tutor had never ventured to trouble me with the proofs of his theory, yet to this day I do not disbelieve it. I am convinced that the minds of men are connected through some deep-lying continuous medium, and that a disturbance in one part is by it secretly communicated to others.'

From these dingy and lonely lodgings Rabindra shifted as a paying guest to the house of a professional coach, one Mr. Barker. He was even more queer, though less pathetic, than the Latin tutor. The only other members of the household were 'his mild, little wife who must once have been pretty' and her pet dog. Whenever Barker wanted to punish his wife he tortured the poor dog. He was a very gloomy and morose man. 'He was once a clergyman and I bet every Sunday he painted lurid pictures of hell to his congregation.' The husband and wife hardly ever exchanged any conversation. They sat silent and glum through the dinner, much to the discomfort of the embarrassed guest. If Barker wanted a second helping of potatoes, he would mumble, 'Some potatoes' (the word 'please' was inaudible). Mrs. Barker would mumble back, 'I wish you were a little more polite.' 'But I did say "please",' Barker would protest. 'I did not hear it,' said the wife. 'It was no fault of mine,' the husband would remonstrate. There the conversation would end in a heavy silence. Mrs. Barker was, however, kind and friendly to the young guest and often sat and chatted with him in the sitting-room. As soon as Barker entered, a silence would descend on the house. One day Mrs. Barker was playing the piano to the guest when the husband entered.

'When are you going to stop?' he asked quietly. The piano stopped.

'I thought you had gone out.'

Later whenever Rabindra asked her to play, she would say, 'Wait till that horrid man goes out.' And yet the household ran smoothly; she worked the whole day and cooked and looked after the house, he worked and earned and gave her the money. There was never a violent scene or upheaval of any sort. But the guest found the atmosphere too heavy.

Providence came to Rabindra's rescue and he received a letter from Satyendranath's wife inviting him to stay with them in Torquay in Devon where the family had taken a cottage for the season. So off he fled to revel in the midst of nature and in the company of children, the two sources of joy which never failed him. The landscape in Devonshire was very attractive. He relished it to the full but wondered why no fountain of poetry was released in him. He began to feel guilty of neglecting his muse and set out one day in earnest '. . . to fulfil my poet's destiny'. He selected a lovely spot on a rock overhanging the sea, with a fringe of pines whose shade '. . . lay spread like the slipped-off garment of some languorous wood-nymph'. There he wrote a poem which he entitled *Bhagnatari* (The Wrecked Boat). 'I might have believed today that it was good, had I taken the precaution of sinking it then in the sea.'

The pleasant interlude over, Rabindra returned to London and joined the London University where he attended Henry Morley's lectures on English literature. He read with him *Religio Medici* and some plays of Shakespeare and was much impressed with the professor's gift for teaching. Henry Morley was in fact the only one of his academic teachers to whom he has paid unstinted tribute. The university education, however, did not last more than three months. During this period of his stay in London he visited the Houses of Parliament and heard Gladstone and John Bright speak on Irish Home Rule. Something in the latter's countenance so attracted him that he kept on gazing at the old man even before he came to know who he was. He noted with regret the plight of the Irish members of the House, who found the House almost deserted whenever one of them got up to speak.

Rabindra's days in London after his return from Torquay were pleasantly spent, for he was lucky in finding a home with a friendly English family, that of one Dr. Scott. When he first arrived at the house only the white-haired doctor, his wife and eldest daughter were there. The two younger daughters, alarmed at the prospect of their home being invaded by a coloured man, had gone off to stay with a relative. They returned only when they were assured that the stranger was harmless. The household was fairly large, with two sons, four daughters, and three maids. In course of time he became a favourite with everyone, including the dog Tabby,[3] who would not eat until he had played with him. In one of his letters home he has given a detailed picture of the daily life of this family whom he grew to love and admire. Mrs. Scott treated him like a son and looked

---

[3] He gave this name to the dog in his famous novel *Sesher Kavita*, published in 1929. English translation, *Farewell My Friend*, Jaico Publishing House, Bombay, 1956.

after him with more affection and solicitude than he had known from his own mother. Her devotion to her husband and family impressed him greatly. 'One thing struck me when living in this family—that human nature is everywhere the same. We are fond of saying, and I also believed, that the devotion of an Indian wife to her husband is something unique, and not to be found in Europe. But I at least was unable to discern any difference between Mrs. Scott and an ideal Indian wife.'

The daughters, too, grew very fond of him, particularly the third one who was more or less of his age and could sing and play on the piano. She taught him several English and Irish songs. In those days table-turning seances for communication with spirits were in vogue and Rabindra would often join the girls in such home-made amusement in the evening. Communication with the dead has always provided a grotesque thrill to the living and in those days when the movies had not been invented there were not many other opportunities of hands communicating with hands under cover of darkness. 'We would place our fingers on a small tea-table, and it would go capering about the room. It got to be so that whatever we touched began to quake and quiver.' Mrs. Scott, who was a pious Christian lady, did not quite like all this and would gravely shake her head and wonder if what the children were doing was right. But she was a kind and affectionate mother and did not wish to be a kill-joy. One of the sisters, perhaps the third one, expressed a desire to learn Bengali and Rabindra was delighted to teach her. He was too young to have ever given serious thought before to Bengali orthography and phonology and had always flattered himself that his mother-tongue, unlike English, had '. . . a conscience and does not delight in overstepping rules at every step'. But while teaching his charming pupil he came across several discoveries which gave him a new interest and insight in the intricacies of his own language.[4]

His earlier observations on English society and in particular the role and ways of its women, which had been mixed with not a little irony and caustic comment, now underwent a change and he began genuinely to admire the charm and strength of character of women

[4] This interest, thus romantically acquired, continued all his life and in 1909 he published a remarkable book entitled *Sabdatattva* (Science of Words).

At Oxford, 1930

On the stage as Valmiki in *Valmiki Pratibha*

In England, 1890

With his eldest daughter and son, 1889

brought up in a free society. This admiration was freely expressed
in his letters written home and published in *Bharati* where he compared the position of women in the two societies, western and his
own, and sought to show how the same sex was a source of strength
to one society and a source of weakness in the other. These outbursts
of admiration for the fair sex in England caused a flutter among the
elders at home who began to wonder if it was wise to let this
impetuous boy loose in England after his elder brother returned
home. The Maharshi was conservative in social outlook and it is
not uncommon that however fervently men may believe that God
is everywhere, they prefer to welcome His presence only in forms
of their own choosing. So a peremptory order went from India
that Rabindra was to cut short his studies and return home with
his elder brother.

Was the youth happy or heart-broken at this turn of events? He
has himself stated in his reminiscences that he was delighted at the
prospect of returning home. 'The light of my country, the sky of
my country, had been silently calling me.' This was no doubt true,
for from the point of view of his creative expression, his stay abroad
had been comparatively barren and he must at times have longed
for the stimulus which had released and fed his powers at home.
On the other hand, it must have been a painful wrench to break
away from the new and sweet attachments he had formed abroad.
'Mrs. Scott took me by the hand and wept. "Why did you come
to us," she said, "if you must go so soon?" ' What the daughters said
he has not told us, but a poem published in *Bharati*—significantly
under an assumed name—and later included in his book *Sandhya
Sangeet* (Evening Songs or Songs of Sunset) gives some idea of what
he felt. Here is a rough and crude rendering of it in English prose,
for what it is worth. The poem is titled *Du-Din* (Two Days).

> Winter had set in, the trees were bare of leaves,
> the earth covered under a white veil, when I,
> a stranger from the east, arrived in this
> western land.
>
> A two-day sojourn it was.

G

The winter is still there, the birds are silent,
the snow falls on the leafless trees. The passionate
kiss of Spring has not yet awakened Nature from its
death-like torpor. But my two days are over and
I must leave.

As I set my face homewards to the east, I ask myself:
Will I ever return to these shores, will I ever again
see the faces I have known! Years will pass and perhaps
one day when I am sitting alone by a river bank in a
far-away land and the sun is sinking to the west, a storm
of memory will of a sudden sweep over my heart and a
lightning flash will reveal a face once familiar and
the echo of an old song will reverberate in the sky.

This face, made as if a million flowers had gone into
its making, and this hair loose and dishevelled will
haunt my sleep night after night and these eyes wistful
with longing will look into mine and a voice broken
with tears will whisper, 'Must you leave? Must you?'

The two-day sojourn is over.

The leafless tree had no time to blossom, the snow
had no time to melt. And yet this two-day interlude
will for ever hold me in its arms, its feel will
never fade from my life.

And O the regret and shame of it!
I came for two days to this land—only to break
a gentle heart![5]

An incident which took place shortly before he left England is
worth recording, not only because of the very vivid impression it
seems to have left on his mind for, though in itself trifling, he has
related it in detail in his *Reminiscences* while omitting many more
important events, but because of its interesting reflection many
years later in his old age. While in England he had come to know

[5] The last two lines were omitted from the published version.

the widow of an Anglo-Indian official who, since Anglo-Indians like to be more English than the English, used to call him Rubi instead of Rabi. An Indian sycophant of her late husband had composed a dirge on the latter which he sent to her, adding that it could be sung to the mode *Behag*. So the widow pestered Rabi to sing it for her. Though the composition was atrocious, Rabi sang it for her in the traditional Indian mode. The lady was enchanted and since then whenever she ran into Rabi at an evening party, she would insist on his singing it, and would bring out from her bag printed copies of the composition. This had grown into such an ordeal that Rabi dreaded the prospect of meeting her. 'Who would have predicted at my birth or at his death what a severe blow to me would be the demise of this estimable Anglo-Indian!'

One day he received a telegram from her inviting him to her house which was at some distance from London. As the telegram was pressing and he was in any case shortly to leave for India, he thought of obliging the lady. So after the university classes, he took a train and arrived at her house at about nine in the evening, hungry and tired. After a cup of tea he was hustled off to a local inn and asked to come again in the morning. After an uncomfortable night at the inn, when he arrived at her house in the morning he was told that a lady who was ill was anxious to hear him sing. So the poor boy was made to stand on the landing of the stairs and serenade to a closed bedroom door.

'That's where she is,' said the widow, pointing to the door.

On his return to London he himself took to bed. The Scott girls begged him '. . . not to take this as a sample of English hospitality' and no doubt did their best to make up for it.

Nearly forty-five years later when Rabindranath, now famous, was convalescing at San Isidore in Buenos Aires as the guest of Victoria Ocampo, he expressed a wish one day to hear some modern European music. His hostess arranged for the Castro[6] Quartet to come out to San Isidro. For some reason Tagore felt depressed that

---

[6] Juan José Castro, now one of the foremost composers of Argentina. His opera *Prosperina and the Stranger* was awarded the International La Scala on the fiftieth anniversary of Verdi's death.

evening and did not come down from his room on the first floor. In the words of his charming and distinguished hostess:

'He just left his door ajar. The musicians sat down to play, with their music-stands before them, in the middle of the hall on the ground floor. I had to limit myself to pointing in the direction of the room upstairs where Tagore was sitting. I could not help smiling to myself remembering an incident I had read in Tagore's *Reminiscences* ... It is true that my friends did not play on a landing before a closed door. Debussy, Ravel and Borodin could reach the poet through a half-open door. I always wanted to tease him a little about this, telling him that without wishing it the young Indian student had had his revenge.'

In February 1880 Rabindra returned home with his brother and his family, having spent about seventeen months abroad. He came back empty-handed, with no academic degree or distinction. The only thing he brought with himself was the unfinished manuscript of a long lyrical drama he had begun in London with the significant title, *Bhagna Hriday* (The Broken Heart). When he landed in Bombay did he look for Anna? No one knows. His reticence will continue to baffle his biographers. Brought up in an age which looked upon mid-Victorian England as the acme of intellectual and moral progress and nursed under the powerful influence of a father celebrated for his religious and moral puritanism, it is hardly surprising that Rabindra was shy and reticent in his relations with women. He continued to be so till the very end, even though the last twenty years of his life were spent in an age which had almost reversed the earlier values and made unashamed exhibitionism seem a virtue.

Although cast in the form of a drama, *Bhagna Hriday* is more a string of lyrics than anything else—a lengthy exercise in lyricism, in thirty-four cantos or scenes, with over 4,000 lines. The plot is very thin and almost reminiscent of the earlier narrative poems. There is the inevitable poet, young, handsome and dream-entranced, breaking others' hearts and not knowing what he himself wants. His friend and companion since boyhood is a girl called Murala who is deeply and secretly in love with him. The poet is too obsessed with his own chaotic ego to notice her love for him, though he values her friendship and shares his 'sorrows' with her. 'I've lost nothing, and yet

I keep on looking—for what? Why this despair when there never was a hope? Whence this wound when no one ever hurt me?' He has seen a beautiful and wayward girl and thinks he is in love with her. She is Nalini—a name that seems to have haunted young Rabi's imagination. But Nalini is a *belle dame sans merci*, who enjoys playing with others' hearts without giving her own. The disappointed poet wanders away. When he returns and finds Murala on her death-bed he realizes that it is she he has always loved. But it is too late. There are several other characters in the drama and they all manage to break each other's heart. Even Nalini finds her heart broken at the end. 'I was playing with others' hearts when suddenly I lost my own. Amid the wreckage of others' hearts I saw mine broken.' There is, as usual, some philosophizing too, as when Murala discovers at the end that '. . . one who owns nothing has everything; the homeless may make the whole world his own; to the friendless no one is a stranger'. But neither the tragedy nor the philosophy is real, for the author was too young to have deeply experienced what he was trying to express. And yet the need to exercise his poetic gift was real and the poem has some lovely lyrical passages which show that the young author was steadily gaining mastery of the form.

Though the poem was never republished and included by him in his collected works, it did help to establish his reputation when it first appeared, for such lyrical ease and romantic abandon were something new in Bengali poetry. The Maharaja of Tripura, a neighbouring state, sent his Chief Minister to Calcutta to wait on the young poet and to convey to him the Maharaja's felicitations on this literary achievement. What surprised the author in his mature years was not that he wrote this long-drawn and over-heated effusion at the age of eighteen and thought it good, but that others thought it good too. 'The curious part of it is that not only was I eighteen, but everyone around me seemed to be eighteen likewise.' He has likened his imagination at that age to the infant's fever when the milk-teeth are cutting their way out. The fever abates only when the teeth are out '. . . and have begun assisting in the absorption of food. In the same way do our early passions torment the mind, like a malady, till they realize their true relationship with the outer world.'

The dedication of this lyrical drama when it was first published in *Bharati* is of interest. It was originally dedicated with a short poem addressed to an unnamed lady the first syllable of whose name being given as He—. The poem is charged with an almost religious intensity of devotion and it is not without significance that it was later turned into a religious hymn (with some modification) and is still included among Tagore's *Brahmo Sangeet* (religious hymns) and sung as such. It may be roughly rendered into English as follows:

You alone I've made my life's polestar, never again to lose my way in this ocean. May you always shine, wherever I be!—your light the balm of my eyes. Your face is hidden in my heart like the image of a goddess in a dark shrine. If ever I go astray, that face will shame me back into the right path again. I lay this broken heart at your feet; let its blood be the red lac on your feet!

It is obvious that the feet at which he offered his 'broken heart' were those of his sister-in-law Kadambari. It is said that her pet-name was Hecate, after the Greek goddess, which explains the anonymous dedication to He—.

This attachment also explains the paradox that this 'broken heart' on his return home was more carefree and happy than it had ever been. He poured himself out in a cascade of songs and wrote his first musical play, *Valmiki Pratibha* (The Genius of Valmiki). This is not a play to be read, as the author has himself warned us. It is to be seen and heard on the stage. Nor is it what in Europe is understood by an *Opera*, for it is not primarily a musical composition. It is a drama in music; the entire dialogue is in verse and every bit of verse a song. It is what *My Fair Lady* would be if Bernard Shaw had written the libretto and composed the music for it. The theme is based on the legend of the first epic poet of India, Valmiki, the author of *Ramayana*. He was supposed to have been a robber-chief who was once moved to pity when he witnessed the grief of one of a pair of cranes whose mate had been shot by a hunter. He broke into verse and in the metre which thus came to him he composed the first Indian epic. In Rabindranath's version it is not the plight of a bird that moves the robber-chief but the piteous cry of a young girl caught by his followers who propose to sacrifice her to the goddess Kali whom they wish to propitiate. It is a favourite idea of Rabindranath's on which he will harp again and again in his writings that the fountain-spring of all poetry, as indeed of every form of true greatness in life, is the awakening of the 'human' in man. His own favourite symbol of the 'human' was either a child or a girl. However, moved to pity, Valmiki rescues the girl, disbands the gang and wanders in search of his true vocation. The goddess Saraswati reveals herself to him and tells him that it was she who had assumed the form of a young girl to awaken his humanity. She gives him the gift of song and says: 'The music of pity which melted your stony heart shall become in your voice the music of humanity softening and chastening a million hearts. Your voice shall resound from land to land and many poets will echo your songs.'

But the chief significance of *Valmiki Pratibha* is neither its dramatic interest nor its poetic merit but its musical innovation. With this play Rabindra led his revolt against the prevailing orthodox tradition in Indian music. Music, like all other arts in India, had become stereotyped, almost fossilized. There is the classical tradition, whether of the north or of the south, which has behind it centuries of devoted discipline and which has, within its limits, attained near-perfection. It is music, pure and abstract, and like all abstract art its appeal is limited to those who have taken pains to understand what may be called its mathematics. It can be very beautiful, hauntingly so, in the hands of a rare master but ordinarily and as practised by virtuosos its appeal is limited. Its counterpart for the popular taste was the traditional religious and folk music, which is being gradually replaced by film-music. The position was not dissimilar in literature where, before the nineteenth century, there was either the great storehouse of Sanskrit classics or the popular religious lyric and ballad. What Rabindra was doing in literature he now tried to do in music. While caring for both the traditions, he respected the inviolable sanctity of neither and freely took from each what suited his purpose. He was not even averse to borrowing from western melodies, although he did very little of that and made his own whatever he took from other sources.

If his creative contribution in music has not received the same recognition as his contribution in literature it is because, in the first place, the classical tradition of music in India, unlike that of Sanskrit literature, is still very alive and vital and there was no vacuum to be filled. In fact, Rabindranath did not attempt creation of new forms in abstract music. What he did was to bring it down from its heights and make it keep pace with the popular idiom of musical expression. In the second place, his own music is so inextricably blended with the poetry of words that it is almost impossible to separate the mood from the words and the words from the tune. Each expresses and reinforces the other. Hence his songs have not the same appeal outside the Bengali-speaking zone as they have in his native Bengal where they have effectively saved the popular taste from degenerating into a craze for that bizarre amalgam of western jazz and native melodies known as cinema music.

When Rabi was a boy he had come across in the house an illustrated edition of Moore's *Irish Melodies*. The boy was fascinated with the illustrations and with the poems which conjured for him a romantic picture of old Ireland. He longed to hear the melodies sung and had to wait till he went to England before he could do so. Some longings, he confessed later, do unfortunately get fulfilled in this life, and die in the process. That is what happened to this particular longing, but not before he had learnt some of these melodies. The echo of some of them can still be heard in the music of *Valmiki Pratibha*. 'The tunes in this musical drama,' he wrote in his *Reminiscences*, 'are mostly Indian, but they have been dragged out of their classic dignity; that which soared in the sky was taught to run on the earth.'

He had heard serious European music, too, during his stay in England and had gradually learnt to appreciate its beauty, but to the end of his life he was '. . . convinced that our music and theirs abide in altogether different apartments, and do not gain entry to the heart by the self-same door'. What he admired about European music was (or what seemed to him to be) its romantic character, '. . . its aspect of variety, of abundance, of the waves on the sea of life, of the ever-changing light and shade on their ceaseless undulations'. In contrast to the abstract quality 'of pure extension' in Indian classical music, the power of European music to translate into

melody the dramatic playfulness and evanescence of life appealed
to his imagination. He had read in Herbert Spencer's *The Origin
and Function of Music* that it is emotion that gives tuneful inflection
to speech. 'Spencer's idea that through a development of these
emotional modulations of voice man found music appealed to me.
Why should it not do, I thought to myself, to act a drama in a
kind of recitative based on this idea?'[7] He tried it out in *Valmiki
Pratibha* and was much encouraged by its stage success. He himself
took the part of Valmiki and his young niece Pratibha that of the
little girl whom the robber-chief rescued. (There is thus a slight
pun on the use of the word Pratibha in the title of the play.) Soon
after the success of this play he wrote another musical drama in the
same mould, also based on an ancient legend of the *Ramayana*
called *Kal Mrigaya* (The Fateful Hunt). This too was successfully
produced—on an improvised stage in the Jorasanko house where all
such plays were originally staged, Rabindra himself in the role of
the blind hermit. 'The enthusiasm which went to the making of
Valmiki Pratibha and *Kal Mrigaya*,' recalled the author in his
reminiscences, 'I have never felt for any other work of mine.
In these two the creative musical impulse of the time found
expression.'

But a richer harvest lay ahead, waiting for the scorching heat of
sun to ripen it. Jyotirindranath and his wife left Calcutta on a long
sojourn; Rabindra could not accompany them. He was lonely and
unhappy. Though he occupied their apartment on the third storey,
he missed the stimulus of his brother's company and the warmth of
his sister-in-law's affection on which he had come to depend so
much. His somewhat ignominious return from abroad, without any
academic achievement to his credit, had not been well received by
several members of the family who looked upon him as a gifted
wastrel. Thus lonely, dejected, love-lorn and obsessed with morbid
fancies, he sought release in self-expression. His sister-in-law was
not there to listen to what he wrote and he felt obliged to please nobody. As a further asset, he discarded paper and pen and took up a
slate and pencil. The assurance that 'one rub will wipe all away' gave
him added confidence and he scribbled away. The sheaf of poems

[7] *My Reminiscences.*

that were thus born was later published as *Sandhya Sangeet* (Evening Songs) and is the first work of Rabindranath to bear the unmistakable stamp of his authentic genius. He had discovered his form and could write as he pleased, unfettered by any examples of the past. 'At last,' said his heart, 'what I write is my own.' He poured himself out, and 'as the stream does not flow straight on but winds about as it lists, so did my verse. Before, I would have held this to be a crime but now I felt no compunction. Freedom first breaks the law and then makes laws which brings it under true self-rule . . . I cut extraordinary capers just to make sure I was free to move.'[8] The public reception was gratifying. It was obvious that a new star had arisen. The author has himself related in his *Reminiscences* how at a society wedding when the chief guest, the celebrated novelist Bankim Chandra Chatterjee, was being garlanded by the host, Bankim Chandra took the garland off his neck and put it on young Rabindra who had just come in, saying to his host, 'The garland to him, Ramesh; have you not read his *Evening Songs*?'

The poems are marked by what a distinguished contemporary philosopher described as '. . . intensive egoistic subjectivity, untouched by any of the real interests of life or society'. They are generally morbid and full of vapours of heated imagination. Some of the titles are expressive of the mood: 'Suicide of a Star', 'Hopelessness of Hope', 'The Wail of Happiness', 'Invitation to Sorrow', 'Unbearable Love', etc. The young poet was in love with sorrow and revelled in the bitter-sweet despair. Not that the sorrow was feigned or imaginary. It was real; the memory of his sister-in-law haunted him day and night; the vacuum in his life was too painful to bear and some of the poems in this collection which are obviously addressed to her are witness enough to the genuineness of his feeling. The title *Evening Songs* also indicates the wistfulness of the mood as also the subconscious foreboding that it was the last phase, the sunset of the first phase of his creative activity when 'I was busy blowing up a raging flame with the bellows of my emotions'. The sunrise was yet to follow.

The first poem is appropriately an ode to evening, pictured as a lonely and mysterious woman, half visible in the shadows of

[8] *My Reminiscences.*

gathering darkness, her dishevelled hair spread out, her face bent over the earth. 'What is it you are softly humming to yourself? Day after day I have listened to it and have failed to catch either its meaning or its melody.' He feels a strange kinship with her which he elaborates in the rest of the poem. In another poem he sympathizes with the plight of a falling star driven to its suicide. In 'The Wail of Happiness' he elaborates on the irony that the more of joy there is in Nature the more the heart craves to share it with another, and failing to do so, the joy becomes a source of sorrow. For lack of love joy itself is joyless. At times he is sick of this all-consuming love which saps manliness and makes a man wait abjectly on a woman's light-hearted moods. 'Away with this love which is not life-giving but soul-destroying. It is a perversion, a poison.'

But can one help loving? No, it is not loving that is wrong; it is the begging of favours, of crumbs of pity, that is degrading. He is angry with his own self, for its abjectness. He will battle with his heart which has led him astray into a mirage of mist and delusion. The flowers bloom as of old but he no longer notices; the birds sing as before but he cannot hear them; the sun rises and yet the day remains dark. What is this destitution, this bankruptcy that has turned this fair world into a desert?

The dedicatory poem in this book is at the end and not at the beginning, as is the usual practice. The Spirit of Evening which he invoked in the first poem, vague and mysterious, has now assumed a concrete and recognizable image. 'Long ago, when I was a child, you wrapped me round with your affection as the evening envelops the earth with its peace. Had the evening taught you its magic spell? For you looked into my heart and all the stars came out. You revealed my own hidden wealth to me, and without singing yourself, you taught me all the songs I know.'

The melancholy expressed in this sheaf of poems is naïve and adolescent but by no means insincere or affected. The author himself who in later years blushed at some of these poems and would have liked to exclude them from his published works, stoutly defended them against the charge of affectation. 'The fortunate possessor of good eyesight,' he commented in his *Reminiscences*, 'is apt to sneer at the youth with glasses, as if he wears them for ornament.' There is a phase in a man's being, he has pointed out, when 'the anguish of vagueness' is its only truth; its expression need not therefore be dismissed as baseless. 'The sadness and pain which sought expression in the *Evening Songs* had their roots in the depths of my being. As one's sleep-smothered consciousness wrestles with a nightmare in its efforts to awake, so the submerged inner self struggles to free itself from its complexities and come out into the open. These *Songs* are the history of that struggle.'

Lonely and dissatisfied he wrote to his father, who was as usual in the Himalayas, asking for permission to go back to England and resume his studies for the Bar. The permission came and on 20 April 1881 he sailed for the second time to England, accompanied by a nephew. On the evening before he sailed he delivered a public lecture in Calcutta, *Music and Feeling*, illustrating his thesis with plenty of songs. It was his first public lecture and he tried to prove, with vocal demonstrations, that the function of music was to express what the words fail to express. He was coming out of his shell into the public eye and had already published a strongly worded pole-mical article, *Death Traffic in China*, in which he condemned Britain for her opium trade in that country. His sympathies were extending far beyond the frontiers of his country and he was already beginning to voice the wrongs of humanity wherever perpetrated. This dualism in him of intense subjectivity and a manly concern with the objective world was a basic characteristic of his per-sonality, from his childhood to his death. The dualism never ceased; the equilibrium of spirit was never totally upset; only the character of the balancing forces changed with age and experience. The egoistic subjectivity and morbid introspection matured into a calm and serene mysticism, while his interest in the objective world, of nature and of men, widened its horizons and deepened in sympathy.

This second voyage to England proved abortive. The nephew, Satyaprasad, who accompanied him, had married recently, and began to feel, as soon as the boat left Calcutta, as wife-sick as he felt sea-sick. By the time the ship reached Madras he had made up his mind to return home but he lacked the courage to face the formidable Maharshi alone. So he persuaded his young uncle to give him the necessary moral courage by sharing the ignominy of a faint-hearted retreat. The uncle seems to have readily complied—whether wholly out of altruism or because he too had left his heart behind, he has not told us. He was, however, aware of the serious consequences of this decision and went all the way to Mussoorie (in the western Himalayas where his father was) to report what he had done. 'I went to him in fear and trembling. But he showed no sign of irritation, he rather seemed pleased. He must have seen in this return of mine the blessing of divine providence.'

From Mussoorie he went to where his brother Jyotirindranath and his wife were staying in a villa on the Ganges in the French settlement at Chandernagore, not far from Calcutta. There he spent some of his happiest days—'. . . those ineffable days and nights, languid with joy, sad with longing'. The villa was known as 'Moran's Garden'. It was a big, rambling house with terraces and stone steps leading to the bank of the river. Often the three of them, the two brothers and the lady who ruled the hearts of both, spent the afternoon in a boat, Rabindra singing and improvising music 'in a veritable frenzy', and Jyotirindranath accompanying on his violin. It was here that Rabindranath first felt the spell of Bengal's river-life which runs through his poetry like the murmur of a lullaby. Here also he wrote those charming and light-hearted essays —random reflections and fancies rather than essays proper—some of which were summarized and quoted in an earlier chapter, besides more serious essays in literary criticism. His first fully-fledged novel, *Bou-Thakuranir Hat* (The Young Queen's Market), was also written here.

Although in poetry and in literary essay the young author had just asserted his individuality and created a form suited to his genius, in creative fiction he was yet to gain confidence. This first novel is a historical melodrama, cast in the mould which Bankim Chandra Chatterjee, then known as the Scott of Bengal, had made popular. No wonder that when it was published, the author received a letter from the famous veteran congratulating him on an achieve-ment which though immature had the promise of genius. The substance of the plot and the significance of the title may be summed up as follows: A brave but cruel King persecutes his son whose only fault is his sympathy with the suffering people. The Prince is finally exiled. On his way to the holy city of Banaras the Prince escorts his sister to her husband's kingdom. On arriving there they learn that the husband had in the meanwhile taken another wife. The disappointed sister accompanies her brother in the exile. The place where they had moored their boat is still known as 'the young queen's market'.

As a work of fiction in itself, the novel has little to recommend it and has not been translated into English. Nevertheless its historical importance is considerable. It is like a little nursery plot in a backyard where the seedlings were tried out which were later transplanted and made to flower elsewhere. Many situations and characters which the author later developed in his dramas are to be found here in their incipient form: a king indifferent to his people's welfare, a prince atoning for his father's wrongs, an old man, simple and jovial, seemingly naïve but rich in intuitive wisdom and humanity who voices the author's philosophy of life, and young women, loving or hating, but always more dynamic and real than the male characters. Another characteristic trait of the author which is evident in this early work is his courage and humanism which always transcended the narrow prejudices of patriotism. The cruel and vindictive King in the novel has been made much of by many Bengali patriots for his courage in defying the Moghul Emperor of Delhi. Rabindranath conceded his courage and showed no less courage himself in painting his real character as a man. Patriotism is only a partial virtue and what seems as courage may only be a form of obstinacy and pride. Real virtue is to be measured by a man's humanity.

After this idyllic holiday in the villa on the Ganges, the two brothers and Kadambari Devi returned to Calcutta. They did not, however, go back to the ancestral house at Jorasanko but took up their residence in another part of Calcutta (near Chowringhee, which was then developing as the West End or the Fifth Avenue of Calcutta) in Sudder Street, not far from where the Museum now stands. It was in this modest house in the very heart of the new metropolis that the young poet had his first deeply felt spiritual experience which burst upon him with the force of a vision and which he himself has described at length, both in his reminiscences and later in the Hibbert Lectures at Oxford University in 1930.[9] Early one morning as he was standing on the veranda of the house watching the rising sun emerge behind the fringe of trees at the end of the lane; 'All of a sudden a covering seemed to fall away from my eyes, and I found the world bathed in a wonderful radiance, with waves of beauty and joy swelling on every side.' All the gloom and despondency which had weighed over and oppressed his spirit, forcing it to turn upon itself in a morbid relish of its own disease, fell from him like a garment cut from end to end. Nothing in the outside world seemed trivial any more. 'The invisible screen of the commonplace was removed from all things and all men, and their ultimate significance was intensified in my mind.'[10]

The experience by itself is not an uncommon one. Most men have had it in a mild form at one time or another, particularly after a long ailment or sorrow, when of a sudden we seem to rediscover life, as it were.[11] But what was uncommon in the case of Rabindranath's experience was its overwhelming intensity and its duration, so that its impact was indelibly marked on his consciousness. It was a prolonged experience, almost amounting to realization, during which he saw and heard everything not only with his eyes and ears but with his entire being. And it seemed an endless wonder. The experience lasted for four days during which he lived at a heightened awareness of his environments, when everything seemed more vivid, more real, more beautiful and more happy.[12] A couple passing arm in arm, a mother playing with her child, a cow sidling up to another and licking its body, all these commonplace sights assumed a significance he had not known before. Everything, however trivial, seemed to claim his attention and to draw him out of himself.

[9] Published as *The Religion of Man*, George Allen & Unwin, London.
[10] *Ibid.*
[11] Here is the clinical evidence of a professional psycho-analyst regarding a call-girl who had attempted suicide: 'She related that when she came home from the hospital she was struck by the beauty of the grass, the sky, the trees, and she decided that she wanted very much to live.' *The Call Girl:* A Social and Psycho-analytic Study by Harold Greenwald. Elek Books, London.
[12] Rather as Mr. Aldous Huxley felt after taking mescalin.

Even a bore whose sight used to freeze him seemed an object of interest when he turned up the next day.

At the end of the fourth day this state of extraordinary elation passed away and with it Rabindra crossed over what he has described as the 'borderland age' where the direct rays of truth hardly ever penetrate, where shadows chase one another:

> There is a vast jungle called the Heart,
> Endless its mazes on all sides,
> Here I lost my way.

5

THE THRESHOLD

On the very day of this remarkable experience Rabindranath wrote the famous poem, *Nirjharer Svapnabhanga* (The Awakening of the Waterfall or Fountain) which may be said to mark symbolically the beginning of his adult career as a poet. As he put it, the poem 'gushed forth and coursed on like a veritable cascade'. Like a frozen cave in the Himalayas his heart had been locked up in its own darkness. Suddenly the sun's rays penetrated the darkness, melting the snow. The freed water rushed forth, gurgling and cascading, leaping over the rocks and striking music out of each obstacle. The poem itself leaps and dances with this ecstasy of self-abandon. In this mood of semi-exaltation, of a rediscovery of the wonder of this world and the joy of living, he wrote a number of poems which were later published as *Prabhat Sangeet* (Morning Songs).[1]

These lyrics mark a considerable advance over his previous work, not only in the healthiness of the poet's mood and outlook but in the mastery of language and metre. In one poem, which he later made the opening poem of the book, he chides himself for having shut himself up so long in a shadowy world of sick fancies, like a canker-worm that eats into the flower in which it is lodged. In another he reviews his own life, how as a child he loved nature passionately, knew the individual characteristics of each coconut tree in the family garden, how he used to watch from the window the aged banyan tree and the bathing tank; how later he lost his way in the wilderness of his heart and nature ceased to be a source of delight,

---

[1] These, as well as the earlier *Evening Songs*, are lyrics and not songs proper such as he composed for *Valmiki Pratibha* and was to compose later. They were called songs to emphasize their lyrical quality. In Bengali language there is no exact equivalent of what is called in English a lyric.

and how he had now suddenly recovered his lost heritage, with widened dimensions. Thus he goes on, in poem after poem, celebrating his new faith with the zeal of a convert till one begins to wonder if this joy was not somewhat infected with the adolescent self-consciousness as was the melancholy which he celebrated in the *Evening Songs*. A patient who keeps on complaining of his liver and a man who insists on proclaiming that his liver is in order, are both obsessed with liver and not quite normal. Rabindranath had yet to attain the spiritual poise which would give his sorrows the dignity of tragedy and his joys the strength of understanding.

Nevertheless, these poems were an authentic herald of the majestic procession that was to follow and in language and metrical movement opened a new path in Bengali poetry untrodden before. Nor is every poem a mere effusion of the new-found joy. In some of them the backbone of thought is already forming which later was to make some of his poems perfect specimens of that blend of feeling, imagination, thought and music which is the mark of the greatest poetry. It was natural for the young man to assume that if the commonplace sights and sounds of a dingy street in Calcutta could bring him so much joy, he would get much more if he visited the Himalayas. So he accompanied his brother and his wife to Darjeeling which commands the view of the magnificent Kangchenjunga peak, the next highest to Mt. Everest.

'But the victory was with that little house in Sudder Street. When, after ascending the mountains I looked around, I was at once aware I had lost my new vision. My sin must have been in imagining that I could get still more of truth from the outside . . . I wandered about amongst the firs, I sat near the falls and bathed in their waters, I gazed at the grandeur of Kanchenjunga through a cloudless sky, but in what had seemed to me these likeliest of places I found it not. I had come to know it, but could see it no longer. While I was admiring the gem the lid had suddenly closed, leaving me staring at the enclosing casket.'[2]

Where then was the beauty that had so recently ravished his heart? What was its secret? Is it an absolute quality residing in the object or is it freshly created each time it is *felt* in the mind of the

[2] *My Reminiscences.*

observer? The poet fancied that what he saw as beauty or felt as music was merely the echo of the rhythm that beats in the heart of the Universe. This idea he expressed, vividly and poetically, in a poem written in Darjeeling which he entitled 'The Echo'. This poem, like several others he was to write later, is tantalizingly abstruse and critics have not ceased to wrangle over its exact import. When it was first published two friends of the author laid a wager as to its real meaning. 'My only consolation was that, as I was equally unable to explain the enigma to them when they came to me for a solution, neither of them had to lose any money over it.'

Commenting on this academic itch to understand everything cerebrally, the author wrote in his reminiscences:

'But does one write poetry to explain any matter? What is felt within the heart tries to find outside shape as a poem. So when, after listening to a poem, anyone says he has not understood, I feel non-plussed. If someone smells a flower and says he does not understand, the reply to him is: there is nothing to understand, it is only a scent... That words have meaning is just the difficulty. That is why the poet has to turn and twist them in metre and verse, so that the meaning may be held somewhat in check, and the feeling allowed a chance to express itself. This utterance of feeling is not the statement of a fundamental truth, or a scientific fact, or a useful moral precept ... If while crossing a ferry you can catch a fish, you are a lucky man, but that does not make the ferry-boat a fishing-boat, nor should you abuse the ferryman if he does not make fishing his business ... The fact of the matter was that a longing had been born within my heart, and unable to find any other name, I had called the thing I desired an Echo.'

Two other poems included in this book also bear the germ of his favourite philosophy that being is becoming, that life is ever moving and renewing itself and that death is what helps it to renew itself. The poems are entitled 'Endless Life' and 'Endless Death'. Life is replenished through death and death never dies. 'Every year I have lived, I have died too.' In another long poem, perhaps the most metaphysical and in some respects the most magnificent in the whole sheaf, Hindu mythology is employed to illustrate the researches of modern science in a cosmic picture of the creation and dissolution of universe upon universe. In the midst of the Great Emptiness, limitless, timeless and lightless, sits Brahma the Creator, his eyes closed in the stony silence of meditation. Suddenly the eyes open and he utters the primeval hymn of creation. The emptiness is filled with burning nebulae and revolving globes of fire. Then Vishnu the Preserver blows his conch and order emerges out of chaos and the earth cools and is filled with life and beauty is born to fill the heart with delight. But the universes tire of revolving in the endless round of the Law and the creation wearied of itself prays to Shiva the Lord of Destruction for the peace of annihilation. Shiva opens his third dread eye and the suns and the moons and the stars are shattered into bits and everything is reduced to nothingness in the cosmic funeral pyre. Once again the Great Emptiness rolls over and Brahma's eyes are closed in meditation.

One of his first public activities in Calcutta was to assist his brother Jyotirindranath in founding the first Literary Academy in India. Jyotirindranath was always exploring new paths and initiating new enterprises, cultural or industrial. The idea in starting this Academy was to enlarge and equip the Bengali language as an adequate instrument of modern thought, particularly scientific thought. Bengali, like other Indian languages, lacked scientific terminology and it was necessary to bring the leading scholars and philologists together to agree on the use of technical terms.[3] So the brothers set to work and founded the Saraswat Samaj, persuading many of the leading scholars and writers—the novelist Bankim Chandra Chatterjee one of them—to join. When Rabindranath went to the great scholar, educationist and social reformer, Pandit Vidyasagar, to request him to join the Academy, the latter told him: 'My advice to you is to leave us out—you will never accomplish anything with big-wigs; they can never be got to agree with one another.' This sound warning, relevant then as now, proved true and the Academy after a good beginning petered out and ceased to exist.

In the summer of 1883 the 'Sudder Street party' shifted to Karwar on the south-western sea-coast of India, now in the State of Mysore, the fragrant land of cardamum and sandalwood. The elder brother

[3] This problem, of considerable national importance, which the two brothers sought to face and tackle in 1882 has not yet been satisfactorily solved in India.

Satyendranath had been posted there as District Judge and here Rabindranath spent some very happy and carefree days, in the company of those he loved most, including the two children of Satyendranath, his playmates of Brighton days. The little harbour of Karwar, ringed with the hills, its crescent-shaped beach fringed with casuarinas, fascinated Rabindranath who loved Nature in every form and mood. Here he wrote his first important drama in verse, *Prakritir Pratishodh* (Nature's Revenge),[4] which whatever its limitations on the stage as an evening's entertainment for a jaded and sophisticated audience, portrays the eternal drama that goes on between spirit and life, between truth and beauty, between reason and love.

A Sanyasi has shut himself up in a cave to attain mastery over his self and to transcend all limitations of nature. The drama opens with the ascetic standing outside his cave announcing his great liberation in a magnificent soliloquy of seventy-five lines, a fierce indictment of life and its seductions. 'I have tasted the bliss which is Lord Shiva's when he wipes away the unclean stain of creation from the emptiness of eternity and sits entranced in his own invincibility.' No more will the lightning flashes of pleasure lure him into the darkness of sorrow, for he has burnt all the senses in the funeral pyre of self-knowledge. He can now proudly walk the earth and pity mankind for their folly. When he comes to the nearest town he sees a little untouchable girl who has lost her parents and whom everyone shuns and drives away, including the temple-priest. She clings to the Sanyasi in her helpless despair; and pity and love which he has long despised are born afresh in him. He is frightened at the prospect of his becoming human and flees from her. When he returns, unable to keep away, he finds her dead. Death sets the seal on his realization 'that the great is to be found in the small, the infinite within the bounds of form, and the eternal freedom of the soul in love'.

There are many other characters in the play but they can hardly be called characters in a drama. They are wayfarers and passers-by, nameless and anonymous, who represent the daily panorama of life in a village or on the highway. Tagore's dramas are full of such anonymous characters or types representing the various segments of

---

[4] An English translation, somewhat mutilated, was published as *Sanyasi, or the Ascetic* in *Sacrifice and Other Plays*, Macmillan & Co., London, 1917.

society, which give him considerable scope for either mouthing his own comments or for merely reminding the audience that whatever drama goes on, the rest of the world continues to exist. These characters use the native dialect and, like some of Shakespeare's rough characters, indulge in crude humour, all of which provides a relief from the high-flown thoughts and superb poetry of the main characters. For this reason, too, Tagore's plays are not meant for the regular, professional, city stage. They were written to be performed in the open and for the joy of it. Many learned critics who believe that a good drama is what can be successfully staged in London or New York have severely condemned Tagore's habit of 'cluttering up' the stage with all sorts of characters who lack 'blood'. But, Tagore would not be Tagore if he were an Arthur Miller or a Terence Rattigan or even an Ibsen or a Shaw. Each creative genius is what he is and we must either understand him or leave him alone, and not wish he were this or that.

The shrewd reader must have guessed that this seemingly metaphysical play was largely the story of the author's own experience, the frozen waterfall in the cave which the human rays melted, the adolescent obsession with self which had shut out for him the lovely pageant of life, seemingly trivial but in truth more real than the crowning of kings. It was a little 'untouchable' girl, plain, unlettered and in rags who took this proud Indian Paracelsus to the gateway of true knowledge.

'In the *Nature's Revenge* there were shown on the one side the wayfarers and the villagers, content with their home-made triviality and unconscious of anything beyond; and on the other the Sanyasi casting away his all and himself into the self-evolved infinite of his imagination. When love bridged the gulf between the two, and the hermit and the householder met, the seeming triviality of the finite and the seeming emptiness of the infinite alike disappeared . . . This *Nature's Revenge* may be looked upon as an introduction to the whole of my future literary work; or, rather, this has been the subject on which all my writings have dwelt—the joy of attaining the Infinite within the finite.'[5]

Having spent the summer and the rainy season in Karwar, the

[5] *My Reminiscences.*

party returned to Calcutta in autumn where they now stayed in a garden-house or villa on Lower Circular Road, near Chowringhee. This was not then a thickly built area as it is now, and in front of the villa where the brothers were staying were the improvised huts of labourers and other lowly folk, this kind of improvised colony of thatch-and-tin being known in India as a Bustee. From his window on the first floor Rabindranath would watch the daily drama of this crowded colony of humble folk; men and women at their various tasks and the children at play. 'To me it was all like a living story.' To the poet's delight was added the artist's eye. 'A faculty of many-sightedness possessed me at this time.' He was curious '. . . to see with the mind what the eye sees, and with the eye what the mind imagines'. As he himself said,[6] 'Had I been a painter with the brush I should doubtless have tried to keep a permanent record of the visions and creations of that period when my mind was so alertly responsive. But that instrument was not available to me. What I had was only words and rhythms, and even with these I had not yet learnt to draw firm strokes, and the colours went beyond their margins.' Nevertheless, the poems he thus wrote, later published as *Chhabi O Gan* (Pictures and Songs) are a remarkable document of his state of mind at this period. He was watching, absorbing and growing and all the time the craftsman was practising new strokes and improving his technique.

The author, who was his own severest critic, has characterized these poems as 'adolescent in sentiment, immature in language'. Had they been leaves of trees, he wrote, they would have in due course fallen off and been forgotten. 'Unfortunately, leaves of books continue to stick fast even when they are no longer wanted.' He had not yet come to grips with life. He was still watching through a window. And yet some of the pictures he has painted in words of the scenes witnessed through the window are extraordinarily vivid. Not all the poems are pictures, however; nor do they all belong to one *genre*. One of them, for example, 'Rahur Prem' (The Love of Rahu) is half symbolic, half metaphysical, and is perhaps the most powerful poem in the whole book, virile, intense and magnificent. Rahu is a popular character in Hindu mythology, a demon, a

[6] *Ibid.*

bodiless planet who is in love with the moon and eternally chases her, occasionally swallowing her, when the eclipse is caused. But he cannot retain his prey and has to let her go. In Rabindranath's poem, Rahu is the sensual, the passionate, the greedy and devouring aspect of love which is ever present like a shadow. Whatever else the young poet had seen or not seen of life at first hand, he had known love. Pure and sublime though this love was, he could not have altogether escaped its agony and torture. This poem bears adequate testimony to it. A few lines are paraphrased below—its rhythm and sweep are impossible to reproduce. It is Freudian love talking to the Platonic:

I understand you don't care for me. It matters little—
for in any case you are and shall ever remain my captive,
your spirit chained to mine in the soul's unbreakable iron.

Wherever you go, in whatever season, I follow you, close
at your heels, a visage of darkness, a vast agony,
a desperate groan, like the discord of a musical instrument
out of tune.

I am your companion from the beginning of time, for I am
your own shadow. In your laughter, in your tears, you
shall sense my dark self hovering near you, now in front,
now behind. At the dead of night when you are lonely and
dejected, you'll be startled to find how near I am seated
by you, gazing into your face.

Wherever you turn I am there, my shadow sweeps over the
sky and covers the earth, my piteous cry and my cruel
laughter echo everywhere, for I am hunger never appeased,
thirst never quenched. I am always there, a dagger in
your breast, a poison in your mind, a disease in your body.

I shall chase you like a terror in the day, like a nightmare
in the night. Like a living skeleton in a famine I shall
stretch my hand before you and pester you to give and give
and give. Like a thorn I shall prick you day and night,

like a curse I shall haunt you, like fate I shall follow you—
as night follows the day, as fear follows hope.

His prose writings continued, polemical diatribes on social and
political issues and thoughtful analysis of literary and philosophical
problems. The latter were published as *Alochana* (Discussions). Those
were happy days, carefree and unburdened with any responsibility,
living with those he loved best and daily feeling his powers grow,
seemingly idle but reaping a rich harvest. The earlier morbidity, the
nameless hunger gnawing at his heart had given way to a robust
and healthy outlook and he was beginning to enjoy the world and
life with all the zest his nature was capable of. Handsome, well-
dressed, and versatile, he strode like a young god, the world at his
feet. But already the fates were laying a snare for him and the days
of irresponsible and overflowing happiness were numbered. His
brother Jyotirindranath was getting more and more involved in his
intrepid and quixotic business enterprises and was no longer able to
look after the family estates. The Maharshi, aloof and remote but
shrewd and watchful like unseen Providence, decided that it was
time that his youngest son was yoked to the family chariot. This
wild and wayward youth must grow into a man and must be made
to face the responsibilities of life. If the Maharshi could himself
attend to both God and the world, there was no reason why his
son should not attend to both poetry and the family estates. But
before he could do so he must be properly broken and yoked in
marriage. And so a silent edict was issued that the family must look
for a suitable bride for the young man.

There is an amusing anecdote preserved in the family regarding
the first hunting expedition for a suitable bride. Word was received
that the head of a principality in the neighbouring State of Orissa
had a daughter of marriageable age to offer to the handsome young
poet of aristocratic lineage. So the two brothers, Jyotirindranath
and Rabindranath, set out to see her and were invited to the ruler's
palace where they met two young ladies, one extraordinarily attractive, the other exceedingly plain. If the brothers hoped that the
attractive one was the prospective bride, the hope was short lived.
They soon discovered that the daughter available for marriage was

the plain-looking girl; the lovely one was the step-mother. After this farcical interlude the ladies of the family took upon themselves, as was the practice, the responsibility of selecting a bride for the youngest son of the family. But they were not free to select whom they liked. The Maharshi, very progressive in religious matters, was extremely conservative in the observance of social forms. The girl must be of Brahmin parentage. But the Tagores themselves, despite their social position due to wealth and intellectual and moral leadership, belonged to a sect of 'degraded' Brahmins known as Pirali. The orthodox Brahmins, proud of their high caste, would not intermarry with them. The choice was therefore limited to a few families belonging to the same Pirali sub-caste in the small provincial town of Jessore. So a second expedition, this time of ladies, consisting of the two sisters-in-law, wives of Satyendranath and Jyotirindranath, accompanied by maids, set out for Jessore to look for a suitable bride for their favourite brother-in-law. Their choice fell on the ten-year-old daughter of one Benimadhav Raichaudhury who happened to be an employee in the Tagore estate.

The family was humble compared to the Tagores. The girl was no beauty and was almost illiterate, having read up to the first Bengali primer only. The fact that two intelligent and sophisticated Calcutta ladies were obliged to select this seemingly commonplace rustic maid as their future sister-in-law shows how the snobbishness of caste and family pride can recoil on itself. Princes have been known to marry ugly princesses because they dared not marry beautiful commoners. History has its ironies and thus this unromantic marriage was arranged for one of the most romantic men of the age. Considering the social traditions that held sway in that period what happened was not surprising. Nor was it surprising that Rabindranath meekly submitted to the choice. For all his dashing romanticism and his dynamic individuality in the field of literary experiments, he was a docile and obedient son and was so much under the spell of his father's personality that not only was the latter's word law for him but he believed that the Maharshi could never be in the wrong.

He was, however, none the worse for the Maharshi's arbitrary and seemingly unreasonable choice of a match for him. The unglamorous bride proved to be an excellent wife, the kind he really needed.

He was not in want of inspiration for his work; his love of life and of this earth was a perpetual stimulus to him. He was so incorrigibly romantic that what he needed from a wife was not further stimulus but an antidote. Had he married a mere beauty he might have tired of her, but he never tired of the protective shade of care and comfort which his wife unobtrusively built around him, the self-effacing devotion with which she helped his genius to its fruition. But we are anticipating. What he himself felt at the time, whether he welcomed the prospect of this marriage or bitterly resented it is not known, for he has left no record of his feelings either in his poems or in any other document. What is, however, of significance is the fact that the family itself does not seem to have taken this wedding very seriously. Normally the wedding of the youngest son of an aristocratic family—and what a son!—would be an occasion of con-siderable festivity in India, but in this case the father himself did not choose to be present although the wedding took place in the family house at Jorasanko. Nor was he far away in the Himalayas for the wedding took place in winter, on 9 December 1883 when the Maharshi was on a boating cruise not very far from Calcutta. Nor could the elder brother Satyendranath and his family be present. It would hardly be unreasonable to surmise that Rabindranath was hustled into a marriage which was arranged at very short notice. Fate also seems to have conspired to turn this wedding into a mere ritual shorn of festivity, for on the very day of the wedding the family suffered a sad bereavement in the sudden death of the eldest son-in-law, husband of Saudamini Devi, the sister who had brought up Rabi in his infancy.

The bride's maiden name was Bhavatarini, a name so old-fashioned that it must have raised then, as it does now, a smile of amusement. After the marriage the name was changed into Mrinalini, a lovely name very likely given by the husband himself—perhaps his only initiative in this episode. Nalini was a name always dear to his heart and somehow Mrinalini seemed to incorporate it. As a matter of fact, he was at this time working on a prose drama of that name. The plot was familiar, a rehash of his earlier adolescent fancies centr-ing round a lovely and true-hearted girl called Nalini. The drama was to be acted by various members of the family and it was decided that each actor would be part author and write his or her own part. The experiment was interesting and original—perhaps too original, for it did not work. In the end Rabindranath had to complete the drama by himself. But before it could be produced a tragedy overtook the family. On 19 April 1884 Kadambari Devi, Rabindranath's favourite sister-in-law who had been his lifelong friend and more than mother to him, suddenly committed suicide. She was only twenty-five. No one knows why. If the secret was known to any members of the family it has died with them. In the absence of any authentic evidence, any surmise or guess would be not only profitless but disrespectful to the memory of one of the finest specimens of Indian womanhood.

This tragedy left a very deep impress on the mind of Rabindranath. It was the first great sorrow of his life, his first experience of the terrible reality of death. He had known his mother's death earlier but he was then too young to feel its impact, and the loss was more than made up for by the affection his sister-in-law had poured on him. But her loss none could fill. For nearly sixteen years, the most impressionable years of his life, she had been his comrade, his confidante, his refuge. After this he was to face death again and again and suffer many bereavements in his life—in fact, within a few weeks of this tragedy his third elder brother died, Hemendranath, who had supervised his education as a boy—but no other loss ever had so profound an impact on his mind and his genius. It did not break him, it made him. It was a churning of the soul out of which he emerged strong and mature. It was a love which left behind no despair, no embitterment, no howling against fate—only a deeper understanding of life and of the meaning of death. But let him speak for himself. [7]

'One of the great blessings of life is the power to forget what cannot come back. This power being fresh and strong in childhood, no wound festers unhealed for long and no scar is left . . . But my encounter with death at the age of twenty-four[8] was a lifelong one, its memory linking itself to each succeeding bereavement in an ever-

[7] The passage which follows has been translated by me from the original Bengali text in *Jivan-smriti*. The author's own English rendering or, to be more correct, Surendranath Tagore's rendering as approved by the author, may be read in *My Reminiscences*.

[8] Actually he was twenty-three.

widening rosary of sorrow . . . I had not realized till then that there could be gaps in life's familiar patchwork of smiles and tears, to which I had clung, unable to see anything beyond it. When death came and what had been there as part of life became suddenly a gaping void, I felt utterly lost. Everything else had remained the same, the trees, the soil, the sun, moon and the stars; only she who was as real as they, indeed far more real than they, for I had felt her touch on every aspect of my being—only she was not there, she had vanished like a dream. This terrible paradox baffled me. How was I to reconcile what remained with what had been?

'The bottomless chasm of darkness which had thus appeared in my life seemed to exercise a kind of fascination over me and to draw me to its brink day and night. I would stand on its edge and gaze below into the darkness, wondering what was left in place of what had been. The human mind cannot understand absolute emptiness and imagines that what is not must be unreal and what is unreal is not. Hence our unceasing search to find something where we see nothing. Just as a plant hemmed in by darkness stretches itself upwards to gain access to light, even so when Death puts up its black screen of negation and says, it is not there, the mind of man struggles desperately to break through the screen of darkness into the light of affirmation. But when one discovers that the way out of darkness is itself shrouded in darkness, what agony can equal this!

'And yet in the midst of this suffocating darkness, there would suddenly blow over my heart, now and again, a breeze of gladness, taking me by surprise. The painful realization that life was not ever-lasting itself turned into a source of comfort. That we were not prisoners for ever within the impregnable walls of life's solid actuality —this indeed was welcome tidings to gladden the heart. I had to let go what I had clung to—as long as I viewed this fact as my own loss I was unhappy, but when I learnt to look at it from the point of view of life being liberated through death, a great peace fell on my spirit... As this sense of detachment grew within me, Nature's beauty assumed a deeper significance to my tear-washed eyes. Her death had given me the necessary distance and detachment to see life and world in their wholeness, in their true perspective, and as I looked at the picture of life painted on the vast canvas of death, it seemed to be truly beautiful.'

Despite a tendency to relish occasional sentimentalizing—a racial more than an individual weakness—Rabindranath had a very robust and virile mind and no sorrow or pleasure, no disappointment or lure of any kind ever made him pause, much less deviate, from the steady pursuit of his vocation. He continued to write, and poems, stories and articles poured from his pen. Except for a few prose poems addressed to her, 'forgotten by the world but never to be forgotten by me,' his literary outburst of this period bears no mark whatsoever of any morbid preoccupation with sorrow. The family was already running a literary monthly, *Bharati*, to which he regularly contributed. To this was now added another monthly magazine called *Balak*, a journal for boys and girls started by his elder brother Satyendranath's wife. Unable to fill the journal otherwise, she put the responsibility of it on her young brother-in-law, who had to provide the monthly fare for its pages in the form of nursery rhymes, poems, stories, dramas and novels. Later in life he was to write a great deal for children and wrote some of the loveliest things ever written for the young, but this was the beginning of it.

He wrote a short historical novel for this journal called *Mukut* (The Crown) which many years later he dramatized for the school children of Santiniketan where it is still acted. But the appetite of a journal is inexhaustible. A demand came for another serial and he could not think of what to write. He was returning to Calcutta from Deoghar and as the railway compartment was crowded and he could not sleep, 'I thought I might as well take this opportunity of thinking out a story for the *Balak*. In spite of my efforts to get hold of the story it eluded me, but sleep came to the rescue instead. I saw in a dream the stone steps of a temple stained with the blood of victims of the sacrifice—a little girl standing there with her father, asking him in piteous accents: "Father, what is this, why all this blood?" and the father, inwardly moved, trying with a show of gruffness to quiet her questioning. As I awoke I felt I had got my story.'

Thus he came to write the novel *Rajarshi* (The Royal Sage), weaving this dream episode into the story of a remarkable King of Tripura, an ancient kingdom on the eastern border of India. The novel, though partly vitiated by historical melodrama, is a powerful indictment of the traditional Hindu ritual of offering animal sacrifice to please the dread goddess Kali. Five years later he used the same plot for a drama in blank verse, *Visarjan*, translated and published into English as *Sacrifice* in 1917. The play is a great improvement on the novel, both as a piece of literary art and as a passionate testament of Rabindranath's humanism and his courage in denouncing what seemed to him stupid or inhuman in the traditions of his own people.

Besides this juvenile magazine, he had to attend to the demands of the other serious literary monthly, *Bharati*, for which he continued to write a number of articles, some of them polemical. The Maharshi, shrewd and watchful as ever, now made him Secretary of the Adi Brahma Samaj (the reformist religious society which he had founded) to yoke this spirited horse more securely to the family waggon. The result was as anticipated by him. Rabindranath who had never before taken much interest in religion,[9] much less in institutional religion, now began to take his new duties seriously. He composed hymns for congregational singing, wrote a paper on Raja Rammohun Roy and several articles propagating his father's religious faith; he even crossed swords with the redoubtable Bankim Chandra Chatterjee who had lately taken to propagating the glories of traditional Hinduism. But the veteran had too genial an affection for the impetuous youngster and the latter too high a regard for the grand old man of Bengali letters for the misunderstanding to ripen, and since both the combatants were intrinsically noble the feud was short-lived. 'At the close of this period of antagonism Bankim Babu wrote me a letter which I have unfortunately lost. Had it been here the reader could have seen with what consummate generosity Bankim Babu had taken the sting out of that unfortunate episode.' Nor did

[9] He has himself recorded in *My Reminiscences:* 'The religious services which were held in our family I would have nothing to do with, I had not accepted them for my own . . . As with religion, so with my emotions, I felt no need for any underlying truth, my excitement being an end in itself. I call to mind some lines of a poet of that time:

> My heart is mine
> I have sold it to none,
> Be it tattered and torn and worn away,
> My heart is mine!'

the younger contemporary fail to respond with equal generosity in recalling the episode in *My Reminiscences*.

Every generation has its illusion of progress and the intelligentsia is divided between those who wish to rush forward and those who wish to preserve what they are used to. But in India of the eighties of the last century this division was sharper, for Western education and the knowledge of modern science were new and utterly different from the traditional forms of knowledge and ways of living. Those who had accepted the new were intoxicated by it and found fault with everything that was old; while those who feared it clung passionately to the placid security of age-old ways. Each side had its case and in a remarkable series of letters supposed to be exchanged between a conservative grandfather and his Western-educated grandson, Rabindranath presented both the cases with such consummate lucidity, convincingness and sincerity that reading them one begins to agree with each case as it is presented. 'However pure and beautiful the mountains from which the river Ganges takes its source,' writes the young man to his grandfather, 'it cannot reverse its current and flow back. It must follow its course through the dusty plains into the sea where lies the fulfilment of its destiny.' The grandfather smiles and congratulating the youngster on his cleverness reminds him: 'Humanity is not flotsam and jetsam to drift along with the waters, following the path of least resistance. Humanity is like a rock in the midst of swirling waters holding aloft its great heritage over the flux.' And so it goes on, argument and metaphor being tossed backwards and forwards, like a ball in a tennis tournament, to the delight of the spectator. All his life Tagore hesitated to take sides in this battle which each generation renews for itself. His imaginative sympathy and understanding of human nature enabled him to appreciate the passionate partiality of both outlooks and he himself entered the lists only when he felt that justice and humanity were at stake. He hated fanaticism of any kind and when he found that an extreme form of reaction was raising its head under the banner of Hindu patriotism and sentimental nationalism, running down everything Western and glorifying everything 'Aryan', he wrote some biting satires which did not add to his popularity but which showed hat t he young man was a master of caustic irony and could wield

a pen as vitriolic as Swift's. But he had an innate distaste for any
kind of public exhibitionism and entered the arena only under
extreme provocation. After each such sally, he retired into his
corner and sought comfort in his muse.

His next book of poems, *Kari O Komal* (Sharps and Flats), showed
how much more worth while it was to attend to his muse than to
engage in public controversies, although for a man of his wide
sympathies and public spirit it was difficult to be a recluse in an ivory
tower. No poet, certainly no Indian poet, ever loved this earth and
his fellow men more passionately and more consistently. The very
opening poem of his new book reaffirmed this faith.

> I do not want to die in this lovely world.
> I wish to live as man among men,
> with the sun shining, the flowers in bloom,
> and perchance some loving heart responding!
>
> How varied is the game of life on this earth,
> its meetings and partings, its laughter and tears!
> Oh to sing of man's joys and pains
> and leave behind a melody undying!

He has himself described these poems as 'a serenade from the
streets in front of the dwelling of man, a plea to be allowed an entry
and a place within that house of mystery . . . Man is overcome by a
profound depression while nodding through his voluptuously lazy
hours of seclusion, because in this way he is deprived of full commerce
with life. Such is the despondency from which I have always painfully struggled to get free. My mind refused to respond to the cheap
intoxication of the political movements of those days, devoid as they
seemed of all strength of national consciousness, with their complete
ignorance of the country, their supreme indifference to real service
of the motherland. I was tormented by a furious impatience, an
intolerable dissatisfaction with myself and all around me. Much
rather, I said to myself, would I be an Arab Bedouin!'[10]

The poems in this volume are considerable in number and cover
a large variety of themes and moods—poems for children, religious

[10] *My Reminiscences.*

songs, patriotic admonitions, love poems and amatory poems which throb with sensuous delight, besides several translations from Shelley, Victor Hugo, Mrs. Browning, Christina Rossetti, Swinburne, Hood, Aubrey de Vere, Moore, Philip Marston, Ernest Myers, Mrs. Augusta Webster and a Japanese poet unnamed. Many of these poems are in variations of the sonnet form. He was gaining increasing command over diction and metrical skill and introduced into Bengali verse beauties hitherto unknown. Despite the variety of themes the main mood of these poems is of delight in life, an eagerness to savour its seductions, a delight and eagerness which at times became an intoxication, like a musk deer drunk with its own perfume, wandering in a forest on a spring night, seeking it knows not what and getting what it neither seeks nor wants. The poet has discovered the mystery of the woman's body and is entranced by its loveliness. There are poems on her arms, her feet, her breasts, her kisses, on the act of love—poems full of naïve wonder and conceits; it is as though a child has found a wonderful toy from which he cannot keep his eyes off, looking at it, now from this side, now from that. For all that, the poems throb with adult blood.

Not all this revelry of the senses can make him forget for long the image of her who had left him for the other shore. Often as he sits alone and looks at the sky, he is overwhelmed by her missing presence. 'In this morning light dreaming in autumn's warmth, I know not what it is my heart desires. Someone is missing and that is enough to make this life a barren waste. My spirit wanders, wailing, she's not here, she's no more. To whom shall I sing my songs, on whose neck shall I put this garland of flowers? At whose feet shall I pour my life, my soul?' Sometimes he is acutely aware of her presence. 'Her glance is there—but where are the eyes? The kisses I feel—but where are the lips?' He understands that desire is the root of all sorrow, a vast snare in which men are enmeshed. 'When I desire another, it is I who am caught in the coil. She does not become mine, I become hers. Trying to bind others, I get bound myself. I loot the earth's treasure to build a prison for myself and my life's boat, loaded with desires, is about to sink.' Now and again he is seized with nausea at the futility of a poet's vocation and he asks himself: What pride is there in a poet's calling? Is it enough merely to sing, like a singing bird in a cage? Is this eternal thirst and chasing after the mirage a destiny worthy of human dignity? I have lived in vain if my life has failed to infuse life in others, if my strength has not served to make others strong. He invokes his guardian angel to make his life fruitful in the service of men. The last poem, entitled 'The Last Word', is significant. The poet feels that there is something more he has to say, saying which he will have said his all. But what that something is he does not know.

He also wrote about this time a light musical play or operetta called *Mayar Khela* (The Play of Illusion).[11] It can hardly be called a drama, being no more than a series of songs or as the author himself described it, 'a garland of songs with just a thread of dramatic plot running through'. Some of the songs are very charming and are popular to this day. The theme, structure and mood of this play are so dominated by feeling rather than action or thought that as soon as one tries to analyse them they melt 'into air, into thin air'. Nevertheless, if the main idea in the play could be isolated it might be summed up as follows: Nature weaves a web of illusions in which we poor mortals are caught. We chase happiness in love and miss both love and happiness.

Is life then nothing more than '. . . such stuff as dreams are made on'? Can one understand life merely by watching it from one's window and by an occasional sally outside it? Not until he crossed over the threshold and lived life fully would the young poet understand its full meaning, its beauty and its tragedy.

[11] *Maya* is one of those Indian words which are untranslatable in any other language. It represents a basic concept in Indian philosophy and is also a term of varying connotations in popular usage. Its standard rendering in English, 'Illusion', is extremely inadequate and unsatisfactory. The term implies the insubstantial nature of what we see and feel with our senses and suggests in one word all (and much more) that is suggested in Prospero's famous speech in *The Tempest*, 'Our revels now are ended . . .'

6

MATURITY

In 1886 when Rabindranath was twenty-five his first child was born, a daughter, Madhurilata; nicknamed Bela, for she was fair and lovely like the white Indian jasmin. Two years later his son Rathi was born. In the beginning of 1889 Rabindranath took his family to Sholapur (a town in south-west India, at present in the State of Maharashtra) where his brother was then the Judge. There he wrote his drama in blank verse, *Raja O Rani*,[1] which may be considered his nearest approach to a Shakespearian model; that is, plenty of action, much of it violent, contrast of characters and an inevitable sub-plot enlivened by intrigue. King Vikram, ruler of a State in the Punjab, is married to a beautiful princess from Kashmir and is so passionately in love with her that he spends his time hovering round her, completely unmindful of the welfare of his State. Taking advantage of his infatuation for the Queen, her relations from Kashmir have managed to grab all the important positions in the State and fatten on their spoils. One who is in charge of Trade relieves the merchants of their profits, 'taking the burden on his own broad shoulders',[2] another who is in charge of Administration 'pats the land on its back with his caressing hand and whatever comes to his touch gathers with care'. The Queen knows nothing of this and when she asks if her relatives are negligent in their duties, she is informed that far from being negligent, they are ever vigilant, 'as vigilant as a thief who has broken into a house'. Complaints reach the King but he has no ear for them, for he has no time to waste over 'vulgar concerns' when life is short and love so sweet. The hungry

---

[1] Later translated into English as *The King and the Queen* and published in *Sacrifice and Other Plays*, Macmillan & Co., 1917. The English version has considerably abridged the original.

[2] The author's irony at the White Man's Burden is obvious.

crowds riot outside the palace crying for bread. 'What is this noise?'
inquires the Queen. 'Nothing, your Majesty. Only hunger—the
vulgar hunger of the poor who were content with half rations and
now find total starvation a little too much, the coarse, clamorous
crowd who howl unashamedly for food and disturb the sweet peace
of the palace.'

The Queen has a conscience, she pleads with her husband who
turns a deaf ear and wishes instead to fold her in his arms. Nauseated
at this spectacle of love whose egoistic lust has blinded her husband to
all sense of duty and humanity, she leaves him and goes to her
brother Prince Kumarasen of Kashmir, to seek his help in ridding
her husband's state of parasites who were sucking the people's blood.
In the meantime, her relatives, getting word through their spies
of the Queen's intentions, had mustered their forces and were con-
spiring to gain command of the palace as well. When King Vikram
learns of his wife's desertion he is livid with rage, his love for her
turns into a passion for revenge, his wounded manliness into a
voluptuous greed for violence and conquest. He puts down the
insurrection and leads his armies into Kashmir to teach Prince
Kumarasen a lesson. None can withstand the fury of his onslaught,
his armies are victorious everywhere and he occupies Kashmir,
Prince Kumarasen and the Queen being forced to hide themselves in
a forest. Prince Kumarasen is too proud to surrender and yet anxious
to appease the tyrant's wrath and spare his kingdom and his people
the hardships of occupation. He therefore sacrifices his life and
arranges that his severed head shall be sent to the King as a peace
offering. The offering is brought to the Court by the proud and
sorrowful Queen who falls down dead as she offers the tribute at the
feet of the throne. Love is a devouring passion and unless chastened
by its obligation to humanity can cause nothing but tragedy.[3]

The conflict in this play is between love and duty, between a vain
and infatuated man and a proud and humane woman. The woman
triumphs by her suffering. In the play *Visarjan* (Sacrifice) also in

[3] Many years later Tagore rewrote this drama, ridding it of many of its loose ends,
and published it as *Tapati*. It was a characteristic of his that he often returned to the
same theme until he was satisfied with its treatment. In both the versions he himself
took the part of the King on the stage.

blank verse, which he wrote soon after, the conflict between man and wife (here, too, a King and his Queen) is placed in an entirely different setting. Here the queen is aligned with forces of reaction against her own husband. The conflict in this play, which is truly dramatic in its intensity, is many-sided: between husband and wife, between temporal power and priestly authority, between the cry of non-violence and the claim of violence, between love and duty, between duty and conscience, between the unwritten law of humanity and the prescribed rule of religion. Here, too, the play ends in tragedy and the loss of an innocent life, but in the process the voice of love triumphs and the Deity dethroned in the temple finds her true place in the hearts of men. The English translation of this drama which was published in 1917 was dedicated by the author '. . . to the heroes who valiantly stood up for peace when the goddess of war demanded human sacrifices'.

All this while, whether he was writing new plays and producing them or indulging in his occasional sallies into political controversy or social reform (in 1887 he read a brilliant paper on the ideals of Hindu Marriage in which he opposed early marriage and pleaded for women's rights) he was restless and unhappy. Now, as later in life, whenever he was in such a mood he wanted to travel. If he could not go far he must at least change his house. He shifted his residence from Jorasanko to Park Street, went to Darjeeling, then Sholapur and Poona on the other side of India, back to Calcutta and then westwards to Ghazipur famed for its roses. Western India, with its rich historical associations, had always exercised a fascination over his mind, and in Ghazipur on the Ganges, with its acres of rose garden, he thought he had at last found a place fit for a poet to live. He took his family, intending his sojourn to be long. But he was soon disillusioned and discovered that 'rose-gardens, when commercialized, were inspiring neither for the *bulbul*[4] nor for the poet'. After a few months' stay he returned to Calcutta, spent some time at Shelidah where his father wanted him to take over the management of the family estates, then at Santiniketan, and finally went back to Sholapur on the other side of India to stay with his brother Satyendranath. There he heard that Satyendranath and his young

[4] Indian nightingale said to be in love with the rose.

friend Loken Palit were planning a visit to England. Forthwith he
decided to accompany them.

In the course of all these wanderings and changes of abode,
a small exercise-book which was always with him was being filled
with poems. Whether he was gazing at the snow-capped Himalayas
at Darjeeling or sweltering in the heat and dust of Santiniketan, the
poems poured forth. The largest number were written in Ghazipur,
whether because or in spite of the roses, it is hard to say. The traditional *bulbul* might have been missing but the nightingale in Rabindranath sang full-throated in melodies unheard before. All this
harvest garnered over a period of a little more than three years was
published later as *Manasi* (Of the Mind) and immediately set the
seal on his reputation. The poet had come of age. Here were no
antics of an adolescent prodigy, no bravado of youthful romance;
these were accents unmistakable and true of an authentic poet, of a
mature mind, which had reached the right depth in the soil of its
genius from where a steady and inexhaustible current would continue to flow. As this book was, however, published after
Rabindranath's return from England, its discussion would be
more appropriate after a brief account of his second visit to
Europe.[5]

Though this time he sent no letters home to be published in
Bharati, he kept a diary which was published after his return as
Yurop-Yatrir Dayari (The Diary of a Visitor to Europe). The diary
is a charming and delightful piece of writing as all his prose writings
in a lighter vein are, full of acute observation and genial humour.
The first entry is dated 22 August 1890, the day the steamer sailed
from Bombay. Musing on the deck and watching the shores of his
land recede, the poet, who had not yet heard of dialectic materialism,
wonders how far the character of poetry is affected by the material
means of communication available in any age. In the days of
Kalidasa a lover separated from his mistress by a few hundred miles

[5] The original manuscript, the slender exercise-book referred to above, is preserved
in the Tagore Museum (Rabindra Sadana) at Santiniketan and contains the following
line in English on the inside cover: 'Think not bitterly of me', followed by author's
full signature in Bengali. Was he apostrophizing the dearly beloved deceased? It
is difficult to say.

had to implore a cloud-messenger[6] to carry his tidings to her and needed several cantos of verse for this purpose. In the steam age a sonnet or a lyric would suffice; in the nuclear age even a couplet would perhaps be too much. But these musings are soon forgotten as the ship heaves and tosses in the monsoon-troubled waters of the Arabian sea. As during his first voyage, Rabindranath took to his cabin and did not stir out—this time for four days.

It was on the last of these four days of ordeal that he had the experience which he described in his letter to his wife dated 29 August. 'On Sunday night I felt my spirit leave the body and I found myself in Jorasanko. You were lying asleep on one side of the big bed, Beli and the baby[7] by your side. I caressed you a little and whispered, "Chhoto Bou,[8] remember that on this Sunday night I left my body to come and see you. When I return from abroad I shall ask you if you could feel my presence." Then I kissed Beli and the baby and came back.'

Later in life he learnt to be a good sailor and did a fair deal of sea-travel, but he never grew to love the sea as he loved the rivers of his native Bengal. The ocean-liner seemed to him 'a castle of indolence' where the passengers did not know what to do with their time. The diary has some amusing descriptions of the passengers trying to kill time with merrymaking. There was a beautiful lady on board who displayed her charms so generously that in the dining-room all the eyes were riveted on her—the jaws were mechanically chewing the food, the eyes were feasting on her limbs. His own too—or else how could he have noticed! The next morning, which was Sunday, while all the other passengers were at their devotions in the chapel, the lady sat on the deck, receiving the devotion of a young and

---

[6] Reference to Kalidasa's famous poem, *Meghaduta* (Cloud-Messenger). Tagore's love and admiration for Kalidasa was second only to his love for the *Upanishads*. No other single poet, eastern or western, influenced his work so much as his great Indian predecessor.

[7] His daughter Bela and his son Rathindranath.

[8] In a joint family (particularly in Bengal) the members generally address each other, not by name but by epithets descriptive of their mutual relationship, as parents are addressed all over the world. The youngest daughter-in-law of the family would thus be known as *Chhoto Bou*, meaning exactly the youngest daughter-in-law. Very often the husband too addresses his wife so.

ardent Christian youth. What amused the young observer was the fact that even while the elderly gentlemen were critically muttering about her 'indecorous clothing' their eyes kept on straying to what they pretended to dislike.

In Italy the grapes were 'lovely, sweet and fragrant', and so seemed the Italian girls with coloured scarves round their heads. Once again he was charmed with the French countryside. 'No wonder these people love their land so passionately.' He was amused by a British passenger who seemed to resent each query of the French customs authorities and merely muttered, 'I don't parlez-vous française'. On arrival in London he took the first opportunity to visit the house where he had spent such happy days of youth with the Scott family. He was disappointed to learn that the family had left the house and no one knew where they had gone. But the youthful love was now a mere memory and London had many other compensations. He heard a light opera at the Savoy Theatre, called *The Gondoliers* and a dramatic adaptation of Scott's *The Bride of Lammermoor* at the Lyceum. English girls would be glad to read what he noted in his diary about their grandmothers—or maybe, great-grandmothers.

'It is a pleasure to walk along the street here. One is sure to see a pretty face. Patriots at home will, I hope, forgive my admiration of these fair faces, their red lips and shapely noses and eyes that reflect the blue of the sky. English girls are, indeed, attractive. This statement may cause jitters among my well-wishers at home and amused smiles among my friends. Nevertheless, I must confess that a lovely face *is* lovely to me. Good looks and a charming smile—what a wonderful human asset they are! Unfortunately, it so happens that in this country I get more than my due share of such smiles.' He is modest enough to explain that these smiles were provoked not by his handsome and manly looks but by the odd dress he wore.[9]

Once again he praises the European society where women, because

[9] During his first visit to England he had adopted the standard British costume of the period; during this visit he wore over the trousers, not the usual coat and neck-tie but the *gala-bund* or the close-collar coat which is today the popular (and also officially sponsored) Indian dress. It is an adaptation of the western coat or a compromise between the Indian *achhkan* and the western coat. Even in this little matter he anticipated the modern practice of his country by more than half a century.

they are accorded their due share of freedom, help to make the nation strong, and contrasts it with the Indian society where woman's sole function seemed to be to serve and pamper man and thereby emasculate him. But though he seemed to be enjoying his stay in London, his muse forsook him. This was to happen again and again in his life. This man of universal sympathies, a world citizen if ever there was one, was so rooted in his native soil that outside India the fountain of his poetry and songs ceased to flow or flowed only in driblets. He could write philosophic essays and deliver brilliant talks, but music which was the food of his spirit turned its face away. Suddenly he notes in his diary on 5 October, 'I am tired of this place, tired even of the beautiful faces. I have therefore decided to return.' His two companions, his elder brother Satyendranath and his friend Loken Palit, were unwilling to cut down their holiday. So he returned alone.

A letter written by him to his niece Indira (who seems to have partially replaced his deceased sister-in-law as his chief confidante) on the eve of his departure from London, dated 10 October, is interesting and significant. What provoked him to this outburst is not known.

'Is man a mere machine made of metal [he wrote] that he should function in strict accordance with rules? So vast and varied is the mind of man, so many its hungers and so varied its claims that it must now and again swerve and reel and toss. This indeed is what makes man human, the proof that he lives, the refutation that he is not a mere bundle of matter. He who has never felt this weakness, who has never wavered on the brink, whose mind is narrow and strait, such a man is not truly alive. What we call instinct, what we always refer to disparagingly in our daily life—this it is that leads us out of the jungle of virtues and vices, our elations and afflictions, into an awareness of the unlimited possibilities of our destiny. One who has never known the turbulence of life, in whom the petals of the mysterious flower within have never opened, such a one may seem happy, may seem a saint, his single-track mind may impress the multitude with its power—but he is ill-equipped for the life's true adventure into the infinite.'

Soon after his return to India on 3 November 1890 the poems of

Manasi were published. Their wide range and sweep of thought, their lyrical beauty and strength (like a rider at ease on a spirited horse, in firm control of his seat, using no whip, the horse obeying the slightest hint of his hand or heel) convinced even his worst critics that here was indeed a poet. According to Rabindranath's British biographer, Edward Thompson (the only English critic who was capable of appreciating him in the original Bengali), 'the prevailing note of the book is quiet certainty; it marks his definite attainment of maturity'.[10] On the other hand, it is interesting to recall that one of his shrewdest critics and one of the sharpest minds of the age,[11] found in these poems 'a mood of despair and resignation' and wrote about it to the author, whose explanation (conveyed in his reply to the letter) is worth quoting:

'I sometimes detect within myself a battle-ground where two opposing forces are constantly in action, one beckoning me to peace and cessation of all strife, the other egging me on to battle. It is as though the restless energy and the will to action of the West were perpetually assaulting the citadel of my Indian placidity. Hence this swing of the pendulum between passionate pain and calm detachment, between lyrical abandon and philosophizing, between love of my country and mockery of patriotism, between an itch to enter the lists and a longing to remain wrapt in thought. This continual struggle brings in its train a mood compounded of frustration and resignation.'

Indeed, a discerning critic will not fail to notice an undercurrent of this mood running through his finest and most characteristic utterances in all the major productions of his literary career. If it is particularly noticeable in *Manasi*, it is because this exquisite sheaf of poems was his first truly adult production. The poems cover five broad categories which were always to remain his major themes, though later the scope was to widen: love poems, poems of Nature, poems dealing with social and national problems, religious and mystical poems and poems which use natural or legendary phenomena or historical anecdotes to embody the author's metaphysics

---

[10] *Rabindranath Tagore: Poet and Dramatist.* Oxford University Press, London.
[11] Pramatha Choudhury, husband of Tagore's niece Indira and one of the most brilliant writers of Bengal.

or philosophy. Needless to say, these categories are not always clearly defined and merge into one another. The human and the divine, love of Nature and of man, intuition and thought so mingle and interpenetrate in his consciousness that in his poetry, as in actual life itself, it is impossible to separate one from the other.

If I were asked what was his most dominant single quality which might explain all the varied aspects of his personality and genius, I should say that he was first and last and above all else a lover.[12] He loved—whether one woman or many or a mere image which he never found, whether God or man, whether nature or humanity. Nothing is, perhaps, more foolish than to treat a poet as a philosopher, to ignore the vagary of his mood and miss the music of his words in a futile attempt to chase the shadow of his thought. Unfortunately, it is precisely these qualities which evaporate in the process of translation into another language.

One of the poems in the book is particularly interesting as illustrative of the havoc that can be caused by inadequate rendering. While Rabindranath was staying in Ghazipur, a British military surgeon became friendly with him and begged him to translate one of his poems into English for him. So he translated one stanza of a poem he had written entitled 'Nishphal Kamana' (Fruitless Desire). This is perhaps his first attempt at an English rendering of his poems and fortunately the manuscript has survived. He himself forgot all about it, for much later in life he made a different rendering of it which was included in *Lover's Gift and Crossing* published by Macmillan, London, in 1918. It is interesting to compare the two versions, both translations of the same first stanza of a poem which runs to nearly eighty lines, to see how many of the current English

[12] In 1926 when Rabindranath Tagore visited Hungary, he was suddenly taken ill and was ordered complete rest by the doctors in Füred on Lake Balaton. While he was convalescing in that charming health resort he was requested to plant a linden tree in the park and to write a verse in the hotel guest book. He wrote in Bengali a verse which he himself translated into English as follows:

> When I am no longer on this earth, my tree,
> let the ever-renewed leaves of thy spring
> murmur to the wayfarers:
> 'The poet did love while he lived'.

The tree still stands in the park, with the poet's bronze bust underneath it.

renderings of his poems are little more than mutilated paraphrases
of the original, retaining hardly any of the charm and magic of the
original and in many cases not even bare skeletons of the whole.
Here's the earlier version done probably in 1890:

> All fruitless is the cry,
> all vain this burning fire of desire.
> The sun goes down to his rest,
> there is gloom in the forest and glamour
>   in the sky;
> with downcast look and lingering steps
> the evening star comes in the wake
>   of departing day
> and the breath of the twilight is deep
>   with the fullness of a farewell feeling.
>
> I clasp both thine hands in mine,
> and keep thine eyes prisoner with
>   my hungry eyes,
> seeking and crying, where art thou,
> where, O, where!
> Where is the immortal flame hidden
>   in the depth of thee!
> As in the solitary star of the dark
>   evening sky
> the light of heaven, with its immense
>   mystery, is quivering,
> in thine eyes, in the depth of their
>   darkness,
> there shines a soul-beam tremulous
>   with a wide mystery.
>
> Speechless I gaze upon it,
> and I plunge with all my heart
> into the deep of a fathomless longing:
> I lose myself.

And this the later version of the same original stanza:

> I clasp your hands, and my heart plunges into

> the dark of your eyes, seeking you, who ever
> evade me behind words and silence.

The paraphrase of the remaining stanzas is equally mutilated. The curious reader may see it for himself in No. 25 of *Lover's Gift*.

In 1887, a ship carrying 800 pilgrims to the holy city of Puri on the eastern coast was wrecked in a storm and sank, all the lives being lost. Rabindranath wrote a poem on this tragedy which is not only one of the best in this collection but is perhaps the best he ever wrote on a sea-storm. It is a magnificent poem whose rhythm heaves and swells like the demented waves of the sea lashed by wind, the imagery and diction conjure up the black terror of the elements, the accents resound with the thunder of doom. But Tagore would not be Tagore if he did not point out at the end that even in the midst of this fearful destruction, the little lamp of love and faith continues to burn in the human heart, which no storm has yet succeeded in blotting out for ever. An adequate rendering in English is beyond the capacity of the present writer who can only attempt a bare digest in paraphrase, to indicate the tenor of the author's mood.

> Annihilation rolls and rocks on the breast of the shoreless
> sea, Nature's festival of terror, the wild wind raging
> and beating its hundred wings, the sky and the sea
> reeling in a drunken embrace. The demons are let loose
> in an orgy of unrestraint, eyeless, heedless, homeless,
> pitiless—out of tune the mad music of Nature, out
> of rhythm its meaningless dance! There stand eight hundred
> men and women huddled on the deck of the reeling ship,
> numb with terror, while beneath the Ogress of the storm
> shrieks, Give! Give! Give! The foaming sea, its
> million arms upraised, roars in chorus, Give! Give! Give!
>
> O God, thou art not. No pity is there, no life—only the
> mad revelry of the elements, merciless, unmindful of human
> suffering, unaware of itself!
>
> And yet in the lap of this insentient, unfeeling Matter,
> man nestles unafraid. Why has the demon of destruction

failed to swallow all his hopes and joys? Why does the
mother leaping to destruction still hold her babe fast
to her breast? Defying the challenge of the elements' fury,
stands the mother—who shall tear the babe from her arms?
Whence this love, this strength in the pitiless flux of
insentient elements?

Pitying and pitiless—the two stand side by side in the
same spot. A fearful riddle! Great terror and great hope
have built a common home. What then is true and what false?
Day and night the question troubles the human heart, now
elating, now depressing. The brute terror of the elements
strikes, heedless of appeals. Then comes love and wrapping
its arms around drives away all fear. Is this a duet of
two Gods, this ceaseless breaking and making, this endless
round of defeat and victory, of victory and defeat?

Another beautiful poem is entitled 'Meghaduta' and was written
on a rainy day in Santiniketan where Rabindranath had spent some
days shortly before his departure for England in 1890. As he watched
the clouds thicken in the sky, he was reminded of his great predecessor Kalidasa who on such a day as this had written his great
poem, *Meghaduta* (Cloud-Messenger), which has made immortal the
love of all lovers throughout the ages whom distance has parted from
their sweethearts. The poem is a new Meghaduta in honour of the
old and shows that Rabindranath was now confident enough of his
genius to claim kinship with the greatest classical poet of his country,
like Dante paying homage to Virgil.

In Santiniketan, too, he wrote another magnificent poem addressed
to Ahalya, the legendary victim of divine intrigue and human
weakness. Ahalya was the beautiful wife of a Rishi. The god Indra
(Indian Zeus or Jupiter), attracted by her beauty—Indian gods, like
their Greek and Roman counterparts, were not only easily excitable
but could be thoroughly unscrupulous—assumed the form of her
husband and seduced her. The husband coming to know of it cursed
the innocent woman who turned into a stone. Centuries later, Rama,
the hero of *Ramayana*, restored her to her human form. The poet
imagines that during this long period of suspension of human

consciousness, Ahalya must have shared the consciousness of the so-called mute, insentient things, for even they have a consciousness though it may differ from the human kind.

And so the poem goes on, hinting and guessing at the secret bonds that unite at some dim level of sub-consciousness the worlds of nature and of man, until the earth's loving hand has wiped away from Ahalya all trace of man-made sin and she rises again from the womb of the great mother, a new-born virgin, bright and beautiful, like the dawn rising over the blue ocean of forgotten memories.[13]

But however much this poet of love and Nature enjoyed nursing his private longings or brooding on the mysteries of Nature, he could never remain indifferent to what was happening in society around him. This patriot and lover was the severest and most bitter critic of the follies of his countrymen. In a poem entitled 'Duranta Asha' (Wild Hopes) he castigates them for being gutless and spineless and yet ever boastful of their past glory and Aryan heritage—'the goody-goody, rice-eating, mother-sucking Bengali', pulling at his hookah and shuffling his dirty cards with a smirk on his face while 'wild hopes hiss like a serpent in the breast'. Rather than this—'O that I were an Arab Bedouin! Beneath my feet the boundless desert stretching endlessly! The horse gallops, the sands fly, I pour myself into the sky, a fire raging in my breast day and night! Spear in my hand, courage in my heart, ever homeless, free as the desert wind!' His gift for humour and irony finds full scope in these satirical poems, in one of which he congratulates the 'patriots' who are engaged in 'building our country' by the easy way of cheering themselves and reviling those who do not cheer them, by filling reams of paper with petitions, always itching for battle, with pen and ink ready at hand. 'Banga-Bir' (Heroes of Bengal) makes fun of the book-worm heroes who have read all about Cromwell and Mazzini and decided that we are as good as the best, for has not Max Müller told us that we are the Aryans?

The most savage of these satires was provoked by an incident in 1888 when a group of these 'patriotic Aryans' fell on a Salvation

---

[13] The poet's own English rendering of this poem is such a mutilation that one wonders how he had the heart to do it. See *Poems* published by Visva-Bharati, Calcutta.

Army preacher and beat him up. His description of this cowardly attack in a long poem entitled 'Dharma Prachar' (Propagation of Religion), how the attack is planned and executed on a defenceless man who refuses to retaliate, how the 'heroes' flee at the approach of police and arriving home, swaggering like warriors from the battle-field, shout at their wives because the food is not ready for their hungry stomachs, is as remarkable for its fierce irony and contempt of his co-religionists as for its eloquent and noble interpretation of the spirit of Christianity. One does not know what to admire more, the author's genius as a satirist or his courage as a humanist. Another poem, reminiscent of Browning's 'The Lost Leader', is full of pain and lofty reproach at the 'lost leaders' who having led the renaissance and opened new horizons had now turned social reactionaries and were justifying every foolish and cruel custom in the name of Hinduism, in particular, child marriage. He reminds them of the early days when as a young boy he had been inspired by their writings and 'today they expect us to bring home, to the music of the wedding pipes, a bride of eight years, to tear open the petals of her unbudded youth, to squeeze all sweetness out of it, to crush a young life under the weight of scriptures and make it one with the dust of the dead past!'

In a very humorous poem he makes merciless fun of a newly-married romantic youth trying to make love to his baby-wife. The more poetic becomes his ardour the more scared is the poor child who starts crying, asking for her nurse, or for plums or for her doll to play with. In a more serious vein he discusses the tragedy of romantic love, which inevitably cools down after the first few years of married life, in two poems in one of which 'The Woman Speaks', full of controlled grief and subtle reproaches, the other where 'The Man Speaks', a plea reasonable and pitiful but more likely to irritate the woman than to console her. Rabindranath's understanding of the woman's heart was always subtler and deeper than of the man's tangle of physical desire and masculine vanity.

Sometimes the pilgrim in his Indian soul comes out and his zest for life weakens, 'sicklied o'er with the pale cast of thought'. It is as though Prospero's wand suddenly breaks and the wonderful panorama of life and this world seems insubstantial. Why all this

J

pain and fever of wanting and striving? Everything melts away like
a shadow. Getting and not getting, they both end in sighs. Sometimes he feels that in all the loves he has ever known, in this life as in
the many past ones,[14] he has been seeking the one true love in many
forms, namely, the love of God, the spirit's ceaseless search, without
its knowing, for its ultimate goal, its merger with the divine spirit.
The religious consciousness, the need of establishing a satisfactory
relationship with the Absolute, the Ultimate, which was to find its
culmination in the *Gitanjali* period, is beginning to stir within him.
But the love of life is still too strong and the mystic consciousness not overwhelming. So he wonders, in a poem entitled 'Ashanka'
(Doubt): 'Is it right to merge all the little loves into this one great
love, to lose the light of a million stars and be dazzled by only one
great light? So many little joys of this world, so much varied beauty,
so much love, so many flowers blossoming at the door, this immense
earth and the sky—is it right to let one great obsession overwhelm
them? Who can say if this be well?'

Strangely enough, he wrote only one small poem in London
during his entire stay there, but the poem is significant and is entitled
'Viday' (Farewell). This is the gist: 'In a boundless ocean floats the
little boat of my life. From your familiar shore blows a soft wind
bringing with it memories sweet and fragrant and full of pain, of
hopeless longings, of secrets unconfessed.'

In a letter written to a friend after the publication of *Manasi*,
Rabindranath wrote in answer to a query as to who was the object
of his love poems in that book: 'Man's cravings are unlimited,
his capacity and reach very limited, and so he builds up in his mind an
image of his desires which he can adore. The beloved in Manasi
poems is of the mind only. It is my first, tentative, incomplete image
of God. Will I ever be able to complete it?'

Whatever the young poet's achievement in the field of letters—
and it was considerable—the Maharshi was adamant that his son

---

[14] It is doubtful if Tagore believed in the theory of transmigration of the soul as
the orthodox Hindus believe. What he believed in was that the human consciousness
has evolved out of several sub-layers of consciousness, whose dim memory survives
in highly sensitive minds, linking the so-called insentient, the animal and the human
worlds.

should also accept his responsibilities as a man and as a son of a
big land-owning family. Rabindranath could no longer evade his
father's command that he should take full charge of the family
estates which were at that time fairly large and spread over a vast
area.[15] The young man had to obey. He had played with the
romantic idea of travelling all over north India in a bullock-cart so
as to watch leisurely and at first hand the vast panorama of his
country's life. Instead he had to make his headquarters in a house-
boat on the river Padma[16] and look after the interests of the family
estates and adjust them, as best as he could, to the welfare of the
tenants. Much as he may have shied at first from this onerous
responsibility, he was later grateful to his father for having yoked
him to it. He not only needed this discipline to make a man of him,
but the years he thus spent in the heart of rural Bengal widened and
strengthened his intimacy with nature which he loved so much and
gave him glimpses into the varied landscape of his country which he
would not otherwise have known. This was rich food for his
poetry.

But even richer was the intimacy he thus gained with the actual
life of the common people, their daily drudgery and constant
struggle against the indifference of nature and the worse indifference
of a rigid social orthodoxy and of an alien political rule. This first-
hand knowledge gave him an insight into the lives of the people and
an understanding of the social and economic conditions which had
limited the scope of these lives. This proved a rich asset to his genius
and provided the real backbone both to his success as a short-story
writer and to his sound diagnosis of his country's social and economic
malaise. The letters he wrote during this period, most of them to his
favourite niece Indira Devi,[17] are a remarkable testament of his
widening sympathies as a man and his deepening sensibilities as a
poet. As they were not intended for publication he wrote freely and

[15] These estates were spread over north-east Bengal and Orissa. The major part
was in what is today East Pakistan.
[16] Padma is but another name of the Ganges when it flows through that part of
the country.
[17] Excerpts from these letters were later published as *Chhinna Patra* (Torn Letters)
in 1912. A selection of these excerpts was translated into English and published as
Glimpses of Bengal, Macmillan & Co., London, 1921.

without any self-consciousness. They provide not only glimpses of Bengal but also glimpses of the author's own development.

The two aspects of nature he loved best, space and flow, the sky and the river, he had here to his heart's content. Unlike Pascal, 'the silence of the infinite space' never frightened him, it beckoned to him as though he could listen to the music of the spheres. Few poets have loved space as he did, anything that stretched beyond the reach of the senses, whether it be the sky or an expanse of water or of bare land. Again and again he talks of his 'hunger for space' and once he wrote, 'Goethe on his death-bed wanted "more light". If I have any desire left at all at such a time, it will be for "more space" as well.' In one of his letters he has described how one evening he was reading an English book on art, beauty and aesthetics. As he plodded through its abstruse definitions and fine distinctions he suddenly felt wearied and dejected as though he had strayed into an empty mirage, filled with mocking voices. He threw the book on the table and as the night was far advanced blew out the lamp with the intention of retiring to bed. No sooner had he done so than the moonlight burst into the room through the open windows. Looking out at the sky flooded with light, he wondered how a little man-made lamp could have successfully shut out all this beauty. 'What had I been looking for in the empty wordiness of the book? There was the very thing itself, filling the skies, silently waiting for me outside, all these hours!'

In a less serious mood he has described in another letter how while he was walking at night on the moonlit sands, his estate manager came to make solicitous inquiries about his meals, etc. 'As soon as the patter of words came to an end, the peace of the stars descended and filled my heart to overflowing.' He was amused at the irony of man's fate, seeking the eternal, himself tied to the ephemeral. The trivial chatter about food seemed discordant in the silence of the night '. . . and yet the soul and the stomach have been living together so long. The very spot on which the moonlight falls is my landed property, but the moonlight tells me that my ownership is an illusion and my landed estate tells me that this moonlight is all emptiness. And as for poor me, I remain distracted between the two.'

He paid frequent visits to Calcutta to see his wife and children.

The family had started a new literary monthly called *Sadhana*[18] in place of the old one, *Bharati*. Though edited by his nephew Sudhindranath, it was obvious that the main supplies had to come from Rabindranath's pen. The pen, fortunately, was now equal to the task and the pages of this journal during the four years of its life are an impressive record of the amazing fecundity and versatility of Rabindranath's genius—poems, dramas, short stories, literary criticism and essays and polemics on almost every conceivable aspect of national and social problems. From now on his work bears the impress of maturity and whatever flowed from his pen came as a flash of surprise, lighting up unknown vistas of thought and expression in the literature of his language. If he continued to experiment— he never ceased to experiment—it was not because he had not found his form but because there is no end to this discovery.

The beautiful drama *Chitrangada*[19] belongs to this period, written in 1891 and published a year later—the only one of his dramas written in spring. 'All my plays except *Chitrangada* were written in the winter.'[20] The spring unfroze the fountain of his poetry and song, which flowed steadily in summer, swelling and heaving when the rains came and became a smooth expanse of waters under the clear autumn sky. But in winter ' . . . lyrical fervour is apt to grow cold, and one gets the leisure to write drama'.[21] And this is a lyrical drama *par excellence*, the breath of spring blows through every line of it, making it languorous with the ecstasy of sensuous delight. Indeed, the play deals with the enchantment of spring and the power of its spell on the senses. In fact, Spring is itself one of the characters in this play, which is one of Rabindranath's most beautiful plays and perhaps the only one that is flawless. Not a line one would like to take away from it; one wishes it were longer—in the original Bengali where every utterance quivers with lyrical passion held in masterly restraint. The play is in blank verse, his last great experiment in that form. The play, too, is very characteristic of the author, in

---

[18] Not to be confused with the title of the philosophical lectures in English which Tagore delivered at the Harvard University, U.S.A., in 1912-13, published by Macmillan & Co. in 1914.

[19] English translation, *Chitra*, Macmillan & Co., London, 1914.

[20] *Chhinna Patra*.   [21] *Ibid*.

the sense that it does not embody a seasonal mood or idea which he outgrew but represents a basic and permanent attitude of his mind and philosophy—his unification of man and Nature, the latter almost an active participant in the drama of life, and the perennial question, what is beauty; what is love; what is the true and enduring basis of man-woman relationship? So characteristic indeed is this play that the author might have written it in any period of his life, in the seventies instead of in his thirtieth year. In fact, he recast it at the age of seventy-five in the form of a sequence of songs, interspersed with stray dialogue, as a musical accompaniment to its performance on the stage as an Indian ballet.

It is interesting to know the genesis of the play as the author recalled it late in life. Once, after one of his very early visits to Santiniketan, while he was returning to Calcutta—it was early April—and watching the receding landscape from the window of his railway coach, he was struck by the profusion of flowers on the wild shrubs and trees that lined both sides of the track. These flowers, so fragrant and lovely to look at, would soon wither and fall in the burning heat of the sun and in their stead the trees, among which were many mango trees, would bear fruit. The flowers were merely the play of spring. Nature's trick to bring about the fruit. Musing on this the young poet said to himself: If a sensitive woman felt that her lover was bound to her solely on account of her physical charms, which were external and short-lived, and not by any qualities of her heart and the need of her life-long companionship, she would discover in her body, not an asset but a rival. This idea intrigued the poet and he felt like giving it a dramatic form. At the same time an episode from the *Mahabharata* floated into his mind. The two jostled in his consciousness until several years later the present drama emerged during his sojourn in a small village in Orissa, called Pandua, where he had gone to inspect his family estates.

The episode as originally recorded in the Indian epic, *Mahabharata*, is simple and bald, devoid of any particular dramatic interest. Here it is: In the course of his wanderings in fulfilment of a solemn vow, Arjuna, the great hero, came to Manipur, the easternmost region of India. There he saw Chitrangada, the beautiful daughter of the King

of Manipur whom the father, who had no son, had brought up as
his heir. Arjuna fell in love with the princess, married her and after a
year a son was born to them. This bare skeleton was filled by
Rabindranath with the flesh and blood of an enchanting romance,
full of deep psychological insight into the relationship of man and
woman. This is the story as it emerged from the crucible of his
imagination:

The princess Chitra who had been brought up as a boy and trained
in the rough art of the battle-field was plain and rugged to look at
and knew 'no feminine wiles for winning hearts'. She could wield
the bow with her hands but not with her eyes. One day while she
was chasing a deer in the forest, dressed in man's hunting costume,
she came upon a man lying across her path. She asked him haughtily
to move aside but he took no heed. Enraged, she pricked him with
the sharp end of her bow. Instantly he leapt up like a tongue of flame
but noticing a girl in hunting costume he merely smiled ironically.
'Then for the first time in my life I felt myself a woman, and knew
that a man was before me.' She asked him who he was. 'I am Arjuna
of the great Kuru clan,' he replied. The princess was stunned. Here
before her was the fabulous warrior whom every damsel of the age
worshipped in her dreams. In her confusion she was tongue-tied and
failed even to greet the great warrior. Contemptuously he walked
away.

The next morning she laid aside her man's garment and decked in
feminine finery sought Arjuna out in the forest and tried to woo him.
But Arjuna repulsed her advances by telling her that he was under
an oath of celibacy and could not touch a woman. Humiliated and
wounded in the core of her being, Chitra broke her bow into two
and invoked, by her penance, Madana, the god of love. Madana
appeared before her with his boon companion, Vasanta, the god of
spring and eternal youth. The princess begged, 'For a single day
make me superbly beautiful, as beautiful as was the sudden awakening of love in my heart. Give me but one day of perfect beauty, and
I will answer for the days that follow.' The gods granted her the
gift of perfect beauty—not for one day but for one whole year.

Chitra was transformed into a maiden of ravishing beauty. While
she was washing her limbs and playing with water on the edge of a

forest pool, entranced by her own beauty, Arjuna saw her and was swept off his feet. Forgetting his vow of celibacy he wooed her. For some months the lovers lived in the perfect bliss of love's abandon. But Chitra was not fully happy. She burnt in her own desire and burnt with shame at the recollection of her own wild ecstasy in Arjuna's arms. 'Shame slipped to my feet like loosened clothes,' she confessed to Madana. 'What fearful flame is this with which thou hast enveloped me! I burn, and I burn whatever I touch.' She was ashamed that she had won her lover with borrowed beauty and feared that she had created a rival in her own body. 'I found that my body had become my own rival. It is my hateful task to deck her every day, to send her to my beloved and see her caressed by him. O god, take back thy boon!' The god assured her that in course of time the season of flowers will yield to the season of fruit and that Arjuna, wearied of the pleasures of the flesh, would himself look for the real woman in her. In the meanwhile, 'O child, go back to thy mad festival.'

And so indeed it happened. The surfeit of pleasure brought about its inevitable reaction and the warrior in Arjuna began to long for a life of action and for a love 'that can last longer than pleasure, that can endure even through suffering'. His heart was restless 'like a serpent reviving from his long winter's sleep'. One day he met some foresters who talked of the warrior-princess Chitra who was as valiant as she was noble, who had a man's valour and a mother's heart. Arjuna began to wonder who this other Chitra was. He asked his fair mistress who told him that the princess was plain and ungainly, devoid of all feminine charm, her very virtues were like prison walls within which languished the woman in her. 'She is like the spirit of a cheerless morning, sitting upon the stony mountain peak, all her light blotted out by the dark clouds. Do not ask me of her life. It will never sound sweet to man's ear.' But Arjuna's curiosity had been aroused and he begged Chitra to let him meet the princess. He also begged her to let him see her own true self. 'I never seem to know you aright. You seem to me like a goddess hidden within a golden image . . . Illusion is the first appearance of Truth.' She advances towards her lover in disguise. But a time comes when she throws off her ornaments and veils and stands clothed in naked dignity. 'I grope for that ultimate *you*, that bare simplicity of truth.'

Chitra, secretly pleased, promised to introduce the princess to him. She begged the gods to take back her false beauty. The gods withdrew their gift and Chitra, restored to her old and true form, appeared before Arjuna and said, 'I am Chitra, the Princess of Manipur—neither a goddess to be worshipped nor a mere female to be used or brushed aside as it pleases a man. If you care to have me as a comrade by your side in the path of danger and daring, if you let me share the great duties of your life, then only you will know my true self.' The play ends with Arjuna's words, 'Beloved, my life is full.'

In the same year in which this lyrical drama was published, Rabindranath wrote and published his first social comedy in prose, *Goray Galad* (Radically Wrong, *lit*. Error at the Start), a comedy of errors interspersed with social satire, its polished and sophisticated wit matching Oscar Wilde's,[22] its farcical spirit as delicious as that of *Charley's Aunt*.[23] It deals with the romantic effusions and matrimonial predicaments of three young intellectuals and their ladies. As usual the women in the drama are far more vivacious and sharply characterized than the men. The plot is simple and straight, unencumbered with any sub-plots or irrelevant intrusions, and the farce runs merrily to its climax without undue strain on the reader's credulity. The dialogue scintillates with wit—its native idiom is untranslatable. There is a passing dig at the contemporary Victorian novel when one of the romantic youths complains of his dull, day-to-day 'vegetarian existence' without a touch of warmth of flesh and says, 'I would much rather cease to be and live as a character in an English novel where I might make love to an Edith or an Ellen or a Leonora. The girl's father will forbid the match, the girl will threaten to commit suicide and finally in the last chapter everything will wind up in the everlasting bliss of matrimony. Thus, at five shillings a copy I'll run into several editions.' There is also an interesting

[22] Who wrote and produced his comedies in London at about the same time, *Lady Windermere's Fan* being produced in 1892, *A Woman of No Importance* in 1893, and *The Importance of Being Earnest* in 1895.

[23] Strangely enough, this too was produced in the same year, 1892.

and ironic anticipation of modern psycho-analyst therapy and the advertising of patent advice and drugs to cure the many ills of love. The wise Hindus knew all about it and the child-marriage was invented as a vaccination against sex neurosis of which a sure symptom is to feel romantic. Whether in poems, plays, novels or other writing, Tagore never missed an occasion to ridicule Hindu orthodoxy and its fantastic pretensions.

It will be impossible within the scope of this volume to list and discuss all his achievements from now on. Only the major landmarks which outline the development of his personality and thought or which bring into special relief some significant aspect of his genius will be referred to. This volume is not intended as a critical analysis of his literary work or as an evaluation of his philosophy of life or as an appraisal of his contribution as an educationist or social reformer or as an internationalist, though none of these aspects can be wholly ignored. This is rather an attempt to trace the growth of a many-faceted but highly integrated personality who, whatever else he was, was above all a man like one of us, though his senses may have been keener, his imagination subtler and his capacities larger. His achievements in the various fields, important in themselves, gain further significance and human interest, if properly related to the various stages and moods of his development as a man.

The portrait that the West made of him, after the publication of *Gitanjali* and his public lectures mainly interpretive of his country's philosophic heritage, was so partial and one-sided as to be almost misleading. He was either a religious mystic suddenly emerging from his ivory tower, a prophet from the pages of the *Old Testament*, or a wishy-washy sentimentalist and intellectual charlatan. He appeared so suddenly on the Western firmament, full-grown and luminous, bearded and robed in the traditional uniform of a divine messenger that the contrary reactions his personality provoked are not incomprehensible. He seemed so wise that intellectuals doubted if he was clever enough or had his wits about him, so humane that he hardly seemed human, so well-chiselled and perfect in every respect that in a mental climate where toughness tends to be equated with strength and guts are more in demand than the spirit, the very perfection seemed unmanly and artificial. Just as pure and whole-

some water tastes insipid to those who are addicted to alcohol or
to coca-cola or sherbets, so a man who is truly human is *persona
non-grata* with he-men and she-women. And yet in the long run
what can replace water? 'I count it enough,' wrote Rabindranath in
a private letter dated October 1891, 'to live and die as a man, loving
and trusting the world, unable to look on it either as a delusion of
the Creator or a snare of the Devil.' And again in another dated
16 June 1892, '... nothing is more beautiful or great than to perform
the ordinary duties of one's daily life simply and naturally'. This
was the real and basic Tagore; all other aspects in their bewildering
variety were the variations on a simple theme, like the shapes and
colours which clouds assume at different times or, to use his own
words, 'like an endless meaning in the narrow span of a song.'

7

A MAN AMONG MEN

Having wooed and won his Muse the man in Rabindranath, like his Arjuna in *Chitrangada*, felt the need of a wider field of activity, of a fuller life as a man among men. The artist in him, too, looked for newer media and modes of expression. The poet's imagination sought for firmer support in realistic observation, as a flowering creeper needs the firm base of a tree to wind upwards. Life in the country brought him in direct contact with the soil of his land, and the daily, prosaic, matter-of-fact business of looking after the estates enabled him to see at first hand how the vast majority of his people lived. An aristocrat by birth and upbringing, he could have been repelled by them, nauseated by their ignorance, their superstitions, their cussed folly in the midst of dire poverty, their placid acquiescence in remediable wrongs, their inability to help themselves. But instead he grew to love them and love gave him an understanding of their helplessness, like a mother's of her crippled child. It widened his social consciousness which had always been sensitive and lively and turned what had hitherto been a more or less theoretical sympathy into a life-long passion to raise these dumb, half-grown creatures to a full stature of their humanity.

How minute was his observation of nature and men and how it stimulated his imagination with image after image may be illustrated by a few excerpts from the letters he wrote during this period. In a letter of June 1891 he describes a gathering monsoon storm which he watched from the deck of his boat.

'The little boats scurried off into the smaller arm of the river and clung with their anchors safely to its banks. The reapers lifted up the cut sheaves on their heads and hied homewards; the cows followed, and behind them frisked the calves waving their tails. Then came an angry uproar. Torn-off scraps of cloud hurried up from the west like panting messengers of evil tidings. Finally, lightning and thunder, rain and storm, came jostling together and executed a mad dervish dance. The bamboo clumps howled as the raging wind swept the ground with them, now to the east, now to the west. Over them all, the storm droned like a giant snake-charmer's pipe, and to its rhythm swayed hundreds and thousands of crested waves, like so many hooded snakes.' And on another day when nature is quiet and subdued: 'From the bank to which the boat is tied a kind of scent rises out of the grass, and the heat of the ground given off in gasps, actually touches my body. I feel that the warm, living earth is breathing upon me, and that she too must feel my breath.'

Fortunately, some of these letters written casually from day to day have survived to give evidence that this poet really and truly did feel in actual life what he had said in his poetry. One does not normally poetize or affect attitudes while writing casual letters to one's young niece, much less would one bore her with descriptions of commonplace scenes unless they seemed so vivid as to cease to be commonplace. 'Two cowherd lads are grazing their cattle just in front of my boat. The cows are munching away with great gusto, their noses plunged into the lush grass, their tails incessantly busy flicking off the flies. The raindrops and the sticks of the cowherd boys fall on their backs with the same unreasonable persistency, and they bear both with equally uncritical resignation, steadily going on with their munch, munch, munch.' In a letter of February 1894 he writes, 'We have two elephants which come to graze on this bank of the river. They greatly interest me. They give the ground a few taps with one foot, and then taking hold of the grass with the end of their trunks wrench off an enormous piece of turf, roots, soil and all. This they go on swinging till all the earth leaves the roots; they then put it into their mouths and eat it up. Sometimes the whim takes them to draw up the dust into their trunks, and then with a snort they squirt it all over their bodies; this is their elephantine toilet.'

Here is a picture of a gypsy camp. 'Right in front of my window, on the other side of the stream, a band of gypsies have ensconced themselves, putting up bamboo frameworks covered over with split-bamboo mats and pieces of cloth ... That is always the gypsies' way—no home anywhere, no landlord to pay rent to, wandering about as it pleases them with their children, their pigs and a dog or two; and on them the police keep a vigilant eye. I often watch the doings of the family nearest me. They are dark but good-looking, with fine, strongly-built bodies, like north-west country folk. Their women are handsome and have tall, slim, well-knit figures; with their free and easy movements and natural independent airs, they look to me like swarthy Englishwomen.'

He might admire the gypsies as he envied the Bedouin, but it was to the peasant of Bengal that his heart went out, who stirred the deeps of humanity in him. It was not pity only, certainly not the kind of pity which is a luxury of the sentimental. It was pity which makes the heart humble and gives understanding to love. 'I feel a great tenderness for these peasant folk—our ryots—big, helpless children of Providence, who must have food brought to their very mouths, or they are undone. When the breasts of mother-earth dry up, all they can do is to cry. As soon as the hunger is somewhat appeased, they forget everything else. Whether the socialist dream of all children sharing alike the heritage of the earth can ever be realized, I know not; but if such an ideal is wholly unattainable and cannot even be made partially feasible, then I must say that the Law which governs human destiny is indeed cruel and man a truly unfortunate creature. If suffering must exist in this world, be it so; but let there be some loophole, some possibility somewhere to spur the best in man to a ceaseless endeavour, to nurse an undying hope. They utter very hard words indeed who maintain that a time will never come when the least of mankind will be provided with a minimum of food and clothing.'

The 'deep concern' was not merely literary and poetic. He did whatever was possible under the circumstances to help these 'big helpless children of Providence' grow into self-reliant adults and thus initiated, two decades before Mahatma Gandhi came on the scene and half a century before the national Government took it up, the first experiments in rural community development. Apart from the fact that the Government at that time was in the hands of foreigners who were interested primarily in maintaining 'law and order', Tagore did not consider it a healthy state of society where the individual had lost his initiative and looked up to the State for help and guidance in matters where he could help and guide himself best. Only where the individual initiative is necessarily restricted for lack of material and technical resources, as in the case of large-scale projects for dams and river control to cope with floods and droughts, the State should and must come in. But if the State did everything for the individual, people would continue to remain 'big, helpless children', if not of Providence, of the State. His pro-gramme of community development was therefore based on the twin principles of self-help and enlightenment. The latter was very important because if the people had lost their initiative it was not only because they had become physically and morally lazy, but because their spirits had been crippled by all sorts of social inhibitions and religious superstitions. They were totally ignorant of the most elementary scientific knowledge and while they believed blindly and abjectly in every kind of religious hocus-pocus they were incredulous of the real miracles of science. There is no misfortune greater than ignorance, no sin greater than to revel in it.

It was this realization, reinforced by painful memories of his own school-days, of a mechanical system of teaching based on 'cram and exam', which gradually obliged him to take upon himself the role of an educationist and social reformer. His first practical experiments in this field were conducted for the benefit of the peasants on his family estates.[1] Many years later when he was working out his educational experiments in Santiniketan, he founded a parallel insti-tution adjacent to the educational colony and named it Sriniketan—a nucleus for experiments in large-scale community development. He strove to build up, through social participation and service, a living communication between the students of his school, the budding

---

[1] Tolstoy had done the same long before Tagore. The affinity between these two outstanding literary geniuses of the age was as remarkable as were their differences. Tolstoy was, spiritually and morally, more akin to Gandhi. Nevertheless it is a great pity that these two literary and intellectual giants—Tolstoy and Tagore—never met or even came to know each other better. Tagore no doubt knew of Tolstoy and admired his unrivalled genius, but it is doubtful if Tolstoy was even aware of his Asian contemporary. If Tagore and Gandhi could understand each other, despite their great differences, the Russian and the Indian would no doubt have done the same—and even better.

intelligentsia who were to become the active citizens of tomorrow, and the peasants rooted in the soil, the solid core of Indian economy and society. So long as the core remained unchanged, India would remain static, whatever the seeming progress among the intellectuals in a few big cities like Calcutta or Bombay.

He therefore wanted to make this awareness of the basic and fundamental problem of India's future as an integral part of the education of the intelligentsia. 'The soil in which we are born,' he reminded them again and again, 'is the soil of our village, the mother earth in whose lap we receive our nourishment from day to day. Our educated *élite*, abstracted from this primal basis, wander about in the high heaven of ideas like aimless clouds far removed from this our home. If this cloud does not dissolve into a shower of loving service, man's relation with mother earth will never become truly meaningful. If all our ethereal ideas float about in vaporous inanity, the seed time of the new age will have come in vain. It is not as if there is no rain but the land remains untilled. It is as if from out our vast country, stretched out like an arid waste, a thirsty cry goes forth heavenward: All your accumulated ideas, your wealth of knowledge arrayed in fine splendour—all this should be mine. Give to me all that is mine. Prepare me so that I may receive it all. Whatever you give will be restored to you a thousandfold.'

These were not mere words of a poet or empty exhortations of a patriot-politician. This was said by a man who had already practised to the full what he now preached. Himself the leading intellectual among his people, his chief concern, as a man if not as a poet, for fifty years, from 1890 to the year of his death in 1941, was the Indian peasant. With his limited resources and in the limited field where he could function, first in his family estates and later in Sriniketan, he helped and made it possible for the peasants to build their own schools and hospitals, roads and water-tanks, set up co-operative enterprises and banks and a system of self-government, thus saving them from the extortions of usurious money-lenders and petty lawyers who fatten on litigation. The handsome amount which he received as Nobel Prize in 1913 was donated by him to his school in Santiniketan and invested in the agricultural co-operative bank he had earlier set up in one of the family estates at Potisar, so that two

Bust by Jacob Epstein, 1926

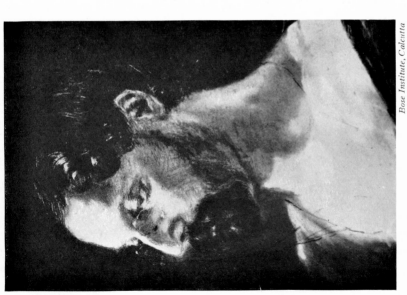

Portrait by Abanindranath, 1896

In Darjeeling, 1914

birds were killed with one stone. The peasants got loans at cheap interest and the school received a fixed annual income.

When his son Rathindranath grew up, he sent him, not to Oxford or Cambridge which the upper classes in India then considered— indeed, still seem to consider—as *the* thing to do, but to Illinois in the United States for training in agricultural science. He sent not only his son, but his son-in-law and another young protégé, a friend's son, whom he loved as his own. In 1906 when he sent his son to Illinois, the United States was not the glamorous country it seems today—at any rate not to Indians of the first decade of this century who fully shared the British prejudice that the U.S.A. was mainly a land of uncouth roughs and rich upstarts. It needed considerable imagination and courage to prefer Illinois to Oxford. Tagore never believed that culture could be acquired in a foreign university; what could and should be acquired is scientific knowledge wherever available. Since India, according to him, needed scientific knowledge for agricultural development more than for any other kind of development—nearly ninety per cent. of the people lived on land—he would rather that Indians should learn to become better farmers in Illinois than better 'gentlemen' in Oxford.

When his son returned after completing his studies, he put him to work on the estate so that he might demonstrate to the peasants the benefits of the American methods of farming. A farm was laid out, new crops and new implements suitable to Indian conditions were tried, and even a small laboratory was set up. A New York lawyer, Myron Phelps, who happened to visit the farm told the son how pleased and surprised he was to find in India 'a genuinely successful American farm'.[2] Later on tractors were introduced, and though at first the peasants eyed the machine with suspicion, they soon learnt to appreciate its benefits. Once they understood how efficient and economic the machine was, there was such a demand for hiring it that more tractors had to be brought in to satisfy the demand.

---

[2] *On the Edges of Time*. Rathindranath Tagore. Orient Longmans, India. Though not written as memoirs in the orthodox sense of the term, the book throws very interesting sidelights on the environments in which the author was brought up and on the personality of his father.

But the problem of village economy in India was—and still is—more complex and could not be solved merely by introducing better methods and implements of farming. The pressure of population is very heavy and the problem is not only how to make the best use of the land but how to utilize the surplus labour that is idle over a great part of the year. Tagore was aware of this problem, as Mahatma Gandhi was later, and he tried to encourage the cultivation of subsidiary crops to supplement the main crop and introduced cottage industries and crafts to keep the labour employed and help the peasants to eke out a better living. In one of his letters to his son, he wrote, 'Please encourage them [the peasants] to grow in their homestead land, on the boundaries of the fields and wherever possible, pineapple, banana, date-palm and other fruit trees. Good and strong fibres can be obtained from the leaves of pineapples. The fruit is also easily marketable. Tapioca can be grown as hedges and the tenants should be taught how to extract food material from its roots. It would profit them if they could be induced to grow potatoes. Try again to sow the seeds of the American maize which have been kept in the office'.[3]

This is not poetry but hard common sense. The author of *Gitanjali* could be as practical and down-to-earth as any American farmer or Bolshevik manager of a collective farm. His only difference from the former was that he used his practical ability to benefit others and not himself, and from the latter was that he did not believe in using force but relied on the power of persuasion. He believed that human beings, however stupid they may seem, can be made to see their own good if the best of their kind helped them to do so. Perhaps he was naïve, perhaps he was an incorrigible optimist, but this was the anchor of his faith in humanity. Indeed so deep-rooted was his faith in man that it might even be said that he believed in God because he believed in man and not *vice versa*.

However, to continue the story. In another letter to his son he wrote, 'I have been thinking which of the cottage industries can be taught to the peasants of this place. Nothing grows here except paddy. They have a hard clayey soil as raw material. I wish to know if pot-

[3] Quoted by Rathindranath Tagore in an article entitled 'Father as I knew him'.

tery can be introduced as a cottage industry. Try to find out if the people of a village can turn out pottery by investing in a small furnace . . . The making of umbrellas is another industry they can be taught. Don't forget to inquire about these matters.' He also discussed with his son the possibility of establishing a rice mill on a co-operative basis. He persuaded the peasants in his estate at Potisar to organize themselves into a welfare community which came to be known as Hitaishi Sabha, covering about 125 villages with sixty to seventy thousand inhabitants. The Sabha raised its own funds to which the Tagore estate contributed, maintained schools, hospitals and other centres of common welfare and was self-governing in its constitution.

All this time while the benevolent land-owner was concerned with the welfare of his tenants, the artist in him was watching the life of the common people, their joys and sorrows, loves and enmities, their little deeds of patience and heroism, their capacity for sacrifice in the cause of family or religion and their cowardly acquiescence in injustice and oppression. Always seeking the great in the small, he found ample material in the lives of the common folk for his short stories. This was a new venture of his in the field of creative expression. He had so far written poems, songs, dramas, novels and essays, in all these he had groped and fumbled till he discovered and achieved his form. But in the short story he showed himself a master almost from the very beginning. He followed no known model or pattern—there was none in his own country and its literary tradition. He was the first Indian to attempt this form proper and though the short story as a literary genre is now very popular with Indian writers, no one has yet equalled him in this art, much less surpassed him. Chekhov and Maupassant were still unknown to him—the only two foreign masters who can be compared to him in this field, though he was as different from them in his technique and mode as they from each other. A distinguished Indian sociologist, himself a gifted and versatile writer, has summed up this difference thus: 'The Russian classics have a candour of the soul, the French have a candour of the mind, and Tagore's have a candour of feeling. If we are ashamed of feeling, Tagore's stories are not for us. If we have no such obsession, they are among the best in the world.'[4]

[4] *Tagore: A Study.* D. P. Mukherji. Padma Publications Ltd., Bombay, 1943.

Many of these stories were suggested by some scene or incident or character he observed while he lived in his house-boat on the river Padma (the house-boat too was named Padma). The genesis of some of them is referred to in the letters he wrote during this period. Wherever there is a village nestling on the river bank there is a *ghat*, stone-steps leading to the water, where men and women, young and old, come to bathe and to gossip. He sees one such ghat, its old stones covered with moss, and wonders how much the stones could tell if they could speak. He had felt the same when as a young boy he had stayed with his elder brother in an old Moghul palace in Ahmedabad. That recollection was later woven in the famous story, *The Hungry Stones*.[5] And so now too the ghat speaks and recalls how a charming little girl used once to come to the river—'... so sweet she seemed that when her shadow fell on the water, I used to wish, if I could only catch that shadow and keep it clasped to my stones! When her feet trod lightly on the stones, the moss on them would shiver with delight.' She was called Kusum, though her playmates called her by many endearing variations of that name. She loved water as though she belonged there. Soon a time came when she ceased coming to the water. The ghat gathered from the talk of her playmates that the little Kusum had married and gone to her husband's home in another village.

Days passed. One day suddenly the stones felt the old familiar shiver of delight, which could only come from the tread of Kusum's feet. But there was no longer the same light music in her step. Kusum had returned to her village—a widow. Some years passed and Kusum gradually grew into a young and lovely woman, '... as the Ganges swells into beauty during the rains'. One day a tall, fair and handsome Sanyasi arrived in the village and took up his residence in the Shiva temple near the ghat. Men and women of the village came to visit the Sanyasi to listen to his discourses, but Kusum was not one of them. On the day of the sun's eclipse many people had gathered from villages far and near to bathe in the holy Ganges, among them some women from the village where Kusum had spent the few months of her wedded life. The ghat heard one of the women say that the

[5] The story bears the title, *Ghater Katha* (Tale told by the Steps).

Sanyasi looked very much like Kusum's husband, to which another said, 'But he's disappeared and supposed to be dead. How can he come back?' A third said, 'But he never had such a long beard!' That settled the issue and the women went their way.

One evening—it was full moon—Kusum came and sat on the steps. No one else was there. After a little while the Sanyasi came out of the temple and was coming down the ghat when he suddenly noticed a lonely woman seated on one of the steps. As he hesitated and was about to turn back, Kusum raised her head and the two looked at each other in the light of the full moon. Recovering herself she pulled the veil down on her face and did obeisance to the Sanyasi who asked, 'What is your name?' Kusum told her name. After this incident Kusum came every evening and brought flowers for worship and listened with rapt attention to whatever the Sanyasi said. Then suddenly Kusum disappeared again and did not come to the ghat or to the temple for a long time. One day the Sanyasi sent for her and she came and sat before him with downcast eyes. When he chid her for her long absence, she said that she had deliberately kept away because she was ashamed of her 'wicked thoughts' and was unworthy to sit beside a holy man. When the Sanyasi cross-examined her she confessed that she had had a dream in which she found the Sanyasi making love to her. Since then the dream had obsessed her as a reality and she was unable to look upon the Sanyasi as other than her husband and lover. The Sanyasi was stunned. When he recovered his poise he begged of Kusum to forget him and disappeared from the village. No one heard of him any more.

Kusum slowly came down the steps and stood looking at the water. 'From her childhood she had loved this river and if now, in her crisis, the river did not take her in its arms, who would! I heard a splash—and then nothing more.'

This is one of his earliest stories and a very characteristic one, in the sense that nature and the so-called inert matter are also part of the story and help to create an atmosphere, a mood, of half pity and half awe, which, rather than the plot, is the essence of the story. In a similar vein *The Highway* tells the story of what it has seen of secret longings and frustrated loves. In almost all these stories the author's tenderness and sympathies seem to be monopolized by women, generally young girls, and little children. His portraits of children and teenagers, whether girls or boys, are drawn with infinite tenderness and an almost uncanny understanding of their young, unformed minds. His adult male characters, on the other hand, are generally drawn with a touch of irony, even when they are tragic. When they are good, virtuous or noble, they are weak and somewhat priggish and pitiful; when they are mean or wicked, they tend to become ridiculous or contemptible. Perhaps the only exception is the Kabuliwalla in the story of that name—but then he was a rough Afghan and not a Bengali.

Tagore seems to have had inexhaustible sympathy and admiration for Bengali women but little for the males of his race. This is more true of his novels than of his short stories and is a defect in the former only, for in the latter he was not concerned with portraiture of personality or development of character but with depiction of a mood, creation of an atmosphere or sudden revelation of an unsuspected aspect of character or motive. This swift and intuitive grasp of a scene or a situation was akin to his lyrical genius and native to his highly sensitive mind which responded quickly to each and every impression or suggestion from the outside. Once a suggestion was registered the imagination worked on it and soon wove a story round it.

And so when the village post-master—an educated young man freshly recruited from the city—came to see him, he could see that the young man was bored in the quiet and sluggish atmosphere and wondered how he lived and spent his time. The famous short story, *The Post-Master*, was born of this casual contact. In one of his letters of February 1891 he has described the individual who was to become immortal in the story. 'The post office is in a part of our estate office-building—this is very convenient, for we get our letters as soon as they arrive. Some evenings the post-master comes up to have a chat with me. I enjoy listening to his yarns. He talks of the most impossible things in the gravest possible manner.' The post-master of the story is also a city-bred young man stationed in a small malaria-ridden village of Bengal. An orphan girl of the village, Ratan by name, who had no one to call her own, worked as his maid-cum-cook. The post-master had very little work and to while away the tedium of long summer evenings he would call the girl and engage her in conversation while he puffed at his native tobacco-pipe. He told her stories of the big city he missed so much and in course of time gave her lessons in reading and writing. The orphan girl who had never known any affection grew deeply attached to her young master and used to wait eagerly for the evening hour.

One day the post-master took to his bed with a severe bout of malaria. Day and night the little girl watched by his bedside and nursed him back to health. The post-master took all this devotion for granted and as soon as he was able to leave the bed, resigned his post and made preparations to leave for Calcutta. When Ratan begged him to take her with him, he laughed, 'What an idea!' When he was about to leave he offered Ratan some money which she refused. She broke down and begging him not to worry about her, ran away out of sight. The post-master sighed as he took his place in the boat, musing, such is life—meetings and partings! But Ratan who knew no philosophy wandered about the post office, disconsolate, the tears streaming down her little face.

That this story had little correspondence with actual facts is obvious from another letter dated sixteen months later. One evening as Rabindranath was about to take up one of Kalidasa's books to read, '. . . the post-master walked in. A live post-master cannot but take precedence over a dead poet . . . So I offered him a seat and gave old Kalidasa the go-by. There is a kind of bond between this post-master and me. When the post office was in a part of this estate building I used to meet him every day. I wrote my story, *The Post-Master*, in this very room. And when the story was published in *Hitabadi* he came to me full of bashful smiles as he deprecatingly touched on the subject.' The fact that there was a city-bred post-master marooned in a village was all that was needed to set the author's imagination working on the problem of human relationship and the possible tragedy of a simple, guileless girl who might take for granted that her affection would be returned.

In the same way he must have often noticed in the streets of Calcutta big, hefty, strangers from Kabul peddling dry fruits and nuts. These men, who were known as Kabuliwallas, were much dreaded by Bengalis who looked upon them as uncouth barbarians who lent money at usurious rates and were ready to kill at the slightest provocation; rough characters who might well steal children and carry them away in the big bags that hung on their huge shoulders. But surely, thought Rabindranath, they too were human and must love their children as parents do all over the world. And so the dreaded Kabuliwalla becomes in Tagore's story of that name one of the most lovable characters in Bengali fiction. The friendship between this big hulk of a man, unlettered and uncouth from the rugged mountains of Afghanistan and the five-year-old Bengali girl Mini with her ceaseless prattle and irrepressible mirth is one of the most moving testaments of human relationship overriding all barriers of race, religion and social prejudice.[6]

These stories are of various kinds and in varying techniques, mainly suggestive and impressionist, dealing with different aspects of Bengali life and depicting different types of characters from many classes and walks of life. Like the letters he wrote during this period when he lived on the river and watched the panorama of his country's landscape and life, they provide realistic and vivid glimpses in the life of his people. They are remarkable for their fine blend of acute observation and lively imagination, of pity and irony, of nature and life, and bear witness to his extraordinary gift for seizing on essentials, his wide humanity, his intolerance of social wrong and injustice and his matchless sense of form. The dumb, patient, seemingly cattle-like and uninteresting people of his country have found their individualities in his stories, which have made immortal the humdrum types of men and women whom in actual life one is apt to ignore.

The India that he depicts is not the falsely romantic India of the Maharajas and tigers, of snake charmers and naked sadhus, the India of Kipling and of the tourist guide books. This was real India, of men and women rooted to the soil for centuries, India in transition where different classes and types are reacting differently to the impact of the machine age. Unlike many of his characters in dramas and novels who are either mere types or his own mouth-pieces, the

Many of these stories were later translated into English and published by Macmillan, London. A screen version of the *Kabuliwalla* won the Government of India Gold Medal as the best Indian feature film produced in 1957.

characters in his short stories are real and vivid, some of them unforgettable. In several cases they first lived in his mind as his companions and he even gave them names before he wove stories round them.

He wrote in one of his letters: 'If I do nothing else but write short stories I am happy and I make a few readers happy. The main cause of happiness is that my characters become my companions, they are with me when I am shut up in my room on a rainy day, and on a sunny day they walk about with me on the bright banks of the Padma. Today since early morning a petulant little girl named Giribala has entered my imaginary world.' Giribala lives in Bengali literature as one of the most lovable specimens of Indian womanhood. Describing a scene on the river bank in one of his letters of July 1891 he wrote: 'One girl in particular attracts my attention. She must be about eleven or twelve, but being well-built and buxom she might pass for fourteen or fifteen. She has an attractive face—very dark, but very handsome. Her hair cut short like a boy's seems to suit her face which beams with intelligence and a frank simplicity. She has a child in her arms and is looking at me with unabashed curiosity—not a dull, stupid stare but lively and straightforward. Her utter lack of self-consciousness and her half-boyish, half-girlish manner, confident and yet full of feminine grace, is singularly charming. I did not know we had such types among our village women.' Her people had come to see her off and were waiting for the boat to take her to her husband's home. So young and lively and yet already burdened with a child and with household cares! How does she react to her mother-in-law's nagging and to the self-complacence of a Hindu husband who takes his wife's devotion for granted? And thus the different types the author has observed are placed in varying domestic situations and their destinies, mostly tragic, are worked out with much sympathy and consummate skill. Pity and irony pervade the mood of these stories, pity for wasted youth and frustrated ideals, for the bud that withers before it blossomed, and irony at man's egoism and at the inhumanity of a social and religious order which debases the living to exalt the dead.

There is the dumb girl Subha who receives more affection and understanding from animals than from her fellow beings; the devoted wife Kumo who loses her eyesight to pamper a conceited husband; the unfortunate Nirupama whose young life was crushed merely because her poor but doting father could not pay enough dowry; there is Kadambini who had the ill luck to revive on her funeral pyre, only to wander forlorn like a ghost, no one accepting the living for the dead until she died and 'by dying proved that she had been alive'; the helpless Mahamaya who could not unveil her face before her lover—a whole gallery of tragic heroines crushed under the wheels of an unfeeling Juggernaut. Not all the women, however, are heroic or tragic. Some of them are, ironically, the protagonists of the very system which has thwarted their lives and warped their minds; some are nagging and cantankerous and drive their husbands to despair, some prefer their jewellery to their husbands' love. Nor are all of them Hindu. One of his most romantic heroines is a Muslim princess who gives up everything for the sake of the Hindu general whom she admires and loves. True-hearted and brave, her final frustration of hope (the title of the story, *Durasha*, means Frustrated Hope) is depicted with masterly irony. Even more romantic is the story of the Moghul princess Amina who is ready to avenge her father's death, only to discover that the Prince of Arakon in whose breast she was supposed to plunge her dagger is the very beloved vagabond Dalia in disguise with whom she had been in love.[7]

Some stories deal with man's lust for gold, some with woman's relentless goading of husband or son to ambition, some with the tragedy of decrepit aristocracy clinging to the illusion of glory long faded, some depict uncommon types like a gifted vagabond whom no lure of riches or comfort or love can bind to a home or an unruly tomboy who grows into a wonderfully mature and loving woman. Some are phantasies in which the natural and the supernatural are so skilfully blended that one wonders whether they are mere stories or subtle explorations of the sub-conscious. One of these relates the story of the skeleton which used to hang in the class-room of the child Rabi for lessons in elementary science.

[7] Twenty years later this story, *Dalia*, was dramatized in English by George Calderon and published under the title, *The Maharani of Arakan*. The play was staged in London on 20 July 1912.

Some stories lay bare the political helplessness of the people and the callous cynicism of the alien rulers, like the beautiful story in which the charming Giribala, referred to earlier, figures. Tagore never wrote 'patriotic' stories intended to incite hatred of the foreigner. He hated foreign rule but believed that as a sick body easily falls prey to outside infection, so a society where the individual has lost all initiative and backbone must invite foreign exploitation. No people can be exploited for long who are conscious of their rights and willing to die in their defence. He was therefore more concerned with rousing in his people a sense of their own dignity than with finding fault with the foreigner.

In a delightful story—a satirical phantasy—which in 1933 he developed into a play called *The Kingdom of Cards,* he relates the experiences of the traditional adventurers of Indian folklore, the Prince and his two boon companions (sons of the city's Merchant and of the Captain of the Guards) who are shipwrecked and stranded on a strange island whose inhabitants are all classified and labelled like a pack of cards. One is Five, another Six, another Jack or Queen; one is Diamonds, another Hearts, another Spades and so on. They sit, rise, fight and make love in strict accordance with a prescribed set of rules which no one understands but everyone obeys. We laugh at the Fives and Sixes without realizing that we are laughing at our own absurdities and imbecilities.

In a letter of February 1893 he wrote: 'Ours is indeed an unfortunate, God-forsaken country where the primary will-to-do is lacking. The capacity to think, to feel, to will is atrophied. The adventure of big striving, of truly and fully living is unknown. Men and women are like shadows flitting about—merely eating and drinking, doing their routine work, smoking and sleeping and endlessly chattering. Our reasoning is infantile and our emotions easily degenerate into sentimentalism. How one misses adult striving and full-blooded living!' How little they know of Tagore who know him only as a romantic poet, a singer of sweet platitudes, a religious mystic and a protagonist of his country's way of life! All that he was, but the visionary never blinked at reality, the idealist's feet were firmly planted on the rough ground and the sweet singer, like Wordsworth's Skylark, was 'true to the kindred points of heaven and home'.

That this combination of realism and idealism did not embitter his mind and make him a cynic is the best testimony to the strength of his spirit.

Strangely enough, during this period when his interest in the life of the common people of his country was most vivid and realistic, his poetry shows the sprouting of that mysticism which was later to grow and suffuse much of his writing. This mysticism was not a creed or a philosophy which he consciously adopted; nor was it an escape from the bewilderment of reality which he found too much. He was never a philosopher, he found no bondage more irksome than that of a closed and formulated system of thought which has an explanation for everything. He had even less respect for fixed creeds. He loved this earth and this life far too passionately ever to turn away from them. The mystery of life never ceased to fascinate him, the pain he suffered, the cruelty and sordidness which he witnessed, instead of causing a revulsion, made him love his kind all the more. 'How artificial and unreal are our notions of sin and virtue!' [he wrote in a letter dated 22 March 1894]. 'There is no higher religion than that of sympathy for all that lives. Love is the foundation of all religions.'

Tagore's mysticism was nothing but his sense of kinship with everything, his innate awareness of the unseen link that binds all the living together as well as the living with the so-called non-living, the seen with the unseen. In that sense this mystic awareness was deep-rooted in his soul from his childhood. It had always stirred within him. Its 'sprouting' at this period of his life in his poetry simply means that his search for this link in his own life, his quest for the guiding Muse of his genius and destiny, the Personality within and above his personality, became more conscious. In a letter dated 24 March 1894 he wrote:

'I am overwhelmed by this awareness of the baffling mystery within me which I can neither understand nor control. I know not where it will take me or I it, I know not what I can do or cannot do. I cannot see, nor am I consulted about, what surges up in my heart, what flows in my veins, what stirs in my brain, and yet I move about and keep up the pretence that I am the master of my thoughts and deeds. I am like a living pianoforte with a complicated network of wires hidden within it, but what makes it play and who comes suddenly to play on it and when and why, I do not know. I can only know what is being played at the moment, whether the keys are struck in joy or in sorrow, whether the notes are sharp or flat, high-pitched or low, whether the music is in tune or out of tune— but wait, do I really know even that?'

Fortunately, he was not a philosopher and was content to be played upon without breaking his head over the why and how of it. In fact, he was disconsolate if no music came. Poetry was his oldest love and whatever his other 'dates' with other Muses, to this one he constantly came back. 'The joy of writing one poem [he said in a letter of May 1892] far exceeds that of writing sheaves and sheaves of prose . . . If I could only write one poem a day . . .' He almost did that. During the seven years from 1894 to 1900 he published as many major volumes of verse, besides several of drama, stories and other prose writing. The first of these volumes of poetry is *Sonar Tari* (The Golden Boat), taking its name from the first poem in the book.

On a rainy day, when the clouds thunder in the sky, the poet is sitting disconsolate on the edge of his field overlooking the river.[8] The golden boat approaches and he dimly recognizes the figure at the helm. The harvest of his field has been gathered and he fills the boat with it. The boat goes on its way, no one knows where, and the poet is left behind on the bank, forlorn. There was a time when a storm of controversy raged in the literary circles of Bengal as to the real meaning of this poem. What is the Golden Boat and who is at its helm? The author himself tried to explain that the Boat symbolized for him Life which collects the harvest of our achievement and goes floating on the stream of time, leaving us behind. The Golden Boat reappears in the last poem of the book, but now the poet has been taken into the boat. His Muse, the Beloved of his dreams, his guardian angel, half known and half unknown, is at the helm. He asks her again and again where she is taking him. She says nothing but,

[8] To the Western reader the picture of a person sitting in the rain and actually enjoying it may not seem convincing. Only those who have lived in the plains of India during the summer can understand what the rains mean to Indians. The best poetry in India has been inspired by the rains.

half smiling, points to the distant horizon where the sun is sinking in the west.

There are several very long and beautiful poems in the book, one on the earth, the mother of all life; one on the sea, the first ancestor of this world out of whose lap the earth itself was born,[9] one on Manas-Sundari, the Beauty behind all beauty, his childhood's play-mate, his youth's dream, and now his very being. There is a lovely and moving poem entitled, 'I will not let you go'. The poet is about to leave on a journey, the household is in commotion, the servants busy packing the baggage, the wife adding this and that in anticipation of every contingency. Only the little daughter sits calmly on the threshold and says as he is about to leave, 'I will not let you go.' These simple words wrung out of the infant's heart sum up for the poet the perennial pathos of life. Everything goes and amid this unceasing flux of life and matter the Eternal cry resounds, 'I will not let you go'.[10]

Much as these poems glow with passion, it is passion suffused with, and subdued by, reflection. This reflective element will hence-forth be increasingly impressed on his poetry, the passion subdued will be the stronger, the thought subtler.

There are many other kinds of poems in the book, charming fairy tales, social satires, poems of nature and poems addressed to his people. In one of these belonging to the last category he attacks the doctrine of Maya-Vada, the favourite thesis of Indian philosophy which regards the universe as Maya or Illusion. 'Alas, my cheerless country, dressed in worn-out rags, loaded with decrepit wisdom, you pride yourself on your subtlety in having seen through the fraud of creation. Sitting idly in your corner, all you do is to sharpen the edge of your metaphysical mumbo jumbo and dismiss as unreal this boundless, star-studded sky and this great, big earth whose lap has nurtured a myriad forms of life, age after age. Millions of living beings make up the vast fair of this world and you, unbelieving dotard, ignore it all as a child's play.' In another he says, 'Much as

[9] At last on the sea-beach at Puri on the eastern coast of India, the poet felt the full impact of the sea's majesty which had previously left him cold during his two voyages to Europe.

[10] An English rendering of this poem by Humayun Kabir may be seen in the Chicago journal, Poetry, Jan. 1959.

you pretend to know, you really know nothing. Even if man be naught but dust, let it be dust. Where can you find the equal of this dust? Do not shut yourself up alone and grow prematurely senile. How will you grow into a man if you do not join in the game of life?' To those who say that all life is a bondage, he answers,' What is not a bondage? The mother's hand which removes the infant's lips from one breast to feed it from the other is a fetter too. All love, all longing for happiness is a fetter—but what a fetter!'

The poet has travelled a long way since he wrote his *Evening Songs* and *Morning Songs* in which he luxuriated in his personal sorrows or proclaimed too loudly his escape from morbidity. In either case it was a personal obsession. Now he is achieving a calm detachment and is learning to discriminate between the self that imprisons and the self that liberates, between the self that separates and the self that unites. What he lost in the flesh he will regain in the spirit and will find in the universal what he sought in the particular. What pain he must have gone through to achieve this reconciliation within himself can be appreciated only by those who have passed through the dark night of the soul. It is interesting to note that the manuscript of *Sonar Tari* which is now in the Tagore Museum at Santiniketan carries the following quotation from Goethe in German:

> Entbehren sollst du,
> Sollst entbehren.

This is followed by his English rendering of the same:

> Thou must do without
> do without ...

The Golden Boat was followed by a collection of poems published in 1896 under the title *Chitra*.[11] Many Bengali readers would consider this volume as the finest fruition of Tagore's poetical genius. There is no doubt that some of the poems in this volume mark the highest reach of his achievement during this period, though his genius was like a mountain range that revealed different peaks in different

---

[11] Not to be confused with the title of the English rendering of his drama *Chitrangada*. The word *Chitra* means the variegated, the many-sided.

weathers.[12] The key to the title of the volume which also indicates the general spirit and tenor of the poems in it may be sought in the very first poem where the poet addresses the universal spirit or Nature as the wondrous Lady whose beauty is manifest in a million forms. But though in the outside world her beauty overflows in many different sights, colours and sounds, within the mind she sits alone, unique—immanent and pervading.

The Universal Spirit or God (or whatever term is employed to embody the concept of the Ultimate) is after all a pure abstraction. To establish any relation of intimacy with it, saints, mystics and poets—and philosophers too—have throughout the ages tried to particularize it as Father, Lord, Beloved, etc. Whether man is made in the image of God or not, God certainly has been conceived in the image of man. Tagore's growing apprehension at this period of life of this Universal Spirit or Reality was intensely personal and he could only visualize it in terms of his own direct perception and need of it. He was, above everything else, a lover who saw beauty in the commonest things, who felt its touch in the outside world and felt it in his inmost being and knew that at some level of the subconscious or the superconscious the two were intimately linked. The same Spirit that suffused and ruled this vast universe dwelt within him and guided his life and genius. He called it Jivan-devata or Lord of my life. In his famous poem of that title he says, 'O my Inmost Being, has your thirst been quenched by coming into my heart? I have crushed my heart, like grapes in the press, and filled your cup with a thousand pourings of joy and sorrow. I have melted the gold of my desires and made of it ever-new images for your transient sport.' He goes on to confess his many limitations and failures and begs the Lord of his life to forgive them. 'How can I, O Master-poet, sing adequately your music?'

Much controversy and ingenuity has been wasted by well-meaning critics in trying to explain or repudiate the validity of this conception

---

[12] Several poems from this collection as well as from *Sonar Tari* were later translated into English and are included in *The Gardener, Fruit Gathering, Lover's Gift and Crossing* and *The Fugitive*—all published by Macmillan & Co., London. As usual many of these translations are little better than mutilated paraphrases of the original.

Portrait drawing by William Rothenstein, 1912

With Mahatma Gandhi and C. F. Andrews at Santiniketan, 1925

of Jivan-devata, forgetting that all poets and men of destiny—indeed, even ordinary men—have at times been aware of two selves within them, one that does, the other that watches and judges. Who has not, at times, begged forgiveness of himself and promised to be truer to himself? If the poet's sensibility is sharper and he is able to voice effectively what we all feel and cannot express—well, that's exactly what is expected of a poet. Rabindranath has no such private and esoteric creed or feelings which we cannot all share. If there is any esoteric Rabindranath whose words are veiled in mystery, it is the creation of his critics. 'Thy words are simple, my Master, but not theirs who talk of You.'

One of the most beautiful poems in the book is an ode to Urvasi, the legendary Feminine of Hindu mythology who seduces saints and captivates the hearts of all men. Rabindranath pictures her as arising out of the foam of the primal ocean when it was churned by the gods—naked and flawless beauty, holding nectar in her right hand and poison in her left. Urvasi is the eternal woman, whom men have always desired but never possessed, for she is 'not mother, not daughter, not bride'. Another poem, tender and exquisite, is entitled, A Farewell to Heaven. It is in the form of a monologue by a soul who has had a long sojourn in paradise as a reward for his good deeds on earth. The term over and merit exhausted, the soul is about to return to earth and compares the chilly joy and unruffled happiness of heaven with the woven web of joys and sorrows which is the life on earth. The poem is one long paean in praise of this lowly earth and its simple human attachments. Let the heaven's face beam with unruffled joy, let the gods sip their nectar! For us mortals the earth is the motherland, the mother who hugs the wicked as well as the virtuous to her breast.[13]

The struggle between the poet's heart enchanted with its own music and his conscience troubled by the plight of his countrymen finds passionate utterance in a long poem entitled 'Turn me back now'. It is a poem such as Mahatma Gandhi might have written had he been a poet. The poet reproaches himself for being content to play the flute all by himself—like a truant boy on a summer afternoon—when everyone else is engaged in some useful task or the other and

[13] Both these poems are long and well-nigh untranslatable.

L

exhorts himself: 'Get up and see where the fires are raging and listen to the wail of your fellow men crying for help, victims of a bloated Pride that licks the blood of the helpless with its million tongues.' He describes the condition of his people, hungry, naked and homeless in their own land, bereft of human rights and bereft even of the will to protest. 'Rise, O poet, and give voice to these dumb, haggard and stupefied faces, bring hope to these tired, emptied and broken hearts. Teach them to raise high their heads and stand united. Those whom they fear are even more scared than they—terrified of their sins. The moment you awaken they will take to their heels; when you stand up and face them, they will slink away like pariah dogs for, despite all bravado, they know in their heart of hearts that they are in the wrong and God is not with them.' The poet begs his Muse not to bewitch him any more with her enchantments, not to rock him any longer on the waves of joy, but to let him turn towards those whose lives are blighted by lack of food, lack of light, lack of air, lack of spirit.

But Rabindranath was not Gandhi. The heroic impulse vented itself in occasional spurts and though he anticipated the Mahatma not only in his ideals but in his field work, he could not be single-minded. He could not be wedded to one ideal and activity, he had a harem of Muses to lure him back. For in the very next poem, written a few days later, he is haunted by memories of the old days, of the champaks and the jasmines that grew round the terrace of his sister-in-law's apartment. 'How sweet it was when she gave those flowers with her hand!' In another poem he regrets that he could achieve nothing, fulfil nothing. 'The *vina* was in my hands, the music was in my mind—who knew that half way through the music, the string would break!' And in the poem, called 'Abedan' (Petition)[14] where he conceives the Dispenser of his destiny, who is also the Dispenser of all men's destiny, as the Queen, he begs her to make him the gardener of her flower garden. He has no heroic ambitions, he lays down his sword at her feet, he wants no robes of honour, all he wants is the duty to '. . . keep fresh the grassy path where you walk in the morning'. 'And what will be your wages?' asks the Queen.

---

[14] Later translated into English by himself and published as the first poem of the volume, *The Gardener*, Macmillan, & Co. London.

'The right to make wristlets of fresh flowers every morning and to slip them over your hands tender as lotus buds.'

In between these two major volumes, *Sonar Tari* and *Chitra*, were published a long poem, *Nadi* (The River) and a lyrical drama in one act, *Viday-abhisap* (The Curse at Farewell). His earlier dramas were in blank verse which he now discarded in favour of run-on and enjambed rhymed couplets, which he found more to his taste. He naturalized this form in Bengali and achieved amazing results with it. As in the case of *Chitrangada*, Tagore takes a simple anecdote, in this instance a mythological one, from the *Mahabharata* and turns it into a conflict of high psychological significance—between devotion to knowledge and duty and the claim of love. The anecdote relates to the ancient feud between the Gods and the Titans. Sukra, the teacher of the Titans, knew the secret of immortality and could restore the dead to life. The Gods, anxious to learn the secret, send Kacha, the young son of their teacher, Brihaspati, to Sukra to be his pupil. Seeing the handsome Brahmin, Sukra's daughter Devayani falls in love with him and persuades her fond father to accept Kacha as his pupil. Having completed his course of study and learnt the art of reviving the dead, Kacha comes to Devayani to bid her farewell. This is the starting point of this short drama which consists entirely of the dialogue between the two. The following summarized paraphrase may interest the reader, for, though the characters are mythological and the setting an ancient hermitage, the problem posed is universal and whatever else may have changed, the woman's heart has remained the same. A modern student learning nuclear science at a foreign university may still hear the same reproach from his professor's daughter, though today her language would be more blunt and downright and might end, not in a curse but in a resounding smack.

'So you've at last attained,' says Devayani, 'what you had hardly hoped for. The knowledge coveted by the Gods is now yours. But tell me, have you nothing more to ask for than permission to depart? Have all your desires been fulfilled—none left lingering in your heart to prick like a hidden thorn?' 'None,' Kacha assures her. 'Then you must be the one happy being in creation,' taunts Devayani. 'Go back to your Paradise and add to its splendour your own triumph. There they are waiting to welcome you back with music and conch shells and flowers. Ah, Brahmin, you have indeed spent hard and dreary days here, drudging in an alien land, with no one to comfort and delight you.' Kacha feels the sting and begs, 'Not thus with a reproach, but with a smile bid me farewell.' 'Smile! This is no Paradise, my friend. Smiles are not so cheap in this world where thirst, like a worm in the flower, gnaws at the heart's core, where desire like a baffled bee hovers round the closed petals of its lotus. Here memory broods and pines in the deserted nook of departed joy. Go and waste no more of your time here.' Kacha tries to pacify her and assures her that the happy association of the days spent in the hermitage would always haunt him. The reminiscences are exchanged and she archly reminds him of how, but for her intervention, her father would never have consented to teach the son of a rival race. He acknowledges the gratitude but she is not content with gratitude, and with subtle feminine suggestions forces him to admit that he loves her and recalls how he used to go out of his way, even neglecting his studies, to woo and win her. 'What made you fetch water for me while I tended the flower beds and why need you have played truant from your studies to pet my little deer? And why need you have sat on the grass beside me, singing songs learnt in Paradise, while darkness hung over the hushed bank of the river, like eyelids drooping on languorous eyes? If knowledge it was you were after, why need you have ensnared in your coils this simple-hearted maiden? Or was it all a well-planned strategy to win access to my father's favour?'

Kacha, unnerved by her passionate utterance, protests that he truly and deeply loves her for her own sake. But duty calls and he must, even at the sacrifice of his happiness, go back to his people and put his knowledge in their service. He begs to be forgiven. 'Forgive! What forgiveness, O Brahmin, is left in the heart of a woman flamed to the fury of a thunderbolt? You will go back to the celestial realm where all regrets will be lost in the pride of your success. But what is left to me here—what ambition or mission can instil a meaning or pride in this thwarted and barren life of mine? In these woods must I drag on the humiliation of an aimless and forlorn existence, where memory with its thousand thorns will prick me at each turn and a secret shame gnaw at the very centre of my being. Shame be yours, O heartless adventurer, who came and sat through the sunny hours in the shade of my life's garden and, to while away time, plucked all its flowers and wove them into a garland, only to snap the thread at the end and scatter all the glory of a woman's heart into dust! Be this my curse at farewell—may the knowledge for whose sake you have spurned me never bear its full reward for you! You shall bear its burden and not enjoy its use, you will teach it but shall never be able to practise it.' What can shamefaced Kacha say in reply save a magnanimous platitude? 'And let this be my parting wish—may all your suffering be lost in its own greatness!'

This charming dramatic fragment was followed by a full-fledged drama, also in verse, *Malini*,[15] a well-constructed play and much more dramatic, in spirit as well as in the development of the situation, than the lyric drama discussed above. It is both the vehicle of an idea and a study of conflicting loyalties—in which respect it may be said to belong to the same class as his earlier play, *Sacrifice*. Here, too, the forces of Brahminism, of Hindu orthodoxy, are ranged against the challenge of compassion, of universal love—in this case as specifically taught by the Buddha.

Though by birth a Brahmin and the son of a great Hindu reformer, Tagore's feeling for Hinduism was strictly eclectic and was more or less confined to his admiration of the philosophic wisdom of the *Upanishads* and the literary heritage of Sanskrit. For Brahminism as such, for its priestly authority and the tyranny of its regimented social organization, he had nothing but contempt. His admiration of the Buddha, on the other hand, was boundless. In the Buddha, according to him, the Hindu race and thought had achieved its finest flowering; in the so-called Hinduism nothing but its own degeneration. He was brought up to despise idolatry and yet he confessed that when he first saw the famous stone image of the Buddha in Bodh Gaya, he could not help bowing down to it. It was not merely the compassion of the Buddha that drew him; it was the rare combination in him of a great intellect, rational and logical, a great heart overflowing with love that made no distinctions, a great

[15] An English translation under the same name was included in *Sacrifice and Other Plays*, published by Macmillan & Co., London, 1917

strength that never wavered or drew back and a great calm and serenity of mind. He was to write many poems and plays drawing on Buddhist legends and motifs; Malini, the King's daughter in the play, is his first major Buddhist heroine.

And yet the most powerful and convincing character in the play is not this lovely and saintly but somewhat shadowy maiden but her chief enemy, the leader of Hindu orthodoxy in whose proud personality is symbolized the strength and obstinacy of his religion. The conflict is not only between obedience to 'moth-eaten scriptures' and a religion of one's choice but between the poetry of pity and the prose of social necessity. 'Pity is beautiful like the yonder moon that casts its spell in the sky, but is that the only enduring reality? Tomorrow the day will break and the hungry multitude will draw the sea of existence with their thousand nets and their clamour will fill the sky. Then this very moon will seem a pale shadow.' But even a deeper conflict is that of personal loyalties. Should one, if faced with a relentless choice, betray one's conscience or one's religion, one's country or one's faith, the pledge of friendship or that of love? There is no answer to these questions and the tragedy of heroic folly must take its course. All that Malini can do is to forgive and ask others to forgive.

The next major volume of verse, *Chaitali*, was published in 1896. Chaitali means a late harvest, the last gleanings of rice gathered in the month of Chaitra (March-April), before the fierce sun of May burns out the last drop of moisture from the earth. It was as though the poet was dimly aware that the period of his life's Spring was drawing to a close, the emotional exuberance and intellectual recklessness of early manhood would soon shed many of its leaves and petals in the hot blasts of an increasing spiritual austerity. Almost all the poems in the volume are short, most of them sonnets; the language is simple, no effort is made to invent new forms and modes; the themes are drawn from the lowly, everyday life he watched on the banks of the Padma or tinged with momentary regrets and memories of the past. A gentle, brooding sadness lurks in the mood of these poems and a dim foreboding of the parting of ways. Before the sense of India's past overwhelms him in the next phase, he will glean a few immortal moments from the immediate present.

A girl scrubbing her pots on the bank, her little brother hovering round, a day labourer returning from work, a decrepit old man hobbling along, a young man washing his mud-covered buffalo and calling it by endearing names—these and many other trivial and fleeting sights are painted in minute detail and with great tenderness. A girl is holding her little brother in her arm, a kid bleats, she picks it up too with the other arm and 'dividing her caresses between them bound in one bond of affection the offspring of beast and man'. There are several poems on the forest. He had always loved the forest but what was merely a lovely phenomenon of Nature before comes now to be invested with a wistful longing for his country's spiritual heritage—it was in the forest that the *Upanishads* were composed and the Indian sages meditated and taught.

Criticism of the social and religious follies of his people must always be there. Addressing his Bengal he says, 'You have brought up your seventy million sons, O fond Mother, as Bengalis—not as men.' In another he rebukes his countrymen's mania for renunciation. 'At the dead of night the aspirant resolved, "I must leave my home and seek my God. Who has beguiled and kept me here?" God whispered, "I." But the would-be ascetic heard it not. Seeing his wife fast asleep, her babe clasped to her breast, he muttered, "What are you if not a snare?" God whispered, "Nought else but I," but none was there to heed. Leaving his bed he cried, "Where art thou, O Lord?" "Here" came the reply. He heeded not. The child wailed in its dream, pulling at its mother. God commanded, "Turn back!" The ascetic ignored the behest. God sighed and said, "Alas, where is my devotee straying, deserting me?" '

Rich and varied as was Rabindranath's poetic output of this period, no less so was his contribution in prose. His short stories, which have already been referred to, created a new form in literature and a standard which has not yet been surpassed in Indian literary achievement—not even by his own later stories. His light, humorous social comedies, particularly the two major ones, *Baikunther Khata* (The Manuscript of Baikuntha) and *Chira Kumar Sabha* (The Bachelor's Club), the former dealing with a kindly old bore who insists on reading out his manuscript to whoever comes his way, a simpleton whom everyone avoids and imposes upon (who has not come across such a type?), the latter with the discomfiture of those who imagine they can do without women, are still popular on the Bengali stage and have never failed to delight and hold the audience.

Besides this creative prose, the range and quantity of his reflective prose of the period is astonishing. There was hardly a subject which he did not cover, including philology and science, and in almost everything he said he opened out new lines of thinking. Though not a philosopher in the orthodox sense of the word, he was without question the most vital thinker of his age in his country. If not logical, his thinking was intuitive, and like a gifted physician he was able to diagnose his country's maladies as no professional educationists, economists, social reformers and politicians of his country succeeded in doing. Even in the field of pure political strategy it was he who first pointed out, in a remarkable paper, 'The Englishman's Fear', that the British Government would play the Hindus against the Muslims and *vice versa* to divide the country and delay India's freedom. Almost every great idea of Mahatma Gandhi—except, of course, his moral and other fads—had been anticipated by Rabindranath nearly twenty years earlier. Even his own countrymen have forgotten their debt to him.

Perhaps the most characteristic and in some respects the most brilliant achievement of his prose in this period is recorded in the pages of a book which is almost unknown outside Bengal, *Pancha Bhuter Dayari* (The Diary of the Five Elements), which consists of dialogues and arguments on life and letters between five points of view humorously represented by the five elements, air, earth, water, fire and ether. The elements are dramatically characterized; fire and water are feminine—inquisitive and emotional, the other three masculine, earth stolid and opportunist, air an idealist and so on. Wit and wisdom, logic and frivolity jostle each other in these pages; the author himself plays the part of a mediator, provoking and clarifying the different points of view, an Indian Plato with a Shavian wink in his eye.

How much greater the author could be when he was truly himself than when he tried to be traditional, in the manner of oriental oracles dispensing wisdom, can be immediately felt by comparing this Diary with another little volume published at the end of this period in which too his wit and wisdom are recorded, not subtly and artistically as in the dialogues of the Elements but obviously and tritely in the form of aphorisms, epigrams and fables in verse. His countrymen love these clever and wise sayings and constantly quote them—wisdom, like medicine, is more palatable when dispensed in the form of tablets—but that the author himself did not attach much value to them is evidenced from the title he gave to the volume—*Kanika* (Trifles). A few examples are given for the reader to judge for himself, bearing in mind that much of their original beauty and metrical effectiveness is necessarily lost in translation. 'We shut the door lest Error should creep in, but Truth wonders, how then can I get in?'[16] 'The handle imagined that all its troubles were due to its being tagged on to the ploughshare and denounced the union, but when it achieved its independence of the plough, the peasant burnt it as useless wood.' 'The game of life consists of both life and death, as walking consists of raising the foot and bringing it down.' 'The net swore, "I shall no longer raise mud." The fisherman retorted,"A lot of fish you'll catch." '

---

[16] Edward Thompson's rendering.

8

A MAN OF GOD

When asked in his old age what he considered his 'best quality' Tagore replied, 'Inconsistency'; when asked what was his 'greatest failing', he replied, 'The same.' He was not being frivolous; he meant what he said. While he was sincere in what he said and did at any time, there was no knowing what he would say and do the next day. He could afford to be inconsistent because he was truthful; he trusted his own genius and was willing to venture into unknown paths, turning his back on his own previous achievement and commitments, at the call of his Jivan-devata. In a letter dated 8 May 1893 he wrote, 'I have never uttered anything untrue in my poetry.' And yet it is precisely in his poetry that seemingly contrary ideas and moods jostle and challenge each other.

'Poets are allowed to lie,' said Pliny the Younger. The fact is that a *really* truthful person must at times *seem* a liar, just as a person who always seems consistent and truthful must *be* a liar. And so even while Rabindranath was writing that he wanted nothing more in life than to be allowed to watch its lovely panorama from his boat on the river, he was getting restless for a more dynamic and crowded existence. Much as he dreaded the din and clamour of the market-place, he was drawn to it again and again and could not stay away from it for long. Much as he might chide the ascetic for leaving his home in search of God when God was already in his home, he himself sought Him everywhere.

Restlessness was in the air. The sleeping giant of nationalism was beginning to stir in his land and the British Government was getting nervous and apprehensive. Beneath its cloak of benevolence the sword rattled. In 1898 the Sedition Bill was passed to stifle all nationalist agitation and the great scholar-patriot, Tilak, was arrested. The poet jumped into the fray and on the day before the

Bill became an Act read his famous paper 'Kantharodh' (The Throttled) at a public meeting in Calcutta. He raised his powerful voice against the repressive policy of the Government and actively participated in raising funds for Tilak's defence. When, soon after, the plague broke out in Calcutta he assisted Sister Nivedita[1] in organizing relief and medical aid for the victims of this dread epidemic. The poet was turning into a healer of his people's wounds and a high-priest of their national aspirations, not only raising his voice but lending an active hand in service at the front.

Parallel to his political activities were his literary offerings of the period—ballads, narrative poems and dramatic episodes recreating his country's past, and its moral heritage. Plato would have warmly approved of him. 'Hymns to the gods and the praises of worthy actions,' opined the Greek philosopher in his *Republic*, 'are the only sort of poetry to be admitted to our state. For if you were to admit the pleasurable muse also, in songs or verses, we should have pleasure and pain reigning in our state instead of law.' Wordsworth too would have approved that

> In his breast the mighty Poet bore
> A Patriot's heart, warm with undying fire.

Two major volumes of this period, *Katha* (Ballads) and *Kahini* (Tales), are not only masterpieces of narrative verse and dramatic dialogue but are a store-house of legends and historical anecdotes culled from the Indian classics, the Buddhist lore and the more recent deeds of heroism and sacrifice in the annals of the Rajputs and the Sikhs. These two volumes are in themselves a new, miniature modern Mahabharata, a noble treasury of India's moral and spiritual heritage, truly national because not exclusively Hindu. The lyric poet, the dramatist and the story teller have combined their genius to make some of these pieces one of Tagore's finest legacies to his people, cherished as much by the young as by the old. They are equally free of sentimentalism and bravado, there is no false glorification of pride in them, no strain of 'Rule Britannia' or 'Heil Hitler';

[1] Margaret Noble, a remarkable and gifted Irish lady who became a disciple of Swami Vivekananda and dedicated her life to the service of the Indian people.

on the contrary the emphasis is on devotion to truth, humility and universal love. Not even in his fiercest outburst of patriotism could Tagore be jingoistic—which may partly explain why among his own people he was never popular, whatever the praises sung after his death.

An idea of his power of seizing on the dramatic possibilities of a situation which is only baldly referred to in the pages of the *Mahabharata* can be had by reading the author's own English rendering in such pieces as 'Karna and Kunti' or 'Gandhari's Prayer' and comparing them with the original reference in the Indian epic. His translation of some other pieces too can be seen in *Fruit-Gathering*. Though the glow of passion and the music of the verse are necessarily lost in the rendering, enough has survived to indicate the kind of poetry he wrote during this period and his growing concern with basic moral and spiritual values. A rich disciple, proud of his wealth, came to the Sikh teacher and offered a pair of gold bangles inwrought with precious stones. The teacher let one bangle slip from his hand into the river below. The disciple jumped into the river to rescue the costly gift. Failing to find it he asked the teacher to point out the exact spot where it had fallen. The teacher threw the remaining bangle into the water and said, 'There!'

Equally significant is the Buddhist tale of the monk Upagupta, a disciple of the Buddha. This handsome young monk was sleeping on the ground outside the city wall of Mathura when suddenly something struck against his chest and he woke up with a start. Vasavadatta, the beautiful courtesan of the city, had stumbled against him in the dark on her way to a tryst with a lover. She flashed her lantern on the monk and seeing what he was and how handsome, she begged him to come to her house, for '. . . this hard and rough ground is no bed for you'. The monk looked at her and said softly, 'O bunch of loveliness, my time is not come yet. Go where you are going now. When the time comes I shall myself come to you'. The days passed and one day as the monk was passing again by the city wall he noticed a woman lying sick on the ground. The beautiful courtesan had caught the small-pox and the townsfolk, scared of the dread disease, had thrown her out of the city and abandoned her outside the walls. The monk sat down beside the unconscious body and raising the woman's head rested it on his lap, poured water on her dry lips, smeared the body with cool and fragrant sandal paste and chanted prayers for her recovery. The woman opened her eyes and asked, 'Who are you, O merciful one?' The monk answered, 'Vasavadatta, I have come to keep my tryst.'

In another poem entitled, 'The loss is negligible', the poet tells the following story: On a winter morning the Queen of Kashi (Banaras) went with her companions to bathe in the Ganges. The wind was chilly and after the bathe the Queen who was in a gay mood felt it would be great fun if she could warm herself near a fire. Seeing a humble cottage near by she ordered her companions to set fire to it. As the flames fanned by the wind shot up high the Queen was delighted and returned to the palace, pleased with a morning well spent. In the meanwhile the villagers ran to the King's court and told their tale of woe. The King sent for the Queen and asked her how she could do a thing like that. The Queen smiled and said, 'The loss is negligible.' The King replied 'You shall judge that for yourself', and forthwith ordered that the Queen be divested of all her jewels and other valuables and asked to leave the palace. 'Go and beg your livelihood,' he said to her. 'Only then you will understand how great was the loss of the poor man whose cottage you burnt down for a moment's pleasure. After you have earned enough to rebuild his cottage for him, I shall take you back as my Queen.'

But 'hymns to the gods and the praises of worthy actions' could not wholly satisfy a poet whose genius was so intensely lyrical and individual. So even while he was re-interpreting his nation's moral heritage to equate it with his own universal and humanist outlook, he was at the same time pouring out his personal agonies and playing with vagaries of thought and form in a series of exquisite lyrics and songs which were published consecutively in three volumes, each a landmark in his own development as well as in the literature of his country. Whatever Plato might have thought of 'the pleasurable Muse', she was Rabindranath's first and last love and whenever he strayed away from her for any length of time, he went back to her with redoubled ardour.

In the very first poem of the next volume, *Kalpana* (Dreams), he is aware of his immense need for space, even when bereft of light, and exhorts his spirit not to give up soaring, however vain the beating of its wings. 'What if the dusk descends and the music is stilled, what if the companions have all flown back to their nests and a weariness creeps over the limbs and all around is wrapt in an ominous veil—even then, my bird, O my blind bird, do not furl your wings, not yet!' His Czech biographer and critic, V. Lesny, considers *Kalpana* '. . . a work of great poetic value, rich not only in inspiration, but also in poetical invention, and so fascinating that the reader believes he hears the poet's heart beat, and thinks and feels with him. At the same time his verses are firmly welded.'[2] There are some beautiful poems on Nature, particularly the magnificent ode to 'The Year's End'. The Bengali year ends in April when the hot winds blow and violent dust-storms sweep over the plains, followed by a merciful shower. On such a day the poem was actually written and one can still hear in its passionate rhythm the convulsive fury of the time-spirit, as it destroys the old and brings in the new. The poet's instinctive and pagan love of nature, his sheer voluptuous delight in its varying moods, is now weighed down with melancholy reflections. He sees a temple in ruins and pity for the deity, neglected and unworshipped, wells up in his heart. Men have found other gods.[3] A lovely poem—which might also have interested Freud— reproaches the god Shiva for having burnt to ashes, in a foolish fit of anger, the love-god Madana.[4] For the ashes, carried away by the wind, are now scattered all over the earth and the anguish of sex repressed never ceases to trouble men. The poet's foreboding of the spiritual crisis and the cross that lay ahead of him is also reflected in several poems. The Lord of Life is becoming increasingly the Lord of All and claiming His dues. 'I threw my heart into this world, you picked it up and have made it your own. I sought sorrow imagining it to be pleasure; you have turned that sorrow into joy.'

[2] *Rabindranath Tagore: His Personality and Work*. Prof. V. Lesny. Translated by Guy McKeever Phillips. George Allen and Unwin, Ltd., London, 1939. Prof. Lesny and Prof. Edward Thompson were perhaps the only two foreign critics who were capable of appreciating Tagore in his original Bengali.

[3] For the author's English rendering of this poem, see *Gitanjali*, No. 88.

[4] Kalidasa has described how the god of love was punished for having dared to interrupt with his arrows the meditation of the Prince of Yogis.

But the pagan will not easily part from his Pan, the lover of life will not readily give up his many loves for the cheerless austerity of an exclusive devotion. For sheer delight in the creation of forms, for light-heartedness of mood, playfulness of thought and liveliness of language, for exquisite frivolity of genius, Tagore never wrote anything finer, whether before or after, than the book of poems with which he closed the fortieth year of his life. As though he had a premonition that half his life was over and before the second, more majestic but sombre, half began he indulged for a brief interlude in the full abandon of a carefree enjoyment of life's fleeting moments. The book was appropriately named *Kshanika* which means what is momentary and fleeting. Even more significant and daring than the lightness of theme and imagery was his use of the language and style to suit his purpose. He took the unprecedented liberty of using freely the colloquial language with its abbreviated sounds and drew such strength, vigour and music out of it that the experiment may be said to have revolutionized the future of Bengali poetry. In the language of the people he found at last his own true language and made it the language of literature.

But this exquisite overflow of high spirits, of genial cynicism and unconcern, was itself a fleeting interlude—his parting gift to the dying century to which he owed so much. His offering to the new century was utterly different. No two books of his are in sharper contrast than these two which followed each other in quick succession, *Kshanika* which marked the end of 1900 and *Naivedya* (Offering) which marked the beginning of 1901. This bunch of one hundred poems, written in about as many days, can claim rank with the world's highest religious poetry. Several of them were included later in the English *Gitanjali*. The gay vagabond of *Kshanika* has become a humble devotee, overweighed with a sense of his responsibility to God and to man. The artist is subdued by the man of God and there is no room in these poems for high flights of imagination or dexterity of thought or emotional exuberance or metrical playfulness.

The naked spirit is humble in the presence of God and speaks in tones of utter simplicity. 'Day after day I shall stand before you, O Lord, with folded hands.' He has realized his own helplessness and will henceforth seek his light only from Him. All else is because He is. 'Let your lamp burn in my home. Mine own only heats the air and throws out foul smoke.' He is not afraid of pain any longer. 'If the door of my heart is locked, break it open, but do not go back. If your call does not reach me in my sleep, wake me up with your thunderbolt.' It is fear that distorts the truth. 'Far as I gaze at the depth of Thy immensity, I find no trace there of sorrow or death or separation. Death assumes its mask of terror and sorrow its pain only when, away from Thee, I turn my face towards my own dark self.' He is not ashamed of his past, for he knows that even in his most carefree and playful days there were moments made immortal with the touch of the Infinite—'Those fleeting moments inscribed with your autograph have survived and the steps that I heard in my childhood's play—today their music resounds in all the music of this world, in the music of sun and moon.' He will wait patiently and will despise nothing, however seemingly trivial, for he knows that '. . . Thy centuries follow each other, perfecting a small wild flower'.

This indeed is the keystone of his spiritual philosophy or intuition —he will see God within himself and also permeating everything in the Universe, big or small, but not as a Super-Entity remote and self-isolated, luring men away from this world or as a jealous Tyrant, scared of Satan and bribing mankind with His favours. God is either everything or nothing. And so even in his most intensely religious and God-conscious mood, he would not turn away from life and this world. 'Deliverance is not for me in renunciation. I feel the embrace of freedom in a thousand bonds of delight.' Love is not the antithesis of duty; on the contrary, it relieves duty of its burden and makes what was dreary pleasurable. Love of God and love of the people are complementary and justify and fulfil each other, as Gandhi was to prove later. Religion and patriotism reinforce each other in these poems; hymns to the Divine are also prayers for his people. He was a patriot, not a nationalist; 'my country, right or wrong,' was never his creed. The ideal that he held aloft for his country and for which he invoked divine aid was also his ideal for every other country and would be echoed by patriots all over the world, whatever their race, nationality or creed.

No ideal can be achieved without suffering and he invokes the

Father of all mankind to '. . . strike, strike mercilessly with Thine own hand and waken India into that heaven' '. . . where the mind is without fear and the head is held high, where knowledge is free, where the world has not been broken up into fragments by narrow domestic walls, where words come out from the depth of truth, where tireless striving stretches its arms towards perfection, where the clear stream of reason has not lost its way into the dreary desert sand of dead habit, and where the mind is led forward by Thee into ever-widening thought and action'. What better ideal can any patriot or saint hold up to his people? He asked for no wealth or riches for his country save the wealth of knowledge and the riches of freedom. He had no patience with those 'patriots' who blamed the foreigner for all the misfortunes of his country and encouraged their people to pity themselves as mere innocent victims. He warned them that '. . . those who perpetrate wrong and those who meekly suffer it, the persecutor as well as the persecuted—they are equally guilty in the eye of God and deserving of contempt'.

A very significant poem in which he denounces nationalism as the 'self-love of Nations' was written on the last day of the last century.[5] The Boer War had deeply disillusioned him about the claims of Western democracies and he saw in its holocaust the ominous warning of worse massacres impending. 'The last sun of the century sets amidst the blood-red clouds of the West and the whirlwind of hatred. The naked passion of self-love of Nations, in its drunken delirium of greed, is dancing to the clash of steel and the howling verses of vengeance.' What pained him even more was that his fellow-poets in the West, instead of voicing the anguished cry of humanity, had joined in the fray. The last two embittered lines of the original Bengali sonnet, which the poet gracefully left out in his own English version, are nevertheless worth quoting in Professor Edward Thompson's competent and faithful rendering:

> Awakening fear, the poet-mobs howl round,
> A chant of quarrelling curs on the burning-ground.

[5] Entitled in English 'The Sunset of the Century', it was published as an appendix to his lectures on *Nationalism*, Macmillan & Co., London, 1918. The extract quoted here is the poet's own rendering.

This volume of one hundred poems, appropriately entitled *Offering*, was dedicated by the author to his venerable, eighty-three-year-old father—no doubt in grateful recognition of the fact that the spiritual and moral wealth enshrined in its pages was in a sense the Maharshi's gift to him. When he read out these poems in manuscript to his father, the latter was so pleased that he gave his son a purse to meet the expenses of the publication of the volume. Many years earlier when Rabindranath was in his youth, the Maharshi had heard that his youngest son had composed some religious songs. He sent for Rabindranath and asked him to sing the songs, one of which—now famous—opened with the lines:

The eye cannot see thee, for thou art the eye within the eye,
the heart cannot know thee, for thou art its inmost secret.

The Maharshi was deeply moved and said,
'If the ruler of this land had belonged to the people and understood their language, he would surely have rewarded the young poet.' In the absence of such a ruler the Maharshi himself gave a handsome purse to the poet.

The Maharshi's influence on his youngest son, though on the whole very wholesome, and even inspiring, was not altogether conducive to the poet's intellectual freedom of mind. In particular, it tended to make Rabindranath socially conservative, like his father. It is noteworthy that the first decade of the new century which was in many respects the most fruitful period in Rabindranath's career was also the period in which he showed the least—comparatively speaking—freedom in his own life from social inhibitions and conventional biases. Could it be that with increasing spiritual and moral sensibility came its hidden parasite, a feeling of self-righteousness? Perhaps the new ardour of patriotism brought a nostalgia for the past, a wishful thinking which saw ancient India as a land peopled mainly with righteous kings, heroic maidens and holy sages discoursing on the eternal verities in sylvan settings. No man can rise entirely above his environments and Rabindranath too, despite his extraordinarily original and dynamic mind, shared to some extent the prejudices and obsessions of the environments in which he lived, more so in this period than in any other.

It is difficult otherwise to explain how one who believed so instinctively and profoundly in the development of personality and who despised so vehemently the tyranny of the Hindu social organization should have been in such a desperate hurry to marry off his two growing daughters, the eldest Madhurilata (Bela) who was only fourteen, the second Renuka (Rani) who had not yet completed her twelfth year. Both the weddings took place in 1901 within a month of one another. Bela was very attractive, lively and intelligent and Rani was a remarkable girl with a will of her own, and the father was very attached to both. Rabindranath was, in fact, a devoted husband and a very loving father, despite his preoccupation with his pen and with many public activities. During this particular year he was not only passing through a spiritual crisis but was also faced with serious financial worries. A business enterprise he had started earlier in Kustia had failed, involving him in heavy liabilities; he was busy raising funds to finance the visit to England of his friend J. C. Bose (later to become internationally famous) who had gone there to demonstrate his discoveries in bio-physics before the Royal Society in London. He also needed funds desperately himself to start his educational project at Santiniketan which he already had in mind at this time. Why then in the midst of so many other and more pressing obligations did he have to precipitate his daughters' weddings, apart from the fact that he had himself earlier denounced without mincing words early marriages?

It is true that it was uncommon in those days, in the class and society from which he came, for girls to remain unmarried after puberty, and yet it could not have been too uncommon for he himself has described in his own novels progressive families of the same period where educated and accomplished daughters made their own choices. It is also true that the Tagores were dubbed as Pirali Brahmins, a tainted caste, and it was not easy for them to intermarry freely with other and more orthodox Brahmin families, but this would be a problem only for those who believed in the sanctity of caste and not for him who had ridiculed all such superstitions. In any case, why need he who was uncommon in every other respect have done a very common thing? This is a question difficult to answer. As though anticipating the question, he wrote a poem at this time (after reading the biography of Alfred Tennyson by his son Hallam Tennyson which had disappointed him) asking his readers not to seek the poet in the man, earth-bound and vulnerable. Let his wish be respected.

Strangely enough, during this very period his mind was occupied with the problem of woman's destiny and the tragedy of her frustrated love. The two novels which he serialized, one *Nashta Nir* (Broken Nest)[6] in the pages of *Bharati* which he was editing, the other *Chokher Bali* (Eyesore)[7] in *Bangadarshan* which he now began to edit, bear ample witness to this preoccupation. Incidentally these two novels laid the foundation of the modern novel in Indian literature. The novels written before these, whether by Bankim Chatterjee or by Tagore himself, were historical romances or social melodramas or a mixture of both. The modern novel proper, whether realistic or psychological or concerned with a problem, begins with these two in Indian literature.

The *Broken Nest* is a tragedy of a busy editor of a daily paper who has little time to spare for his very young and romantic wife. The bored wife seeks solace and stimulus in the company of her husband's young cousin, a lively and versatile youth. They inspire each other to write and both prove to be quite promising. The inevitable complications arise and when the boy goes away to England for higher studies, the wife is disconsolate and, imagining that he did not care enough for her, is broken-hearted. The naïve and good-natured husband assumes that she is disconsolate because she has not had enough of *his* attention. He tries to make up for it, only to discover the bitter and humiliating truth. The happy nest is broken. One wonders how far the author, in tracing the development of this emotional entanglement with its tragic climax, was drawing on his own reminiscences. However that may be, the problem discussed is of universal interest. Is the wife, young and immature, to blame if the husband takes her affection and loyalty for granted and leaves her romantic longings exposed to others' attention? The problem assumes special interest in the context of the

---

[6] Though included later in his volume of short stories, it is really a short novel.

[7] An English translation, entitled *Binodini*, has been published by Sahitya Akademi, New Delhi, 1959.

Hindu joint family where tradition has always permitted a tender and affectionate familiarity between a married woman and her husband's younger brother. In fact, the customary Indian term indicating this family relationship (*devar*, derived from Sanskrit) means, literally, a second husband. Whether levirate or any other primitive social practice has kept its odour in this word is for anthropologists to discuss.

The problem analysed in *Chokher Bali*, which is a fully-fledged and a better constructed novel, is more subtle and is posed in a more complex setting. The story is simple and is simply told. It centres round the dilemma of human relationship and describes what takes place behind the staid façade of a well-to-do, middle-class Bengali home of the period, where a widowed mother lives with her only son on whom she dotes. One would imagine that nothing much ever happens in a home like that with its numerous inhibitions and restricted social contacts, and in fact nothing happens that may not happen in any Indian home. And yet passions, savage and violent, are roused within hearts seemingly placid, and battles rage until the home is nearly burnt down without flame or smoke being visible to the outside eye. There are only six characters in the novel—the fond mother, devoted and jealous, the pampered son, vain and self-centred, the simple untutored wife who needed the shock of great sorrow to mature into a woman, the pious aunt who finds refuge in religion, the loyal friend so virtuous and heroic that he seems rather a prig, and the young, beautiful and vivacious widow who gives the name to the English version of the novel. Of all women characters created by Tagore in his many novels, Binodini is the most convincing, vital and full-blooded. In her frustrations and suffering is summed up the author's ironic acceptance of the orthodox Hindu society of the day.

A beautiful, talented and well-educated girl cannot get a husband because the affectionate father had spent what little he had on her education and could not save enough for the dowry. In panic— since an unmarried girl over twelve years of age was a social disgrace to a respectable Hindu family of the day—she is married off to a poor and sickly nobody who dies soon after, leaving her stranded in an unsympathetic environment. Conscious of her beauty and her wit, she rebels against the unjust privations of a bleak and humiliated existence to which as a widow she is condemned for life and asserts her right to love and happiness. She burns her fingers and nearly burns up a home. If in the end she retires from the contest it is not because she is defeated or crushed but because she disdains a victory achieved at too sordid a cost. Her tragedy is a lasting shame to the Hindu conscience.

Tagore was to write several other novels some of which are much better known than this and as literary achievements far surpass it; in them his poetic imagination, the range and play of his intellect, his intuitive understanding of human nature and his inimitable flair for style find more mature scope. But in no other novel of his—the short stories excepted—is he a better story-teller. In no other novel has he watched the human drama with such gentle and calm irony, without the intrusion of poetic rhapsodies or intellectual dissertations. In no other novel has he accepted the kinship between sex and love with such frank sympathy—the white lotus of love rooted in the dark slime of desire.

Altogether the first year of the present century is a very significant year in Tagore's life, significant in every respect, from the point of view of his literary achievement, his spiritual development, his public commitments and his struggles as a man. The year marks the end of his freedom as an individual owing no obligations save to his Muse and to his family; from now on his soul will be increasingly pledged to God, the baffling God of the Hindu metaphysics who is both Redeemer and Mephistopheles in One. The lover will become a teacher and the poet will don the robe of a prophet. He will struggle and suffer, his devotion will bear a richer fruit and his ambition its bitter weeds. He will rise through suffering and his life will attain a fullness and his stature a magnificence unsurpassed in his age.

He hardly knew what was coming. All he knew was that he could no longer continue looking exclusively after the family estates, that destiny was calling him to a larger field of activity. Life in Calcutta with its incessant clamour and distractions was too noisy and distasteful. He needed proximity to nature and earth (he breathed freely only in open spaces), he needed quiet for his work and he needed activity to fill the leisure between writing. What better place than

Santiniketan to suit all his requirements? His father had already built a house there, a retreat for quiet and meditation, and had later added a temple, a large hall with walls of coloured glass and a bare floor with no image or other paraphernalia of any particular ritual or rites.

In 1898 Rabindranath had taken his wife and five children, three daughters and two sons, to his estate house in Shelidah and had taken in his own hands their education. Although he had engaged an English tutor for his eldest son, he himself was the principal teacher of all his children. Having suffered from bad teaching in his childhood, he had thought much, and written also, on the fundamentals of teaching and now he gained a new insight by putting his principles into practice. But teaching one's children haphazardly is not enough; he needed a wider field for systematic experimentation and he thought, why not shift to Santiniketan and start a small experimental school there? His imagination had already been caught by idealized pictures of *tapovana* or forest hermitages or asramas in ancient India where learned sages lived with their disciples and taught them the practice of simple living and high thinking. The very word *upanishad* is derived from this close association of the teacher with his pupil. He would thus revive the ancient ideal and people his country once again with sages and heroes. He would also replace the soulless and mechanical system of education which the British rulers had imported from the Victorian slums by a new and creative one in which both teaching and learning would be pleasurable. He would combine the ancient with the modern and re-create the old in terms of the new.

On 22 December 1901 he inaugurated his school at Santiniketan with five pupils, among them his eldest son, and as many teachers. He named it Brahmacharya Asrama, after the ancient forest hermitages. The orthodox must have squirmed at this sacrilege, for of the five teachers three were Christians, one of them an Englishman, his son's previous tutor. But that was always Tagore's way—to interpret tradition in his own fashion, to honour the dead on his own terms, with the result that he won the support neither of the orthodox who looked askance at him as an impertinent innovator nor of the radicals who considered him too ancient. He had to stand alone—a position ideal for a poet but inconvenient for a social reformer who needed money and men for his institution. Even his admirers and well-wishers were inclined to believe that the school was at best a poet's whim. He found it difficult for a long time to get enough funds or enough pupils for his school, even though both tuition and boarding were almost free. He had to sell his house at Puri and part of his personal library to meet the expenses, while his wife magnificently parted with her jewellery to help him carry on. This gracious lady, gentle and loving, always ready to efface herself, was a source of great strength to him in his work and was a mother to all the children in the school. The life in the asrama was simple to the point of austerity, the children had to attend to all their needs themselves which involved not a little manual labour, and the food served was very simple and vegetarian. Mrinalini Devi, who was an excellent cook, would sometimes prepare special dishes and delicacies with her own hands as a treat for the children.

The school, however, was not a poet's whim. It was his sadhana, a new medium of creative striving for the good of his people, his one epic which he continued to work on till the end of his life and which grew with his growth, remaining unfinished. A poet's dream it undoubtedly was, for who but a poet could '. . . bring the earliest tidings of the unborn flower to a sceptic world'? How else explain the paradox that just when he had established an unrivalled position in the then metropolis of India and won applause even from his detractors he chose to adopt the vocation of a schoolmaster—the latest among the despised castes of India—in a neglected corner of Bengal! That he did so and preferred the hardships of a life of stark simplicity (Santiniketan then had little to offer by way of what are known as the amenities of civilized life) to the easy ways and glamorous society of Calcutta is evidence enough, if such were needed, that the new vocation was in the nature of a mission and not of play.

He had always been deeply interested in problems affecting the welfare of his people and of such problems none seemed more deserving of his attention than the prevailing system of education which, instead of developing, stunted the mind of the growing generation. He was the first to see through its limitations. It seemed to him wrong that the child, instead of being encouraged to express himself freely and happily in his mother-tongue, should be forced from an early age to master the intricacies of a foreign idiom, thus expending all the resources of his tender and undeveloped mind in trying to balance himself on crutches, in the meanwhile forgetting the use of his limbs. He had not forgotten his own school days when 'we had to sit inert, like dead specimens of some museum, whilst lessons were pelted at us from on high, like hailstones on flowers'.

'Poor Bengali child,' Tagore had written a decade earlier, 'there is surely no one so unfortunate as he! At an age when children of other lands are happily munching sugarcane with their newly-cut teeth, the Bengali child is seated on a school bench, his thin, stunted legs dangling from the pleats of his dhoti, and treated only to that other cane with no more tasty accompaniment than the master's harsh abuse. The natural consequence of this system is that the power of digestion in every sphere of life is weakened. The bodies of these sons of Bengal remain stunted for lack of sufficient games and whole-some food, while the intellectual digestive apparatus is equally undeveloped. We pass our B.A. and M.A. examinations, we cram ourselves with loads of learning, but the intellect gains neither vigour nor maturity . . . The ideas with which we thus stuff ourselves for some twenty years or more enter into no chemical combination with the lives we live, with the result that our minds present a fantastic appearance. Some of our ideas remain as it were gummed on, while others fall off in course of time. Just as savages take pride in painting and tattooing their bodies, hiding the glow of their natural health, so we go strutting about, our bodies smeared with an alien English learning which has hardly any connexion with the inner reality of our life. We swagger about with a few cheap, flashy English words, bringing out profundities of English learning at inappropriate times and in completely wrong places, unable even to see ourselves as unwitting actors in an absurd farce . . . It follows inevitably from the present system of education that the acquirements in which we pass our whole childhood fit us for nothing but a clerkship or a trade, and that we have no use for them in our everyday life at home, but take them off and fold them away in a box along with our office turban and *chaddar* . . .

'And so the domestic feud between learning and life goes on

growing, each bitterly and incessantly mocking at the other, till between his stunted living and his bloated learning the life of a Bengali is reduced to a farce . . . There is a story of a poor man who used to gather alms bit by bit all the cold weather, but was no sooner able to buy warm clothes than the hot weather would set in—and by the time he had laboured through the hot weather and bought his summer clothes, it would be almost winter again. At last a kind god took pity on his misery and offered him a boon. "I want only one thing," the man cried. "Save me from this topsy-turvydom. All my life I have been getting my winter clothes in summer and my summer clothes in winter. If you could only put this anomaly right, I shall have nothing left to wish for!" That prayer is ours too. Save us from our topsyturvydom, and we shall be content. All our misery is due to the fact that we cannot make our winter clothes coincide with winter nor our summer clothes with summer. Otherwise we have all we need. Let us therefore ask this boon of God, that our possessions may be rightly matched—rice with hunger, clothes with winter, language with thought, and learning with life. We are like Kabir's fish: We have water, yet we are athirst; the world sees it and laughs.'

The child's mind is extraordinarily aware of the things he sees around him and is much more receptive than his teacher's to sense-impressions. He learns with his limbs and with his senses long before he learns with his brain. He must therefore be provided with an environment which will stimulate and feed his curiosity and make his introduction to the world around him easy and joyful. He should be encouraged to *do* things for himself and should lean as little as possible on his teacher. The idea and practice of teaching through some form of activity or craft was first developed at Santiniketan long before Mahatma Gandhi incorporated it in his system of what is known today in India as Basic Education.

The best teacher, according to Tagore, is nature. The classes in his school were therefore held in the open, under the trees, and the students were encouraged to study and love nature in its changing moods and phases. Education in the sciences, in which he greatly believed, must arise naturally from the study of nature and the training of the senses, which develop the child's curiosity and his aptitudes. No less important, said Tagore, is the influence of music and of the fine arts in training the child's emotions and his sensibility. Education to be real must be of the whole man, of the emotions and the senses as much as of the intellect. Man in his fullness is not limited by the individual but overflows in his community. And so in his school, along with training in individual initiative and self-reliance, equal emphasis was laid on community service and corporate action. The school was run almost as a small self-governing community.

Education is not a plant that can be made to grow as an exotic variety in the hot-house. If it does not strike roots in the soil and adapt itself to the natural environments, it has little value for the people as a whole. It was a painful and humiliating fact that the intelligentsia of that generation—to some extent even of this—were borrowing their pattern of thought and behaviour, indeed even of their feelings, from the West, particularly Britain, thereby justifying Tagore's charge that the '. . . educational institutions in our country are India's alms-bowl of knowledge; they lower our national self-respect; they encourage us to make a foolish display of decorations made of borrowed feathers . . . Once upon a time [he reminded his countrymen] we were in possession of such a thing as our own mind. It was living. It thought, it felt, it expressed itself. It was receptive as well as productive. That this mind could be of any use in the process, or in the end, of education was overlooked by our modern educational dispensation.'

Life never imitates, it assimilates, and so he warned his people that '. . . if the whole world grows at last into an exaggerated West, then such an illimitable parody of the modern age will die, crushed beneath its own absurdity'. It was an obvious truth and yet it needed reiteration by him that '. . . for proficiency in walking it is better to train the muscles of our own legs than to strut upon wooden ones of foreign make, although they clatter and cause more surprise at our skill in using them than if they were living and real'. A man may digest all the knowledge contained in the pages of the *Encyclopaedia Britannica* but if he does not know himself and his immediate environments he can hardly be considered wise or even intelligent. However scientific a system of education, however broad its sympathies and universal its outlook, it must adapt itself to indigenous needs, economic and cultural, it must '. . . break open the treasure-trove of our ancestors and use it for the commerce of life'.

And last but not least: To ensure that the emphasis on individual self-expression and the development of the personality does not degenerate into a sharpening or bloating of the ego, with its inevitable cupidity and self-aggrandizement and thereby defeat the very aim of true education, the individual consciousness must be charged with that sense of the One, the impersonal and universal Over-all (call it God or Law or Historical Will or whatever term one prefers), pervading and uniting all life and nature, which is the common and, one may say, the one redeeming feature of the various faiths of mankind. Mere *intellectual* conviction of the unity of mankind or of the common destiny of any particular race or class, however effective as an instrument of policy, is insufficient by itself to subdue the tempest of man's ego. Thought has to be realized as religious feeling before it can gain access to that basement of the consciousness where operates in silence and in obscurity the power-house of the mind. This was the basic core of Tagore's religious thought, which remained constant amid the many colours and textures its outward shape assumed. At the time when he started his school he was under the spell of the *tapovana* ideal, monastic discipline tempered with poetic licence, which was his own peculiar interpretation of the past. What was unreal about it gradually fell off; what was real survived. Later on, he even made the school co-educational; and the boys and girls who were taught there—many of them occupying positions of high distinction today—were by no means monks and nuns.

These were the main principles of his educational ideal which he tried to implement with his very limited material resources and in a very humble beginning. It was not that having established the school, he left it to his assistants to run it, himself occupied with higher things. He was never an armchair idealist; what he believed in he did himself, pouring all his energy and his heart into it. He not only supervised all the details of the school-and-asrama administration but participated in all its activities and himself taught the children. Finding that there were no suitable primers and textbooks available in Bengali, he wrote them himself and encouraged his colleagues to do the same. Apart from his considerable output of children's literature—poems, dramas, stories, fairy tales and fables, which he probably would have written in any case, for he loved children— he wrote and compiled several volumes of systematically planned and graduated primers and textbooks which were later taken up and used by several other schools in Bengal. The poet could drudge as well as sing. He was content with small beginnings and did not know himself that this little asrama would one day grow into a full-fledged university and a world-known seat of international studies. Even when it had grown into such, his special and tender solicitude was always reserved for his first love, the little nucleus of a children's school, in perpetual danger of being swamped by more spectacular rivals.[8]

As though to test the sincerity and strength of His new devotee, God sent him, as He had done to His servant Job of the Old Testament, a series of bereavements and afflictions. Within a few months of his finding a new home in Santiniketan, his wife, Mrinalini Devi, fell seriously ill and was taken to Calcutta where she died on 23 November 1902. Recalling the tragedy, her eldest son, Rathindranath, writes: 'Mother had realized that the end was near even before the doctors had given up hope. The last time when I went to her bedside she could not speak, but on seeing me the tears silently rolled down her cheeks. That night we children were all sent to bed in another part of the house. But my sister Bela and I could not go to sleep. A vague

[8] For an authentic description of the school by one of Tagore's distinguished foreign colleagues, see *Shantiniketan: The Bolpur School of Rabindranath Tagore*, by W.W. Pearson, Macmillan & Co., London, 1917. There are several books in Bengali of reminiscences of ex-pupils of the school and innumerable anecdotes current. One of them is worth recalling. Tagore had strictly forbidden corporal chastisement in any form; nevertheless, occasionally an exasperated teacher had recourse to it for some of the boys were very wild. As a matter of fact, in the early days many of the boys were problem children whom the parents found it hard to control at home. So they were conveniently sent to the poet's school. One day the poet's eldest brother Dwijendranath, the genial philosopher and mathematician who spent his last years in Santiniketan, was strolling in the grounds and noticed a teacher smacking one of the boys. He immediately sent the teacher a slip of paper in which he had scribbled some doggerel in Bengali, meaning: Let me remind you, dear brother, that you cannot, by beating, turn an ass into a horse, although you can easily beat a horse into an ass.

fear kept us awake. Early in the morning we went up to the terrace overlooking the room where mother slept. An ominous silence hung over the house, the shadow of death seemed to have crossed its threshold with stealthy steps during the night. That evening my father gave me mother's pair of slippers to keep. Vicissitudes of life, pain and afflictions never upset the equanimity of father's mind. His inward peace was not disturbed by any calamity, however painful. Some inner resources gave him the power to face and to rise above misfortunes of the most painful nature. After mother's death father devoted himself with renewed zeal to the affairs of the school at Santiniketan.' The son goes on to testify that his father '. . . bore even physical pain with uncommon fortitude. Once when he was stung by a scorpion he sat quietly with his leg stretched out before him, trying to imagine it was not *his* limb that was in pain but a separate entity that had nothing to do with his real self. The success of this experiment gave him power to resist pain, both physical and mental, throughout his life.'

Pain is not the less real because one bears it with equanimity. In this case the pain was perhaps made more poignant by a touch of regret that he had not fully appreciated and repaid the wife's devotion while she lived. It had been an arranged, and not a romantic, marriage and it is possible that he had suffered rather than welcomed her when she first came into his life. She was neither beautiful nor glamorous in any way; unlettered and unsophisticated, she was, moreover, too young to be his companion. She was only eleven when they married, while he was twenty-two, a handsome and dashing young man, intoxicated with his own genius. But she grew and what she lacked by way of glamour she more than made up for by her simple and unostentatious ways, her affectionate and generous nature which made everyone welcome to her home and her remarkable aptitude for the household arts.

For twenty years she looked after him with unstinted devotion and bore him five children. Though young and living in the midst of an aristocratic and sophisticated society, she dressed very simply and wore almost no jewellery and cheerfully adapted herself to her husband's austere ideals. She grumbled only when he tried to prevent her from dressing her children in fine clothes. Nor could it have been easy to put up with her husband's whims and inconsistencies. On the one hand he insisted on simplicity and economy, on the other he expected his visitors and guests to be entertained lavishly. Fortunately her culinary ingenuity and resourcefulness were equal to all occasions and even celebrated gourmands of the day never forgot her dishes having once tasted them. Whenever they travelled the poet would insist on her taking the minimum of luggage and would particularly frown at the sight of kitchen utensils and other cooking aids. She would say nothing but would quietly smuggle in whatever she could in innocent-looking cases, remarking smilingly, 'What an impossible man! As soon as we reach the other place, visitors will call and he will expect me to produce delicacies for their palate out of nothing!'[9]

Nor did she remain unlettered for long. She soon acquired proficiency not only in her own language but in English and Sanskrit as well. At her husband's persuasion she translated into Bengali an abridged version of the *Ramayana* from the original Sanskrit. She also acted on the stage in his play *Raja O Rani* (The King and the Queen) and gave an excellent interpretation of the role she was assigned. No wonder then that she won her husband's heart in the end, who gave ample proof of his devotion when she took to bed. For two months he nursed her day and night, refusing to engage a professional nurse. There were no electric fans in those days and contemporary witnesses have left on record their admiration of the husband who was always at the patient's bedside, his hand-fan moving gently over her. When she died he spent the whole night on the terrace walking up and down, having given strict orders that no one was to disturb him.

As usual his feelings found expression in his poems only. These were published in a small volume of twenty-seven poems remarkable for their tenderness and depth of feeling and for their simplicity of utterance. Some critics have noted with regret a lack of adequate passion in these elegies, but they must be very naïve indeed who

[9] It is said that years later when Tagore was an old man he was once persuaded to attend a spirit-calling seance. The psychic medium announced that the spirit of Mrinalini Devi was in the room. The planchette moved and scribbled the following query addressed to the poet, 'Are you still as foolish as you used to be?'

imagine that a man's feeling for his wife, after twenty years of living together, should still palpitate with unrestrained passion. However that may be, the husband's sincerity of sorrow at a loss that was irreplaceable and that was felt from day to day is very evident and is movingly expressed without an excess of self-pity. 'My night has passed on the bed of sorrow, and my eyes are tired.' She died before he could repay her for the many gifts he had received from her and now all he can do is to offer to God what was meant for her. 'Her night has found its morning and Thou hast taken her in Thy arms; and to Thee I bring my gratitude and my gifts that were for her.'[10] Absent-mindedly he looks for her everywhere in the house, only to realize that he will never again see her on this earth. 'My house is small and what once has gone from it can never be regained. But infinite is Thy mansion, my Lord, and seeking her I have come to Thy door.' He finds among her belongings a bunch of letters written by him to her, carefully preserved like a great treasure, and is deeply moved. He prays that her memory may bring order into his life as she had brought order into his home.

Grief disguised is more potent than grief expressed. Few among those who do not know would suspect that Tagore's poems on children so full of innocent delight were written during a period of great dejection and anxiety. Within a few months of his wife's death his second daughter Renuka, whose early marriage he had precipitated, fell seriously ill and the doctors advised a change of climate in the mountains. The father took her and the two youngest children, daughter Mira and son Samindra, now motherless, first to Hazaribagh and then to Almora in the Himalayas. He had not only to nurse the ailing daughter but to look after and entertain the two youngest ones who, in the absence of the mother, clung to him. For their sake he had to hide his own grief and anxiety and to share their little interests and listen to their prattle. Thus he wrote poems which were published in a volume entitled *Sisu* (The Child), 'A collection of poems about children, unique in the literature of the world', to quote the estimate of the Czech savant, Professor Lesny.

Undoubtedly they rank with the finest poetry written, not *for*

---

[10] Some of these poems can be read in *Fruit-Gathering*.

but *about* children, in any language of the world. As many of these poems are available in English translation in *The Crescent Moon*, the foreign reader can judge them for himself—keeping in mind that they are not meant to amuse children; their chief value, apart from the exquisite poetry necessarily lost in translation, being that they help the adult in his understanding of the wonderland of the child's mind.[11] 'On the seashore of endless worlds children meet . . . They know not how to swim, they know not how to cast nets. Pearl-fishers dive for pearls, merchants sail in their ships, while children gather pebbles and scatter them again. They seek not for hidden treasures, they know not how to cast nets.' Which child would like to be told this about himself, even if he understood what it meant? Only saints and poets know what 'Heaven lies about us in our infancy!'

In September 1903, nine months after her mother's death, Renuka died, at the age of thirteen. This precocious, moody and uncommon girl was very dear to the father who felt her loss very deeply, though he gave no outward expression of his grief. Instead he buried himself in his work and continued to fill the pages of his literary journal, *Bangadarshan*. Strangely enough, it was during this period that he contributed serially to the pages of this journal what may be described as perhaps the only novel he wrote merely for the sake of entertaining the reader with an ingeniously constructed story, unburdened with philosophy or any kind of sophistication, and not ending on a tragic note—*Nauka Dubi*, translated into English as *The Wreck*. It is a story based on the dilemma of mistaken identity resulting in an exchange of wives, delightfully told and interspersed with descriptions of nature of extraordinary loveliness. Those who think that a story to be good must be probable may find fault with it; but then so must they with most classics written before the nineteenth century. Sophisticated and over-civilized critics do not approve of this novel. Edward Thompson found it 'incredibly bad'. On the other hand, Professor Lesny considered it 'one of Tagore's best novels . . . homogenous . . . full of action, and the human interest is very powerful'. The popularity of this novel may

[11] As a matter of fact, children are more interested to read about adults than about themselves, which explains the popularity of the American Comics.

be gauged from the fact, that with the exception of *Gitanjali*, no other book of Tagore's has been translated into so many languages.

Four months after the death of his daughter Renuka, the poet suffered another grievous bereavement. A young and brilliant poet, Satis Roy, whom Tagore loved as his own son and who, an idealist like himself, had joined his school staff at Santiniketan, and might in course of time have been his right hand, suddenly died of small-pox. The whole school had to be shifted to Shelidah for the time being, for fear of the epidemic. Financial difficulties made it increasingly difficult to run the school and Tagore was obliged to sell to the Hitabadi Publishing House the rights of publishing a limited edition of his collected works for the paltry sum of Rs. 2,000/- only (400 dollars). Soon after, his father, the Maharshi, died at the ripe old age of eighty-eight on 19 January 1905. The death of this remarkable and towering personality marks the end of a very significant period in Indian history—the age of religious and cultural renaissance, of intellectual and moral giants who paved the way of India's political awakening. Henceforth political and not moral or intellectual ideals will dominate the Indian scene, despite the great dreams of Gandhi and Tagore.

Lord Curzon, the strong-headed Viceroy of India, provided the necessary provocation and challenge in the last year of his office, 1905, by his proclamation of the partition of Bengal, thereby beginning the process of driving a wedge between the two major religious communities in the country which ultimately resulted in the partition of India forty-two years later amid a holocaust of violence and terror unprecedented in Indian history. Tagore had already warned his people of this danger and now he jumped into the fray, making fiery speeches, composing patriotic songs and leading huge processions in protest against the vivisection of the country. Students were being expelled from colleges for no other crime than the temerity to sing patriotic songs; to provide for their education he and some other leading educationists formulated and put into operation a scheme for national education and set up a Council of which the celebrated Indian philosopher-yogi Aurobindo Ghosh became the first Principal. It was for this Council that Tagore delivered his famous series of lectures on the principles of literature which were later published as *Sahitya* (Literature). He had hoped that by leading the popular discontent against foreign rule he would succeed in harnessing the newly-aroused passion for national freedom to a constructive programme of national regeneration. He had planned and outlined such a programme in a series of remarkable lectures and essays in which he anticipated almost every basic principle of what later became a nation-wide mass movement of non-violent non-co-operation under the dynamic leadership of Mahatma Gandhi.

But Tagore was no Gandhi; he lacked the latter's infinite patience, his calm judgement and unruffled will, his genius for strategy and his unrivalled gift of leadership. He rode the storm majestically for a time, but as soon as it raised its inevitable howl of violence, he retired from the battlefield, a sadder and a wiser man. He was severely criticized for having abandoned the struggle which he had so heroically inspired, but be it recalled to Tagore's credit that he was never deflected from what he thought was his duty by public abuse. That too was heroism. Indeed, he did well to retire, for he was no match for unscrupulous politicians who would merely have exploited his presence in the struggle for their own benefit. He preferred to meet these politicians on his own ground and he did so brilliantly in his later novels. His patriotic songs, however, continued to inspire the national struggle, although these songs are remarkably free of any trace of jingoism or incitation of crude passions, as the following samples may show: 'Let the earth and the water, the air and the fruits of my country be sweet, my Lord! Let the homes and marts, the forests and fields of my land be full, my Lord! Let the promises and hopes, the deeds and words of my people be true, my Lord! Let the lives and hearts of the sons and daughters of my nation be one, my Lord!' Another song, very popular even today, which the underground revolutionaries loved to sing and which may also be taken as his own answer to them in anticipation of the parting of the ways, says: 'If no one answers your call, if all are afraid and turn away, even then, O unlucky one, open wide your heart and speak out alone! If no one holds the light in the stormy and troubled night, even then, O unlucky one, let the pain light its lantern in your heart and let that be your only light!'[12]

Whether his retirement from the battlefield was a loss to the national movement or not, it certainly was a gain to Santiniketan and to literature. Apart from a large number of articles on social and political problems, on education, literary criticism, folk literature and the philosophy of words and sounds, he wrote a number of humorous and satirical sketches and completed his next major volume of verse which was published as *Kheya* (Crossing). The title is symbolic of the poet's mood of wistful expectancy, of waiting for the ferry to cross over to the other bank. The many bereavements and disappointments he had recently suffered had only served to steel his fortitude and to prepare him for the change that was coming. He had fondly imagined that his Lover would leave behind on the bed a garland of flowers, but no, what he found instead was a sword, sharp and heavy. If God wants him to take up arduous duties in life and not merely to while away the idle hours singing, he will do so. Most of the poems (some are songs) are dreamy and symbolic; eleven of them were later included in his English *Gitanjali*, and a few others in *The Gardener, Fruit-Gathering* and *Lover's Gift and Crossing*.

In India after the rainy season is over in September, a few clouds still linger in the autumn sky; they give no rain and serve no obvious purpose except that occasionally they give colour to the sunset. And so the poet feels that he is like an autumn cloud uselessly floating in the sky, waiting for the sun to melt away its vapour and to dissolve it into emptiness. But if it pleases the sun to paint this 'fleeting emptiness' with colours, then let it be so. He will surrender his all to God and will withhold nothing. What he held as his own became a burden and a shackle, what he gave to God came back as wealth untold. 'Prisoner, tell me who wrought this unbreakable chain?' 'It was I,' said the prisoner, 'who forged this chain with great care. I thought my chain would bind the world, leaving me free. And so I laboured at it, day and night, beating the iron in fire. When the chain was ready, I discovered that I had bound myself in its shackles.'

[12] This was one of Mahatma Gandhi's favourite songs and was often sung at his evening prayer-meetings.

The poet describes himself as a beggar girl who was on her begging round when the Prince stopped before her and stretching his hand, said, 'Give me something.' She blushed with shame. What could she give him? She took out a copper coin from her miserable bag and placed it in his hand. When she returned home and opened the bag, she found a gold coin in place of the one she had parted with. 'Oh, why did I not give my all?' she wailed. In another poem he is a woman waiting at night for her lover. 'At the dead of night came the King of the dark chamber.' This symbolism he elaborated later in his famous drama known in English as *The King of the Dark Chamber*.

In November 1907 came the crowning tragedy of his family life. His youngest son, Samindra, a lovely and gifted boy who might have become something like his father, suddenly died of cholera at the age of thirteen, five years to the day after the death of his mother. In the course of those five tempestuous years Tagore suffered an almost total break-up of his family life. He lost his wife and two children; of the three surviving ones, the eldest daughter lived with her husband outside Bengal, the eldest son had been sent to the United States the previous year for training in agricultural science, and the third daughter Mira had been married a few months earlier. With the untimely death of his youngest son, he was reduced to utter loneliness. Loneliness amid the crowd is even more oppressive and so for a time he retired into solitude on his estate at Shelidah. That was the only visible expression of the heavy hand of sorrow that lay on his heart. He had learnt not to muddy the waters of his Muse with his personal grief; his verse was increasingly becoming his offering to God, the language of his communication of a higher love.

He had never been very popular with his own people; he was too far above their current prejudices and passions and too far ahead of his time. Even his literary genius had won but a grudging and limited admiration and it is said that for a long time pundits and purists used to set passages from his writings to schoolboys saying, 'Rewrite in correct and chaste Bengali.' The only time he rode on the crest of popularity was when he led the agitation against the partition of Bengal, but that was for a brief while only and now he was blamed for having let down his people and was less popular than ever. He had alienated the ruling authorities who issued secret circulars asking the Government servants and loyalists not to send their children to his school or help it in any way. He was a political suspect and was being watched.[13] He was thus forced, as much by outer circumstances as by an inner necessity, to stand alone, to rely entirely on his inner resources, to stand face to face with God. His religious poetry of this period which culminated in the passionate sincerity and utter simplicity of *Gitanjali* was wrung out of his heart's blood. His religious insight, like that of all great saints and mistics, was born of deeply experienced sorrow and loneliness.

The most remarkable aspect of his religious insight was that it made him love this earth and this life the more. He sought God not merely in the privacy of his soul but in every manifestation of His play in the outside world. The son he lost in his home he found again in all the boys of his Santiniketan; in their zest for living he recovered his own. How well he did so can be seen in the play he wrote for them in 1908—*Saradotsav* (Autumn Festival). The play is one long riot of innocent delight, a hymn to the joy of living and, as aptly pointed out by Edward Thompson, might have been written as a symbolic commentary on Emerson's wise words, 'Give me health and a day and I will make the pomp of emperors ridiculous.' It is still a favourite with the boys of his school for whom it was composed and is acted in the open air, as many of Tagore's plays were intended to be, for in them nature is not merely a background but almost a participant.

This was followed by another play, *Prayaschitta* (Atonement), very different in theme and mood from the previous play, though also in

[13] He has himself related how once when a family acquaintance had gone to the Jorasanko police station in Calcutta to report a theft, an intelligence agent came in and reported to the chief on duty, 'Rabindranath Tagore, Class B, Number 12 has arrived in Calcutta from Bolpur.' Tagore must have told this story to Ezra Pound whom he came to know in London some years later, for when the present writer met the distinguished American poet in Rapallo in 1959 the latter, who was in a reminiscent mood, said, 'Rabindranath, whose words on numerous (unprinted) occasions are worthy of record, once told me, "In my country I am suspect Number 12 Class B."'

prose interspersed with songs. It is not a play of feeling but of action, full of strife and intrigue and the clash of interests, although an idea and a moral run through it as they do in all Tagore's plays. It is a dramatization of his first and very early novel, *The Young Queen's Market*, with the addition of a new character who is the prototype of Mahatma Gandhi and anticipates the latter's campaign of non-violent civil resistance and non-payment of taxes as the people's answer to the tyranny of an unjust ruler. The play was Tagore's answer to his compatriots who had accused him of deserting the political battle-field. It was not desertion but renunciation, the spirit of which is most movingly portrayed in the last scene of the play. He was to return to this same theme later in a much more powerful play.

The poet was in a full frenzy of the dramatic phase of his career and it was inevitable that he should dramatize the most intense experience of his life—his adventure with the Divine. He had sought God in beauty and had found Him in sorrow. Is Truth merely Beauty and Goodness or is it also the Terrible? √hat is the soul's relation to God? Must we approach Truth on its own terms or on ours? These are the questions the poet has sought to answer in this his most symbolic and in a sense his most characteristic play, *Raja*.[14] Several critics, even in his own country, have found fault with Tagore's plays on account of their symbolism, their excess of lyricism and the introduction of wayside scenes and characters not strictly relevant to the plot. They apply to his plays standards learnt from their study of the Western, in particular the British, drama, forgetting that Tagore sought neither to follow any known models nor to cater to any standardized public taste. He created his own forms as well as his own public.

It is remarkable how an imaginative foreign critic sometimes understood him better than many of his own countrymen, as may be seen from the following quotation from Ernest Rhys's biographical

---

[14] The play is available in English rendering (*The King of the Dark Chamber*, Macmillan & Co., London, 1914) and need not therefore be discussed in detail. The reader can judge it for himself. The principle followed in the present study is to refer to books available in English in very general terms and to deal a little more fully with works not known to foreign readers.

study:[15] 'The dramatic critics have complained over this tendency in Indian playwrights, as if in great drama, in Aeschylus, in Sophocles, in Shakespeare, in Goethe's *Faust*, there was not any attempt to find lyrical alleviation on the road to the dramatic climax. Moreover, the east has fostered a drama of its own, congenially influenced by the musical affinity of its themes. It does not, like our English stage, look for the comedy of differences or the sheer tragedy of circumstance . . . We have to reckon with the tradition of a stage as well as with the temperament of a playwright in judging a kind of drama so new to us. Rabindranath Tagore may break the rules of our common stage-practice, but he breaks none that govern the leisurely drama of the open air and the courtyard, which he and his fellow play-wrights in India have in mind.'

This philosophic allegory (*Raja*) was followed by two other plays written in quick succession in 1911, very different from each other and from the previous dramas, although the central character in both of them is a young boy. Tagore not only loved children but believed profoundly in the natural wisdom of their innocent and whole-hearted acceptance of life. Of these two new plays, *Dak Ghar* is well known in its English translation, *The Post Office*, and was successfully staged in London by the Irish players in 1913.[16] W. B. Yeats, who was present at the performance, testified, 'On the stage the little play shows that it is perfectly constructed, and conveys to the right audience an emotion of gentleness and peace.' Even Edward Thompson, who has severely criticized the play for its 'substructure of sentimentalism' admits that its 'language is of an unsurpassable naturalness' and that the play as a whole is 'within its limits an almost perfect piece of art. It does successfully what both Shakespeare and Kalidasa failed to do, brings onto the stage a child who neither "shows off" nor is silly.'

The other play, *Achalayatan* (The Immovable), has not been published in English, and is indeed untranslatable. The play is a

---

[15] *Rabindranath Tagore*, Ernest Rhys, Macmillan & Co., London, 1917.

[16] It has also been well received on Paris stage in André Gide's exquisite rendering, *La lettre du roi*. Since then the play has been produced in many capitals of Europe. As late as 1949 the present writer saw its production in Rio de Janeiro in an excellent Portuguese rendering by the distinguished poetess Cecilia Meireles.

rollicking satire on 'the institution of fixed beliefs' which is Hindu society and is one long unsparing mockery of its absurd orthodoxies. The central character is a small boy by name Panchak who has been enrolled by his elder brother, a pillar of orthodoxy, as a novice in a monastic order which is Achalayatan, the Castle of Conformity, surrounded by high walls and cut off from the rest of the world. The poor boy who suffers from irrepressible curiosity and mirth is looked down upon by the inmates as an incorrigible dunce and is constantly reprimanded for his habit of singing. 'What merit is there in singing? Even the birds can sing.' He is always playing the truant and hobnobs with the surrounding tribes of peasants, workers and such other low-caste untouchables and finds pleasure in their innocent games, their honest labour and in their lust for living. Finally the Great Teacher whom the monks and elders fear but have not known arrives on the scene and himself leads the low-caste tribes against the Achalayatan whose high walls are razed to the ground for ever. It may well be imagined how severely the author was criticized and abused for this play by his compatriots and co-religionists who had no difficulty in recognizing themselves as the inmates of 'a vast lunatic asylum'.

But Tagore was no embittered Swift who delighted in belittling his fellow men nor one of those revolutionaries who in their impatience with the old order would trample underfoot the good along with the bad. He loved his country and its heritage too well to despise all traditional values. How fair he was in his defence of both the old and the new is evident in the novel which he wrote and published at this period and which many consider his best, *Gora*. *Gora* is more than a mere novel; it is the epic of India in transition at the most crucially intellectual period of its modern history. Though not so vast in its scope and sweep of events nor so rich and varied in its gallery of portraits, it is to Indian fiction what Tolstoy's *War and Peace* is to the Russian. No other book can claim so masterly an analysis of the complex of Indian social life with its teeming contradictions, or of the character of Indian nationalism which draws its roots from renascent Hinduism and stretches out its arms towards universal humanism. Nor is it any the less interesting as a novel. The characters are well drawn, not as individual freaks but as types, clearly recognizable, and their conflicts both as between themselves and within themselves as living and growing characters are delineated with great insight and sympathy. Despite the abundance of polemics in the book, inevitable in view of its very theme, the author does not lose the thread of the main narrative whose interest is sustained to the end.

It is worth recalling how this novel came to be written. His brief but hectic experience of active political agitation had set Tagore brooding on the character of Indian nationalism, the sources of its inspiration and its future direction. He had himself grown with its beginnings. The first impact of the modern age had made itself felt in India as a ferment in the religious and social consciousness of the people. Raja Rammohun Roy was its chief apostle. Inspired by him, Rabindranath's father, the Maharshi, carried the movement forward and laid the foundation of the main schism in Hindu society, between the progressives and the orthodox. Among the progressives were genuine intellectuals and humanists as well as those who merely aped the foreign ways in the name of progress. Since the British patronized the latter they became a new class of social snobs and upstarts, a type still very common, though they have adopted many modifications in dress, manners and slogans. Among the orthodox too were two main types, those who were sincere in their patriotism and pride and those who merely kept up the façade of orthodoxy either out of self-interest or sheer superstition. All these four types are clearly portrayed in the novel with their many variations and individual idiosyncrasies. The author gives each type its due and is as fair and eloquent in the defence of tradition as he is rational and devastating in his criticism of it.

It is said that the main character in the novel, Gora, who gives the title to it, was suggested to him by the personality of Sister Nivedita, the Irish lady who became a disciple of Swami Vivekananda, the eloquent apostle of neo-Hinduism. Those who have read her books[17] know what a passionate advocate she was of everything Hindu. Tagore who liked and admired her for her sincerity and courage must often have smiled when she preached orthodoxy to him—

[17] *The Web of Indian Life.* William Heinemann, London, 1904. She wrote several other books too. Her real name was Margaret Noble.

more Hindu than the Hindu. Once when she was staying as his
guest at his Shelidah estate, she would insist, when they sat out on
the deck of the house-boat in the evening, that he tell her a story.
So he began telling her the story of Gora and later wrote it down.
Gora is an Irish foundling whose parents were killed in the so-called
Sepoy Mutiny of 1857. A kind Brahmin lady finds the baby and
brings it up as her own. Gora, handsome, impulsive and passionate,
grows up to be a fervent believer in Hindu orthodoxy and a vehe-
ment champion of the caste system. In his crusade for what he
believes is the only true and divinely ordained faith, he alienates
his only friend and is ready to sacrifice the girl he loves. The anti-
climax comes suddenly when he discovers that he is of foreign blood
and therefore, in terms of his own faith, worse than an untouchable.
He has no place whatsoever in the orthodox Hindu society by which
he had sworn. This realization brings him to his senses and he
understands the true meaning of religion. 'Today I am really an
Indian. In me there is no longer any opposition between Hindu,
Mussulman and Christian. Today every caste in India is my caste,
the food of all is my food.'

The right understanding of his country's history and true destiny
which he made his hero realize at the end of this novel was also
directly voiced by Tagore in a beautiful hymn to India which he
wrote about the same time. It is too long to be quoted here, but a
few lines may give some idea of it.

> Awake, my mind, gently awake
> in this holy land of pilgrimage
> on the shore of this vast sea of humanity
> that is India.
> Here I stand with arms outstretched
> to hail man—divine in his own image—
> and sing to his glory in notes glad and free . . .
>
>
> No one knows whence and at whose call
> came pouring endless inundations of men
> rushing madly along—to lose themselves in the sea:
> Aryans and non-Aryans, Dravidians and Chinese,

Scythians, Huns, Pathans and Moghuls—
all are mixed, merged and lost in one body.
Now the door has opened to the West
and gifts in hand they beckon and they come—
they will give and take, meet and bring together,
none shall be turned away
from the shore of this vast sea of humanity
that is India.

Two years later he elaborated the idea in a brilliant thesis which he
first delivered as a public lecture in Calcutta and later published as
Bharatvarshe Itihaser Dhara (The Course of Indian History). In the
same year, 1912, he echoed the sentiment in a famous song which is
today the official national anthem of India. Because the hymn was
addressed to 'Thou Dispenser of India's destiny' who 'bringest the
hearts of all peoples into the harmony of one life' calling men of all
races and religions, from the East and West, 'round thy throne',
some of his compatriots who were bent on maligning him spread
the story that the hymn was addressed to the British King, George V,
who was to visit India the same year. How the British King could
be addressed by anyone as the 'Eternal Charioteer' who drives
'man's history along the road rugged with rises and falls of Nations'
passes understanding. Actually the hymn was sung for the first time
at the twenty-sixth session of the Indian National Congress, the
political party that won India's freedom and is in power today.

All the pain and suffering, the bereavements and rebuffs, the
struggles and mortifications, both in the world and in his mind,
which this poet, who had begun his career as a dashing and gay
cavalier, went through in the first decade of this century were finally
resolved and sublimated in the songs that poured forth from his full
and chastened heart in 1909 and 1910 and published as *Gitanjali*
(Handful or Offering of Songs) in the latter year. Fifty-one of these
157 songs were later translated by him into English and included
in the English book of that name which made him world-famous.
They are too well known to need any introduction or commentary
here beyond the testimony of his countrymen that they are even
sweeter to sing than to read. The language is as simple and the feeling

as sincere as the thought is sublime. As he said in one of them, 'My song has put off her adornments. She has no pride of dress and decoration. Ornaments would mar our union; they would come between thee and me; their jingling would drown our whispers.'

Love of God and love of man, strength in sorrow and humility in joy, an innocent wonder that hides centuries of thought, invest these songs with an appeal that is both universal and perennial. The very first song (of the original Bengali volume) strikes the keynote of the poet's mood: 'May I never celebrate myself in my achievement! Let only Thy will be fulfilled in my life!' This is not the passivity of a defeated and therefore resigned will. Such passivity is but the penury of the heart. His constant prayer is for strength—the strength to bear his joys and sorrows lightly, to make his love fruitful in service, the strength which will never bend its knee before the insolence of might nor ever disown the lowly and the lost, the strength which raises the mind high above daily trifles—such is the strength he will surrender to his Lord with love. Love is the key-word. He loves God because he loves the world and when the time comes for him to bid it farewell, his last words will be of thankfulness that what he saw on this earth was unsurpassable. In one remarkable poem included in this volume he hears the rumbling of the darkening clouds in the West, a foreboding of the Balkan War and the catastrophe that followed. 'I see the clouds gather in the sky of mankind; they thunder and they march in formation. Fiercely their hearts beat and they trample under foot all boundaries. What drives these clouds, mass on mass, to clash and to thunder? I see the clouds gather in the sky of mankind.'

Fifty years of a rich and fruitful career closed in 1911. As though aware that the major phase of his development was at an end and an entirely new chapter was to begin, he wrote his reminiscences (*Jivansmriti*) of the earlier days up to the threshold of manhood. Why he did not bring them up to date, why he left the most dramatic years of his life out of the picture it is difficult to say. Nor are these memoirs a chronicle of events as in a diary. As he himself put it, while introducing them, 'Life's memories are not life's history, but the original work of an artist.' The artist is an impressionist and what he paints on the mind's canvas does not exactly reproduce what actually happened. 'The two correspond but are not one.' Some outlines are blurred and some of the colours laid on '. . . come passion-tinged from his heart; thereby unfitting the record on the canvas for use as evidence in a court of law'.

9

NOBEL PRIZE

The high had proved a little too high, the heroic a little too hard on the flesh. Eleven years of struggle without respite on many fronts had yielded a rich harvest, but the strain had been very great, both on his body and his mind. The high tension at which he had lived brought its inevitable reaction and the fiftieth birthday found Rabindranath sick in body and weary in spirit. Twice before, once in early youth and again a few years later when he was at a loose end as to the choice of a career, a visit to the West had proved helpful and stimulating. Now again at the crossroads, he looked wistfully towards the West. He had never been anti-West even in his most patriotic and introspective phase and had drawn inspiration and sustenance as freely from the values of Western civilization as from the past of his own country. He took freely because he knew he could give back richly. So in the beginning of 1912 he made preparations for his third voyage to Europe. This time he looked upon it as a pilgrimage rather than as a holiday. More even than the hope of recovering his health, it was the prospect of meeting at first hand the live minds of the West that drew him.

In the meanwhile the intelligentsia of Bengal made up for their past neglect of their greatest poet by celebrating his jubilee in a grand manner by a public reception and address on 28 January 1912 in the Town Hall of Calcutta, under the auspices of the Bangiya Sahitya Parishad (Bengal Academy of Letters). A well-known Calcutta monthly, the *Modern Review*, described the reception as 'an unparalleled ovation—the first time that such an honour has been done to a literary man in India'. The poet was deeply moved, although this gratification was soon followed by the shameful scandal of many parents and guardians withdrawing their wards from Santiniketan, under pressure of a confidential circular issued by the British Government (in the name of the Government of East Bengal and Assam) declaring the school at Santiniketan as '. . . altogether unsuitable for the education of the sons of Government servants'. As though to assure him that the British Government did not represent the West an American lawyer, Myron H. Phelps, visited Santiniketan about this time and published in the papers a glowing account of the school and its humane methods of teaching.

Tagore was due to sail from Calcutta on 19 March, but suddenly fell ill on the night before his departure and the doctors forbade an immediate voyage. His luggage was already on board and had to be sent back from Madras where the ship halted next.[1] He was disappointed at this unforeseen cancellation of his voyage and sought consolation and strength, as of old, by retiring to Shelidah on the banks of his beloved river Padma. It was here that he began to translate, for the first time, some of his *Gitanjali* songs into English. But let him tell the story in his own words.[2]

'You have alluded to the English translation of *Gitanjali*. I cannot imagine to this day how people came to like it so much. That I cannot write English is such a patent fact that I never had even the vanity to feel ashamed of it. If anybody wrote an English note asking me to tea, I did not feel equal to answering it. Perhaps you think that by now I have got over that delusion. By no means. That I have written in English seems to be the delusion. On the day I was to board the ship, I fainted due to my frantic efforts at leave-taking and the

[1] His son's account of this ill-fated voyage is worth quoting: 'The evening before the boat sailed there was a party at Sir Ashutosh Chaudhuri's palatial residence, where a performance of father's operatic play, *Balmiki Pratibha*, was given . . . Father, of course, had to be present. We came back late at night. Instead of going to bed father sat down to write letters for the remainder of the night. In the early hours of the morning we found him to our dismay on the verge of collapse. Doctors had to be hurriedly summoned. All our luggage had been sent on to the boat the previous evening. A big crowd of friends had gathered at the Chandpal Ghat jetty to see him off. Their surprise could well be imagined when the boat left with our belongings but the owners were not to be seen.' *On the Edges of Time*, Rathindranath Tagore. Orient Longmans, India.

[2] What follows is an excerpt from his letter dated 6 May 1913, London, addressed to his niece, Indira Devi. The original letter was in Bengali. The translation quoted above is by Indira Devi and was published in *Indian Literature*, Volume II, Number 1. Sahitya Akademi, New Delhi.

journey itself was postponed. Then I went to Shelidah to take rest. But unless the brain is fully active, one does not feel strong enough to relax completely; so the only way to keep myself calm was to take up some light work.

'It was then the month of Chaitra (March-April), the air was thick with the fragrance of mango-blossoms and all hours of the day were delirious with the song of birds. When a child is full of vigour, he does not think of his mother. It is only when he is tired that he wants to nestle in her lap. That was exactly my position. With all my heart and with all my holiday I seemed to have settled comfortably in the arms of Chaitra, without missing a particle of its light, its air, its scent and its song. In such a state one cannot remain idle. It is an old habit of mine, as you know, that when the air strikes my bones, they tend to respond in music. Yet I had not the energy to sit down and write anything new. So I took up the poems of *Gitanjali* and set myself to translate them one by one. You may wonder why such a crazy ambition should possess one in such a weak state of health. But believe me, I did not undertake this task in a spirit of reckless bravado. I simply felt an urge to recapture through the medium of another language the feelings and sentiments which had created such a feast of joy within me in the days gone by.

'The pages of a small exercise-book came to be filled gradually, and with it in my pocket I boarded the ship. The idea of keeping it in my pocket was that when my mind became restless on the high seas, I would recline on a deck-chair and set myself to translate one or two poems from time to time. And that is what actually happened. From one exercise-book I passed on to another. Rothenstein already had an inkling of my reputation as a poet from another Indian friend. Therefore, when in the course of conversation he expressed a desire to see some of my poems, I handed him my manuscript with some diffidence. I could hardly believe the opinion he expressed after going through it. He then made over the manuscript to Yeats. The story of what followed is known to you. From this explanation of mine you will see that I was not responsible for the offence, which was due mainly to the force of circumstances.'

This authentic account of how the English *Gitanjali* came to be

o

written needs only one minor correction. It would not be correct to say that he wrote nothing new during this period of convalescence. In fact, he wrote several songs which were later published as *Gitimalya* (Garland of Songs) and of which seventeen were included in translation in English *Gitanjali*. In some of these songs, untranslated, the poet's disappointment at the abortive voyage and his restlessness find vivid expression.

'Within my mind I sit and gaze at the far-away, steady-eyed . . . Overhead in the sky the swans fly in formation towards their strange home in a foreign land . . . I sit on the bank idling away the hours waiting for the ferry which fails to turn up . . . Above the yonder mansion in the west the half-moon is dreaming and within my mind I hear the call of a flute from far away.' Again, 'Now is the time to set the boat afloat on the waters. Ah me, the weariness of waiting on the bank is intolerable . . .' He rebukes himself for this impatience. 'It is only when I give up the helm that Thou wilt take it over. What is to be will be. Why this futile grabbing?' In the meanwhile he will sing songs to his Lord. 'Now that all tumult is banned, let us whisper to each other, Thou and I. Let the heart murmur its secret in song.'[3] The very first poem of the English *Gitanjali* is from this collection: 'Thou hast made me endless, such is thy pleasure. This frail vessel thou emptiest again and again, and fillest it ever with fresh life.' So too the parting words in the poem No. 93: 'I have got my leave. Bid me farewell, my brothers. I bow to you all and take my departure.'

At last the convalescence was over and Rabindranath was well enough to risk a voyage. After spending a few days in Santiniketan he sailed for London from Bombay on 27 May 1912 accompanied by his son Rathindranath and the latter's wife, Pratima. Fortunately the voyage was calm and he had enough rest and leisure to continue his translations of *Gitanjali* songs.[4] In London the party put up in a

[3] The author's own English rendering is somewhat different and less literal. See English *Gitanjali*, No. 89. The colloquial Bengali word used for 'whisper' is far more pictorial and expressive: *Kanè Kanè*. Literally, from ear to ear.

[4] The only amusing interludes being provided (as described by Rathindranath) by a young Santiniketan boy on his way to Harvard for higher studies, who shocked everyone by his unconventional ways, particularly by his habit of walking on the deck bare-footed, and by a lady-passenger who was caught helping herself to mangoes

Bloomsbury hotel. A minor mishap, recalled by his son, might have changed the course of events. He was carrying his father's brief-case which contained among other papers the manuscript of the English *Gitanjali*. While travelling in the Underground from Charing Cross to Bloomsbury, he left behind the brief-case in the compartment and realized his mistake on the following morning when his father asked for it. Fortunately the brief-case was recovered at the Lost Property Office.

It was the English painter Sir William Rothenstein who served as midwife to the the birth of Tagore's fame in Europe. Rothenstein had visited India in 1910 and had come to know the artist-brothers Abanindranath and Gaganendranath well during his stay in Calcutta. He had already heard of them in Banaras from Sir John Woodroffe and Sir Harry Stephen. The fact that neither of these two distinguished Englishmen who knew India well had mentioned anything to him about Rabindranath shows how little the poet was known in his own country outside the strictly limited literary circle of Bengal. 'I was attracted, each time I went to Jorasanko,' writes Rothenstein,[5] 'by their uncle, a strikingly handsome figure, dressed in a white *dhoti* and *chadur*, who sat silently listening as we talked. I felt an immediate attraction, and asked whether I might draw him, for I discovered an inner charm as well as great physical beauty, which I tried to set down with my pencil. That this uncle was one of the remarkable men of his time no one gave me a hint.'

A little later, on his return to London, Rothenstein came across, in the pages of the *Modern Review*, the English translation of one of Tagore's short stories which impressed him. He wrote to his friends in Calcutta inquiring if any more such translations were available. In response he received a few translations of poems done by Ajit Chakravarty, a colleague of Tagore's on the staff of the Santiniketan school. 'The poems, of a highly mystical character, struck me as being still more remarkable than the story, though but rough

---

in Tagore's cabin while he was asleep. 'Knowing that father was fond of mangoes, we had brought a basket of Alfonsoes and these were kept in his cabin. The delicious smell coming out of the open door must have proved too tempting for the lady.'

[5] *Men and Memories* (1900-1922), by William Rothenstein. Faber & Faber, Ltd. London.

translations. Meanwhile I met one of the Kooch Behar family, Promotto Loll Sen, a saintly man and a Brahmo of course. He brought to our house Dr. Brajendranath Seal, then on a visit to London, a philosopher with a brilliant mind and a childlike character. They both wrote to Tagore, urging him to come to London; he would meet, they said, at our house and elsewhere, men after his heart.'

And so when Tagore came to London where he hardly knew anyone else, almost the first thing he did was to call upon Rothenstein and, knowing his interest in his poems, gave him the notebook in which he had scribbled his translations. 'That evening,' writes Rothenstein, 'I read the poems. Here was poetry of a new order, which seemed to me on a level with that of the great mystics. Andrew Bradley, to whom I showed them, agreed: "It looks as though we have at last a great poet among us again," he wrote. I sent word to Yeats, who failed to reply; but when I wrote again he asked me to send him the poems, and when he had read them his enthusiasm equalled mine. He came to London and went carefully through the poems, making here and there a suggestion, but leaving the original little changed.'

What Yeats felt about these poems he has himself recorded in the beautiful introduction he wrote for the first limited edition of *Gitanjali* published by the India Society of London on November 1 of the same year. 'I have carried the manuscript of these translations about with me for days,' he wrote, 'reading it in railway trains, or on the top of omnibuses and in restaurants, and I have often had to close it lest some stranger would see how much it moved me. These lyrics—which are in the original, my Indians tell me, full of subtlety of rhythm, of untranslatable delicacies of colour, of metrical invention—display in their thought a world I have dreamed of all my life long. The work of a supreme culture, they yet appear as much the growth of the common soil as the grass and the rushes.'

Yeats's appreciation of these poems encouraged Rothenstein to call a few friends to his Hampstead house on the evening of 30 June when Yeats read out the poems in 'his musical ecstatic voice' to a choice gathering which included Ezra Pound, May Sinclair, Ernest Rhys, Alice Meynell, Henry Nevinson, Charles Trevelyan, Fox-

Strangways and others. It was at this gathering that Tagore first met Charles Freer Andrews who became his lifelong friend and associate. Andrews, who was at that time a missionary attached to the Cambridge Brotherhood,[6] has left his own record of that memorable evening: 'I walked back along the side of Hampstead Heath with H. W. Nevinson but spoke very little. I wanted to be alone and think in silence of the wonder and glory of it all. When I had left Nevinson I went across the Heath. The night was cloudless and there was something of the purple of the Indian atmosphere about the sky. There all alone I could think of the wonder of it:

On the seashore of endless worlds children meet.
On the seashore of endless worlds is the great meeting of children.

It was the haunting, haunting melody of the English, so simple, like all the beautiful sounds of my childhood, that carried me completely away. I remained out under the sky far into the night, almost till dawn was breaking.'

May Sinclair wrote in a letter to Rabindranath: 'May I say now that as long as I live, even if I were never to hear them again, I shall never forget the impression that they made. It is not only that they have an absolute beauty, a perfection as poetry, but that they have made present for me forever the divine thing that I can only find by flashes and with an agonizing uncertainty . . . You have put into English which is absolutely transparent in its perfection things it is despaired of ever seeing written in English at all or in any Western language.'

Tagore, however, was not in England when *Gitanjali* was published. Though his stay in England during this visit was not long—a little over four months—it was very hectic and fruitful, thanks to Rothenstein and the warm affection he received from his other British acquaintances and friends. It was almost as if in anticipation of this that he had written in *Gitanjali*, 'Thou hast made me

[6] Later he resigned from the Brotherhood, though he continued to live the dedicated life of a missionary, albeit free-lance, all his life. He was also closely associated with Mahatma Gandhi and had many admirers in India who interpreted the initials of his name, C.F.A., as Christ's Faithful Apostle.

known to friends whom I knew not. Thou hast given me seats in homes not my own. Thou hast brought the distant near and made a brother of the stranger.' Among other celebrities, he met Bernard Shaw, H. G. Wells, Bertrand Russell, John Galsworthy, Robert Bridges, John Masefield, Sturge Moore, W. H. Hudson (whose books he had greatly admired) and Stopford Brooke. 'Tagore's dignity and handsome presence,' wrote Rothenstein, 'the ease of his manners and his quiet wisdom made a marked impression on all who met him.' He himself was much struck by '. . . the breadth of view and the rapidity of thought that he found among his new friends', and said, 'Those who know the English only in India do not know Englishmen.'

When he met Bertrand Russell the latter abruptly asked him, without any preliminary small talk, 'Tagore, what is Beauty?' 'The question came so suddenly,' writes Tagore's son who was present, 'that father kept silent for a minute and then explained his ideas on aesthetics which he later developed in "What is art?" in his book *Creative Unity*. I could not judge whether father's exposition satisfied Bertrand Russell because after listening with rapt attention he left just as suddenly as he had come.' They met again in Cambridge when it was the British philosopher's turn to talk. Lowes Dickinson has described the meeting: 'It is a June evening, in a Cambridge garden. Mr. Bertrand Russell and myself sit there alone with Tagore. He sings to us some of his poems, the beautiful voice and the strange mode floating away on the gathering darkness. Then Russell begins to talk, coruscating like lightning in the dusk. Tagore falls into silence. But afterwards he said, it had been wonderful to hear Russell talk.'

His first meeting with Bernard Shaw is worth recounting as recalled by Rothenstein: 'But they [Shaw and Tagore] did meet, though I was away when the Shaws came to dinner. My wife told me that Shaw was rather outrageous, while his wife was all admiration—"Old Blue-beard," said Shaw to mine while he was leaving, "how many wives has he got, I wonder!" Nearly twenty years later, at a reception given to Tagore by Evelyn Wrench and Yeats-Brown, the two met again, now white-headed and white-bearded, and sat and talked together, two noble-looking elders.'

Rothenstein proposed to the India Society that they should print, for its members, a selection of Tagore's poems for which Yeats agreed to write an introduction. It was thus that *Gitanjali* was first published in English in a limited edition of 750 copies only. Later on, Rothenstein persuaded George Macmillan to publish a popular edition. This was before the award of the Nobel Prize when some persuasion was necessary to make the publishers undertake the risk of publishing the work of an unknown Indian. 'Macmillans, after some hesitation, finally published all Tagore's books, to his profit and their own.' There were many critics, both in Great Britain and in India, who found it hard to believe that Tagore who had not published anything in English before could write so well in that language and attributed the success of *Gitanjali* to Yeats having drastically revised or rewritten the poems. This impression is still current in some quarters and it is therefore desirable to quote what Rothenstein had to say about it, since he should have known better than anyone else, for he had not only read the original manuscript before sending it to Yeats but the final manuscript as it emerged from Yeats's hands was with him and should still be in his family. 'I know that it was said in India that the success of *Gitanjali* was largely owing to Yeats's rewriting of Tagore's English. That this is false can easily be proved. The original manuscript of *Gitanjali* in English and in Bengali is in my possession. Yeats did here and there suggest slight changes, but the main text was printed as it came from Tagore's hands.'

In October 1912, Rabindranath sailed for the United States, accompanied by his son and daughter-in-law. The son who had earlier graduated from the University of Illinois persuaded the father to spend some quiet months at Urbana, hoping to take this opportunity of completing his own thesis for the doctorate. A house was rented not far from the College where the family settled down for the winter. It was here that Tagore wrote his first original serious prose in English, later delivered as Lectures at Harvard University and published as *Sadhana* (Realization of Life).[7] In these lectures he

[7] Parts of these lectures were first delivered as talks at various Unitarian chapels under the auspices of the Unity Club. This book, *Sadhana*, was dedicated to Ernest Rhys, as *Gitanjali* was dedicated to William Rothenstein.

interprets, in his own fashion, 'the ancient spirit of India', as revealed in the utterance and example of her sages. Profound and beautiful as these lectures are, one wonders what made him dole out this characteristically Tagorean blend of philosophy, poetry and sermonizing to his American audience. As it was, he not only failed to find an adequate response in a continent known for its generous responses, but was actually misunderstood. The average American who had read his people's history as an uninterrupted march of prosperity and 'progress' and who naïvely imagined that if there was any 'happiness' it was to be found in his land, resented being told the meaning of 'joy' by a foreigner coming from an unhappy and joyless land. Here is an instance of this typical reaction voiced by an American paper (*News*, Newark, N.Y.), some time later.[8]

'Did Mr. Tagore ever stop to join a crowd which was watching men hoist a safe or put in a plate-glass window? If he did or mingled with a thoughtful group observing a total stranger search for engine trouble in his car, he was in the midst of happy men. It is hard in fact to imagine where Mr. Tagore got his wrong ideas about us. He obviously never saw the happy smiling faces of American throngs making their way workward and homeward with their eyes full of the elbows of people they never met before. He cannot have looked in on the United States Senate while a merry filibuster was on. Where indeed has Mr. Tagore been? The inevitable conclusion is he has been attending banquets ever since he came to America, listening to toastmasters and after-dinner speakers.'[9]

[8] For this and several other quotations from foreign journals, I am indebted to Dr. A. Aronson's book, *Rabindranath Through Western Eyes* (Kitabistan, Allahabad, 1943). This study is a painstaking but rather partial analysis of the reactions in the foreign press to Tagore's sudden rise to fame and his later journeys to the West. It is a pity that no comprehensive and adequate study has been made of this vast and unexplored field.

[9] On the other hand, the distinguished Czech savant V. Lesny saw much wisdom in these essays. 'These opinions, which are by no means a new philosophy or a thoroughly worked-out system, contain no puritan homilectics. Tagore, who is unshakable in his faith in man, wishes to oppose the world-wide opinion that man is essentially sinful and must be saved by God's grace, and to emphasize that there is a divinity in man and that this is man's glory. With *Sadhana* the poet benefited Hinduism also. Not only did he make it widely known in the world, but he also pointed out to conservative circles in India how to infuse new life into Hinduism.'

It was while he was in Illinois that the India Society edition of
Gitanjali was published in London in November 1912. The book
was on the whole well received in the British press. The *Times
Literary Supplement* wrote: '. . . and in reading these poems one feels,
not that they are the curiosities of an alien mind, but that they are
prophetic of the poetry that might be written in England if our
poets could attain to the same harmony of emotion and idea. That
divorce of religion and philosophy which prevails among us is a
sign of our failure in both. . . As we read his pieces we seem to be
reading the Psalms of a David of our own time. . . Some perhaps
will refuse to fall under the spell of this Indian poet because this
philosophy is not theirs. If it seems to us fantastic and alien, before
we despise it we should ask ourselves the question: What is our
philosophy? We are very restless in thought, but we have none that
poets can express.'

Indeed, critics were not wanting who refused 'to fall under the
spell of this Indian poet'. One of them wrote in *New Age*, London,
'any of us could write such stuff *ad libitum*; but nobody should be
deceived into thinking it good English, good poetry, good sense,
or good ethics'. Some critics patted themselves on the back that the
British had civilized the Indians so well that the latter could write
such good stuff. 'The chief significance of Mr. Tagore's triumph,'
wrote a critic in the *Birmingham Post*, 'is that it marks the culmination
of the development of an offshoot of English literature, the importance of which has not been sufficiently recognized.'[10] The general
reception of *Gitanjali* in the British press was, however, over-
whelmingly favourable and the author was naturally pleased about

---

The following paragraph from a letter written by Tagore, on 24 January 1918, to
his American publisher, Mr. George P. Brett, the Macmillan Co., New York, is of
interest in this connexion: 'It has given me great pleasure to learn the opinion of Mrs.
Winston Churchill about my book *Sadhana*. It is the best reward for an author to
know that his writings have a value for his readers not merely because of their
literary merits, but because they are helpful for the more intimate purposes of life.'

[10] I am reminded of what an Indian friend who was a student in Cambridge before
the last war reported to me. His kindly old professor had invited him to dinner at
his house. When the batter-pudding was served at the end, the professor asked him
if in India they had a sweet of the same kind. When my friend replied in the affirmative, the professor remarked, 'I didn't know we had introduced that too.'

it. Writing to Rothenstein from Urbana, 19 November, he said,
'I am so glad to learn from your letter that my book has been
favourably criticized in the *Times Literary Supplement*. I hope the
paper has been forwarded to me and I shall see it in a day or two.
My happiness is all the more great because I know such appreciation
will bring joy to your heart. In fact, I feel that the success of my
book is your own success. But for your assurance I never could have
dreamt that my translations were worth anything, and up to the
last moment I was fearful lest you should be mistaken in your
estimation of them and all the pains you have taken over them
should be thrown away. I am extremely glad that your choice has
been vindicated and you will have the right to take pride in your
friend, supported by the best judges in your literature.' And yet, as
the author of *Rabindranath Through Western Eyes* has pointed out, the
latest edition of *Who's Who* of December 1913, that is, after the
award of the Nobel Prize, did not include Tagore's name, and as
late as 1916 the *Cambridge History of English Literature*, Volume XIV,
did not even refer to him in its article on Anglo-Indian literature.

Nor need one be shocked at it, much less make a grievance of it,
for in his own country, outside the small Bengali reading public,
Tagore was hardly better or even as well known. And even among
his own people in Bengal, he had had worse detractors. His countryman Basanta Kumar Roy, who was then living in the United
States and who later published his biography in that country,[11]
tells us that several young Bengalis in the United States were furious
when they read the following statement by an English missionary
published in an English review: 'For many centuries no such poet
and musician has appeared in India.' Though today such a statement
might not be contradicted in India, at that time, it needed a brave
man to say so. One of the Bengalis (referred to by Basanta Kumar
Roy) '. . . shouted in true American fashion, "D—n it." ' Others
cited many other Bengali poets, among them Nabin Sen and D. L.
Roy, as much greater than Tagore. 'His love lyrics,' they went on
to say, 'are poor imitations of the poems of our Vaishnava poets of
old, and his philosophy is the philosophy of the *Upanishads*. Let

[11] *Rabindranath Tagore: The Man and His Poetry*. New York, Dodd, Mead &
Co., 1916.

the Europeans and the Americans rave over Tagore. But there is
nothing new for us in his writings.' Considering the grudging
appreciation Tagore received from his own people, what is surprising
is not that several critics and circles in the West ignored him or
judged him wrongly, but that so many recognized his stature
immediately and gave such ungrudging praise.

At any rate Tagore's name was sufficiently bandied about in the
English papers after the publication of his book for its reputation to
have crossed the Atlantic. Although the ordinary American citizen
was hardly aware of his obscure existence in Urbana, invitations
from academic and other circles began to pour in, and Harriet
Monroe published six poems of *Gitanjali* in the December issue of
the Chicago magazine *Poetry*, perhaps the first journal in the West
to publish his poems. This was followed by an invitation from the
University of Chicago for a lecture. It was while Tagore was still in
Urbana that Basanta Kumar Roy came to visit him and asked him
how he liked America and its people. Tagore praised the country
and its climate—he had enough of both space and sunshine which
he missed in England—and expressed his admiration of the people's
drive and efficiency, 'unrivalled businessmen, splendid organizers
and agriculturists, and matchless engineers', adding that he, however,
wished he saw more evidence of people's interest in culture, 'even
though agriculture suffered a little'. Roy reminded him that staying
in that small provincial town he had hardly had any opportunities
of meeting many cultured people who in any case were scattered all
over that vast continent and 'not focused in one place as in Paris,
Berlin or London'. Roy said that he had come to persuade Tagore
to translate more of his works into English, for he felt certain that
when his writings became known, 'You will sooner or later win the
Nobel Prize for Poetry. No other man in India or Asia has won that
laurel.' Naïvely Tagore inquired, 'Are the Asiatics eligible for the
Prize?'

Perhaps the doubt was not so naïve after all, for when the Prize
did come, there were rumblings of protest in many quarters of the
West that an Asian had received it. 'The awarding of the Nobel
Prize for literature,' wrote an American paper, 'to a Hindu has
occasioned much chagrin and no little surprise among writers of

the Caucasian race. They cannot understand why this distinction was bestowed upon one who is not white.'[12] The *Globe* of Toronto, Canada, wrote: 'It is the first time that the Nobel Prize has gone to anyone who is not what we call "white". It will take time, of course, for us to accommodate ourselves to the idea that anyone called Rabindranath Tagore should receive a world prize for literature. (Have we not been told that the East and the West shall never meet?) The name has a curious sound. The first time we saw it in print it did not seem real.' The *Times*, Los Angeles, complained that young modern writers in Europe and America had been discouraged by the award of the Prize '. . . to a Hindu poet whose name few people can pronounce, with whose work fewer in America are familiar, and whose claim for that high distinction still fewer will recognize'.[13]

In January 1913 Rabindranath came to Chicago where he stayed as the guest of Mrs. William Vaughan Moody. 'This contact,' writes his son, 'led to a much cherished friendship lasting until the death of this remarkable woman, whose house was the refuge of many would-be artists and writers and a great attraction to all persons of eminence visiting the United States.' After lecturing on the 'Ideals of the Ancient Civilization of India' at the University of Chicago and on 'The Problem of Evil' at the Unitarian Hall, Tagore went to Rochester to attend the Congress of Religious Liberals where he spoke on 'Race Conflict'. Here he met the German philosopher Rudolph Eücken who had come from Germany for the Conference and who had become a warm admirer of *Gitanjali*. From Rochester Tagore went to Boston where he delivered the series of lectures on the ideals of ancient India, later published as *Sadhana*. In these lectures he pointed out that while '. . . the West seems to take a pride in thinking that it is subduing nature, as if we are living in a hostile world where we have to wrest everything we want from an unwilling and alien arrangement of things . . . India put all her

[12] *Rabindranath Through Western Eyes*, by A. Aronson, p. 4.
[13] I have no doubt that several other papers in the United States reacted differently and welcomed the award generously. Unfortunately, no serious analysis has been made of the press reactions in different countries based on adequate and comprehensive study.

emphasis on the harmony that exists between the individual and the universal'.

After visiting New York Tagore returned to London in April 1913 where he delivered a course of lectures at the Caxton Hall. When he had arrived in London a year earlier, he was an unknown stranger. Now he had become a sensation and a curiosity. His play *The Post Office* was staged and three more volumes of translations were published before the year was over: *The Gardener*[14] which he dedicated to W. B. Yeats, *The Crescent Moon*, dedicated to Sturge Moore, and the play *Chitra*, dedicated to Mrs. Vaughan Moody. None of these books can be considered particularly religious or philosophical and might have been expected to give his foreign readers a better perspective to his work. But the first impressions are always more vivid and lasting and Tagore would henceforth continue to be regarded as primarily a religious poet and a philosopher. His own biblical personality and august mien and his insistent harping on the ideals of the ancient forest-sages helped to confirm the one-sided impression. Ezra Pound who saw him as one poet sees another tried to correct the distortion but his was a lone voice. Reviewing *The Gardener* in the *Freewoman*, he wrote: 'Why the good people of this island are unable to honour a fine artist as such; why they are incapable, or apparently incapable, of devising for his honour any better device than that of wrapping his life in cotton wool and parading about with the effigy of a sanctimonious moralist, remains and will remain for me an unsolvable mystery. I think what I am trying to say about these poems is that one must read each poem as a whole and then re-conceive it as a song, of which you have half forgotten the chords. You must see them not as you see stars on a flag, but as you have seen stars in the heaven.'

Rothenstein too had sensed the danger, for he records in his memoirs: 'It was pleasant to see homage paid so readily to an Indian; nothing of the kind had happened before. I was concerned only lest Tagore's saintly looks, and the mystical element in his poetry, should attract the *schwärmerie* of the sentimentalists who abound in England and America, and who pursue idealists even more

---

[14] There is no Bengali book of his of that name. Selections from several volumes of verse are included in it. Similarly with *The Crescent Moon*.

hungrily than ideals. Tagore had, indeed, all the qualities to attract such.' The danger became more real after the award of the Nobel Prize and the glare of publicity it focused on him. Till then his reputation was more or less confined to literary and academic circles and had to encounter considerable resistance and apathy even there. To quote Rothenstein again: 'Fox-Strangways wanted Oxford or Cambridge to give Tagore an honorary degree. Lord Curzon, when consulted, said that there were more distinguished men in India than Tagore. I wonder who they were; and I regretted that England had left it to a foreign country to make the first emphatic acknowledgement of his contribution to literature.'

And yet England had paved the way for that 'emphatic acknowledgement' and the Nobel Prize Committee in Sweden could hardly have taken notice of Tagore if his English admirers had not rated his poetry so high. Indeed, the first formal proposal of Tagore's name for the Prize was made by Sturge Moore.[15] England also helped Tagore to recover his health which had broken down under the stress of the strenuous years in India. In July 1913 he was admitted to a nursing home in London for a surgical operation which was successful. In September Tagore sailed from London for his home in India, having achieved both fame and health. 'Before Tagore left for India,' writes Rothenstein, 'Yeats and I arranged a small dinner in his honour. After dinner we asked Tagore to sing *Bande Mataram*,[16] the nationalist song. He hummed the tune but after the first few words broke down; he could not remember the rest. Then Yeats began the Irish anthem—and his memory, again, was at fault; and Ernest Rhys could not for the life of him recollect the words of the Welsh national anthem. "What a crew!" I said, when I too stumbled over *God Save the King*.'

It was while Tagore was in Santiniketan that the news came, on

[15] During my visit to Stockholm in July 1959 (made possible by a Rockefeller grant) the courtesy of the Curator of the Royal Library enabled me to see the original file in which Sturge Moore's letter is recorded. The letter reads as follows: Sir, As a Fellow of the Royal Society of Literature of the United Kingdom, I have the honour to propose the name of Rabindra Nath Tagore as a person well qualified, in my opinion, to be awarded the Nobel Prize in Literature. T. Sturge Moore.

[16] Perhaps the most popular nationalist song in India. Its words were written by Tagore's predecessor, the famous novelist Bankim Chandra Chatterjee. The tune which gave it currency as a song was Tagore's contribution.

13 November, of the award of the Nobel Prize to him for his *Gitanjali*. The news was received with no small surprise and much rejoicing all over the country. In the little asrama at Santiniketan the children, who hardly knew what the Nobel Prize was but understood that their beloved teacher had been honoured by the world, went wild with joy. What did the poet himself feel? No doubt, he felt elated and proud and happy—and above all, justified. He would not have been human if he felt otherwise. The patriot in him felt happy, too, that his country's name had been put on the world's literary map and felt proud that he was the reason of it. But the poet in him was far too sensitive not to feel a misgiving, that his days of peace, of quiet and uninterrupted pursuit of his vocation as a poet and as a teacher of little children, of intimate *tête-à-têtes* with his God, were over.

Five days later later he wrote to Rothenstein: 'The very first moment I received the message of the great honour conferred on me by the award of the Nobel Prize my heart turned towards you with love and gratitude, I felt certain that of all my friends none would be more glad at this news than you. Honour's crown of honours is to know that it will rejoice the hearts of those whom we hold most dear. But, all the same, it is a very great trial for me. The perfect whirlwind of public excitement it has given rise to is frightful. It is almost as bad as tying a tin can at a dog's tail making it impossible for him to move without creating noise and collecting crowds all along. I am being smothered with telegrams and letters for the last few days and the people who never had any friendly feelings towards me nor ever read a line of my works are loudest in their protestations of joy. I cannot tell you how tired I am of all this shouting, the stupendous amount of its unreality being something appalling. Really these people honour the honour in me and not myself.'

The thought rankled in his mind and the patriot found it humiliating that the majority of his countrymen had needed the stimulus of foreign recognition to turn their grudging appreciation of his service to their language and literature into adulation. This sad and bitter thought found public expression on 23 November when a large deputation of 500 distinguished citizens of Calcutta representing diverse professions and interests came by a special train to

Santiniketan to offer him the nation's felicitations. In blunt but poetic words the poet told them that he could not accept a homage that was so unreal. Those among his audience who had always been his warm admirers understood for whom the snub was meant; the rest, thus deflated, never forgave him for what they considered his 'inhospitable reply'. How right Tagore was in his estimate of these people's capacity to understand him was immediately proved by a violent spate of attacks on him in the Calcutta press for his ungracious sin of calling a spade a spade. However, it brought him the unexpected support of a leading patriot-politician of the day, Bipin Chandra Pal, who wrote in his paper, *Hindu Review*: 'No man of Rabindranath's position and sensibilities could have been less bitter under similar circumstances . . . the rebuke of his reply was neither undeserved nor undignified.'

Though the Prize was awarded on the merits of an individual work whose poetic excellence and high idealism were almost universally acknowledged, the fact that it was given to an Asian invested the award with a significance which such awards do not normally have and made it look almost like a unique phenomenon. It was received everywhere with a shock of surprise and turned Rabindranath from an individual into a symbol—a symbol of the West's recognition of Asia's neglected humanity and its potential resurgence. Tagore was the first to impress vividly on the intellectual consciousness of the West the fact—now amply demonstrated—that the 'mind' of Asia was living and would have to be reckoned with as a vital entity and not merely as an interesting specimen in a museum. 'That the very name of a poet,' wrote a French writer a little later,[17] 'who in his country enjoyed such a reputation should have been almost ignored by the whole of Europe until these last few years, goes to prove the limits of human glory. It also proves the narrowness of our civilization and points out—whatever one may say—its provincialism . . . The knowledge that these ideals are different from ours, at least makes us aware of the relativity of our European concepts. We do not sufficiently realize that millions of human beings are fed on different ideals from ours, and yet live.'

[17] Jean Guehenon in *La Revue de Paris*. See Aronson's *Rabindranath Through Western Eyes*.

Two faces. Drawing by Tagore

Dear Gurudev,

This is early morning 3 o'clock of Tuesd. I enter the fiery gate at noon. If you can bless the effort, I want it. You have been to me a true friend because you have been a candid friend often speaking your thoughts aloud. I had looked forward to a firm opinion from you one way or the other. But you have refused to criticise. Though it can now only be during my fast, I will yet prize your criticism, if your heart condemns my action. I am not too proud to make an open confession of my blunder, whatever the cost of the confession, if I find myself in error. If your heart approves of the action I want your blessing. It will sustain me. I hope I have made myself clear.

Y.C.P. 20 9/32.

my love

mkgandhi

8.5.

Visva-Bharati, Santinikete

Mahatma Gandhi's letter to Tagore, written before he began his fast on 20 September 193

Apart from this salutary reaction there were certain other rather amusing reactions which also may illustrate in a different fashion 'the relativity of our European concepts'. These were, needless to say, confined to less imaginative and 'patriotic' elements in the different countries. The *Birmingham Post*, proud of its imperial consciousness, rejoiced that 'Indian-English poetry cannot well be ignored henceforward seeing that two of its representatives have been the only English authors who have won the annual Nobel Prize for literature'. Strange bed-fellows, Kipling and Tagore![18] The *Irish Citizen* hailed it as a vindication of the Irish literary movement. 'These poems [referring to *The Gardener*] take their place, without question, not far from the summit of "English literature".' They are, perhaps, the forerunners (in conjunction with the poems of W. B. Yeats and Æ) of the greatest movement in European Literature yet experienced—its coming emergence from the low levels of "realism" and intellectualism merely, to the plane of its true voice as the exponent of a divine humanity.'

Devout and hopeful Christians saw in Tagore's poems the promise of a coming dawn. 'We have been waiting anxiously,' wrote the *Baptist Times*, 'for some indication of the effect of Christian ideas on a truly representative Hindu mind. Here, surely, is the person we have been longing for—one sent before the chariot of the Lord to make His path straight. And when we remember that this poet's every word is eagerly caught up by waiting millions, may we not venture to assert that the new, the Christian, India is already at the door?' It needed the courage and clarity of mind of a Dean Inge to remind his co-religionists that 'Tagore is not a Christian; but his attitude reminds us that there was a time when Christianity was an Asiatic creed—it was the time of the original Gospel. Again and again he seemed to be more Christian than the Christians.' Then there were, as always, the usual clever people who believe they can see through everything. Some of them saw in the award the

[18] One wonders if the humour and the irony of this struck any contemporary cartoonist. It must also be said in fairness to the English poet that his famous line that 'Never the twain shall meet' has been made notorious by being torn out of context. For the poet goes on to say that when two brave men meet, coming from opposite ends of the earth, all differences are wiped away—'There is neither East nor West, border nor breed nor birth.'

ingenious British hand trying to boost the glory of the Empire; others fancied that the Swedish literary circles, being pro-German, had deliberately tried to embarrass the British ruling classes. There is no end to human cleverness.

The actual fact, however, was simple and innocuous enough and has been authentically recalled by the distinguished Swedish Academician Anders Österling:[19] 'T. Sturge Moore, an English author and a member of the Royal Society, had submitted his [Tagore's] name for consideration for the prize. The minutes of the Selection Committee show that this proposal came as an interesting surprise for the Swedish Academy. It is true that Harald Hjarne, the then Chairman of the Committee, was unwilling to commit himself and expressed the opinion that it must be difficult to decide how much in Tagore's enchanting poetry was his own personal creation and how much must be attributed to the classical traditions of Indian literature. Therefore the Committee gave serious consideration in the first place to another author who had been proposed, Emile Faguet, the French literary historian and moralist.

'However, Tagore's candidature had gained enthusiastic supporters within the Academy. One of them was Per Hallström, whose fine essays show that his newly-awakened admiration led to penetrating study. The happy outcome of the debate was without doubt largely due to a written contribution made by Verner von Heidenstam, who was himself awarded the Nobel Prize three years later. Writing of Gitanjali, which Tagore himself had presented in English and which Heidenstam had also learnt to know in a Swedish-Norwegian translator's rather inadequate rendering, he said, "I was deeply moved when I read them and I do not remember having read any lyric writing to equal them during the past twenty years or more. They gave me hours of intense enjoyment, it was like drinking the water of a fresh, clear spring. The intense and loving piety that permeates his every thought and feeling, the purity of heart, the noble and natural sublimity of his style, all combine to create a whole that has a deep and rare spiritual beauty. There is nothing in his work that is controversial and offensive, nothing vain, worldly and petty,

[19] In an article contributed to the Tagore Centenary Volume published by the Sahitya Akademi, India.

and if ever a poet may be said to possess the qualities that make him entitled to a Nobel Prize, it is he . . . Now that we have finally found an ideal poet of really great stature, we should not pass him over. For the first time and perhaps for the last for a long time to come, it would be vouchsafed us to discover a great name before it has appeared in all the newspapers. If this is to be achieved, however, we must not tarry and miss the opportunity by waiting till another year." '

No two regions could be more different from one another than the tropical lowlands of Bengal and the snow-capped highlands of Scandinavia, in physical climate and social environment. The fact that, despite these vast differences, the poems written in the Ganges delta found a response in the heart of a Scandinavian as sensitive, sincere and deep as any in the hearts of Tagore's own countrymen is a vindication not only of the universal quality of *Gitanjali* poems but of Tagore's almost fanatic faith that a single heart beats in the breast of mankind, despite the barriers built by patriots, politicians and priests. No less profound was the impression made by these poems on a young and unknown lad of fifteen in an even more remote but no less remarkable region, who was to win much later a Nobel Prize for himself—the distinguished novelist, Halldór Laxness. Recalling this impression he writes,[20] 'This strange, distant and subtle voice at once found its way to the very depths of my youthful spiritual ear; and ever since, at given moments, I feel its presence in the innermost labyrinths of my mind. In my country as elsewhere among western readers the form and flavour of the *Gitanjali* had the effect of a wonderful flower we had not seen or heard of before; its great attraction was a direct stimulus for many poets to undertake new experiments in lyrical prose. Even as far as the Scandinavian countries there was a vogue in lyrical prose directly originating from the newly-acquired knowledge of Tagore. I, among others, tried my hand at this form in my youthful days, but without success, perhaps because I did not realize that *Gitanjali*'s form is entirely secondary to its substance. I guess this was the common reason why most of Tagore's disciples in the West were bound to fail. The physical foundation of Tagore's poetry, the

[20] *Ibid.*

tropical warmth and growth, was lacking in our environment to make this kind of poetry imitable here . . .

'What an enviable god, this god of Tagore: the Great Friend, the Beloved, the Lotus flower, the unknown man playing a lute in the boat yonder on the river! A god akin to Tagore's can be found in the Jewish biblical poetry belonging to the Mediterranean Basin; you meet him occasionally in the *Tao-teh-king* of China; but here in Europe He has hardly had a representative since the Middle Ages when medieval monks, like the author of *The Imitation of Christ*, were locking themselves up contemplating the mysteries in narrow cells and chapels—without open air and the fragrance of nature. Nowadays our god in the West is either the director of the Big All World Firm Inc., or the primitive imaginary playmate of the childish mind. He is the one we cry to in the hours of precipitate danger and in the hour of our death. This is why a spiritual reality like Tagore's probably shall remain only one more eastern wonder to the western mind yet for a long long time to come.'[1]

[1] Although Mr. Laxness has used the word 'Lute', it is no doubt wrong. No one plays a lute in India. The word used by Tagore is 'flute'.

IO

A WORLD CITIZEN

The best gift which Tagore brought back from his visit to England was not the great honours that were showered on him—for great honours are great burdens in the end—but the friendships he made with some of the finest minds of the West. They broadened his humanist sympathies which were already broad enough, and deepened his understanding of the intellectual and spiritual urges that have spurred the western mind to great achievement. Henceforth he was more a world-citizen than an Indian. He was a world-citizen not because he became world-famous but because he felt with the world. There have been many men world-famous who were world-scourges, and many who have failed to see beyond their noses. But Tagore made the world's destiny his own and felt the agony deeply if there was suffering or injustice in any part of the world. This world-consciousness which was very real in him exposed him to not a little misunderstanding in his own country.

Of his many foreign friends the two who came to be most closely associated with him and his work in Santiniketan at this time were the two remarkable Englishmen, Charles Freer Andrews and William Winstanley Pearson. Andrews's first meeting with Tagore on the evening when Yeats read out the *Gitanjali* poems has already been referred to in the last chapter. Pearson was already in India then. He came from an old Huguenot family, with its firm tradition of Christian piety and independence of spirit. He had studied philosophy at Oxford and botany at Cambridge and had come to India as part of a British missionary educational enterprise. But being more Christian than missionary both he and Andrews broke away from their organizations in order to be free to serve the people in the spirit of Christ as they understood it. As Andrews put it, Tagore revealed to him '. . . an inner vision of beauty that I saw with the eye of the spirit. It went far beyond the bounds of this temporal and material world . . . He broke through the dull routine of outward form that had imprisoned me up to that time, and thus set me free.' Through Andrews his friend Pearson also came to know of Tagore and the school at Santiniketan, with its atmosphere of freedom and reverence for life.[1] Both of them became Tagore's associates and lifelong friends.

Gandhi, not then a Mahatma and, in fact, hardly known even in his own country, was at that time engaged in his lone and heroic struggle against racial discrimination in South Africa. He had launched his first great experiment in non-violent mass civil disobedience. Tagore who had anticipated, with the true insight of a poet-seer, the advent of the Mahatma in his dramas and verse, was already with him in spirit, and when Andrews and Pearson left Santiniketan, on 30 November 1913 for South Africa to study the Passive Resistance movement on the spot, they carried with them his best wishes to Gandhi for the success of his mission. 'Let me dwell for a moment longer,' recalled Andrews some years later, 'on these early days when Willie Pearson and I had just left Santiniketan, and had landed in South Africa. During that period of new spiritual vision and illumination thoughts of the Poet and his *Asram* would come clearly before us in all our conversations. It was the first full flush of our common enthusiasm and love for him and it coloured all our existence with its own bright hues. The very sky itself seemed more glorious as we spoke about him and shared our thoughts together. This was also for us both the happy moment of discovery of a new friendship with Mahatma Gandhi. These two affections were blended into one in a very intimate manner. Often under the

[1] It would be no exaggeration to say that not only Pearson but many Indians outside Bengal came to know and appreciate Tagore through Andrews. It was he who was the first and the main link between Tagore and Gandhi and helped them to see one another in their true dimensions. Even while Tagore was still in London and had not yet become a sensation, Andrews had written articles in English-language papers in India about him. Before that hardly anything had appeared in the Indian press outside Bengal about him, except the translation of one short story in a Hindi magazine. It is therefore, in a sense, as true to say that Europe gave Tagore to India as to say that India gave him to the world. The first translations of *Gitanjali* and of several other works of Tagore in many Indian languages were from English.

stars at night we would sit in the silence and then speak to one another in quiet accents of the wonderful evenings we had spent with our *Gurudev*[2] on the terrace outside his little room at Santiniketan. Those were golden moments and Mahatma realized with deep sympathy our own hearts' devotion to the Poet. He often spoke to us of his own great longing to meet him. Thus we were all drawn together into a single circle of affection.'[3]

The end of the year 1913 was marked by Calcutta University conferring a D.Litt. (*Honoris Causa*) on Tagore at a special convocation held on 26 December. It had been an eventful and exciting year, rich in rewards and honours, but poor in creative achievement, the only year in the decade which closed with it in which not a single new book of his was published in Bengali, the language of his creative expression. The three books published in London, *The Gardener*,[4] *The Crescent Moon* and *Chitra*, were all translations. Several songs were, however, written by him during this year, some during his sojourn abroad and some in India. The only one written in the United States in the beginning of the year is significant for its employment of the metaphor of buying and selling. The poet imagines himself carrying his burden of wares and hawking them from place to place. The King threatens to take his wares by force, the aged millionaire offers to buy them with gold, a lovely maiden tempts him with a smile, but the burden remains—until a child

[2] *Lit.* Holy Teacher, an epithet by which the pupils at Santiniketan addressed Tagore.

[3] *The Golden Book of Tagore*, Calcutta, 1931.

[4] May Sinclair's impression of the poems in *The Gardener*, conveyed in a letter dated 17 October 1913 addressed to the poet, is interesting: 'It is, to me, quite the most wonderful book of modern "secular" love-poems that there is, and I think you have done very wisely in bringing them out between *Gitanjali* and *The Crescent Moon*. I made a note of those I love best—such a long list! [Here follows a list of 24 poems.] I would not have thought it possible to carry in any translation the atmosphere, the very colour and smell and life of India, and this is what you have done. And yet I feel a greater loss in these poems in not knowing the original than I felt in reading the *Gitanjali* and *The Crescent Moon*.' A delicate and graceful hint that the English rendering of these poems was not of the same high quality as in the other two books—a judgement which every sensitive reader will confirm. One wishes that Tagore had taken the hint and stopped further translations of his poems which became increasingly inadequate. But as Shakespeare has said, 'Wishers were ever fools.'

playing with a sea-shell pulls him by the sleeve and says, 'All this is mine.' He is relieved of his burden only when he hands over his wares, without any payment, to the child to play with.

These songs which he continued to write (both words and music) and which were published in 1914 in two volumes, *Gitimalya* and *Gitali*, are some of the finest he ever wrote and continue the religious strain of *Gitanjali*, though the mood was changing. His faith had gained firmness, his confidence in man's destiny was now more robust and his acceptance of life and its responsibilities more gladsome. As he says in one of them, the thorns in his life would find their meaning when the rose blossoms. In a sense his songs are his greatest gift to his people, not only because their joy is equally shared by the literate and the illiterate, by the young and the old, but because through them he has expressed all the finest nuances of mood and feeling in the simplest and sweetest of words. They are his 'offerings' in the true sense of the word and because they are the intimate whispers of his soul, their appeal is so universal. He often said in his old age that while all his other achievements might be forgotten, his songs would continue to be sung.

Once a young and impertinent teacher at Santiniketan asked him bluntly, 'You talk so much of God, are you sure He is?' After a moment's silence, Tagore gently replied, 'No. All I can truthfully say is that at times I have felt His presence—more deeply and intimately when I am seized by a new song than in any other mood.' He said the same thing in one of these songs: 'My song touches Thy feet where Thou standest on the other shore—but me Thou eludest ever.' He is assured that his God wants him to love this world. 'If the heart were not meant to love, then why hast Thou filled the morning sky with songs, why this wonder of the stars in the sky, why these beds of flowers on this earth, why these whispers in the wind?' He knows that he is going to be caught more and more in the turmoil of work and asks reproachfully, 'If Thou needs must bind me with work, why then must Thou distract me with so much beauty?' He is uneasy and not sure what the future has in store for him. 'I was going along my lonely path when the light in my hand went out. This sudden storm which is driving me into the darkness is now my only companion. I have lost my known path and I stumble, not knowing when and where this night will find its morning.' He must face the struggle and not be scared of suffering. 'How will you conquer sorrow if you shun it? The poison must burn itself out in its own fire. Be not afraid of the fire; once it burns itself to ashes, there will be no more burning then.'

The nostalgia for the past which had temporarily overwhelmed him in the early years of the century had now faded and his old manly faith in the forward march of life, in the free commerce of minds which enrich themselves by giving and taking had been fully restored. This is evident from a letter[5] he wrote to Sturge Moore on 1 May 1914: 'Our school is closed, and after a long interval of a busy time a full day has been given to me to spend as I like. I took up your book—*The Sea is Kind*—finishing it at one sitting. It will be difficult for you to imagine this blazing summer sky of ours with hot blasts of air repeatedly troubling the fresh green leaves of a tree whose name will be of no use to you. This is as unlike the climate and the country where your poems were written as anything could be. I feel your environments in your poems. There is in them the reticence of your sky, the compactness of your indoor life and the general consciousness of strength ready to defy fate. Here in the East the transparent stillness of our dark nights, the glare of the noonday sun melting into a tender haze in the blue distance, the plaintive music of the life that feels itself afloat in the Endless, seem to whisper into our ears some great secret of existence which is uncommunicable.

'All the same, nay, all the more, your literature is precious to us. The untiring hold upon life which you never lose, the definiteness of your aims and positive reliance you have upon things present before you, inspire us with a strong sense of reality which is so much needed both for the purposes of art and of life. Literature of a country is not chiefly for home consumption. Its value lies in the fact that it is imperatively necessary for the lands where it is foreign. I think it has been the good fortune of the West to have the opportunity of absorbing the spirit of the East through the medium of the Bible. It has added to the richness of your life because it is alien to your temperament. In course of time you may discard some of its doctrines and

[5] I am indebted to Mrs. Elinor Wolf of Philadelphia for a copy of this letter of which she owns the original.

teachings but it has done its work—it has created a bifurcation in your mental system which is so needful for all life growth. The Western literature is doing the same with us, bringing into our life elements some of which supplement and some contradict our tendencies. This is what we need.

'It is not enough to charm or to surprise us—we must receive shocks and be hurt. Therefore we seek in your writings not simply what is artistic but what is vivid and forceful. That is why Byron had such immense influence over our youths of the last generation. Shelley, in spite of his vague idealism, roused our minds because of his fanatic impetuosity which is born of a faith in life. What I say here is from the point of view of a foreigner. We cannot but miss a great deal of the purely artistic element of your literature but whatever is broadly human and deeply true can be safely shipped for distant times and remote countries. We look for your literature to bring to us the thundering life flood of the West, even though it carries with it all the debris of the passing moments.'

About this time Tagore's young friend, Pramatha Choudhury, who had married his niece Indira, started a literary magazine, *Sabuj Patra* (Green Leaves), which, as its name shows, represented a movement for new experiments in literary writing. Though Choudhury, whose pen-name was Birbal after the witty courtier of the Emperor Akbar, was a brilliant writer himself the main burden of maintaining the prestige and popularity of the journal fell upon Tagore's shoulders. As though he needed this incentive, he responded to the pressure with an abundance of literary output as remarkable for its quality as for its variety—poems, short stories, essays and novels. The stories he wrote at this period do not have the freshness and charm which mark the stories he wrote in the nineties when he lived in his boat on the Padma and watched 'the lights and shadows and colours' of the landscape and life on its banks with gentle affection and ironic sympathy.[6] These later stories deal with middle-

[6] He himself loved these early stories best and re-reading them in later years felt that a loveliness had passed away from his life which would never come again. As he confessed in 1932, 'When I came face to face with nature in the villages of Bengal my days overflowed with happiness. That joy runs through these simple, unadorned stories . . . I have now come away from the loving hospitality of rural Bengal, with

class life and its problems, in particular the tragedy of woman in a Hindu household, and if they lack the aroma of fresh fruit they have the appetizing smell of strongly flavoured cheese. The author's irony in exposing the cowardice and selfishness of the smug Hindu husband is as subtle and sharp as his courage in denouncing injustice perpetrated in the name of holy scriptures and tradition is admirable.

Haimanti, the brave daughter of a noble father in the story of that name finds deliverance in death; the clever, beautiful and strong-willed Mrinal who had a mind of her own redeems the futility of her existence by asserting her freedom to renounce her husband and home. The story which is entitled *A Wife's Letter* is in the form of a letter she writes to her husband when she leaves him after fifteen years of suppressed agony. She is Tagore's Nora flinging her manifesto of independence in her husband's face. Needless to say, the author was severely abused in the Bengali press for this indictment of his society—abused by the very leaders who were clamouring against political injustice. In a third story, called *Aparichita* (The Unknown Girl), he shows how a Bengali girl when well educated is more than a match for the namby-pamby youth who imagined he was doing her a favour by condescending to marry her. All these stories are in the first person singular and the central character in each is made to reveal his or her own inmost feelings. Another very beautiful story is *Boshtami*—the story of a woman who had renounced her home to become a devotee of God. Tagore had actually known such a woman in a Bengal village and he later described her, with much respect and feeling, in his *Creative Unity*.

The summer holidays were spent in Ramgarh in the Himalayas. At first he was happy and felt as though he had till then been 'living on half-rations'. 'My life is full,' he wrote to Andrews. But soon an uneasiness crept over him, followed by an intense agony, a premonition that a great disaster was about to overtake the world he loved so much. There were no menacing clouds in the political horizon and the great war when it came, came suddenly in August. How and

---

the result that my motor-car-riding pen will never again know those cool and shady sylvan paths of literature.'

why he should have sensed its advent, is difficult to explain. That he felt it and felt it agonizingly is obvious from the letters he wrote and from the testimony of those who were with him and around him at that time. 'God knows it is the death pang that is tearing open my heart,' he wrote to Andrews.[7] He also expressed the mood in a poem. 'Look, there comes the all-destroying. The flood of agony spreads out in a sea of pain, the thunder roars in the dark and the lightning flashes amid the blood-shot clouds—a lunatic shaking with laughter in his sport of death!' But the lunatic's challenge must be taken up and men must fight to preserve the honour of humanity. 'The trumpet lies in the dust. The wind is weary, the light is dead. Ah, the evil day! Come fighters, carrying your flags, and singers with your war-songs . . . From thee I have asked for peace, only to find shame.'[8]

The poet was restless and, as usual when he was so, kept on the move from place to place, now Santiniketan, now Shelidah, now Darjeeling, Agra or Allahabad. In the meanwhile the war broke out in Europe. He did not look upon it as a European misfortune in which Asia was not concerned, much less gloat that England's difficulty was India's opportunity. Nor did he take sides. To him the war seemed as a wound in the breast of humanity, its pain and horror to be shared by all its limbs, however seemingly far removed. In an address to his students at Santiniketan he emphasized that as the sins of fathers are visited on children, so all humanity must share both the guilt and its punishment for whatever crimes are committed by man anywhere.

In a beautiful poem he said, 'All the sorrows of the earth, all its sins and crimes, its heart-breaks and its lust for violence, have swelled like a tidal wave overleaping the banks, blaspheming the skies. Nevertheless, O ye brave and afflicted ones, hold on to your oars and steer your boat over the howling, demented waves, with hope undying in your breasts. Whom do you condemn, my Brother? Bow down your head—the sin is yours and mine. It is the ulcer in the heart of Time that has burst at last. The poisonous fumes of the

---

[7] A selection from his letters to C. F. Andrews was published in 1928: *Letters to a Friend*, George Allen & Unwin, London.
[8] *Fruit-Gathering*.

faint heart's funk, the bully's insolence, the vulture's greed, the rancour of the disinherited, the accumulated insults to the divine in man—these have at long last burst through the flesh of Time, scouring earth and sea with their foul breath of destruction.' The catastrophe is not the revenge of a vindictive fate, it is a penance, an atonement which must bring redemption in the end. 'If death does not yield its deathless prize, if truth is not gained in battling with sorrow, if sin does not die in the shame of its exposure, if pride does not break under the weight of its intolerable pomp, then what hope sustains the hearts of these millions who leave their homes to face death like stars seeking their oblivion in the morning light? The blood of the brave, their mothers' tears—shall all this wealth be lost in the dust of the earth and not win heaven? Will the heaven's treasury not repay this debt?—the night's penance not end in the dawn?'

This and many other poems, including a sonnet on Shakespeare, he wrote during these uneasy, anguished but faith-filled months, which were all published in 1916 in a slender volume called *Balaka* (The Flight of Cranes). This volume, appropriately dedicated to Pearson—the spirit of these poems is itself one long dedication to the World-spirit—marks one of the great peaks which Tagore periodically scaled in his Himalayan pilgrimage. 'The poetry of *Balaka*,' writes a distinguished historian of Bengali, 'is truly grand, in the grandest scale possible for the lyric. We had seen nothing like it before, not even the gorgeous *Urvasi*.'[9] The book takes its name from the poem written in Kashmir where the author, watching in the evening '. . . the curving stream of Jhelum glimmering in the dusk like a scimitar', is suddenly roused from his reverie by 'the lightning streak of a sound hurtling across the void' and looks up to see a flock of cranes (or swans or wild ducks—the Bengali word is ambiguous) winging their way to somewhere unknown. This flight symbolizes for him the latent motion in all motionless things,

[9] Prof. Sukumar Sen, *History of Bengali Literature*, published by Sahitya Akademi, India. Though the poet himself translated several of these poems in *Fruit-Gathering* and *Lover's Gift and Crossing*, and the complete volume was translated in 1955 by a well-meaning admirer of Tagore's and published by John Murray, London, in the Wisdom of the East Series, the present writer feels that it is better not to attempt the impossible. The author's own attempt was suicidal; ours can only be murderous.

the passage of the time-spirit, the unending quest of life and of the soul, the eternal cry in the heart of the universe: 'Not here, not here, but somewhere else.'

The echo of this cry reverberates through all the poems in the volume which, whatever their theme and form, are all hymns to the endless wonder of the motion that keeps all things in a flux, renewing and surpassing themselves—whether the object addressed is Shah Jahan, the builder of the immortal Taj Mahal or the beloved angel of the poet's life, the deceased sister-in-law, Kadambari. He must have chanced upon an old photograph of hers, for the poem is addressed to it.[10] The memory is painful, but instead of luxuriating in the sorrow of his loss as he would have done in his youth, the poet finds comfort in the thought that in a sense she is even more real in his life now than before. 'If you are not before my eyes, it is because you are the very light that shines in them—you are the green in the earth's green, the blue in the heaven's blue, the inmost rhythm in the harmony of my universe. No one knows—not even I—that you are the music in my songs, the poet within the poet.'

The same idea, of life perpetually renewing itself, of Winter throwing off its mask to reveal itself as Spring, he embodied in a delightful fantasy which he wrote for his boys at Santiniketan—*Phalguni* (The Cycle of Spring). The play was staged both at Santiniketan and in Calcutta, Tagore playing the double role of the Poet and the blind Minstrel. The plot is very thin, in fact there is hardly a plot at all, just enough to provide an excuse for a riot of song, dance and gaiety to express the author's mood in spring. The excuse is a King who having discovered a couple of grey hairs in his head is scared at the prospect of death and wants to seek comfort in philosophy. His court poet diverts his mind by staging for him a play in which a group of young urchins pursue the old man Winter and disrobe him, only to discover that he is none other than Spring.

It is difficult to classify this fantasy, but let the author speak for

[10] This lovely poem for which the poet later composed music is known in Bengali as *Chhabi* (Picture). Some competent and well-meaning Bengali critics have insisted that the poem was inspired by a photograph of the poet's deceased wife. A good instance of how wishful thinking affects sober judgement.

himself. When the King asks what kind of entertainment the Poet has arranged for him, the latter replies, 'It is the very thing, but whether it is a drama or a poem or a play or a masque, I cannot say.' When the King wonders if he would be able to understand it, the Poet answers, 'What a poet writes is not meant to have any sense.' The King is puzzled. 'What do you mean?' he asks. 'Is there no philosophy in it?' 'No, none at all, thank goodness.' More puzzled the King asks, 'What does it say, then?' 'Nothing,' answers the Poet. 'It merely shouts, I exist!—like the first cry of the new-born babe.' When the King inquires about the stage sets and décor, he is told, 'Truth looks tawdry when she is over-dressed . . . Our only background is the mind. On that we shall summon up a picture with the magic wand of music.' The merit of the play is to be sought neither in its plot nor in the characters nor in the dialogue but in the lovely songs and the spirit of gay abandon which suffuses the whole play. 'Is it your custom,' the Watchman asks one of the characters, 'to answer questions by songs?' 'Yes,' replies the latter, 'otherwise the answer becomes unintelligible.' It is forty-five years since this fantasy was acted on the Calcutta stage by actors who were all amateurs, but those who saw it then never forgot the experience.

Soon after he had completed the writing of *Phalguni* Tagore had his first meeting with Gandhi, in March 1915. Having done his work and won his fight in South Africa Gandhi had returned to his country but had not yet made up his mind what he was going to do or even where he was going to stay. He had earlier disbanded his Phoenix colony and school in South Africa and had sent the boys, about twenty, to India. Andrews, who was the link between the two great men, had suggested that these boys should be accommodated in Santiniketan until Gandhi came and made his own arrangements for an asrama. Tagore readily agreed and the boys had been in Santiniketan some months when Gandhi came to see them. It must have been very interesting to watch these two sets of boys living side by side; Tagore's little Ariels, singing and dancing and romping about, and Gandhi's little saints, too wise and sober for their age. But the two got on splendidly and Tagore grew to love Gandhi's boys as his own. He found them 'very nice' and 'very lovable', but as he wrote in a letter to Andrews, he wished they were not so 'completely nice'.

Although Gandhi stayed for hardly a week in Santiniketan and had not yet become the Mahatma whose mere name was to cast a spell in later years, he left a permanent impress of his personality on the inmates of Santiniketan. This was his second visit to Santini-ketan; he had come a month earlier when Tagore was not there. The teachers and pupils of Santiniketan had given him a very warm welcome on his first visit and had given their voluntary labour to repair the main road along which he was to come and had erected arches all along the way. Tagore's eldest brother, Dwijendranath, the philosopher-mathematician, lovingly known as Borodada (Eldest Brother) to everyone, had warmly received Gandhi whom he greatly admired. Indeed he had, almost instinctively, seen the Mahatma (Great Soul) in him even before his younger brother and the rest of the country discovered it. He used to tell Rabindranath, 'Rabi, you do not understand. This man will deliver India.'

The six days that Gandhi spent in Santiniketan not only laid the foundation of a lifelong friendship between him and Tagore, the two giants of modern India, but brought into relief the contrast between their personalities and the dynamics of their idealism. So glaring and seemingly irreconcilable seemed this contrast that their respective admirers found it difficult to see through it. Beneath this mask of contrast was a kinship so deep and subtle that only they themselves were aware of it, barring a few common friends and admirers of exceptional sensibility, like Andrews or Jawaharlal Nehru. The so-called disciples or 'devout followers' of each saw mostly the grimace in the mask and not the smile concealed behind it. In his characteristic, matter-of-fact and practical manner Gandhi looked around, made friends with all, put his finger on the weak spots and tried to show Tagore how to implement his own ideals better. 'You believe in simplicity and self-reliance,' he told the inmates of the asrama in so many words. 'Excellent, I too believe in these virtues. But how can you achieve self-reliance without self-help and how can you be simple when you live on others' labour?' He told them that they must do wholly without hired labour or service and take upon themselves the responsibility of r 23-4-39.

Santiniketan
19/9/37

Dear Mahatmaji

The first thing which welcomed
me into the world of life after the period
of stupor I passed through was your message
of affectionate anxiety. and it was fully
worth of suffer the cost of sufferings which
were unremitting in their long persistence.

With grateful love
Rabindranath Tagore

Tagore's letter to Mahatma Gandhi after his illness in 1937

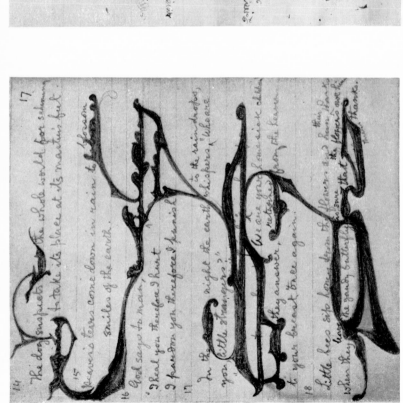

Specimens of erasure in manuscript. Left, English and right, Bengali keeping the asrama clean, as they kept their own bodies clean, and of running all its services including the cooking of food, washing dishes, etc. The young are always drawn to new adventures and both the pupils and the teachers warmly welcomed Gandhi's advice. When Tagore was approached for permission, he smiled and said, 'It is an interesting experiment.' And so on 10 March 1915 the experiment was launched. On the following day Gandhi left for Rangoon. That the experiment did not last very long must have surprised neither Gandhi nor Tagore. They were both realists and human, each in his way. The memory of this experiment survives in the observance of 10 March every year as Gandhi Day (Gandhi Punyaha) when all the paid servants are given a holiday and the teachers and pupils do all the cooking themselves and give an annual spring-cleaning to the asrama. A typical example of recurrent symbolism in Indian tradition.

Before Gandhi left Santiniketan he placed his finger on one more weak spot and spoke frankly to Tagore about it. He had noticed that in the asrama refectory separate seats were provided for Brahmin boys. That Tagore, who had spared no sarcasm against the curse of Brahminism, should himself tolerate its snobbery in his own sanctuary shocked Gandhi and he remonstrated against it—rightly. The practice was in fact a relic of that phase of social conservatism or reaction in Tagore's spiritual development during the period when he had founded the asrama on the monastic ideals of the ancient forest hermitages. That this was so is proved by the fact that the practice was abolished later and is no longer tolerated in Santiniketan. But at the time when Gandhi spoke of it to Tagore, the latter had either not yet realized the anomaly of it or was unwilling to admit his own limitation, for he justified the practice by saying that he did not believe in forcing others to do anything against their wishes. If the Brahmin pupils willingly sat at the same table with others he would be happy, but he would not compel them to do so. He must have known that he was wasting a noble argument over a poor cause. Tagore never believed in tolerating injustice or evil and considered such tolerance not as a measure of large-heartedness but of laxity of conscience, the chief bane of the Hindu social consciousness.

These two small incidents throw light on the basic characters of

Q

these two remarkable products of modern India, the saint who strove to make politics holy and the poet who made holiness seem beautiful. Gandhi's practice was always in advance of his ideology; Tagore had wings to his thoughts and feet to his practice. However firm and unfaltering the feet they could not keep pace with the wings. Gandhi, the stern ascetic, was more humane than the humanist; a kill-joy in theory he brought joy to millions of human hearts. Tagore, the pagan-lover, saw heaven where Gandhi failed to see it. These two faces of modern India, one rugged, one beautiful, both equally luminous, represent the two aspects of Indian *sadhana* or realization of life's truth. No one felt their impact more or understood their inner kinship better than the noble Englishman, C. F. Andrews. Let him estimate them whom he loved so well:

'Personally, I have never in my whole life met anyone so completely satisfying the needs of friendship and intellectual understanding and spiritual sympathy as Tagore. His very presence always acts as an inspiration. To be with him, to be at unison with him in some creative work, is a privilege, which it is very difficult to state in words. Indeed, it has been by far the greatest privilege of my life. No one has been more fortunate than I have been in personal friendships. Side by side with the friendship with the poet, I have had the supreme happiness of a second personal friendship with Mahatma Gandhi. His marvellous spiritual genius has appealed to me in a very different way. For his character, in his own way, is as great and as creative as that of Tagore himself. It is, however, of more ascetic order. It has about it rather an air of religious faith of the Middle Ages than that of modern times. Tagore is essentially a modern; Mahatma Gandhi is the St. Francis of Assisi of our own days.'

The Governor Lord Carmichael, who at the beginning of 1914 had formally handed over to the poet the Nobel Prize Diploma and Medal on behalf of the Swedish Academy, visited Santiniketan on 20 March, nine days after Gandhi had left. Having won recognition abroad, Tagore had become respectable in the eyes of the British Government in India. Gone were the days when the Government servants were warned not to send their children to his school. Now the highest British dignitary in Bengal came to pay his respects. Tagore gave the honoured guest a fitting reception and elaborate arrangements were made in the asrama to welcome him. Some 'patriots' criticized Tagore for honouring the representative of foreign rulers. Poor Tagore, whatever he did seemed wrong in the eyes of his countrymen. He was abused for his radicalism, maligned for his conservatism. He whose poetry expressed the heart of his country through the ages, who loved the very dust of the soil where he was born, never really won the hearts of his contemporary compatriots. They never forgave him for not sharing their superstitions, the biggest of which was the patriotic delusion that they were God's chosen people. Tagore loved his country and his people, but made no secret of the fact that he admired the British character more than the Indian. This his compatriots never forgave him. For this history will honour him.

Tagore was sensitive and vulnerable to public criticism and was in that respect less robust than Gandhi or his Irish contemporary Bernard Shaw. However brave the reflections in his writings on the vanity of fame or popular goodwill, actually he was deeply hurt by unjust criticism, and mostly the criticism was unjust, if not malicious. In a letter to Andrews dated 1 February 1915 he tried to analyse this susceptibility: 'You are right. I had been suffering from a time of deep depression and weariness. But I am sane and sound again, and willing to live another hundred years, if critics would spare me. At that time I was physically tired; therefore the least hurt assumed a proportion that was perfectly absurd. However, I am glad that there is still that child in me who has its weakness for the sweets of human approbation. I must not feel myself too far above my critics. I don't want my seat on the dais; let me sit on the same bench with my audience and try to listen as they do. I am quite willing to know the healthy feeling of disappointment when they don't approve of my things; and when I say, "I don't care," let nobody believe me.' Ten years earlier he had sung in a song: 'They call you mad. Wait for tomorrow and keep silent. They throw dust upon your head. Wait for tomorrow. They will bring their wreath.' The tomorrow took a long time to come.

That he was 'sane and sound again', whatever the previous fit of depression, was true, for he was writing at that time for the journal *Sabuj Patra* the famous four chapters which were later published as the novel *Chaturanga*,[11] a magnificent testament of the sanest and soundest common sense. Compact, well-knit and tense, this short novel is one of Tagore's best and has been described by a competent critic as 'a work of art without blemish'. There are only four chapters and four characters in the book, one of whom tells the story. The central character is Sachish, a young and ardent idealist whose quest for truth and inner fulfilment is traced through different phases. He has grown up under the influence of his uncle Jagmohan whose keen rationalism and innate nobility of mind had turned him early in life into an atheist and a positive-humanist. Jagmohan's God-denying humanism is contrasted in the first chapter with his brother's God-believing meanness and cupidity.

Sachish, revolted by his father's degenerate orthodoxy, is a fervent follower of his uncle's way of life. He comes across a young girl, an orphan, who had been seduced by his own elder brother and thrown on the streets. He takes the girl, now pregnant, to his uncle's house who gives her shelter and treats her as his daughter. To safeguard her future Sachish offers to marry her. But the girl, though she is grateful to her benefactors, is really still in love with her seducer and prefers to commit suicide to the shame of marrying anyone else. This incident comes as a shock to Sachish's cultivated belief in human rationalism. Soon after, the city of Calcutta is scourged by plague and as there are not enough hospitals in the city the humanitarian uncle turns his own house into a hospital for the poor, himself nursing the victims. He catches the dread disease and dies. 'He deserved it,' comments his orthodox brother.

Sachish is disconsolate after his uncle's death and wanders about in search of a faith to fill the void in his life. He falls into the company of a so-called Vaishnav saint and becomes his disciple. Vaishnavism is a religion which seeks to realize God by a life of emotional self-abandon. Tagore who loved the poetry it inspired had a wholesome contempt for the emotional self-exhibitionism in which its practice had mostly degenerated and found in this novel an excellent

[11] *Lit.* Four limbs or divisions. The word also means chess.

opportunity to show how religious emotion divorced from humanism is little better than a form of self-hypnosis or an opiate. However, Sachish was happy in his 'escape' until a young and lively widow, an unwilling and rebellious disciple of the Guru, distracts his attention. This girl, Damini, like Binodini of the earlier novel *Chokher Bali*, is a character so real that no reader having known her can ever forget her. Damini loves Sachish but cares little for the Guru, the façade of whose piety does not deceive her. Sachish, who believes that human love is a snare, tries to avoid her but cannot help being conscious of her. Once when the party was spending the night in a cave, Sachish could not sleep, being haunted by a vague dread of some primeval beast hidden in the cave about to creep over him with its clammy paws. Just then he felt a touch on his feet. In panic he kicked hard. It was Damini who had received the kick in her breast.

Unable to escape from thoughts of Damini, Sachish finally begs her to save him and release him from her spell, not only by going away but by voluntarily renouncing her desire for him. She understands with her woman's insight the hell he is passing through and understands also that in his frame of mind, having known love only as the beast of desire that stood between him and his quest, he is incapable of accepting her love in its true meaning. She gives up her chase of him and marries the fourth character in the novel, Sribilash, the narrator, who is deeply in love with her. She fills his days with happiness, but not for long, for she dies soon after—the kick she had received in the cave had caused an injury from which she never recovers. Her renunciation of him releases Sachish not only from her spell but from his obsession with a religious pursuit that was little better than an escape. He returns to his humanitarian mission in Calcutta, a sadder and a wiser man.[12]

In the same year as *Chaturanga* was published his major novel of this period, *Ghare Baire* (The Home and the World), in which too each of the three major characters reveals his or her own thoughts in a diary. The setting is the political excitement in the stormy years

---

[12] This exquisite novel was translated and published in English as *Broken Ties* but seems to have made no impression on the foreign reader. Perhaps the setting and the problem discussed were too Indian.

of the first decade of the century when Tagore himself had been drawn into its vortex for a time. This novel is his answer to the critics who had accused him of desertion. So powerful was the answer, so vividly true the portrayal of the unscrupulous politician who juggles with ideals that the novel only provoked worse abuse. The author was accused of being both immoral and unpatriotic. For three long years after its publication the critics continued to tear the novel to pieces—a tribute to its impact on their minds.

The atmosphere of the novel is tense and dark with the turmoil of passion, the darkness scintillating with brilliant sparks as flints of opposing thoughts strike against one another. It is a clash all along, within a society in transition, clash of the old with the new, of realism with idealism, of the means with the end, of love claimed as of right and love given of free will, of home-bred virtue with the wild wind from the outside. Although a poet's manifesto, the novel is equally a testament of Gandhi's philosophy of non-violence, of love and truth, of his insistent warning that evil means must vitiate the end, however nobly conceived. Reading it one understands, better than any exposition can demonstrate, how akin Tagore was to Gandhi in spirit whatever the seeming differences in their forms.

The plot, like all Tagore's plots, is very simple—the usual, age-old triangle, two men and a woman. Nikhil, the titled nobleman, owning vast estates in the country, is an unusual representative of his class, too noble to be a noble, although Tolstoy had already made the type familiar, both in his life and in his novels, and Tagore himself had tried to live up to it when he was managing his family estates. Nevertheless, the character, as it emerges in the novel, is less convincing than the other two—which might be taken to show that as a novelist Tagore could not rise to that dispassionate calm of self-analysis which Tolstoy had attained. Nikhil who is compounded of the Maharshi's religious insight, of Gandhi's political idealism and of Tagore's own tolerance and humanism, is too shadowy to be real and too flabby to be heroic as he is intended to be. His friend and protégé, Sandip, the Machiavellian patriot, the unscrupulous politician, the splendid wind-bag and shameless seducer is, on the other hand, far more real—except that he speaks a language which only a Tagore could put in his mouth.

Bimala is Nikhil's wife, an ordinary, domesticated type who becomes extraordinary when her senses and her vanity are aroused —a real and convincing character. She comes under the spell of Sandip's fiery eloquence; the admiration soon warms into attraction under the hot breath of Sandip's sensual vitality. 'So long I had been,' writes Bimala in her diary, 'like a small river at the border of a village. But the tide came up from the sea, and my breast heaved; my banks gave away and the great drum-beats of the sea waves echoed in my mad current. I could not understand the meaning of that sound in my blood.'

Sandip was unscrupulous and dynamic; his philosophy was at once nihilist and Nietzschian. 'The impotent man says,' he noted in his diary, 'what is given to me is mine. And the weak man assents. But the lesson of the world is, whatever I can grab is mine ... Every man has a natural right to possess, and therefore greed is natural. What my mind covets my surroundings must supply.' Nikhil knew what was going on between his wife and his friend and could easily have put a stop to it, but he valued love only when given out of free will and in open competition with the outside world and not as an obligation or under duress. What happens between the three, let the reader find out for himself, for the book is available in English translation—*The Home and the World*.[13]

A significant title in more senses than the one employed for the novel. Tagore himself was tossing between his love of his home and the lure of the world. Having tasted the sweets of fame abroad, it was difficult to subsist for long on the insipid or sour fare at home. All through the year 1915 he played with the idea of visiting Japan and wrote in a letter to Rothenstein on 4 April, 'I give up Japan—at least for the present. Not for any sudden failure of courage or enthusiasm but for the same blessed reason that brings a modern war to its halt. My finance is hopeless, mainly owing to the European

[13] Yeats, who had read and admired the novel when it was published by Macmillan in 1919, told Tagore when he met him in July 1920 that '*The Home and the World* was very true of Irish society at the present time. All the problems apply equally well to his country. He asked if it had not stirred up strong feelings in India, for he was sure it would have done so in Ireland, if a similar book were written by an Irish writer.' Quoted from Rathindranath Tagore's 'diary' as published in *On the Edges of Time*.

complication.' But he did not have to give it up for long. On 3 May 1916 while the war was still on, he sailed for Japan, accompanied by Andrews, Pearson and a young Indian artist, Mukul Dey. He travelled by a Japanese ship and was much impressed with the discipline, efficiency and friendliness of the captain and the crew. As he put it, his taste of Japan began with a Japanese ship, as the taste of Indian food begins at the finger-tips. Those who use knives and forks miss one of the pleasures of eating, as those who marry through matchmakers miss the pleasure of courtship.

In Rangoon, where the party halted for two days, he was charmed with the gay-coloured Burmese women who work harder than their men. 'They are like flowers blooming all over the land, on its branches and on its ground—nothing else meets the eye.' Commenting on their grace and dignity, he noted in his diary, 'It is because the women here have been freed from this cage of exclusive domesticity that they have gained such completeness and self-reliance. They do not have to apologize for their own existence. As they are loved for their womanly grace, so are they respected for the easy dignity of their strength. I first realized that work gives true grace to womanhood when I saw Santal women.'[14] In Hong Kong he was even more impressed with the grace and strength which physical labour, well regulated, can impart to the human body. Watching the Chinese labourers at work on the quay, their half-bare bodies glistening in the light, he wrote: 'Their bodies were spare and perfectly moulded, not the slightest superfluity anywhere . . . Work seemed to vibrate from their bodies like music from lutes . . . This I can say with emphasis, that no woman's figure could be more beautiful than these men's figures, because such perfect balance between strength and grace is rarely found in women.' What he then noted down about the future of China is worth recalling. 'Seeing such strength, skill and joy of work thus concentrated in one place, I realized what an amount of power is being stored throughout the land in this great nation. When such an immense power gets its own modern vehicle, i.e., when science comes under its control, what power on earth will

[14] Santals are an aboriginal tribe in Western Bengal and Bihar. The diary written in Bengali was published later as *Japan Yatri*. The English translation of passages quoted here is by Indira Devi.

be able to offer it resistance? Then to its genius for work will be added the materials to work with. All the nations that are now enjoying the fruits of the earth dread that awakening of China, and want to put off that day unwelcome for them.'

On 29 May the party reached Kobe where the poet was very warmly received. He was happy to meet his old acquaintance Taik-wan, the famous painter, who had been a guest at the Tagore house in Calcutta and who had now come to receive him. Tagore stayed in Japan for a little over three months, visiting several places, though most of the time he stayed in Hakone, from where he made occa-sional trips to Tokyo for his lectures at the University of Keio-Gijiku. Many aspects of Japanese life and landscape attracted him; in particular the people's sense of discipline, their fortitude of body and mind, their self-restraint in expression, their innate love of beauty and the unrivalled charm of their women. Commenting on the fact that he '. . . never heard anyone singing in the streets since I have been here', he noted in his diary: 'The hearts of these people are not resonant like a waterfall, but silent like a lake. All the poems of theirs that I have hitherto heard are picture-poems, not song poems.' He analysed one of them: *'Ancient Pool, Frogs leaping, Splash of Water*. Finished! No more is necessary. The mind of the Japanese reader is all eyes. An ancient pool, dark, silent, deserted by man. As soon as a frog leaps into it, the sound is heard. That it is heard proves how silent the pool is.'

The influence of these poems, remarkable for their brevity, may have worked on his mind when he yielded to the requests of young ladies and girls (who can resist their exquisite grace and courtesy?) to inscribe something on their fans or autograph books. These stray epigrams or verses were later collected and published as *Stray Birds*.[15] Some are translations of his Bengali verses and some were written directly in English. They are by no means literature of any high quality, though many of them are interesting in themselves. Some of them are quoted below as specimens: 'Once we dreamt that we were strangers. We wake up to find that we were dear to each other.' 'You smiled and talked to me of nothing and I felt that for this I had

---

[15] Published by the Macmillan Company of New York, 1916. The volume was dedicated to the author's host in Japan, T. Hara of Yokohama.

been waiting long.' 'I cannot choose the best. The best chooses me.'
'Every child comes with the message that God is not yet discouraged
of man.' 'He who is busy doing good finds no time to be good.'
One was prophetic of Japan's future: 'Your idol is shattered in the
dust to prove that God's dust is greater than your idol.' Another has
an interesting history as recorded by Andrews:

'One incident is vividly recalled to my mind which I personally
witnessed in Japan. When he was in that country, he was asked on
one occasion to write a short poem concerning a deed of violence
which had been committed by two chiefs of rival clans. They had
fought from dawn till evening on a grassy plateau, high up in the
hills near Hakone. A great rock overshadowed the place. When the
sun had set on that day of battle both the warriors had fallen dead,
smitten with many wounds and the ground had been covered with
their blood. The leaders of the Japanese people, who had come to
the spot with the Poet, asked him to write an epigram in a few
words commemorating the heroic occasion. I could see, at that
moment, the strained anguish of the Poet's face as he quickly grasped
the incident just as it had occurred and shrank back from it in his
own mind in horror. In a moment with a quick gesture, he wrote
these words: "They hated and fought and killed each other: And
God in shame covered their blood with His own grass." The beauty
of the thought was only equalled by its daring.'

Though the Japanese welcomed Tagore with real and warm-
hearted enthusiasm—the poet-seer from the land of the Buddha—the
enthusiasm cooled off considerably when he warned them in his
lectures against imitating not the humane values of the Western
civilization but its lust for power and its blind worship of the state-
machine in the name of the nation. 'Europe is supremely good in
her beneficence where her face is turned to all humanity; and Europe
is supremely evil in her maleficent aspect where her face is turned
upon her own interest, using all her power of greatness for ends
which are against the infinite and the eternal in Man.' He compli-
mented the Japanese for being modern but reminded them that
'True modernism is freedom of mind, not slavery of taste. It is
independence of thought and action, not tutelage under European
schoolmasters. It is science but not its wrong application in life.' He

told them: 'Never think for a moment that the hurts you inflict upon other races will not infect you, or that the enmities you sow around your homes will be a wall of protection to you for all time to come.'[16] The ruling classes of Japan did not forgive him for having warned them, as a friend of their people, of the bitter fruit in store for their nation for the sin of their own megalomania. But though the ruling classes frowned on him and jibed at the impertinence of a representative of a slave-nation trying to teach a free people what freedom meant, the intelligentsia of Japan have never ceased to respect Tagore for his courage in saying what he did.

In September 1916 Tagore sailed for the United States arriving in Seattle on 18 September. Before leaving Japan he had received an invitation from Canada to visit Vancouver on the way. He declined the invitation on the ground that he could not accept honour from a country which discriminated against his countrymen in its immigration policy. The incident of the *Komagata Maru*, when a large party of revolutionary-minded Indians, mostly Punjabis, had chartered a Japanese ship in 1914 to emigrate to Canada and had not been permitted to land there and had been forced to return to India where they had to face brutal treatment from the British authorities on landing, had aroused strong feelings in India and the resentment had rankled in Tagore's mind. His declining the invitation provoked caustic comments in the British, Canadian and American press.

This second visit to the United States had been sponsored by the Pond Lyceum in connexion with a lecture-tour from coast to coast. These lectures were published in two volumes, one *Nationalism*, already referred to, the other *Personality*, comprising six lectures; 'What is Art', 'The World of Personality', 'The Second Birth', 'My School', 'Meditation' and 'Woman'. While these latter were greatly appreciated, embodying as they do some of Tagore's profound reflections on art, education, religious philosophy and the divine potential in the human personality, his forthright denunciation of nationalism as a cult provoked violent attacks in the American press. The *Detroit*

---

[16] This lecture was later included and published in the volume *Nationalism* (The Macmillan Co., New York, 1916). The book was dedicated to C. F. Andrews.

Journal warned the people against '. . . such sickly saccharine mental poison with which Tagore would corrupt the minds of the youth of our great United States'.

The relentless schedule of an organized lecture tour and the tempestuous rhythm of American life to which he was not used and which jarred on his sensibilities proved a strain on Tagore's health, aggravated by an ugly incident instigated by his own countrymen during his stay in San Francisco. Some excitable young Indians, more patriotic than intelligent, belonging to a revolutionary organization known as the Gadar Party, had misconstrued his denunciation of nationalism as betrayal of Indian nationalist aspirations. Tagore had been knighted by the British Government the previous year and these impetuous patriots, putting the two together, assumed that this Indian knight was a British agent who had been sent to the United States to blacken his own nation. A rumour was set afloat that the Gadar Party had issued secret instructions for his assassination, with the ironic result that the U.S. authorities, with the best of intentions, had to provide special protection to the distinguished visitor against his own compatriots.[17] Tagore was deeply hurt and mortified by this episode and became more homesick than ever. He terminated his contract for the lecture-tour prematurely and sailed for Japan in January 1917.

Tagore's first visit to the United States three years earlier had been happier. He was then less known and had stayed for a period in a quiet university town and had enjoyed in Chicago and New York the friendly hospitality of Mrs. William Vaughan Moody whom he admired and in whose house he had opportunities of meeting artists and intellectuals at leisure. On his first visit he had come for the love of it and because he wanted to know America and her people. This time he came, tempted by the prospect of raising money which his school at Santiniketan sorely needed. However unselfish the object for which he needed funds, the fact remains that there is an incongruity in the role of a prophet running down

---

[17] The irony of this episode reached its climax when, a year later, Mr. Gourlay, then Private Secretary to the Governor of Bengal, told Andrews that the British Intelligence Service had reported that Tagore was in secret collusion with the Gadar Party and had, in fact, gone to the United States to make contact with German agents there.

materialism and asking to be paid for it. Tagore was far too sensitive not to have felt the prick of humiliation in this anomaly. A man who could write at the height of his fame: 'Praise shames me for I secretly beg for it' has already redeemed his failing by his sincerity.

His lectures on Nationalism were also ill-timed. Though he was right, prophetically right, in what he said and must be admired for his courage in courting abuse, the time was inauspicious. Europe was in the throes of a great calamity and thousands of young men were dying on its battlefields and, right or wrong, they believed they were giving their lives for their hearths and homes; the tide of British sympathy was rising fast in the United States and very soon American lives would be sacrificed. It was hardly the time to expose what seemed holy and heroic as a vast delusion caused by 'Evil incarnate'. What would today find an echo in the minds of millions of men and women all over the world who have known the horrors of two wars was then a voice in the wilderness.

After a month's stay in Japan on his way back, Tagore returned to India in March 1917. There he saw the face, not of aggressive nationalism but of piteous nationalism being trampled underfoot by the very country whose youth were dying elsewhere in defence of their own nation's privileges. And yet it was a brave British lady whose voice was at that time the most eloquent raised on behalf of India. Annie Besant, who had advocated Home Rule for India, was interned by an order of the Madras Government. Tagore, who admired her for her many great qualities, made a public protest against her internment. He was once again being drawn into the political arena of which the stormy centre was no longer confined to Bengal. He was now too important to be left alone by his people and, as ever, too impatient to keep quiet when he saw his people suffer. At a public meeting in Calcutta he captured the hearts of the audience with his patriotic song freshly composed: 'Thy trumpet call has spread all over the earth and the heroic from all lands have gathered round Thy seat. The day is come. But where is India? She lies on the dust in dishonour, deprived of her seat. Remove her shame and give her a place in the House of Man, O Lord ever awake!' At the end of the year when the Indian National Congress met for its annual session in Calcutta he recited on the opening day a long poem which has come to be known as 'India's Prayer'. He received a great ovation from all the political leaders gathered on the occasion.

Tagore's health was breaking down; the mental strain had proved too great, not only the strain of work and engagements but the deeper strain of the dilemma within him, the perpetual struggle between the poet and the prophet. In a letter of 24 January 1918 to James Cousins, the Irish poet, he wrote: 'I must write these few lines to thank you for your books though I am forbidden to read or write letters for at least two months. But the Defence of the Realm Act has no direct connexion with this imposition. The possibility of a breakdown with which I have been threatened has suddenly overtaken me at last and it has come to me as a relief to know for certain that I am entitled to all the undisputed rights of the sick.'[18]

In a letter of 27 January addressed to Edward Thomson, then with the Indian Expeditionary Force, Mesopotamia, he is more analytical. 'Sometimes it becomes a problem to choose between things which

[18] In another letter of the same date he writes to Prof. Rudra: 'Thank you for your letter. I believe that the poor boy has been released by this time. But the sentence of internment has been passed upon me by the medical authority and I am not allowed to carry on correspondence for some time. Of course this letter is an infringement of that order. My doctor has declared that I am suffering from mental fatigue, so I am in that happy state when my conscientious objection to work of all kinds will be considered as valid.' The phrase 'sentence of internment' is in ironical reference to the Defence of the Realm Act under which many young men were being 'interned' on suspicion of their connexion or sympathy with the revolutionary underground movement. That the doctor's orders enjoining complete rest were observed more in the breach than otherwise is obvious from several other letters, written, all in his own hand, on that very date. One of them, addressed to Gandhiji, in reply to the latter's query, is of particular interest in view of the language controversy in India which has persisted to this day. 'Dear Mr. Gandhi, I can only answer in the affirmative the questions you have sent to me from Motihari. Of course Hindi is the only possible national language for interprovincial intercourse in India. But about its introduction at the Congress I think we cannot enforce it for a long time to come. In the first place, it is truly a foreign language to the Madras people, and in the second, most of our politicians will find it extremely difficult to express themselves adequately in this language for no fault of their own. The difficulty will be not only for want of practice but also because political thoughts have naturally taken form in our minds in English. So Hindi will have to remain optional in our national proceedings until a new generation of politicians, fully alive to its importance, pave the way towards its general use by constant practice as a voluntary acceptance of a national obligation.' (Until recently people in the North used to refer to all who lived in the South, whether in Madras or Trivandrum, as Madrasis or people of Madras.)

I can do best and things that challenge my attention because they are needful. The vision of a larger time and life is obstructed at every step by the clamorous present for those who are poor in means and opportunities and we are most often denied the option of choice in our works. This not only leads into poor results but also into fatigue and discouragement. This is what is wrong with me. I live in a time and place which cannot wait for the fruit season of my life, but must lop off its branches for the building of its momentary huts. Unfortunately this has to be attended to, and it becomes useless to claim exemption from sacrifice because it is inappropriate.'

The political situation in the country was getting increasingly out of hand. Tagore's warning to his people was unhappily coming true. For lack of adequate constructive channels, the impetuosity of the Bengali youth driven underground was exploding in terrorist activities. The British Government, now confident of its victory in Europe, thanks to the American participation in the war, retaliated brutally. Violence must be put down with greater violence, hatred met with greater hatred. This age-old philosophy of power was working its havoc and illustrating the truth of Tagore's maxim: 'The clumsiness of power spoils the key and uses the pick-axe.' Tagore who had never believed in violence and terrorism, even for legitimate patriotic ends, and had courted unpopularity by raising his voice against it,[19] could not remain indifferent to the suffering of these brave young men under the heavy hand of British repression. How much he strove on their behalf privately—apart from his impassioned public protests—is indicated by the following letter addressed to Mr. Gourlay on 18 February 1918 when he was still under doctors' orders not to exert himself in any way:

'When I wrote to you last I thought it would be of no loss to anybody in the world if I gave up my attempt at rectifying wrongs and stuck to literature. But occasions come when to remain in the shelter of one's own special vocation becomes a crying shame. And a particularly harrowing account of the helpless condition of a state prisoner having come to my notice from a trustworthy source,

[19] He had already demonstrated its folly in *The Home and the World* and was to show its tragedy in another novel published in 1934, *Char Adhyaya* (Four Chapters). This too brought him considerable abuse from Bengali patriots.

I am compelled to write to you again. The case is that of Jyotish Chandra Ghosh of Hooghly who is in the Berhampur Lunatic Asylum.

'I am informed that he lies motionless on his back day and night in an unconscious condition, his look vacant, jaws firmly set, legs rigid and crooked, probably paralysed. He can neither open his mouth nor speak and does not respond to any outside stimulus, however strong. It is said that he has been in this condition for the last six months or so, and that during that period, or longer, he has been artificially fed. The force applied for this purpose does not rouse him to a least sign of consciousness and the only thing which shows that he is alive is that he breathes.

'After repeated and unaccountable refusals one of his relatives was given permission to see Jyotish at last. I do not wish to discuss what suspicions our people entertain about such cases as this, though these suspicions, whether legitimate or not, should never be ignored. But in the name of humanity I would appeal to His Excellency the Governor of Bengal to look into the case personally and not be satisfied with any report from subordinate functionaries, medical or ordinary. For the sake of humanity I would also urge that the prisoner's mother should now have the consolation of nursing her son in her own home, or if that cannot be, in any other place chosen by Government where he can have the best possible medical treatment.'

Be it recorded to the credit of the Governor that he did look into the case personally and did his best to rectify the wrong.

There were many such cases that he espoused and each caused him considerable emotional stress for he felt others' suffering very acutely.[20] Added to this strain was the anxiety caused by the serious

---

[20] All the time he was also looking after his school in Santiniketan, even thinking of expanding its scope and activities, writing for the literary magazine *Sabuj Patra*, coping with the demands of a literary and cultural club set up at his Calcutta family residence, called Vichitra Club, and responding to innumerable other demands on his time. As an instance of the last, I am quoting two small letters, written in answer to queries, which are of particular interest. Writing on 9 February 1918, to Mr. Kingsley Well of Wesley College, Madras, who had asked for advice regarding the production on stage of the drama *Chitra*, Tagore said: 'All that I can suggest about the performance of *Chitra* is that, instead of having painted scenery at all, only a

illness of his eldest and most dearly loved daughter Bela, who died in May the same year. On 28 February he wrote to Pearson who was then in China: 'I have come once again to Calcutta from Santiniketan, for Bela's condition has grown worse. Death is the obverse side of life, it is one with it, and I do not look upon it with any particular fear. But disease is evil, and when we do not know how to fight it, it makes one's heart rebellious.'

How quickly Tagore's mood could change is illustrated by another passage in the same letter in which he informs Pearson of an invitation he had received from Australia. It would be recalled that hardly a year and a half had passed since he had declined a similar invitation from Canada. The immigration policy of Australia was no better. However, he wrote: 'I had a letter from Sydney University asking me if it were true that I would not visit Australia if I was wanted there. I have written in answer that it would be wrong on my part if I refused to accept any invitation sent to me in right spirit. I think pride of patriotism is not for me. I earnestly hope that I shall find my home everywhere in this world before I leave it. We have to fight against wrongs and suffer for the cause of righteousness

---

blue curtain for a background can be used. There should be a raised platform in the rear for the scenes where Madana appears. The lights will be concentrated upon that part when it is used and shifted to the front part when other scenes are being acted. *Chitra* being a lyrical drama it depends more for the effectiveness of its representation upon the imaginative and emotional fervour of the acting than upon anything extraneous. Judicious employment of coloured lights will add to its effect.' The other letter dated 14 April is addressed to Mr. Anderson who had sent him metrical renderings of two *Gitanjali* poems: 'I have greatly enjoyed reading two of my *Gitanjali* poems done into verse by your friend and thank you for sending them to me. It was the want of mastery in your language which originally prevented me from trying English metres in my translations. But now I have grown reconciled to my limitations through which I have come to know the wonderful power of English prose. The clearness, strength and the suggestive music of well-balanced English sentences make it a delightful task for me to mould my Bengali poems into English prose form. I think one should frankly give up the attempt at reproducing in a translation the lyrical suggestions of the original verse and substitute in their place some new quality inherent in the new vehicle of expression. In English prose there is a magic which seems to transmute my Bengali verses into something which is original again in a different manner. Therefore it not only satisfies but gives me delight to assist my poems in their English rebirth though I am far from being confident in the success of my task.'

—but let us have no petty jealousies and quarrels with our neighbours because we have different names.'[21]

Mr. Montagu, the Secretary of State for India in the British Cabinet, was in India in the early part of 1918 to study the situation on the spot and make his recommendations to his Cabinet on the desirability of associating Indians in the government of their own country. He had invited the leaders of public opinion to submit their schemes to him. Tagore had no scheme to offer but in a long letter addressed to Mr. Montagu on 6 April he made certain general observations some of which are worth quoting here, as they throw light on his political thinking. He had always maintained—and in this he and Gandhi were at one—that self-government to be real must be won from within and not received as a gift. So he wrote:

'Morally considered, the worst of all human relationships is that of the giver and the receiver—at least, it is almost as bad as that of the parasites and their victims. And therefore I have ever felt it my duty to warn my countrymen against taking to such a slippery path of moral degradation. What I have always proposed to my country-men is to organize ourselves to help our own people in all depart-ments of life ... It is of higher importance to a people to be able to feel that they are actively serving their own country than that they are being well governed. It is not at all flattering to us, and far less to the British rule in India, that after more than a century of Western dominion we are still considered unfit to serve our country in its internal administration . . . We must fully realize the hand of providence in the advent of the English in India before we can be reconciled to it, and this can only happen if its moral significance shines above all purposes of selfish gain. If such a great ideal has not been evolved out of the long British rule in India, then it is a failure not only for us but for England. And I feel sure that, in as far as this British rule represents mere power over a subject race and exploita-tion of a foreign country, it has been the sure cause of degeneracy to the English people whose greatest strength was love of freedom and of humanity.'

[21] Soon after this Pearson was arrested in China and deported to England at the instance of the British Government for his alleged anti-British activities. Tagore was deeply perturbed by the news.

But the British were not holding India as an exercise in moral responsibility and were not to relax their hold till India threatened to become more a liability than an asset to the Empire. Nor did they need a certificate of good conduct from Tagore. They were always as convinced of their moral infallibility as they were of the invincibility of their Empire. The success in the European war had only bolstered up that conviction and flushed with it they answered the Indian challenge with the notorious Rowlatt Acts which '. . . sought to perpetuate the extraordinary repressive powers conferred on the Government during the war, for doing away with ordinary legal procedure and for authorizing imprisonment without trial'. This brought into the battlefield Mahatma Gandhi, who turned what were hitherto sporadic outbursts into an organized mass movement of civil disobedience.[22]

'The Government put down the movement with a heavy hand, the blackest stain on its record being in connexion with a prohibited meeting of citizens at an enclosed place called Jalianwalla Bagh at Amritsar. Troops under General Dyer fired 1,600 rounds of ammunition into the unarmed crowd who had no means of exit. Even according to official estimates 379 persons were killed, and 1,200 wounded who were left untended. Martial law was proclaimed in the Punjab; and the subsequent inquiries revealed a gruesome picture of shootings, hangings, bombing from the air and extremely severe sentences passed by the tribunals during the reign of terror.'[23]

The massacre took place on 13 April 1919, but so strict was the censorship on press, so heavy the iron curtain, that no news of the tragedy and the subsequent horrors was made public for several weeks. When the news trickled through and reached Tagore he was so perturbed that, cancelling an important engagement in Santiniketan, he hurried to Calcutta and invited the political leaders to

[22] On 8 April 1919 Gandhi was arrested while on his way to Delhi. On 12 April Tagore addressed an open letter to him calling him for the first time Mahatmaji: 'Through panic or through wrath our authorities have shown us their claws . . . In this crisis you as a great leader of men have stood among us . . . You have come to your motherland in the time of her need . . . to lead her in the true path of conquest . . . Freedom can never come to a people through charity . . . We must win it before we can own it.'

[23] An Advanced History of India. Macmillan & Co., London, 1950.

organize a public meeting of protest over which he offered to preside, but so terror-stricken were the people that his offer came to nothing. He then did what his countrymen have never ceased to be grateful for. He lived up to his own song written years ago: 'If they are afraid and cower mutely facing the wall, then O thou of evil luck, open thy mind and speak out alone.' Without telling anyone and without taking even his own son into confidence, he wrote a letter to the Viceroy, Lord Chelmsford, on the night of 29 May, resigning his knighthood. The letter was published on the morning of 2 June.

'The very least I can do for my country,' he wrote, 'is to take all consequences upon myself in giving voice to the protest of the millions of my countrymen, surprised into a dumb anguish of terror. The time has come when badges of honour make our shame glaring in the incongruous context of humiliation, and I for my part wish to stand, shorn of all special distinctions, by the side of those of my countrymen who for their so-called insignificance are liable to suffer a degradation not fit for human blessings.'

It was not the renunciation of knighthood, which in any case added little to his stature, but the courage with which he voiced his people's anguish which fear had hushed in every other breast that gives its historic importance to the letter quoted above. It was a gesture which restored the self-respect of the nation and gave his people courage and faith at a time when they were sorely needed. The British ruling authorities never forgave what they deemed an unheard-of impertinence.

II

WORLD IN ONE NEST

The sweet singer who had been content with his lone pilgrimage between his nest and the sky had now been caught in the world's mesh. The messenger of freedom will himself no longer be free. To *be* good would no more suffice; he must *do* good. He had won the world and the world in turn had won him. He would now seek his home everywhere in the world and would bring the world to his home. And so the little school for little children at Santiniketan became a world university, Visva-Bharati,[1] a centre of Indian culture, a seminary for Eastern studies and a meeting place of the East and the West. The poet selected for its motto an ancient Sanskrit verse: *Yatra visvam bhavati eka-nidam* which means, 'Where the whole world meets in one nest.' 'Visva-Bharati,' he declared, 'represents India where she has her wealth of mind which is for all. Visva-Bharati acknowledges India's obligation to offer to others the hospitality of her best culture and India's right to accept from others their best.'

The idea had germinated in his mind since his last tour of Japan and the United States and he made his first public announcement and exposition of it at a special gathering in Santiniketan on 22 December 1918. On almost the same day[2] three years later the university was formally inaugurated. During this period the nuclei of several branches of learning and the arts were laid; in course of time they grew and expanded and several more were added. The university, like its predecessor the school, was no doubt the

[1] *Visva* in Sanskrit means the world in its universal aspect; *Bharati* is knowledge, culture, wisdom. *Bharat* is the ancient, traditional name for India and so the compound *Visva-Bharati* has a secondary suggestion: India where she is universal.

[2] This day which in Bengali calendar corresponds to 7 Poush was held sacred in Tagore's memory as the day on which his father, the Maharshi, had been formally initiated as Brahmo. It does not always correspond with 22 December.

product of a poet's dream, but like many dreams when it materialized it turned out to be a pointer to reality. Tagore had always believed that '. . . on each race is laid the duty to keep alight its own lamp of mind as its part in the illumination of the world. To break the lamp of any people is to deprive it of its rightful place in the world festival.' Once India had such a mind which was lit by its own flame, fed with its own oil. Today the university graduates had become little better than 'the eternal rag-pickers at other people's dustbins'.

Tagore did not believe that there are different knowledges and different truths for different peoples; in fact, he was convinced of its opposite. But he did believe that though knowledge is one and universal, different people must assimilate it and make it theirs in their own way, suited to their condition—just as different people have different diets suited to their soil, climate and taste, though the principle of nutrition is one. 'The mischief is,' as he put it,[3] 'that as soon as the idea of a university enters our mind the idea of a Cambridge university, Oxford university, and a host of other European universities, rushes in at the same time and fills the whole space. We then imagine that our salvation lies in a selection of the best points of each, patched together in an eclectic perfection. We forget that the European universities are living, organic parts of the life of Europe, where each found its natural birth. Patching up noses and other small missing fractions of our features with skins from foreign limbs is allowed in modern surgery; but to build up a whole man by piecing together foreign fragments is beyond the resources of science, not only for the present time, but let us fervently hope for all time to come.'

To the glib-tongued politician who complained '. . . that the only thing wrong in our education is that it is not in our absolute control, that the boat is sea-worthy, only the helm has to be in our own hands to save it from wreckage', his reply was: 'The same weakness in our character, or in our circumstances, which inevitably draws us on to the slippery slope of imitation, will pursue us when

---

[3] In his lecture, *The Centre of Indian Culture*, first published by the Society for the Promotion of National Education, Adyar, Madras, 1919. Republished by Visva-Bharati, 1951.

our independence is merely of the outside. For then our freedom will become the freedom to imitate the foreign institutions, thus bringing our evil fortune under the influence of the conjunction of two malignant planets—those of imitation and the badness of imitation—producing a machine-made university, which is made with a bad machine.' Though a visionary, Tagore's genius was constructive, the bent of his mind practical, so that he was never content with an idea until he had tested its validity by giving it concrete shape. If he found fault with anything he must demonstrate how to set it right. Often he burnt his fingers, but who can light a torch if he is afraid of burning his fingers?

The seed he planted grew and has continued to grow. The future will judge its fruit, but whatever the yield, its value is to be measured not only in itself but in the influence it has had on the climate of education all over the country. Santiniketan and Visva-Bharati survive far beyond the geographical boundaries.

Tagore now had an additional incentive or excuse to travel. He needed it. He was restless. The world's adulation was like an intoxicant; he wanted more of it. It is true that it was necessary for him to travel to secure for his project both publicity and material resources, but the necessity was welcome because of an inner and personal need. In a letter of 15 April 1918 written to a young girl in whom he had discovered a little playmate of the spirit, he was frank about it. 'You may have read in books that some birds leave their nests at certain times and fly away over the sea. I am such a bird. From time to time something calls me from beyond the ocean and my wings flutter. So I have arranged to board a ship at the beginning of May and cross the Pacific Ocean.'[4] But for some reason the foreign tour did not materialize. He had therefore to content himself with travelling in his own country. He made an extensive tour of South India visiting several towns where he lectured on his educational ideals. This was followed by a tour of Western India in 1920 when he presided over the Gujarati Literary Conference in Ahmedabad and spent some time with Mahatma Gandhi at his newly-founded asrama on the bank of Sabarmati.

[4] *Bhanusinher Patravali* (Letters written to Ranu Mookerji).

The period, 1917–1919, hectic with political and educational activities, was comparatively sterile in new literary creations. The only two important and original works in Bengali written during this period were *Palataka* (Fugitive), a volume of tales in verse, published in 1918, and *Lipika* (Sketches), prose-poems, reflective and allegorical, published much later in 1922. The list of his publications in 1917 contains not a single Bengali book but all English translations: *My Reminiscences, Sacrifice and Other Plays, The Cycle of Spring, Personality* and *Nationalism*. But though comparatively meagre in volume, the character of his Bengali compositions of the period is not only of a very high quality but marks a new departure in technique, opening a fresh field for experimentation.

Palataka consists mainly of stories in verse, told very simply and directly in colloquial style, the metre free and easy, adjusting itself to the tempo of the narrative. The stories themselves are little, sad episodes from life told with a rare delicacy of feeling which while it never degenerates into sentimentalism bears witness to his great sympathy with suffering. Written in the same year in which his eldest daughter Bela died, they bear unmistakable traces of this personal sorrow—a sorrow which, because it was accepted with resignation and humility, has deepened his sympathy with all living things and given him an understanding of all sorrow. Four of these poems were translated by him and included in *The Fugitive*.[5]

The other volume, *Lipika*, written in 1919, is of an altogether different kind. It consists of short pieces or sketches, some descriptive, some allegorical, some reflective, some satirical and some reminiscent. They are written in prose, but a prose which has all the rhythm and beauty of poetry. It is possible that the author wanted consciously to capture in Bengali prose the beauty of rhythm and expression he had unconsciously achieved in his English translations of *Gitanjali*. On the other hand, these pieces are strangely reminiscent of the prose-poems he had written thirty-five years earlier as dedicatory offerings to the memory of his sister-in-law after her sudden and tragic death in 1884 and which were published as *Pushpanjali* (Offering of Flowers). Her thought is certainly present in some of

---

[5] Published by the Macmillan Company of New York, 1921. Dedicated to W.W. Pearson. This volume also contains twenty pieces from *Lipika*.

these pieces with their tender and wistful brooding as he looks back on the long road he has left behind, strewn with memories like lost melodies.

There is no self-pity or rancour of grievance in these reflections which are instinct with wisdom that comes of 'sorrow that has now turned into peace'. The general and dominant mood, however, is one of reflection rather than of feeling, of calm intellectual detachment, of a playful subtlety of thought which occasionally drifts into conceits. The satirical pieces are full of irony and wisdom without bitterness. One of them called *The Parrot's Training* exposes the folly of mechanized education against which he had protested all his life. It is worth quoting:[6]

Once upon a time there was a bird. It was ignorant. It sang all right, but never recited scriptures. It hopped pretty frequently but lacked manners.

Said the Raja to himself: 'Ignorance is costly in the long run. For fools consume as much food as their betters, and yet give nothing in return.' He called his nephews to his presence and told them that the bird must have a sound schooling. The pundits were summoned, and at once went to the root of the matter. They decided that the ignorance of birds was due to their natural habit of living in poor nests. Therefore the first thing necessary for the bird's education was a suitable cage. The pundits had their rewards and went home happy.

A golden cage was built with gorgeous decorations. Crowds came to see it from all parts of the world. 'Culture, captured and caged!' exclaimed some in a rapture and burst into tears. Others remarked, 'Even if culture be missed, the cage will remain, to the end a substantial fact. How fortunate for the bird!' The goldsmith filled his bag with money and lost no time in sailing homewards.

The pundit sat down to educate the bird. With proper deliberation he took his pinch of snuff as he said, 'Textbooks can never be too many for our purpose.' The nephews brought together an enormous crowd of scribes. They copied from books, and copied from copies, till the manuscripts were piled up to an unreachable height. Men murmured in amazement: 'Oh, the tower of culture so high that its end is lost in the clouds!' The scribes, with light hearts, hurried home, their pockets heavily laden. The nephews were furiously busy keeping the cage in proper trim. As

[6] The English translation is by the author himself and was originally published by Thacker, Spink & Co., Calcutta, 1918. Republished by Visva-Bharati in 1944.

their constant scrubbing and polishing went on, the people said with satisfaction, 'This is progress indeed!'

Whatever may be the world's other deficiencies, it is never in want of faultfinders; and they went about saying that every creature remotely connected with the cage flourished except only the bird. When this remark reached the Raja's ears, he summoned his nephews and said, 'My dear nephews, what is this that we hear?' The nephews said in answer: 'Sire, food is scarce with the fault-finders and that is why their tongues have gained in sharpness.' The explanation was so satisfactory that the Raja decorated each one of the nephews with rare jewels.

The Raja, at length desirous of seeing with his own eyes how his Education Department busied itself with the little bird, made his appearance one day at the great Hall of Learning. From the gate rose the sounds of conch-shells and gongs, horns, bugles and trumpets, cymbals, drums and kettle-drums, tomtoms, tambourines, flutes, fifes, barrel-organs and bag-pipes. The pundits began chanting *mantras* with their topmost voices, while the goldsmiths, scribes, supervisors, and their numberless cousins of all different degrees of distance, loudly raised a round of cheers. The nephews smiled and said: 'Sire, what do you think of it all?' The Raja said, 'It does seem so fearfully like a sound principle of Education!'

Mightily pleased, the Raja was about to remount his elephant, when the fault-finder from behind some bush cried out: 'Maharaja, have you seen the bird?' 'Indeed, I have not!' exclaimed the Raja, 'I completely forgot about the bird.' Turning back, he asked the pundits about the method they followed in instructing the bird. It was shown to him. He was immensely impressed. The method was so stupendous that the bird looked ridiculously unimportant in comparison. The Raja was satisfied that there was no flaw in the arrangements. As for any complaint from the bird itself, that simply could not be expected. Its throat was so completely choked with the leaves from the books that it could neither whistle nor whisper. It sent a thrill through one's body to watch the process.

This time, while remounting his elephant, the Raja ordered his State Ear-puller to give a thorough good pull at both the ears of the fault-finder.

The bird thus crawled on duly and properly to the safest verge of inanity. Its progress was satisfactory in the extreme. Nevertheless, nature occasionally triumphed over training, and when the morning light peeped into the bird's cage it sometimes fluttered its wings in a reprehensible manner.

And, though it is hard to believe, it pitifully pecked at its bars with its feeble beak. 'What impertinence!' growled the Kotwal.[7] The blacksmith with his forge and hammer took his place in the Raja's Department of Education. What resounding blows! The iron chain was soon completed, and the bird's wings were clipped. The Raja's brothers-in-law looked black and shook their heads saying, 'These birds not only lack good sense, but also gratitude!' With textbook in one hand and baton in the other, the pundits gave the bird what may fitly be called lessons. The Kotwal was honoured with a title for his watchfulness, and the blacksmith for his skill in forging chains.

The bird died.

Nobody had the least notion how long ago it had happened. The fault-finder was the first to spread the rumour. The Raja called his nephews and asked them: 'My dear nephews, what is that we hear?' The nephews replied, 'Sire, the bird's education has been completed.'

'Does it hop?' the Raja inquired.

'Never!' said the nephews.

'Does it fly?'

'No.'

'Bring me the bird,' said the Raja.

The bird was brought to him, guarded by the Kotwal and the sepoys and the sowars.[8] The Raja poked his body with his finger. Only the inner stuffing of book leaves rustled.

He would be an optimist who said that the satire has altogether lost its relevance, even outside India. Two other little satires may be referred to in passing—*Trial of the Horse* and *Old Man's Ghost*. The former is really the trial of Man whose cupidity and craftiness ignore nature's design, harnessing all things, living and non-living, to his own use. When the gods wake up from their periodic fit of slumber and discover what man has made of creatures who were designed for other purposes, they frown in anger. Brahma, the chief of the gods, who is in charge of this special portfolio, warns man: 'Unless you set free my horse I shall take care that he grows the teeth and claws of the tiger.' 'That would be ungodly,' protests man, 'thus to encourage ferocity.' Summoning logic and scientific evidence, man explains to Brahma that the horse is not fit for free-

[7] The Police Chief.   [8] Cavalry—the sepoys making the infantry.

dom and that it is precisely in the interest of equestrian well-being that man had to invent the harness. The Old Man's Ghost is obsession with Past which rides on the shoulders of Present, glorification of national culture and unreasoning dread of change.

Besides these two major works, *Palataka* and *Lipika*, Tagore wrote a large number of songs during this period and made a fresh stage-adaptation of one of his earlier plays. Another interesting contribution of this period, not intended as literature, is a series of charming letters he wrote to a young and lively schoolgirl whose bubbling spirits seemed to have stirred the memory of his own playful youth.[9] Apart from the playful and whimsical style of these letters they are of interest as throwing light on the poet's day to day routine of living in Santiniketan. Here is a specimen:

'Lunch is over and I am leaning against a cushion in my corner. The sky is dark with heavy clouds and . . . their shadow rests on the green fields in front of me, filling my eyes with a profound peace. Even as I am writing the rain has descended . . . and the distant line of green trees is half veiled, as though the forest goddess has pulled her scarf over her face. I can't tell the exact time, for I have banished from the wall the clock that used to hang in front of me. Its conduct of late had forfeited my trust, it behaved wrong, it sounded wrong and many a time I came to grief by following its advice about meal-time and bed-time. I can't say that it couldn't have been put right but since the clock was made to look after time I don't see why I should waste time to look after the clock. However, I guess it's about one or half past. Soon it'll be time for my class . . .

'In the meanwhile Andrews was very ill, causing us much anxiety. One night he took it in his head that he had cholera; that very night I sent a man to Burdwan[10] to get a doctor, but within a few hours Andrews felt so much better with the medicine[11] I had given him that early in the morning I had to send a telegram to Burdwan to save the doctor the trouble. You know, of course, that the lines in

---

[9] These letters were published in book form in 1930, entitled *Bhanusinher Patravali.*
[10] The nearest big town, about thirty miles or so away.
[11] Homoeopathic. Tagore believed in Hahnemann's system and had read many of his books.

my palm say that I have the gift of healing. However that be, the Saheb is fully recovered and is running about as usual—though without the Japanese kimono he used to wear . . . I am busy as ever. In the morning, as you know, I teach three classes, after which I have my bath and lunch, and then sit down to write letters if there are any pending. Then I prepare notes for the next class until tea. In the evening when the sun sets I sit alone and quiet on my terrace— occasionally some boys turn up and ask me to read out some poem to them . . . I wake up as the first faint hue of light peeps through the eastern door of my bedroom, rousing the first flutter of wings in the trees and tinting the clouds with gold. Soon after at 4.30 a.m. the school bell rings and I too leave my bed. After a wash I sit down to my prayers on the stone seat facing the east. As the sun slowly rises, its first rays touch me as with a blessing. We have an early breakfast, for at 6.30 all the inmates of the asrama, young and old, assemble in the open field in front of the school and sing a hymn in chorus before the classes begin . . . How peacefully my day passes! I love to work for these boys, because they are not conscious of the value of what we do for them. They accept our service as simply and naturally as they accept the light from the sun—not as one bargains for things in a market-place. When these boys grow up and make their own careers—may be, they will keep with them a memory of these open spaces, this avenue of *sal* trees, this abundant light of the sky, this free, wild wind and this silent worship of God under the open sky, morning and evening.'[12]

It was nothing unusual with Tagore to write long letters to little children. He loved the young and never failed to reply in his own hand when any of them wrote to him, from whatever land. On 2 March 1914 a schoolgirl (presumably very young because her writing is in childish scrawl) wrote him the following letter from The Park School, Buffalo, N.Y.:

My dear Mr. Tagore,
We are the third and fourth grades in an open-air school. We have been

[12] There were no compulsory congregational prayers for the school children, but twice each day, at sunrise and at sunset, the children would seat themselves in meditation and observe silence. They were free to pray or to indulge in day-dreams.

reading your poems in *The Crescent Moon* and have enjoyed them very much. This morning we had for our reading lesson *The Farther Bank*. Are you the little boy that wanted to be the boatman of the ferry-boat when you grew up? Very sincerely, Susan Bass.

The poet answered on 7 August:

My dear little friend,

I must thank you for your letter which has given me great joy. When I wrote the poems of *The Crescent Moon* in Bengali I never thought that a time would come when I should translate them for my little readers across the sea. I am glad that they have won your heart, and that you have rightly discovered who the boy was who had hoped one day to be the boatman of the 'ferry-boat' which carries love from the East to the Western shore.

With love,
Your affectionate friend,
Rabindranath Tagore.

Here is another, dated 15 February 1918, addressed to Rothenstein's daughter Rachel, then a little girl:

My dear little friend,

It is very sweet of you to think of me and send me your greetings of love. It is so much more life for me to know that I live in a definite little corner in the heart of a little girl on the other shore of the sea. It is such a pleasure to muse upon this miracle that you will know me at once when you see me and we shall with utmost ease settle down to talk about things which are of no importance at all to anybody. Very likely you will press me to stay on till tea-time or even to dinner. Possibly we shall never meet, but that is a minor detail.

On the other side of this card you will find a copy of an Ajanta picture copied by a student of my school who is visiting the cave. It still speaks to us though it speaks across the silence of forgotten ages.

My love to you,
Your affectionate friend,
Rabindranath Tagore.

Unknown to Tagore, a kindred spirit 'on the other shore of the sea' felt and said the same things about war and nationalism—with even more courage, for Romain Rolland was in the midst of the conflagration in which his own country was deeply involved. 'Truth is the same to all nations,' he said, 'but each nation has its lies which it speaks of as its idealism.' Rolland had been impressed by Tagore's lectures on Nationalism delivered in Japan in 1916 and immediately recognized in him a spirit akin to his own, one who was like him 'above the battle' where hatred and violence drive nations to mutual slaughter and yet not above the battle where the spirit of man defends its banner against unreason and passion. He had translated portions of these lectures into French and had used them in his articles during the war. The war was over; he now wrote to Tagore in June 1919 asking him to add his signature to the Declaration of Independence of the Spirit which Rolland had drafted on behalf of the European artists and intellectuals. 'I could wish,' he wrote, 'that henceforth the intellect of Asia might take a more definite part in the manifestation of the thought of Europe. My dream will be that one day we may see the union of these two hemispheres of the spirit; and I admire you for having contributed towards this more than anyone else.'

Tagore signed the Declaration on 26 June and in a letter dated exactly two months later Rolland wrote to him: 'The reading of *Nationalism* has been a great joy for me; for I entirely agree with your thoughts, and I love them even more now that I have heard them expressed by you with this noble and harmonious wisdom which, being your own, is so dear to us. It gives me profound pain (and, I might say, remorse, if I did not consider myself a human being rather than a European) when I consider the monstrous abuse which Europe makes of her power, this havoc of the universe, the destruction and debasement of so much material and moral wealth of the greatest forces on earth which it would have been in her interest to defend and to make strong by uniting them to her own. The time has come to react. It is not only a question of justice, it is a question of saving humanity. After the disaster of this shameful World War which marked Europe's failure, it has become evident that Europe alone cannot save herself. Her thought is in need of Asia's thought, just as the latter has profited from contact with Europe's thought. These are the two hemispheres of the brain of mankind. If one is paralysed, the whole body degenerates. It is necessary to re-establish their union and their healthy development.'

On 15 May 1920 Tagore sailed for England, accompanied by his son and daughter-in-law. He had been playing with the idea of a foreign tour since 1918 and now at last the opportunity came. On the same boat travelled the Aga Khan. The strange boat-fellows seemed to have been congenial company to each other for, as the poet's son testified, they had long discussions on Sufism and often the Aga Khan recited to him verses of the great Persian poet Hafiz. Back in England Tagore was happy to meet his old friends and to make new ones. He was, however, pained to find that the atmosphere was not so cordial as on his earlier visit before the war. Much had happened since then. Tagore's condemnation of war, his outspoken comments on the British rule in India and, above all, his renunciation of the knighthood had resulted in a cooling off of the earlier warmth. But even before these political considerations came into play, some British intellectuals had resented the praise that had been lavished on an eastern poet. Strangely enough, it was D. H. Lawrence, himself a votary of the dark and primitive mystery of life, who voiced this resentment most strongly.

'I become more and more surprised,' he wrote on 24 May 1916 to Lady Ottoline Morrell,[13] 'to see how far higher, in reality, our European civilization stands than the East, India or Persia ever dreamed of. And one is glad to *realize* how these Hindus are horribly decadent and reverting to all forms of barbarism in all sorts of ugly ways. We feel surer on our feet, then. But this fraud of looking up to them—this wretched worship-of-Tagore attitude—is disgusting. "Better fifty years of Europe" even as she is. Buddha worship is completely decadent and foul nowadays: and it *was* always only half civilized.'

As against this rather savage outburst must be quoted the touching tribute in the following excerpt from a letter written to Tagore by the mother of the young English poet Wilfred Owen, who was killed one week before the war was over and the news of whose tragic death reached the mother on Armistice day.

[13] *Collected Letters*, Heinemann. Quoted in Aronson's *Rabindranath Through Western Eyes*.

'It is nearly two years ago that my dear eldest son went to the war for the last time and the day he said goodbye to me—we were looking together across the sun-glorified sea—looking towards France, with breaking hearts—when he, my poet son, said those wonderful words of yours—beginning at "When I go from hence, let this be my parting word"—and when his pocket book came back to me—I found these words written in his dear writing—with your name beneath. Would it be asking too much of you, to tell me what book I should find the whole poem in?'[14]

Among the new acquaintances Tagore was happy to make in London was the romantic and heroic soldier Lawrence of Arabia, who told him that he was ashamed to go back to that country because the British Government had let him down by betraying the promise he had made to the Arabs on its behalf. While discussing India's problem Lawrence told Tagore that the only way to win the respect of an Englishman is to hit back harder than he hits, for then he would come to his senses and recognize the other as a brother. Another charming acquaintance was Sybil Thorndike who recited a poem, specially composed for the occasion by Laurence Binyon, at a meeting arranged by the East and West Society at Caxton Hall to welcome Tagore. 'Such a beautiful voice!' wrote Tagore's son in his diary. In Cambridge Tagore met Lord Roberts, Lowes Dickinson and the brilliant economist Keynes, and spent a weekend with Muirhead Bone at Petersfield.

From London Tagore was to leave for Norway and Sweden from where invitations had been received. The passage had been booked from Newhaven to Bergen in Norway and the party was to sail the following day when an interesting incident intervened. A charming and accomplished lady who had been introduced to Tagore by a well-known Orientalist a few days earlier and who professed great interest in Eastern philosophy, had ingratiated herself in Tagore's good opinion and offered to act as his secretary during his Scandinavian tour, claiming that she knew almost everyone worth knowing in those countries. On the day before the party's departure, it was revealed to Tagore that the lady was a government spy.

[14] The full letter which is dated Shrewsbury, August 1st, 1920, is given in *On the Edges of Time*, Rathindranath Tagore.

Tagore was so upset at the discovery that he immediately cancelled his trip to the Scandinavian countries and left for Paris instead. The incident is recorded by his son who writes that a few days after the party arrived in Paris, he '. . . received a pile of cuttings, taken from newspapers in Bergen which I have carefully preserved. Big headlines and front page descriptions of our arrival at Bergen and even photographs of the party disembarking from the boat!'

In Paris the party stayed as guests of a rich Jewish banker and philanthropist, Albert Kahn, at Autour du Monde, Boulogne sur Seine. The surroundings were spacious and attractive and after weeks of stay in a flat in the Kensington Palace Mansions in London, Tagore felt relaxed and at ease. He loved space and was always more happy in a cottage in Santiniketan than in a palace in Calcutta. In Paris he was given a reception at the Musée Guimet and made the acquaint-ance of Bergson, the Comtesse de Noailles and the Comtesse de Brimont, both poetesses of repute, Le Brun and the famous Orientalist Sylvain Levi who later visited Santiniketan as the first foreign visiting professor of Visva-Bharati. The Comtesse de Noailles, who became very friendly with Tagore, told him that she was with Clemenceau on the day when war was declared and related how they both read together from André Gide's French rendering of *Gitanjali* to find consolation and strength in its pages. Tagore himself was deeply moved when he visited the battlefields of France near Rheims and saw the indiscriminate devastation caused. He could not sleep that night and wrote to Andrews: 'It was a most saddening sight; the terrible damage deliberately done, not for any necessities of war but to cripple France for ever, was so savage that its memory can never be effaced.'

From Paris Tagore went to Holland where he visited several places, his lectures attracting vast audiences. He was warmly welcomed by the Dutch writer Frederik van Eeden, who was also his Dutch translator. The acquaintance thus established ripened into a long friendship. 'This fortnight,' wrote Tagore to Andrews, 'has been most generous in its gifts to me . . . Altogether Europe has come closer to us by this visit of ours. . . Now I know more closely than ever that Santiniketan belongs to all the world and we shall have to be worthy of this great fact.' But Europe devastated by war could show her generosity only in her warmth of affection. Deeply as Tagore was touched by it, he needed funds and material resources for his new university at Santiniketan. He was caught in the paradox of his own idealism. He who denounced materialism needed the benefit of materialism to propagate his idealism. So he wrote to Mr. Pond in the United States offering his engagement for a lecture tour. Mr. Pond cabled back regretting his inability to do so in view of the prevailing American opinion which had turned unsympathetic to Tagore in the meanwhile, under the influence of British propaganda. Chastened by the rebuff Tagore wrote to Andrews, 'You must have heard by this time that our American tour has been cancelled. The atmosphere of our mind has been cleared at a sweep of the dense fog of the contemplation of securing money. This is deliverance.'

He was wise and sensitive enough to understand his own contradictions but not strong enough, like Gandhi, to face their challenge without respite. The temptation to blur the differences with a wash of noble sentiments which came to him too easily was sometimes great and often led him to pitfalls from which he was saved only by his extreme spiritual sensibility and his innate sincerity. After visiting Belgium where he was received in audience by the king, he returned via Paris to London where his daughter-in-law had undergone an operation. In London he suddenly decided that he must visit the United States, 'for they must listen to the appeal of the East'. He had worked himself up into a mood to which the Americans would probably have responded gladly and generously—thirty years later. As usual he ran ahead of his time.

He landed in New York and stayed at the Algonquin Hotel. There was no dearth of publicity or of engagements, social or for lectures, as soon as the public came to know of his arrival.[15] He addressed several gatherings, both in New York and other places. A

---

[15] The following anecdote quoted by Dr. Aronson from Lady Benson's book of reminiscences, *Mainly About Prayers*, is worth re-quoting: 'My hostess explained to me that Tagore was a Yogi and his creed forbade him to look upon a woman's bare arms and neck. I felt horribly uncomfortable and immodest, especially as I had been given the honoured place beside him, so I carefully draped my table napkin over the shoulder next to him.'

New York journal of 22 November 1920 reported about his lecture, *A Poet's Religion*, at the Brooklyn Civic Forum: 'Never has the Forum had as large an audience as that which turned out to hear the famous writer from the East. Hundreds were turned away.' But in so far as he had any hopes of raising large funds for his university he was sorely disappointed. Some friends had been sympathetic, which led him at first to build high hopes, for he wrote in a letter home, 'Things are working well, and I have cause to be sanguine of success.' But the elation was short-lived, and the grapes having proved sour he wrote to Andrews, 'This visit of mine to America has produced in me intense contempt for money.'

He had asked for it and ought to have known better than to go about in a foreign country with a begging bowl, even though for a good cause, when he himself had chided the politicians of his country for begging favours from the British Government. Visva-Bharati was a great idea but once an idea becomes an institution it becomes a form of possession with its inevitable vested interest and, as Gandhi pointed out so wisely, possession is incompatible with true freedom of mind and pursuit of truth. The basic motive of the visit being materialistic, however altruistic the end in view, its obscure consciousness must have rankled in his mind, depriving him not only of the stimulus of watching a new phase of Western civilization at work but blurring his proper understanding of it. The pent-up resentment burst out unexpectedly at a farewell meeting which the Poetry Society had organized in his honour. After a short discourse on literature he suddenly gave vent to his grievance at having been unjustly maligned, first as a British agent and later as a secret German agent. However unfair the accusations and insinuations made against him in the American press and in a whispering campaign instigated by British propaganda, this was hardly the occasion to make a public grievance of it. So unfortunate was the effect of this outburst that his son who was present and who had been mainly instrumental in persuading him to undertake this visit to the States, noted in his diary: 'This was the first time, I thought, he lost his dignity. I was moved to tears, it hurt me terribly. It seemed a tragedy to me.'

There is no doubt that Tagore's name had been unnecessarily

dragged into what was known as the German-Indian Conspiracy Trial which took place in San Francisco in 1918. Taking advantage of it, the British authorities and their press henchmen in India had made insinuations suggesting Tagore's complicity with German espionage. His ill-fated visit to San Francisco in 1916, when a rumour had been circulated that some of his countrymen planned to assassinate him, had left a scar on his memory. The very arrangements made by the police to protect him had been a source of humiliation. The *San Francisco Examiner* of 6 October 1916 had reported: 'Word of a plot to assassinate Sir Rabindranath Tagore, Hindu poet and Nobel Prize-winner, reached the police yesterday and led to extraordinary precautions to guard him in his apartments at the Palace Hotel and at the Columbia Theatre where he lectured in the afternoon.' In the same issue was published a letter from one Gobinda Behari Lal, M.A. (University of California), who was later involved in the German-Indian Conspiracy Trial and sentenced to imprisonment, from which the following excerpt may be cited: 'Sir, Will it not be interesting for you to know what the Hindus think of Tagore? They do not think he represents in any sense the ideas, sentiments or feelings which they at present entertain in regard to political, economic or philosophic issues. The heart of India is in the Anti-British revolutionary movement, which is rapidly transforming India along modern lines. But Mr. Tagore stands aloof from this movement just as Goethe stood aloof from the German war of liberation a century ago.' Interviewed by a representative of the *Los Angeles Examiner* the poet is reported to have said, 'As for a plot to assassinate me, I have the fullest confidence in the sanity of my countrymen, and shall fulfil my engagements without the help of police protection. I take this opportunity emphatically to assert that I do not believe that there was a plot to assassinate me, though I had to submit to the farce of being guarded by the police, from which I hope to be relieved for the rest of my visit to this country.'[16]

These memories were painful and humiliating enough. When on top of it the British authorities in India spread their insinuations Tagore was deeply hurt and, taking the democratic and humanitarian

[16] Quoted in the *Modern Review*, Calcutta, June 1918.

professions of the American President seriously, he sent a cable on 11 May 1918 to President Wilson: 'Newspapers received concerning Conspiracy Trial San Francisco implicating me. I claim from you and your country to protect me against such lying calumny. Rabindranath Tagore.' As far as is known, the cable was not even acknowledged.

This third visit was, however, fruitful in many personal and human contacts he made, which were after all of far greater value than the million dollars he failed to raise. He renewed old and valued acquaintances and made new ones, among them the two remarkable ladies, Hellen Keller and Jane Addams.[17] Even more valuable was the foundation laid in Mrs. William Vaughan Moody's house in New York of a lifelong friendship with Dorothy Straight and the young Englishman Leonard K. Elmhirst, whom she later married and who was at that time a student of Agriculture at Cornell. Tagore had heard of this young English idealist from a common friend and sent him a telegram to see him in New York.[18] The friendship thus begun grew with the years and Elmhirst later became not only his chief associate in the development of the Rural Reconstruction Institute at Sriniketan but he and his wife continued to help the

[17] 'Perhaps the most valuable contribution,' wrote Jane Addams later, 'which can be made to our perplexing age is a revelation of the essential unity and validity of all human experiences, that our intellectual and emotional understanding may approach our commercial and political arrangements . . . Rabindranath Tagore has met all these requirements of genius combined in a man who is at once a poet, a philosopher, a humanitarian, and an educator.' *The Golden Book of Tagore*.

[18] Mr. Elmhirst recalls, 'The day before, quite out of the blue, I had received a cryptic telegram addressed to me at Cornell University, "Come and see me in New York, Rabindranath Tagore." I was in the middle of my second year at Cornell where at the close of the first world war I had gone to study agriculture. To earn my board and lodging I was trying to teach English part time to first-year students. But my ambition was to return to India where, after being invalided out of Mesopotamia in 1917, I had begun to study at first hand some aspects of the many-sided problems of Indian agriculture and rural life. I wanted very much to return and to work, neither as a servant of the Imperial British Government nor as a missionary, but rather with an Indian and preferably in association with someone like Tagore and in an Indian village. At the time I had no idea how to bring myself to the notice of a man of such distinction and whose writings in English I had so much admired. The dramatic effect on my mind of a first reading of *Gitanjali* six years before, when I had just finished my studies for a degree in history at Cambridge, had never receded from my mind.'

Institute with generous financial assistance even after Elmhirst's return to his country. So the visit was not fruitless in the long run, even from the point of view of his university.

In March 1921 Tagore returned to London. Despite the obvious chill in the general British attitude, his personal relations with individual friends had continued to be cordial and having once known the English mind at its best, he never ceased to respect the British character, despite many political disillusionments. The best type of Englishman, he had said, is the best type of humanity, and now he confessed in a letter to Andrews, 'With all our grievances against the English nation, I cannot help loving your country which has given me some of my best friends.'

From London where he stayed for about three weeks, Tagore flew to Paris, his first experience of air travel. This time he met Romain Rolland whom he had long wished to see. He also made the acquaintance of Patrick Geddes, the Scottish biologist and sociologist whom he grew to admire. 'What so strikingly attracted me in Patrick Geddes,' he wrote later, 'was not his scientific achievement but, on the contrary, the rare fact of the fullness of his personality rising far above his science. Whatever subjects he has studied and mastered have become vitally one with his humanity.' From Paris Tagore went to Strasbourg and addressed the newly-established French University where Sylvain Levi was professor, on 'The Message of the Forest'. Proceeding to Geneva he spoke at the Rousseau Institute on 'Education'. While he was holidaying at Lucerne to spend his sixty-first birthday in the midst of nature's beauty, he received the good news that a committee formed in Germany, consisting of eminent writers and scholars, among them Thomas Mann, Rudolf Eucken, Hermann Jacobi, Count Keyserling and Gerhart Hauptmann, had celebrated his birthday with a gift of a large collection of German classics to the Visva-Bharati Library. Deeply touched, Tagore wrote: 'The generous greeting and the gift that have come to me from Germany on the occasion of my sixty-first birthday are overwhelming in their significance for myself. I truly feel that I have had my second birth in the heart of the people of that country who have accepted me as their own.'

After brief visits, with lecture engagements, at Hamburg and

Copenhagen,[19] he went to Sweden in response to a long-standing invitation from the Swedish Academy. After his address to the Academy the Archbishop of Upsala said, 'The Nobel Prize for literature is intended for the writer who combines in himself the artist and the prophet. None has fulfilled these conditions better than Rabindranath Tagore.' In Stockholm Tagore witnessed the performance on the stage of the Swedish version of his play *The Post Office*, was received by King Gustavus V and met many distinguished persons, among them Selma Lagerlof, Knut Hamsun, Karl H. Brating (first President of the League of Nations) and the famous explorer Sven Hedin whom Tagore greatly admired.[20]

From Stockholm Tagore came to Berlin where he addressed the University on 2 June. 'Scenes of frenzied hero-worship,' reported a local paper, 'marked a public lecture given by Rabindranath Tagore. In the rush for seats many girls fainted.' So large was the number of persons turned away that the lecture had to be repeated the following day. The lecture was recorded, but unfortunately the University archives were bombed and destroyed during World War II. A portion of the record containing the concluding paragraphs of the speech was, however, salvaged after the war and a tape-copy of it was presented to the Sahitya Akademi (National Academy of Letters, India) by a delegation of German writers who visited India some time ago.

[19] His lecture at the Copenhagen University was followed by a spectacular ovation from the students who later made a torch-light procession in front of his hotel singing national songs till late at night.

[20] In 1931, on Tagore's seventieth birthday, Sven Hedin wrote to him, 'My dear friend Rabindranath Tagore, is it really true that you are only seventy years old! Judging from your work, your wise thoughts and the influence you have had upon our time, one would believe you were much older. I remember so well when our great poet, Dr. Verner von Heidenstam, first told me you had got our Nobel Prize for the year 1913, and how happy I was that the greatest thinker and philosopher of my beloved Asia had been honoured . . . Several years later you came to Stockholm to deliver the public lecture that every receiver of a Nobel Prize has to give. Our Academy at that occasion gave a dinner in your honour . . . In 1929 I again had the honour and pleasure of meeting you in Tokio, and again we had a long talk about the extraordinary and deplorable situation in the world. We found it a great pity for the whole humanity that our time did not possess one single really capable and wise statesman, a man whose actions were dictated entirely by righteousness, justice and love.'

In Munich Tagore met Thomas Mann, Kurt Wolff (his publisher in German) and several other men of letters and learning. Moved by the physical privations which the people of Germany had to face in the wake of the Armistice, he donated the proceeds of his lecture for the benefit of 'famished children' of Munich. The strain, physical and emotional, of the German tour weighed heavily on Tagore's health and he longed to return to India to the quiet of Santiniketan. But though he resisted the pressure of several other invitations he could not decline the one received from the Grand Duke of Hesse to be his guest at Darmstadt. He also wanted to see the German philosopher Count Hermann Keyserling whom he had met in India during the latter's visit in 1911.[21] He stayed in Darmstadt for nearly a week during which there were no official programmes, no receptions and no formal lectures. But crowds used to gather in the grounds attached to the palace and every morning and evening Tagore would come out and meet them and invite questions which he would answer, Count Keyserling acting as interpreter. He was deeply impressed, not only with the warm affection with which the common citizens welcomed him but with their genuine interest in philosophical and metaphysical problems.

On a Sunday the Duke and Count Keyserling took him out for a drive to a park outside the town where they sat on a stone bench on a little hillock. Soon the holiday crowd gathered and formed themselves into a massed circle round the slope. 'Without any encouragement,' reports the poet's son who was with him, 'they burst into song. Song after song followed for nearly an hour. There must have been a crowd of about two thousand. There was nobody to lead them and yet a choir of two thousand voices sang without hesitation and in perfect harmony. Such a performance would be unthinkable outside Germany. This spontaneous ovation from the

---

[21] Keyserling was perhaps the first foreigner to recognize and appreciate Tagore's genius. The recognition was almost intuitive, for at that time he had merely met Tagore and had not read any of his works. Later, as the acquaintance ripened, his admiration of Tagore grew. 'Rabindranath Tagore is the greatest man I have had the privilege to know,' he wrote in 1930. 'He is very much greater than his world reputation and above all his position in India imply. There has been no one like him anywhere on our globe for many and many centuries . . . he is the most universal, the most encompassing, the most complete human being I have known.'

common people, so beautifully rendered, touched father very deeply.'[22]

One other incident is worth recalling. There was an artists' club in Darmstadt whose members complained that the Indian poet had been monopolized by a different sort of people and invited him to their club. He went. The room was noisy and crowded, the tables loaded with tankards of beer, the air thick with cigar fumes. The members did not rise to welcome the guest. The poet, however, rose to the occasion and without showing any resentment made himself at home with the artists and answered their questions freely. As he spoke the tankards were gradually removed and hidden under the tables, the cigars were put out and the audience listened to him with almost reverential attention. Tagore later remarked that he had never experienced a greater triumph. Altogether the week spent in the little German town proved both restful and exhilarating for him.

This enthusiastic reception given to an Indian poet in Germany was naturally suspect in British and French eyes. The English correspondent of the *Daily Telegraph* reported that 'the ovation accorded to the poet at Hamburg was propagandist in origin, contrived by German industrialists to cultivate a good opinion among Indian intellectuals as a stepping stone towards the capture of the Indian markets'. And a French paper, *L'Eclair*, wrote: 'Rabindranath Tagore is a kind of Hindu Tolstoy. As one might have expected, Germany uses him for propaganda purposes; and he exalts pan-Germanism in a whole-hearted and painstaking manner for which the press beyond the Rhine pays him unanimous homage.' The paper goes on to prove its charge by quoting the following message sent by Tagore to Dr. Rudolf Eucken, conveniently omitting the 'ifs'. '*If* it be the destiny of Germany to go through the penance for the sin of the modern age and come out purified and strong, *if* she can know how to make use of the fire that has scorched her for lighting up the path to a great future, to the aspiration of the soul for its true freedom, she will be blessed in the history of humanity '[23]

[22] *On the Edges of Time.*
[23] For a fuller account of the 'other side' see Dr. Aronson's *Rabindranath Through Western Eyes.* The present author is inclined to think that this book, though an

From Germany Tagore went to Vienna where he gave two lectures and then to Prague where he spoke both at the Charles University and at the German University. His visit led to a warm personal friendship with the eminent Indologists Professors M. Winternitz and V. Lesny, both of whom were later invited by him as visiting professors at Visva-Bharati, Santiniketan. Lesny was the first foreign scholar to translate Tagore's writings from the original Bengali. His translation of a selection from Tagore's poetry and prose was published in Czech as early as 1914 under the title *Rabindranath Thakur: Ukazky Poesie A Prosy*. After his visit to Santiniketan he wrote a biography of the poet which has been referred to earlier in this book. Tagore was also happy to make the acquaintance of Karel Čapek and the composer Leos Janáček. Because of these contacts and friendships he retained a very warm affection for Czechoslovakia. But though the visit was stimulating and happy, Tagore was tired and homesick and returned to India in July 1921, after an absence of nearly fourteen months.

If he imagined that he was returning to peace and quiet, he was soon to be disillusioned. India was seething with unrest, the somnolent masses were at last being roused by the magic wand of Gandhi,[24]

---

excellent document of scholarly research, is somewhat one-sided and suffers from the author's hatred of the Nazi régime. The book was published in 1943 and the bias of the author, who is of German and Jewish origin, is not unnatural. It is true that the popular German estimate of Tagore underwent a drastic change after Hitler's assumption of power, and Tagore was denounced as un-Aryan and even made to be a Jew 'whose real name was Rabbi Nathan'. Nevertheless, it is not necessary to dismiss all popular feeling as spurious simply because it changes with altered conditions. The British and American popular estimates of Japan, China and Russia have undergone violent changes. Nor was the German admiration of Tagore unmixed. Many conservative rightists resented his denunciation of nationalism and one of their spokesmen, Arthur Schurig, dubbed Tagore as early as 1921 as 'a British paid agent undermining Germany' and a tool in the hands of the 'Bolshevist conspiracy' against the German race.

[24] Before launching his campaign of non-co-operation, Gandhi had returned (a year later than Tagore's renunciation of knighthood) the Kaiser-i-Hind medal to the British Government, with these words 'I can retain neither respect nor affection for a Government which has been moving from wrong to wrong to defend its immorality.' Tagore's own gesture too was a form of non-co-operation which had even preceded Gandhi's.

who had given a call for a nation-wide movement of non-co-operation with the British régime which he dubbed as 'satanic'. Tagore
had known about it while he was abroad, the press and in particular
Andrews had kept him well informed of what was brewing, but he
now experienced the storm at first hand. He had himself prayed for
years, in his poems, songs and plays, for such a deliverer who would
give voice to the dumb, strength to the unarmed, and he fully
endorsed Gandhi's insistence on non-violence.[25] But actuality
hardly ever corresponds with the idea, and however much one may
welcome a storm, it is none the less distressing when the dust and
the grit get into the eye. Gandhi, though a more incorrigible idealist
than Tagore, was also a revolutionary leader of men and was obliged
on occasions to over-dramatize a situation and exaggerate certain
aspects of it to rouse adequate mass fervour. Like Nelson he often
held the telescope to his blind eye and truthfully declared that he
saw nothing. But Tagore who merely watched, and that too with
an eagle eye, saw everything. And there was much to make him
uneasy.

A sudden upsurge of patriotic zeal in a people who had not felt it
for a long time and had hardly any historical memories of such
phenomena was bound to result in an exaggerated sense of self-
righteousness and a contempt for everything foreign, in this case
particularly British or Western. Tagore, who had been denouncing
this very aspect of nationalism in other countries, found the sight
extremely painful in his own. Only a few months earlier he had
written to Andrews from New York: 'The complete man must
never be sacrificed to the patriotic man, or even to the merely
moral man. To me humanity is rich and large and many-sided.'
Not that the Mahatma believed otherwise. He too said, 'My religion
has no geographical limits. I have a living faith in it which will
transcend even my love for India herself.' Again, 'For me patriotism
is the same as humanity. I am patriotic because I am human and
humane. My patriotism is not exclusive. I will not hurt England or
Germany to serve India . . . A patriot is so much less a patriot if he
is a lukewarm humanitarian.' But it was not in this light that the vast

[25] Tagore had written in September 1920, 'We need all the moral force which
Mahatma Gandhi represents, and which he alone in the world can represent.'

majority of his followers took their patriotism. Disciples take from
the Master not what he wishes to give but what they wish to take.

There were certain other aspects too of the non-co-operation
campaign which jarred on Tagore's sensibility. He hated the sight
of excited crowds gloating over bonfires of foreign-made cloth.
He pitied the students being made to give up schools and colleges
to become pawns in the hands of politicians. He refused to believe
that spinning was the sole panacea for India's economic ills, though
he had always pleaded for the revival of cottage industries, including
spinning.[26] He could spin yarns, he once said jokingly, more easily
than yarn, and looked upon the Congress propaganda for spinning
as itself a big political yarn. Andrews, who loved Gandhi as deeply
as he loved Tagore, summed up the latter's reaction thus: 'Rabindranath Tagore felt that the popular attitude had become one of
wild excitement rather than deep moral conviction. As he expressed
it in a remarkable phrase, it shouted to him, it did not sing. It was
an outburst of pent-up feelings leading to violence of speech and
action, rather than the sustained power of soul-force . . . A further
divergence was the poet's inability to take any part in the Khaddar
movement, because it appeared to be put forward as a universal
panacea for India's poverty, while he regarded it only as an accessory
method of rendering help.'

Without directly referring to the Mahatma or criticizing his
leadership, Tagore gave eloquent expression to his faith in the
necessity of intellectual and moral co-operation between India and
the West in a public lecture in Calcutta entitled *Sikshar Milan*
(Meeting of Cultures) on 15 August—a significant date in India's
history, for on that day twenty-six years later Britain handed her
sovereignty over India back to her own people. So isolated was
Tagore even among his own people in Bengal that his speech provoked a rejoinder from the popular Bengali novelist Sarat Chandra,
in an article entitled *Sikshar Virodh* (Conflict of Cultures). Undaunted, Tagore elaborated and pressed his point of view in another

[26] Not that anyone else, except Gandhi, really believed in the all-sufficing
efficacy of spinning, but it had become a ritual of patriotism to which even today
symbolic homage is paid by Congress leaders who swear by it in the same breath
with which they propagate large-scale industrialization.

public lecture, *Satyer Ahwan* (Call of Truth), a magnificent testament of his faith. This brought a rejoinder from Gandhi himself in a famous article published in his political weekly, *Young India*, under the caption 'The Great Sentinel'.

Soon after, Gandhi visited Calcutta and on 6 September 1921 the two had a long conference behind closed doors in the poet's house at Jorasanko, the only other person present at the interview being Andrews. No authorized report exists of what talks the two had, but it was understood that Gandhi had come to persuade Tagore to give active support to his political movement. It was equally well understood later that the two parted as friends, agreeing to disagree. In the meanwhile crowds had gathered outside the house and eager to show their sympathy with what Gandhi stood for and to teach their world-minded poet a lesson had collected large bundles of foreign cloth from near-by shops and set up a bonfire right in the midst of the open courtyard attached to Tagore's house. Leonard Elmhirst has related that Tagore himself some time later gave him a gist of his conversation with Gandhi on that memorable day. It seems that when Gandhi asserted that his whole movement was based on the principle of non-violence, Tagore said, 'Come and look over the edge of my veranda, Gandhiji. Look down there and see what your non-violent followers are up to. They have stolen[27] cloth from the shops in the Chitpore Road, they've lit that bonfire in my courtyard and are now howling round it like a lot of demented dervishes. Is that non-violence?'

Elmhirst further relates[28] that Gandhi began by saying, 'Gurudev, you were yourself a leader and promoter of the Swadeshi movement in India over twenty years ago. You always wanted Indians to stand on their own feet as Indians and not to try to be poor copies of English-

[27] Mr. Elmhirst has explained that the poet deliberately used the word *stolen* instead of *snatched* because ' . . . as he [Tagore] pointed out, it was the wholesale agents who imported the cloth and committed the first sin, and it was the shopkeepers who were trying to meet the demands of the public. The logical behaviour from Mr. Gandhi's standpoint would have been to have purchased the cloth first and then burnt it! But to take the cloth from a shop by force and not pay for it was, from the Poet's point of view, stealing and not snatching.'

[28] In an article 'Personal Memories of Tagore' in the *Tagore Centenary Volume*, published by Sahitya Akademi, India.

men. My Swaraj movement is the natural child of your Swadeshi. Join me and strengthen it.' Tagore answered, 'Gandhiji, the whole world is suffering from a cult of selfish and short-sighted nationalism. India has always offered hospitality to all nations and creeds. I have come to believe that we in India still have much to learn from the West and its science, and we still, through education, have to learn to collaborate among ourselves.' Finally, when Gandhi pleaded with the poet to take to spinning, as an example to the rest of the country, the latter smiled and said, 'Poems I can spin, songs I can spin, but what a mess I would make, Gandhiji, of your precious cotton!'

The best statement and exposition of differences in the outlooks of these two great minds of India is given by a foreigner—Romain Rolland, who was himself great enough to appreciate and interpret them. His words will bear repetition:[29]

The controversy between Tagore and Gandhi, between two great minds, both moved by mutual admiration and esteem, but as fatally separated in their feeling as a philosopher can be from an apostle, a St. Paul from a Plato, is important. For on the one side we have the spirit of religious faith and charity seeking to found a new humanity. On the other we have intelligence, free-born, serene and broad, seeking to unite the aspirations of all humanity in sympathy and understanding.

Tagore always looked upon Gandhi as a saint, and I have often heard him speak of him with veneration. When, in referring to the Mahatma, I mentioned Tolstoy, Tagore pointed out to me—and I realize it now that I know Gandhi better—how much more clothed in light and radiance Gandhi's spirit is than Tolstoy's. With Gandhi everything is nature—modest, simple, pure—while all his struggles are hallowed by religious serenity, whereas with Tolstoy everything is proud revolt against passion. Everything in Tolstoy is violence, even his doctrine of non-violence.

Yet it was inevitable that the breach between the two men should widen . . . At the time he [Tagore] was not only the 'poet' but the spiritual ambassador of Asia to Europe, where he had asked people to co-operate in creating a world university at Santiniketan. What an irony of destiny that he should be preaching co-operation between Occident and Orient at one end of the world, when at that very moment non-co-operation was being preached at the other end!

[29] *Mahatma Gandhi*, Romain Rolland, 1924.

Non-co-operation clashed with his way of thinking, for his mentality, his rich intelligence, had been nourished on all cultures of the world.

Romain Rolland quotes the following passage from Tagore to illustrate the catholicity of the latter's approach: 'All humanity's greatest is mine. The *infinite personality of man* (as the *Upanishads* say) can only come from the magnificent harmony of all human races. My prayer is that India may represent the co-operation of all the peoples of the world. For India, unity is truth, division evil. Unity is that which embraces and understands everything; consequently it cannot be attained through negation. The present attempt to separate our spirit from that of the Occident is tentative of a spiritual suicide. . . The present age has been dominated by the Occident, because the Occident had a mission to fulfil. We of the Orient should learn from the Occident. It is regrettable, of course, that we had lost the power of appreciating our own culture, and therefore did not know how to assign Western culture its right place. But to say that it is wrong to co-operate with the West is to encourage the worst form of provincialism and can produce nothing but intellectual indigence. The problem is a world problem. No nation can find its own salvation by breaking away from others. We must all be saved or we must all perish together.'

'In other words,' comments Rolland, 'just as Goethe in 1813 refused to reject French civilization and culture, Tagore refuses to banish Western civilization.' Rolland was not the only great European to sense a resemblance between Goethe's universalism and Tagore's. More recently Albert Schweitzer has estimated Tagore's thought thus:[30] 'In Tagore's magnificent thought-symphony the harmonies and modulations are Indian. But the themes remind us of those of European thought. His doctrine of

[30] The present writer had the privilege of spending a day with this noble European in his little picturesque home-village, Günsbach, on 13 September 1959. Returning from the village he had a feeling that it was not a visit but a pilgrimage. There was something of both Gandhi and Tagore in this saintly philosopher. The best of men are everywhere akin. The passage quoted above is from his *Indian Thought and its Development*, English edition, A. & C. Black, London, 1936. When the present writer asked him if he still believed in what he had written (originally in 1935) about Tagore, he replied in the affirmative.

With Mahatma Gandhi and Kasturba at Santiniketan, 1940,
in the antie-chamber of the mud cottage, Syamali

Oxford University Convocation at Santiniketan, 1940, with Dr. Radhakrishnan, Sir Maurice Gwyer and Mr. Justice Henderson

Soul-in-all-things is no longer that of the *Upanishads*, but that of a mode of thought under the influence of modern natural science . . . But the Goethe of India gives expression to his personal experience that this is truth in a manner more profound, more powerful and more charming than any man has ever done before him. This completely noble and harmonious thinker belongs not only to his own people but to humanity.'

Gandhi's mind was no less hospitable to inspiration from outside —he himself had acknowledged his debt freely and with gratitude to the Sermon on the Mount and to the writings of Thoreau, Tolstoy and Ruskin—but his being a one-track mind the range of such inspiration was necessarily limited, whether foreign or native. That he did not wish to shut his mind against all influence from outside was expressed by him beautifully in the following passage: 'I do not want my house to be walled in on all sides and my windows stuffed. I want the cultures of all lands to be blown about my house as freely as possible. But I refuse to be blown off my feet by any . . . Mine is not a religion of the prison-house. It has room for the least among God's creations. But it is proof against insolent pride of race, religion or colour.'[31]

What Tagore, however, feared was not the Mahatma's spirit of exclusion—he knew that the latter was above it—but that of his followers who would not scruple to appeal to any prejudice or passion to work up the fever of nationalism. He explained his misgivings to his students in Santiniketan some of whom had been swept off their feet by the Mahatma's appeal to non-co-operate. 'What does the boycotting of schools and colleges amount to?' he asked. 'What sacrifice are the students called upon to make?—not sacrifice for more complete education but for no education.' He was consistent in his opposition to drag students into the muddy waters of politics. More than a decade earlier when he himself was a leader of the Swadeshi movement in Bengal, a group of young students came and told him that they were prepared to give up their studies if he asked them to do so. When he flatly declined to do so, they went away in anger, doubting his patriotism.

An incident that took place in his own university of Visva-

[31] *Young India*, 1 June 1921.

T

Bharati during the period of non-co-operation excitement illustrates how tolerant Tagore could be and how liberal and humane was his ideal of education. The students' union had organized a public debate on the merits of Gandhi's appeal for non-co-operation and had requested Tagore to preside. He did. After a long debate wherein one set of speakers spoke for the Mahatma's point of view and another for Tagore's, when the votes were taken it was found that the former won by a majority. In his presidential remarks Tagore said that nothing could have made him happier than the result of the debate, for it had vindicated his basic principle of education. He had taught his students, not to conform but to think freely for themselves.

Tagore's misgivings and protest against what he feared was 'blind obedience' that might 'crush, in the name of some outward liberty, the real freedom of the soul' were eloquently voiced in the lecture referred to earlier, later translated into English and published in the *Modern Review* under the caption 'The Call of Truth'.

'Tagore's noble words,' comments Rolland, 'some of the most beautiful ever addressed to a nation, are a poem of sunlight, and plane above all human struggles. And the only criticism one can make of them is that they plane too high. Tagore is right from the point of view of eternity. The bird-poet, the eagle-sized lark, as Heine called a master of our music, sits and sings on the ruins of time. He lives in eternity. But the demands of the present are imperious.' Gandhi replied to the poet's challenge in a powerful rejoinder published in his English journal, *Young India*. He hailed the poet as the 'Great Sentinel' whose warnings against moral dangers must be listened to with respect; but, goes on Gandhi, his misgivings are not justified. Finally, worked up into a moral passion, he admonishes the poet for fiddling when the house is on fire. Let the Mahatma speak:

'When all about me are dying for want of food, the only occupation permissible for me is to feed the hungry. India is a house on fire. It is dying of hunger because it has no work to buy food with ... To a people famishing and idle the only acceptable form in which God can dare appear is work and promise of food as wages. God created man to work for his food and said that those who are without work were thieves. We must think of millions who today are less than animals, almost in a dying state. Hunger is the argument that is drawing India to the spinning wheel.

'The poet lives for the morrow, and would have us do likewise. He presents to our admiring gaze the beautiful picture of the birds in the early morning singing hymns of praise as they soar into the sky. These birds had their day's food and soared with rested wings in whose veins new blood had flowed the previous night. But I have had the pain of watching birds who for want of strength could not be coaxed even into a flutter of their wings. The human bird under the Indian sky gets up weaker than when he pretended to retire. For millions it is an eternal vigil or an eternal trance. I have found it impossible to soothe suffering patients with a song from Kabir . . .

'Give them work that they may eat! "Why should I, who have no need to work for food, spin?" may be the question asked. Because I am eating what does not belong to me. I am living on the spoliation of my countrymen. Trace the source of every coin that finds its way into your pocket, and you will realize the truth of what I write. Everyone must spin. Let Tagore spin like the others. Let him burn his foreign clothes; that is the duty today. God will take care of the morrow.'

'Dark and tragic words these!' comments Romain Rolland. 'Here we have the misery of the world rising up before the dream of art and crying, "Dare deny me existence!" Who does not sympathize with Gandhi's passionate emotion and share it? And yet in his reply, so proud and so poignant, there is nevertheless something that justifies Tagore's misgivings: *Sileat poeta*, imposing silence on the person who is called upon to obey the imperious discipline of the cause. Obey without discussion the law of Swadeshi, the first command of which is, Spin!'

Soon after writing the above, Rolland wrote to Tagore: 'I have just finished a pretty long essay on Mahatma Gandhi, based on the volume of collected articles in *Young India*. I shall have it published in the review *Europe*, as well as in several German and Russian reviews . . . I have conceived for the man Gandhi himself and his great heart burning with love, an infinite love and veneration. In a chapter of my essay I have taken the liberty, according to your admirable published essays, of recalling the position which you have taken up with regard to Gandhi, and the noble debate of ideas which has been evoked between you. The highest human ideals are confronted therein. One is reminded of a controversy between a St. Paul and a Plato. But transported to India, its horizons have expanded. They embrace the whole earth, and the whole of humanity joins in this august dispute. In my conclusion I have shown you united in the feeling for the beauty (even for the fruitful necessity) of the sacrifice of self through love. It may gratify you to know that your thought is the nearest to mine that I feel actually in the world and that the soul of India, as expressed by your luminous spirit and the ardent heart of Gandhi, is for me a larger native land in which my limbs stretch themselves free from the bonds of fanatical Europe which have bruised them.'

Unwilling to prolong an unnecessary and futile debate with a man whose character he deeply respected and whose advent on the scene he had hoped for and predicted, Tagore kept silent and retired to his favourite retreat in Santiniketan. Had he not earlier admonished himself? 'If you cannot march in step with your compatriots in the greatest crisis of their history, beware of saying they are in the wrong, and you in the right! But give up your place in the ranks, and go back to your poet's corner and be prepared to meet with ridicule and public disgrace.' And so he went back—not to sulk, but to sing. In the darkness of his defeat he saw a smile and heard a voice that said, 'Your place is with the children, playing on the beaches of the world, and there I am with you.'

A series of beautiful child-poems were the result, which were later published in 1922 as *Sisu Bholanath*, lyrical interpretations of the child-mind, reminiscent of the poems he had written two decades earlier which had been later published in English as *The Crescent Moon*. In a letter to his niece Indira Devi he said: 'I wrote these poems to give respite to my mind from its obsession with adult responsibilities. I have tried to express in them what had of late persistently recurred to my mind, namely, that the meaning of my life was summed up in its foreword which said that I was born as a child in the playground of this world. When with age we are increasingly caught in the fever of our sense of responsibility, we are inclined to look down upon play and take pride in building up an antithesis between work and play. We forget that thereby we malign the Creator of the universe, who functions without toil, who is supreme bliss because He is free of all obligations.'

But the respite was brief and intermittent. Santiniketan clamoured for his attention. Pearson returned to Santiniketan on 26 September, after an absence of five years. With him came Leonard Elmhirst, the young Englishman whom Tagore had met in New York. He had accepted Tagore's invitation to organize the Rural Reconstruction Centre in Sriniketan. He brought with him adequate funds for the purpose made possible by the generosity of Dorothy Straight. Through her America at last made a generous response to Tagore's appeal. Soon after, the French savant Sylvain Levi arrived as the first visiting professor to Visva-Bharati and organized a department of Tibetan and Chinese studies, the first in any Indian university. Tagore himself used to attend Levi's classes. On 23 December 1921 Visva-Bharati was formally inaugurated and the land, buildings and other properties at Santiniketan were legally transferred to it by a trust deed. Tagore also made a gift to it of the copyright and its benefit on his Bengali books. The Nobel Prize money had already been donated by him to the school.

In the midst of these excitements Tagore continued to brood on the political scene in the country until the subconscious churning of the mind found its dramatic expression in the symbolism of a play which he wrote in the early part of January 1922. The play, which is in a sense a noble tribute to the personality of Gandhi and his campaign of non-violence, is named *Mukta-dhara* (Free Current).[32] The background of the play is the political subjection of the people of Shiv-tarai to the neighbouring kingdom of Uttarakut. Mukta-dhara is the mountain-spring whose waters rush down the slopes of Uttarakut and irrigate the plains of Shiv-tarai. In order to enforce his authority more effectively by controlling the source of the people's economic well-being, the King of Uttarakut has had a

[32] The author gave the title *The Waterfall* to his English rendering published in the *Modern Review*, May 1922. Marjorie Sykes's competent English translation is available in the Oxford University Press publication, *Three Plays of Rabindranath Tagore*.

huge dam erected to prevent the waters of Mukta-dhara from flowing into the plains below, its engine-tower dominating the landscape and out-soaring the trident of the temple of Shiva which was on a mountain-peak. The play opens with the King and the citizens of Uttarakut preparing to participate in a festival in honour of the Machine—very proud of their achievement and heedless of its consequences to the poor people whose lands would be deprived of water.

The Crown Prince, however, professes open sympathy with the subject people and rebels against the callousness of his own people. His character provides the main psychological interest of the play, with his love of freedom and justice involving him in a conflict of loyalties. He determines to sacrifice his life in an attempt to liberate the imprisoned waters of Mukta-dhara by forcing the dam at a point which he happened to know was weakly constructed. He succeeds. The leaping torrent of water breaks free and carries away the Prince's body in its turbulent sweep. The socio-political motif of the play, if such there is, seems to dissolve at the end in an undefined sense of mystic self-fulfilment, as in some of Ibsen's later plays.

The author has reintroduced in this play that remarkable character, the Ascetic Dhananjaya, prototype of Mahatma Gandhi, who first appeared in his drama *Prayaschitta* (Atonement), published in 1909. In that play as in the present one, Dhananjaya exhorts the subject people to resist the ruler's unjust claims non-violently and fearlessly. 'As soon as you hold up your head and say, It does not hurt, the roots of violence will be cut . . . Nothing can hurt your true manhood, for that is a flame of fire. The animal that is the flesh feels the blow and whines.' Perhaps no other play of Tagore expresses his political convictions with such directness and vigour. Technically, too, the drama is not burdened with sub-plots or extraneous incidents, though the usual panorama of humanity is there, for the true stage, according to Tagore, is the world. Against the grim background of the towering menace of man's diabolical skill, symbolized in the Machine, pass and repass processions of men and women, tyrants and sycophants, idealists and humbugs, rebels and their servile agents and the multitude of anonymous humble folk, with their quaint humour and unsophisticated wisdom. Indeed, it is these wayfarers and spectators rather than the main actors who hold the stage for most of the time. Very little of the real action takes place before our eyes; much of it we witness indirectly through the reactions on the minds of these spectators on stage.

The drama is rich in meaning and suggestions which may tempt critics to attempt a variety of interpretations. But the author has gently warned his readers against missing the main significance of the play, which is psychological and lies in the growing identity in the Prince's mind between his own imprisoned spirit and the dammed current of Mukta-dhara. The final desperate act of sacrifice, the awesome nature of the consummation sought and achieved by the Prince, which brings the play to its close, leaves one with a sense of the tragic grandeur of man's spirit, silencing all contentions for the moment. What happens to the people of Shiv-tarai we have forgotten to inquire.

This remarkable play was never staged. The author read it out to a group of friends in Calcutta in January 1922 and later made preparations to stage it, but before the play could be staged the news came in March of Mahatma Gandhi's arrest, trial and sentence of rigorous imprisonment for six years. The preparations were abandoned and never revived.

12

OLD WORLD AND NEW

Tagore's dream of making Santiniketan a nest where kindred spirits would gather from different parts of the world was coming true. What was originally planned as a hermitage was becoming a cosmopolitan beehive. Besides the three remarkable Englishmen, Andrews, Pearson and Elmhirst, there was the French savant Sylvain Levi and his wife. He was soon followed by the no less eminent Orientalist Moritz Winternitz of the German University in Prague and later by Professor V. Lesny of the Charles University. Among other distinguished visiting scholars may be mentioned Stella Kramrisch, art historian and critic (now on the staff of the University of Pennsylvania, U.S.A.), F. Benoit, a French-Swiss linguist, L. Bogdanov, a Russian scholar of Persian and Pehlevi, Arthur Geddes from Scotland, Stanley Jones and Miss Gretchen Green from the United States, and Miss S. Flaum, a Jewish lady who had graduated from the University of Columbia. Whether this variegated beehive produced more honey than buzzing, it is difficult to say. The atmosphere was certainly stimulating; the poet was susceptible to atmosphere and attached value to symbols. Much pioneering work was also done of which the benefit was reaped, not only by Visva-Bharati but by many other universities.

The stimulus, however, was enough for the poet to imagine that the world was becoming one and that he had only to travel more to win men's hearts for his ideal. There is hardly any illusion more exhilarating than the consciousness that one is healing the world's wounds and Tagore was neither the first nor the last of great men to come under its spell. Nor is there any doubt that the gain in moral and intellectual consciousness, both to his country and to the rest of the world, from this missionary zeal was considerable and not to be ignored. He was one of the most sincere and eloquent protagonists of international understanding and humanism of the modern age who sought to achieve on the moral plane what the ill-fated League of Nations and its successor, U.N.O., have tried to achieve on the political. He risked unpopularity at home and suffered ridicule and jeers for his faith in one world long before that faith became a world fashion.

A greater sacrifice was the loss he risked in his creative and spiritual progress. He was never again to recapture that passionate and single-minded devotion to his Muse, the loving and careful observation of the seemingly commonplace aspects of life and nature, the simple and unsophisticated humility of the reed waiting for 'Thee to fill with music'. The poet was losing to the prophet, the singer to the preacher. The 'endless meaning in the narrow span of a song' was dissolving in the endless preaching over the wide span of the world. One sometimes wonders whether Tagore would not have been a greater poet and also perhaps a greater man (assuming that true greatness is to be measured in terms of spiritual and intellectual integrity) if he had spent the later part of his life, like the earlier, in comparative obscurity and had not received the Nobel Prize and had not founded the Visva-Bharati. But 'ifs' are a futile proposition. 'With an "if" you might put Paris in a bottle,' says a wise French proverb.

It would be untrue to suggest that Tagore ceased to be creative. He never did till the last day of his life and was still to achieve new and unpredictable heights as a creative artist. Even during his comparatively sterile periods he produced enough to make a writer famous. Nevertheless, it is true that something was missing in his later works, that rare something which comes from exclusive devotion to one's art, from ceaseless striving for perfection, something that cannot be defined and categorized. There were several reasons for it. Constant travel, public addresses and a ceaseless crusade for a new outlook, which also became a campaign for raising funds for Visva-Bharati, were a distraction hardly conducive to a meditative or creative mood. Secondly, since he could no longer give his personal and undivided attention to the teaching of his school children, he tried to make up for it by writing for them songs and dramas and organizing seasonal festivals, with music and dance, in which they could participate. He wrote some beautiful pieces and initiated festivals which have since become a rich repertoire of cultural heritage. (It is truly amazing how much one man did for his people.) But the quality inevitably suffered. He was writing for an uncritical clientele who applauded whatever he did. Gradually he came to be surrounded by a flock of admirers, many of whom were little better than courtiers and sycophants, who were like a solid wall which stood between him and the real world. This is a danger which celebrities all over the world have to face, but nowhere is it more fatal than in India, the traditional land of idolaters. The idol breakers become idols themselves. Even Gandhi who was so ruthless with himself and free from any trace of humbug in his personal life, could not wholly escape the insidious poison of the parasites who clung to him.

Rothenstein, a sincere friend, sensed the danger and recorded with sorrow in his diary: 'No man's company gives me more pleasure than Tagore's; but among his disciples I am uncomfortable; easy idealism is like Cézannism or Whistlerism—no, away with the smooth talkers, with those who wear bland spiritual phylacteries upon their foreheads! These men who specialize, as it were, in idealism give me the sense of discomfort that I feel among other men who do not practise but preach. I marvel always at Tagore's patience with such, who weaken his artistic integrity by flattery, as they weakened Rodin's. Degas, Fantin, Monet and Renoir closed their doors against such half-men, parasites and prigs. I imagine Tolstoy's house to have been infected by these, to his wife's despair.'

Rothenstein understood, but not all were so understanding. Many—and among them artists who ought to have had a surer intuition—misunderstood Tagore on this account, mistaking the mantle for the man. Typical of such is Jacob Epstein's estimate as recorded in his memoirs.

'I am he that sitteth among the poorest, the loneliest, and the lost.'

This quotation from *Gitanjali* was strangely contradicted by my sitter, whose handsome, commanding presence inspired in his followers awe and a craven obedience . . .

He posed in silence and I worked well. On one occasion two American women came to visit him, and I remember how they left him, retiring backwards, with their hands raised in worship. At the finish of the sitting usually two or three disciples, who waited in the ante-room for him, took him back to his hotel. He carried no money and was conducted about like a holy man . . .

The manners of Tagore were aloof, dignified and cold, and if he needed anything only one word of command escaped him to his disciples.

It has been remarked that my bust of him rests upon the beard, an unconscious piece of symbolism.[1]

In this phase of restlessness, even during the period Tagore was in India, he spent almost as many days outside Santiniketan as in it. The world had become his stage and Santiniketan an ideal studio for rehearsals. Its international character was emphasized by the students and staff celebrating the third centenary of Molière's birth in February 1922. In July Tagore presided at Shelley Centenary Celebrations in Calcutta. In August and September his new musical dramas *Varsha-mangal* (Rains Festival) and *Saradotsav*[2] (Autumn Festival) were presented on the Calcutta stage. These compositions which are a peculiar amalgam of poetry, drama, music and dance were written for community celebration of the seasons of the year and breathe of the open air and the simple joy of living. They were not built on any pattern, the folk and classical traditions intermingle in them as freely as do philosophy and frivolity, religious mysticism and a running commentary on contemporary affairs. As an example of the last the following dialogue may be quoted from *Vasantotsav* (Spring Festival):

King: Poet!
Poet: Yes, Your Majesty!
King: I've run away from the Cabinet meeting.
Poet: Excellent. But how did such a sound idea strike your Majesty?

---

[1] *Let there be Sculpture*. Published by Michael Joseph Ltd., London, 1940. Epstein had made a study of Tagore's head in 1926. The quotation from *Gitanjali* has been painfully distorted by the author to suit his purpose. The actual poem is full of humility and means the very opposite of the construction put on it by Epstein. 'My heart can never find its way to where Thou keepest company with the companionless among the poorest, the lowliest and the lost.'

[2] New version of an earlier production.

King: The financial year is closing and the treasury is almost depleted. As soon as the ministers sit in council, they want more and more for their departments. So the only way is to escape.

Poet: So much the better.

King: For whom?

Poet: For the country.

King: How?

Poet: If the ruler stands aside from time to time, the people get a chance to govern themselves.

In September 1922 Tagore left for a long tour of western and southern India, visiting Bombay, Poona, Madras and a number of other important towns in the south, finally crossing over to Ceylon. Everywhere he was fêted and the public thronged to hear him speak. On his way back he revisited Gandhiji's asrama at Sabarmati in Ahmedabad. The Mahatma was in jail, and Tagore in his address to the students and inmates of the asrama dwelt at length on 'the true meaning of sacrifice which Gandhiji represents'. His simple and homely address is instinct with deep respect for the Mahatma's personality. After spending about two months in Santiniketan, he again left for a tour of north and west India, going as far west as Karachi and Porbundar, the birthplace of Gandhi in Kathiawar. Returning to Santiniketan in April, he left soon after for Shillong to spend the summer in that lovely hill-station of Assam. He had only to stay quiet to be creative and so, while in Shillong, he commenced writing a remarkable play which he named *Rakta-Karabi*, later translated and published in English as *Red Oleanders*, in 1925.

This play, like the earlier one, *Mukta-dhara*, shows Tagore's increasing concern with the basic problems of modern civilization. While the earlier play was concerned with the diabolical use of technological knowledge, symbolized in the Machine, for colonial exploitation, this one raises the more fundamental issue of the free spirit of life set against the more terrible machine of a highly organized and mechanized society which turns men into robots, reducing names to numbers. The age-old struggle between the individual and the state, between the liberative impulse and the compulsive will, between free intelligence and cold, calculating intellect, which has assumed sinister proportions with the development of the 'scientific technique', is the theme of this play. The treatment is characteristically Tagorean, half realistic, half allegorical, logic and mysticism weakening each other and making the dramatic conflict more suggestive than convincing.

The kingdom of Yakshapuri flourishes on gold mining and forced labour. Its King lives behind locked doors, veiled in mystery and awe. In his name the Police Chief rules the land with a ruthless exercise of the whip and a judicious use of religious superstition. It is the same cord, says a victim, that makes the whip and binds the rosary. Into this 'brave new world' comes a young and wilful girl, Nandini, who fears no one and whose beauty charms everyone. She upsets the whole order, not only making the workers rebellious but luring the King himself out of his hiding. When he sees what his henchmen have made of his people, he himself leads the revolt against his own generals—but not before Nandini's beloved companion, a brave and carefree youth, Ranjan, who refuses to be conscripted, is killed.

The play, begun in Shillong, was completed during Tagore's tour of western India in the autumn of 1923. Elmhirst who had accompanied him on the tour has given the following very valuable account of the author's mood which inspired the play:[3] 'Day by day, as we travelled, he would spend his spare hours reading, or dreaming about the new play he was then busy writing. When we arrived at the State of Limbidi he began to complain sadly that he had come to the last scene of the last act of his latest play and that having lived so long on such intimate terms with the characters of his invention, he could not bear to bring the play to a sudden end or say to these people his final farewell. "I have delayed the guillotine for one more day," he would say, "but fall it must." When this work was finally published as *Rakta-Karabi* (or Red Oleanders) I found to my surprise that it was dedicated to myself. The present translation into English does not, it is said, do full justice to the quality of the original Bengali.

'Twelve months later Tagore enlarged to me upon the ideas he had tried to incorporate in the play, but he also hinted that it was

[3] I am grateful to Mr. Elmhirst for sharing this valuable reminiscence with me and for permitting me to publish it.

originally the human relationship between himself and myself and W. that had given him the embryonic idea on which his imagination had set to work ...

'At Tagore's home in Calcutta, where I usually stayed, it was a well-established custom to pay a call, across the courtyard, upon his three nephews, early in the morning following one's arrival. Two of them, Gaganendranath and Abanindranath, would be painting and all three would be discussing the affairs of the large world, on the veranda of their enchanting home. An extra *huqa* would be lit and brought for me from an avenue of *huqas* ready and equipped in the entrance hall. Then, whilst the smoke bubbled sweetly through the water, I would be accosted with a witty tirade of questions. "What has happened," one of them would say, "to our Rabindranath? Whence this outpouring of new poems of a fine and notable vintage? Whence this new inspiration? Is there a cause? Of course there must be. We guessed it ..."

'In discussing the meaning of the play with Tagore a year later in Argentina he used the following words: "Nandini [the heroine in the play] is this touch of life, the spirit of joy in life who, matched with Ranjan, the spirit of joy in work, together embody in themselves the spirit of love. Love in union, union in love, a harmony before which the discord of greed is scattered as under a spell." At the end of his exposition I find a postscript in the notebook: "Elmhirst, you must come back to India and play Ranjan and Nandini will bend over you and put a feather in your hair ..."

'One of the most difficult of all aspects to portray of this many-sided personality is that which encompassed and expressed the artist. He used to disclaim any knowledge as to the source of this bubbling spring of energy that found an outlet all through his life in the making of poetry, music, songs, dramas or paintings. He knew that to deny this power would be fatal, and that not to let it bubble up the way it wished would risk serious mutilation of some vital part of his being. When the spirit was on him any unnecessary frustration was intolerable. I have heard him humming to himself in the bathroom, then suddenly call his Bonomali, or "blue jewel" of a servant, and say: "Fetch Dinu Babu[4] immediately and tell him to stand

---

[4] His grand-nephew, Dinendranath Tagore, the gifted musician who noted down

outside my bathroom window and be ready to take down a new song, words and tune together." '

For whatever reason, whether Tagore's use of symbolism was alien to the Western mind (even as early as 1915, the *Athenaeum* had ascribed the beauty of *Gitanjali* to 'a certain paralysis of judgement before the trance, the mirage of the East') or whether his popularity on the European Continent, in particular in Germany, had alienated the sympathy of the English-speaking world, the fact remains that when *Red Oleanders* was published, it made no sense to English readers. The *Sheffield Telegraph* wrote: 'Mr. Tagore is too serious a writer to be suspected of publishing absolute nonsense on purpose, so one must suppose that he did it by accident. Presumably he is able to follow the workings of his brain, and it would be very interesting to hear from him just what it is all about.' Even the *Times Literary Supplement* commented: 'Many of the lofty utterances of Nandini and the Voice are so devoid of meaning that one is constantly aware of the emptiness of such symbols as the tassel of oleanders, the network in front of the Palace, and the caves of Yaksha town.'

Even *Chitra*, which is a straightforward play with no more symbolism than should be familiar to Shakespeare's admirers, provoked the following homily from a critic in the *Bulletin* of Sydney, Australia: 'Bernard Shaw would have made a modern social comedy of it and carried more conviction. These poetic romances are better in their natural setting, chanted by a solitary loin-clothed spokesman to the thumping of a drum while a posse of dancing girls makes sensuous explanatory movements.' The loyalty of the Commonwealth countries is touching, and probably no Englishman would have expressed himself about Tagore's novel *Gora* as the outraged correspondent who wrote in the *Natal Mercury*, Durban, 24 July 1929: 'My God! Shall I ever forget that awful book? It is . . . a kind of inversion of Kipling's *Kim*, in which the author tries to point the opposite moral. It is utterly without the genius

---

the poet's musical compositions and preserved the notations for posterity. Tagore who generally forgot the tunes soon after their original composition was grateful to 'Dinu Babu' for recording, preserving and teaching them and referred to him lovingly as 'the Treasurer of my songs'.

of Kipling—long, turgid, meandering, in which what plot there is is continually lost sight of in a mass of side issues and irrelevancies. "The Poet," in fact, is the sort of writer that a few silly people talk about, but nobody reads . . . But why should we rack our poor Western brains, inventing phrases whereby to describe a literary impostor, when the incomparable Gilbert gives us all we want . . .'[5]

The zeal of a pilgrim-ambassador had possessed Tagore. Not content with touring in his own country, he now thought of visiting China. Nearly a thousand years had passed since the last band of Buddhist monks had carried their Master's message of compassion and peace to that land. Tagore wanted to restore the ancient cultural link between the two countries which had been snapped for so long. India has never had, nor is ever likely to have again, so noble and distinguished a roving ambassador. An invitation had been received from the President of the Universities Lecture Association of China, Mr. Liang-Chi-Chao, a distinguished scholar and one of the brilliant band of revolutionary reformers who had succeeded in establishing the Republic. Welcoming Tagore and his party in Peking in April 1924, he summed up in an exquisite phrase the quintessence of the Buddha's message for which his country was indebted to India: 'To cultivate sympathy and intellect, in order to attain absolute freedom through wisdom, and absolute love through pity.' Conditions in south China were still disturbed on account of the civil war, and though Tagore had received a very warm invitation from Dr. Sun Yat Sen to visit him, the party could not get to Canton and the two never met.

Tagore was hardly known in China, and mischievous reports had been spread that he was a reactionary harping on the past, and an enemy of the Western civilization, opposed to scientific thought and material progress. The Chinese youth who had recently come under the spell of Western civilization and hoped to overtake Japan in the race for material progress, had therefore at first resented Tagore's visit to their country and had even tried to organize a boycott of his meetings. Elmhirst who had accompanied Tagore on

[5] For all the five quotations I am indebted to Dr. Aronson's *Rabindranath Through Western Eyes*.

At Santiniketan, 1938   *S. Shaha*

Vinod Kothari

On his way to Calcutta for an operation, 25 July 1941. This is
perhaps the last photograph taken of him

Self-portrait

this visit recalls: 'It was not until we had met with the scholars at Peking that the Chinese progressives suddenly realized how much common ground they shared with Tagore. Like Dante and Chaucer in their own day and age, Tagore and Hu Shih were both determined to use the vernacular of their peoples as the ordinary medium for literary expression rather than some classical dialect that had been the monopoly of a limited group of literati. One leading Chinese scholar jumped up to embrace Tagore across the supper table, and expressed with deep emotion the feeling that he could now share with him in a common fellowship of suffering, and even of persecution at the hands of the old guard of the classical literati.'

Tagore's lectures in China, delivered mostly extempore,[6] show with what understanding and sympathy he approached the Chinese mind. He was personal, reminiscent and friendly, and though he was as usual blunt and forthright in his opposition to war, national rivalries and the fetish of indiscriminate worship of material progress, he soon disarmed all hostile criticism and won over the progressive intellectuals. 'For centuries,' he reminded them, 'you have had merchants, soldiers and other guests, but, till this moment, you never thought of asking a poet. Is not this a great fact—not your recognition of my personality, but the homage you thus pay to the springtime of a new age? Do not, then, ask for a message from me. People use pigeons to carry messages; and in the wartime, men valued their wings not to watch them soar but because they helped to kill. Do not make use of a poet to carry messages. Permit me, rather, to share your hope in the stirring of life over this land and I shall join in your rejoicing. I am not a philosopher; therefore keep for me room in your heart, not a seat on the public platform. I want to win your heart now that I am close to you, with the faith that is in me of a great future for you, and for Asia, when your country rises and gives expression to its own spirit—a future in the joy of which we shall all share.'

But to expect Tagore to refrain from giving a message would be to expect the sun to give warmth without light. His whole life was

[6] On the basis of notes taken by his companions and reports published in the Chinese papers, these texts were later collected and published as *Talks in China*, Visva-Bharati, Calcutta, 1925.

U

itself a message which may be summed up thus: Take from the West the best gifts it has but do not imitate it, for imitation is fatal. And so he exhorted the youth: 'I say again that we must accept truth when it comes from the West and not hesitate to render it our tribute of admiration. Unless we accept it, our civilization will be one-sided, it will remain stagnant. Science gives us the power of reason, enabling us to be actively conscious of the worth of our own ideals. We have been in need of this discovery to lead us out of the obscurity of dead habit, and for that we must turn to the living mind of the West with gratefulness, never encouraging the cultivation of hatred against her. Moreover, the Western people also need our help, for our destinies are now intertwined. No one nation today can progress, if the others are left outside its boundaries. Let us try to win the heart of the West with all that is best and not base in us, and think of her and deal with her, not in revenge or in contempt, but with goodwill and understanding, in a spirit of mutual respect.'

But he warned them not to be dazzled by the temporary spectacle of power and wealth won through violence and exploitation: 'Nations that have relied thereon have either been destroyed, or are even now reverting to barbarism. It is co-operation and love, mutual trust and mutual aid which make for strength and real progress in civilization ...' In the long run, he reminded them, society is sustained by moral values which may change from time to time but remain moral none the less. Evil may seem to triumph but not for ever, and he quoted his favourite Sanskrit verse which says:

> With the help of unrighteousness men do prosper;
> With the help of unrighteousness men do
> gain victories over their enemies;
> With the help of unrighteousness men do
> attain what they desire;
> But they perish at the root.

Tagore was pained to see that the younger generation's attitude to Japan was warped by their fear and hatred of the Tokyo war party and, in Elmhirst's words, 'He kept telling them, "You do not know the real Japan at all until you have seen their artists at work, watched their *No* plays and dances, attended their ceremonies and until you have seen how the thousands of factory workers in Kobe will spend two-thirds of their dinner hour walking to and from a famous garden to enjoy and appreciate the beauties of nature before being tied once again to their machine." As a direct result of this challenge three distinguished Chinese scholars accompanied us to Japan and on their return held an exhibition in Peking of the art and craft work, ancient and modern, that had been presented to them by our Japanese friends.'

Tagore returned to India in the latter half of July via Japan where he stayed for about six weeks and gave several lectures. His visit to China and Japan led to the first conscious attempt in the history of Asia to formulate the idea of Asian unity by the organization of an Asiatic Association in Shanghai in September of the same year. Reporting this event the *Christian Science Monitor* of Boston wrote: 'There is on foot an important movement to establish Asiatic concord through the common culture of Asiatic nations . . . It has been accentuated by the recent Japanese exclusion legislation in the United States and stimulated by the recent visit to the Far East of Rabindranath Tagore, who preached the doctrine of idealism opposed to western materialism. The new feeling is shown in the formation of Asiatic associations in the principal centres, the first of which is located in Shanghai. Its formation affected all the Far East, especially Japan. At the inauguration representatives of all Asiatic countries were present. Inspiration for the movement is acknowledged to Tagore whose teachings permeate the issued declarations.'[7] As has been aptly pointed out by Pulinbihari Sen in *Visva-Bharati News*, 'This convention was thus a predecessor to the Asian Relations Conference held in Delhi 23 years later,' in the year of India's independence. Surprisingly enough, no mention was made of Tagore at this latter conference held in his own land. He was then dead and the idea had been taken over by politicians whose memories are proverbially short.

Hardly two months at home, then again to the other side of the world. The occasion was an invitation from the Republic of Peru

[7] Quoted in 'Asia Must Find her Own Voice' by Pulinbihari Sen, *Visva-Bharati News*, June 1947.

to attend the centenary celebrations of her attainment of independence. So he sailed once more, this time to the New World, with Elmhirst again his companion. On the eve of his departure he received a letter from a young Bengali girl begging him to keep a diary of his voyage. This humble request from a comparative stranger somehow touched a chord in the poet's mind, and he not only kept the diary but the creative mood once more overflowed, both in prose and verse. The very first poem he wrote on the voyage, soon after he left India, is significant. The poet's heart is still young and not all the robes of a prophet can hide the lover underneath. An English paraphrase of the poem is attempted below, necessarily bereft of the haunting rhythm and diction of the original:

> Silent and sleepless the night. Your head bent low,
> the tears flowing. Gently you kissed my hand and
> said, 'If you go away, my world will become a desert
> waste wailing in a void without end. This lonely load
> of dumb grief is death more deadly than dying.'

> I held your face against my heart and murmured,
> 'If you go away, the lightning-pain of separation
> will rend my sky with your flashes and this bereaved
> heart and these eyes bereft of your sight will become
> the sport of sorrow. But far as you go, dearest, you
> will find your way back to the inmost chamber of my
> heart, vindicating your sovereign right over it.'

> The seven-starred constellation listened to our whispered
> pledges as our words floated over the clusters of
> *rajanigandhas*.[8] Then with silent steps came death
> and took you away beyond all reach of sight, sound
> or touch. And yet this void is no void. It glows with
> the embers of pain and with this fire I build my world
> of dreams in songs dipped in light.

During the voyage across the Atlantic Tagore suddenly fell ill and had to disembark at Buenos Aires where a heart specialist advised absolute rest for some time. In the meantime letters were received

---

[8] Tuberose. The native name of this favourite Indian flower means 'perfume of the night'.

from Romain Rolland and Andrews warning him 'to beware of all kinds of possible dangers and political complications in Peru', as his companion Elmhirst has put it. Tagore did not know a soul in Buenos Aires, but fortunately the charming and talented Victoria Ocampo offered her hospitality and he was happy to find refuge in an attractive and secluded villa in San Isidro on the bank of the river Plate. The visit to Peru had to be cancelled on the doctors' advice. Nor was Tagore sorry about it, for on this visit the poet had triumphed over the prophet and he was very content and happy to watch the river from the balcony of the villa and be looked after by so charming and devoted a hostess. It was a real devotion, the devotion of a young and ardent spirit to its ideal and not the fussing of a society lady eager to capture a lion. Recalling the visit in an excellent article, Victoria Ocampo writes:[9]

'The week Tagore had meant to spend at San Isidro became a month and twenty days, for the doctors still insisted on the importance of rest. . . I did not actually live at Miralrio.[10] I slept at my father's home close by. But I went to Miralrio every day and often lunched or dined there, for I had no cook at home, my servants having been lent to Tagore. I wanted this man, whom I admired and revered, to feel as much at home as possible. I thought that my constant presence in the house might have disturbed him. And I would have gladly torn my heart out to please him.

'Nevertheless, every moment I spent away from Miralrio seemed to me irremediably wasted. I had had incredible good luck but . . . I dared not take full advantage of it.

'Split between shyness and avidity, scruples and eagerness not to lose a single crumb of this "presence", I often had—to console myself for not daring to importune Tagore—long talks in the kitchen with the cook, or in the pantry with Jose, the butler and his wife Filemena. They were happy people who lived at Miralrio and spent their whole time at the Poet's service. I envied them . . .

'Thus I came, little by little, to know Tagore and his moods. Little by little he partially tamed the young animal, by turns wild or

[9] Written at the request of the present writer and published in the *Tagore Centenary Volume*.

[10] Name of the villa where Tagore stayed.

docile, who did not sleep, dog-like, on the floor outside his door, simply because it was not done.'

Even God is moved by such devotion—so the saints assure us. Tagore was only human. He was deeply touched and grateful. That he was also happy in a truly creative sense is evidenced by the over-flow of poetry, tender and exquisite, which he wrote during his stay at San Isidro and for some time after. These poems were published in 1925 under the significant title *Puravi*, which is the name of a lovely evening mode in Indian classical music. The volume was dedicated to Vijaya (the Sanskrit parallel of Victoria) by which name Tagore used to address his hostess. 'I am sending you,' he wrote to her from Calcutta when he sent her a copy, 'a Bengali book of poems which I wish I could place in your hands personally. I have dedicated it to you though you will never be able to know what it contains. A large number of poems in this book were written while I was in San Isidro ... I hope this book will have the chance of a longer time with you than its author had.' It is interesting to know that he himself described these poems as 'the best of their kind, [enshrining] the memory of those sunny days and tender care—the fugitives made captive'.

Victoria Ocampo has related an incident which throws light on how or why many of Tagore's later English renderings of his poems came to be little better than précis or even disfigured paraphrases: 'Tagore had doubts as to the Westerner's capacity of understanding Eastern thoughts, or at least he had them at times. I remember that on an afternoon during our stay at the estancia Chapadmalal he wrote a poem. I came into his room at the moment when he was finishing it ... "It is nearly tea-time," I said. "But before going down, please do translate this poem for me." Leaning over the pages spread out before him, I could see, undecipherable, like the traces of birds' feet on the sand, the delicate, mysterious patterns of the Bengali characters. Tagore took up the page and started translating, literally, he told me. What he read, hesitating sometimes, seemed to me tremendously enlightening. It was as if by miracle or chance, I had entered into direct contact, at last, with the poetic material (or raw material) of the written thing without having on the pair of gloves translations always are. Gloves that blunt our sense of touch and prevent our taking hold of the words with sensitive bare hands. All-important words because only the poet can build with them a fragile bridge between the intangible and the tangible, between the intangible reality of poetry and the tangible unreality of our matter-of-fact daily life.

'I asked Tagore to put the English version into writing later. On the next day he gave it to me, written in his beautiful English handwriting. I read the poem in his presence and could not conceal my disappointment. "But such and such things you read to me yesterday are not here," I reproached him. "Why did you suppress them? They were the centre, the heart of the poem." He replied that he thought *that* would not interest Westerners. The blood rose to my cheeks as if I had been slapped. Tagore had of course answered as he did because he was convinced of being right, never dreaming that he could hurt me. I told him with a vehemence I seldom permitted myself with him (though impetuosity is natural to me) that for once he was terribly mistaken.'

How lovingly some of these poems written in San Isidro 'encircle', to quote the author's own phrase, the memory of days spent with Vijaya, may be guessed from the English renderings made by Kshitis Roy.[11]

Sixteen years later, shortly before his death, the memory was still fresh and the poet, now aged and ailing and waiting for the end, enshrined it in one of his last poems (*Sesh Lekha*): 'How I wish I could once again find my way to that foreign land where waits for me the message of love! The dreams of yesterday will wing their way back and fluttering softly build their nest anew. Sweet memories will restore to the flute its lost melody ... Her language I knew not, but what her eyes said will for ever remain eloquent in its anguish.'

On 4 January 1925, the poet and his companion Elmhirst bade goodbye to their hostess and sailed from Buenos Aires.[12] Writing to her a few days later from the Italian ship *Giulio Cesare*, Tagore

---

[11] Formerly Director, Tagore Museum, Santiniketan. *Poems from Puravi.*

[12] With them also sailed the armchair in which Tagore used to sit and recline as he watched the River Plate and talked with his charming hostess. It remained his favourite chair till the end of his life and he even wrote a poem on it. The chair is still preserved in the Tagore Museum at Santiniketan.

explained why he could not stay longer with her. 'You have often found me homesick; it was not so much for India, it was for that abiding reality in me in which I can have my inner freedom. It becomes totally obscured when for some reason or other my attention is too much directed upon my own personal self. My true home is there where from my surroundings comes the call to me to bring out the best that I have, for that inevitably leads me to the touch of the universal. My mind must have a nest to which the voice of the sky can descend freely, the sky that has no other allurements but light and freedom. Whenever there is the least sign of the nest becoming a jealous rival of the sky, my mind, like a migrant bird, tries to take its flight to a distant shore. When my freedom of [access to] light is obstructed some length of time, I feel as if I am bearing the burden of a disguise like the morning in its disguise of mist. I do not see myself, and this obscurity, like a nightmare, seems to suffocate me with its heavy emptiness. I have often said to you that I am not free to give up my freedom—for this freedom is claimed by my Master for his own service. There have been times when I *did* forget this and allowed myself to drift into some easeful captivity. But every time it ended in catastrophe and I was driven by an angry power to the open—across broken walls.'

Every great artist or spirit is fundamentally lonely. As Tagore confessed in a letter to Elmhirst, 'I carry an infinite space of loneliness around my soul through which the voice of my personal life very often does not reach my friends—for which I suffer more than they do. I have my yearning for the personal world as much as any other mortal, or perhaps more.' That is why artists often seem more egoistic and callous in their personal relations than they perhaps really are. Not only is it difficult for personal intimacies to break through this 'infinite space of loneliness' round the soul, but they fear the very possibility of its happening and dread to give themselves away. The fear looms the greater when they become famous. It is doubtful if Tagore achieved a real spiritual intimacy with anyone after the death of his sister-in-law. He welcomed inspiration but avoided deep commitments. He wanted to keep himself free, for, as he himself put it, 'This freedom is claimed by my Master for his own service.'

What exactly this service was that his Master claimed from him, he himself could never be sure. Sometimes it was some hard task in the world of men calling for missionary zeal, whether in the field of education or politics or peace; sometimes, on the other hand, he felt that God wanted no other service from him except to sing. He hurried away from Buenos Aires, for he felt guilty that he should be happy and enjoying himself when his country needed him. And yet when he reached his own land he realized that this happiness had been creative, and that in the long run he did more good by being creative than by being merely constructive. He expressed this feeling very charmingly in a letter to Victoria Ocampo from Santiniketan in August of the same year: 'You express regret in your letter that I could not continue to stay at that beautiful house near the river till the end of the summer. You do not know how often I wish I could do so. It was some lure of duty which drove me from that sweet corner with its inspiration for seemingly futile idling; but today I discover that my basket, while I was there, was being daily filled with shy flowers of poems that thrive under the shade of lazy hours. I can assure you, most of them will remain fresh long after the time when the laboriously built towers of my beneficent deeds will crumble into oblivion.'

'The journey from Buenos Aires to Genoa,' writes Elmhirst, 'was both peaceful and productive but we were not at all prepared for the official fuss and reception that welcomed us on our arrival in Italy. Mussolini had apparently decided to make what political capital he could out of Tagore's visit and he was determined to bring Tagore to Rome, if he could, by sending a special reception committee to capture him. Luckily we had to travel via Milan where we were cared for by good friends who warned us of the political danger of his public appearances, and these were, in consequence, apart from one visit to the Scala, cut out altogether. Tagore had, I realized later, always hoped to form his own individual judgement of Mussolini when a suitable opportunity might arise, but he was now homesick for Santiniketan and so agreed to take ship direct from Venice as soon as a boat was available. Duke Gallarati Scotti and his wife took considerable risks both in Milan and later, to steer us safely past all the political schools and entanglements, and at last

Tagore was happily settled in his chair, on a boat in Venice, homeward bound for India.'

A few days after his return to his country, his elder brother Jyotirindranath died. The loss of this gifted brother who had been his friend, guide and philosopher at the beginning of Tagore's literary career, must have moved him deeply, though he kept his feelings to himself. He had suffered so many bereavements that death had ceased to be a stranger. 'Through death and sorrow,' he had said again and again, 'there dwells peace in the heart of the Eternal.'

In May of the same year (1925) Mahatma Gandhi visited him at Santiniketan, to try once again to convert him to his favourite thesis that the way to Swaraj lay through the *charkha* (spinning wheel) and *khadi* (hand-spun cloth). Tagore received him, as usual, with great cordiality and respect, and when he led him to his room which had been tastefully decorated with fresh leaves and flowers, the Mahatma smiled and asked, 'Why bring me to this bridal chamber?' The poet replied with a smile, 'Because Santiniketan, the ever-young queen of our hearts, welcomes you.' But the mission was not fruitful. Tagore could not be convinced that the *charkha* was or could ever be anything more than one of the many necessary village crafts. Later on he explained and elaborated his viewpoint in an article, 'The Cult of the Charka' published in the *Modern Review*.

The article is a sober and wise plea for a rational outlook and a reasoned diagnosis of the grinding poverty of India's millions. Hard work, co-operative effort and a judicious use of the scientific technique, pleaded Tagore, can alone eradicate hunger, and not merely a mechanical and ritualistic spinning on a primitive wheel. 'If the cultivation of science by Europe has any moral significance, it is in its rescue of man from outrage by nature—not in its use of man as a machine, but its use of the machine to harness the forces of nature in man's service. One thing is certain, that the all-embracing poverty which has overwhelmed our country cannot be removed by working with our hands to the neglect of science. Nothing can be more undignified drudgery than that man's *knowing* should stop dead and his *doing* go on for ever.'

Today such a plea would be taken for granted and, indeed, the various Five Year Plans of the Government of India are based precisely on such a programme and not on a blind acceptance of the mythical efficacy of the *charkha*. But at the time when Tagore wrote, his was almost a lone voice in the wilderness and he was reviled for his presumptuousness in challenging what seemed a gospel truth. Even a distinguished scientist like Sir P. C. Ray took Tagore to task for daring to doubt the magic of the spinning wheel. As Tagore remarked, 'Even where hands are reluctant to work the spindle, mouths are busy spinning its praises.'

Tagore had been deeply hurt by the Mahatma's statement that Raja Rammohun Roy was 'a pygmy' compared to some other great men of India. How deeply the poet respected the Mahatma, even while differing from him radically, can be seen from the following words quoted from the same article: 'It is extremely distasteful to me to have to differ from Mahatma Gandhi in regard to any matter of principle or method. Not that, from a higher standpoint, there is anything wrong in so doing; but my heart shrinks from it. For what could be a greater joy than to join hands in the field of work with one for whom one has such love and reverence? Nothing is more wonderful to me than Mahatmaji's great moral personality. . . . The difference in our standpoints and temperaments has made the Mahatma look upon Rammohun Roy as a pygmy, while I revere him as a giant. The same difference makes the Mahatma's field of work one which my conscience cannot accept as its own. That is a regret which will abide with me always. It is, however, God's will that man's paths of endeavour shall be various, else why these differences of mentality?

'How often have my personal feelings of regard strongly urged me to accept at Mahatmaji's hands my enlistment as a follower of the *charka* cult, but as often have my reason and conscience restrained me, lest I should be a party to the raising of the *charka* to a higher place than is its due, thereby distracting attention from other more important factors in our task of all-round reconstruction. I feel sure that Mahatmaji himself will not fail to understand me, and keep for me the same forbearance which he has always had.'

This provoked a rejoinder from the Mahatma in his weekly, *Young India*, under the heading 'The Poet and the Charkha'. Tagore wrote a personal letter assuring him that '. . . even if you have hit me hard in the cause of what you think is Truth, our personal relationship based upon mutual respect will bear that strain'. Gandhi thanked Tagore '. . . for your sweet letter'. This assurance was borne out to the end and the deeper affinity that linked the Mahatma and the Poet survived the many differences in their temperaments and outlooks. Twenty years later when the Mahatma visited Santiniketan for the last time, four years after the death of Tagore, he said: 'I started with a disposition to detect a conflict between Gurudev and myself but ended with the glorious discovery that there was none.' The glorious discovery was mutual.

Despite many public engagements and controversies, the literary output continued unabated. Besides many poems and songs of startling freshness and vigour, he adapted for the stage his earlier humorous drama, *Chira Kumar Sabha* (The Bachelors' Club) which was produced professionally at the Star Theatre in Calcutta. Those who find fault with the mystical or symbolic element in Tagore's plays would do well to see this one, a comedy as delightful and realistic as any ever written. Besides this, he dramatized two of his earlier short stories, *Karma-phal* (Fruit of Action) as *Shodh-bodh* (Final Reckoning), a social satire depicting the moral distintegration caused by inordinate pursuit of social ambition and *Sesher Ratri* (Last Night) as *Griha-pravesh* (Home Coming), a sentimental tragedy. He also wrote, at the request of Count Keyserling, a paper in English on the Ideals of Indian Marriage, which was included in the latter's publication *The Book of Marriage*.

In the winter of 1925, Mussolini, still eager to woo the Indian poet, sent the two distinguished Orientalists Carlo Formici and Giuseppe Tucci as visiting professors from Italy to Visva-Bharati, with a collection of valuable Italian books as a gift to the university. Before the year ended Tagore presided over the first session of the Indian Philosophical Congress in Calcutta where he spoke on the philosophic significance of the folk cultures and folk religions of India. Soon after, in the beginning of the new year, he went to Lucknow to attend the All-India Music Conference. In the midst of the music festival came the news of the death of his eldest brother Dwijendranath, the gentle and amiable philosopher-mathematician. One by one the links with the past were snapping. Dwijendranath was a true philosopher who took even his own vast learning and talents philosophically and neither paraded the former nor made much of the latter. He was Borodada (eldest brother) not only to Rabindranath but to all, including Gandhiji who was much attached to him. Of no one was it more true than of him what Plato made Socrates say: 'In reality then those who pursue philosophy rightly, study to die; and to them of all men death is least formidable.'

At the invitation of the University of Dacca, East Bengal (now East Pakistan), Tagore delivered a series of lectures at the university and also visited several towns in that region. Returning to Santiniketan he wrote a prose-drama in four acts, *Natir Puja*[13] (Worship of the Dancing Girl), based on an old Buddhist legend which he had earlier used in a poem. This is one of Tagore's simplest and most moving plays, free from symbolic abstractions and intellectual complexities which make some of his other plays at once puzzling and fascinating. The main action centres in a simple religious emotion which rises to a high pitch of ecstasy as the story ends in a tragedy of martyred devotion.

Srimati, the palace dancing-girl of humble origin, is a devotee of the Buddha and insists on offering worship at the altar where the Buddha had once sat and preached, although the King Ajatasatru, who is an enemy of Buddhism, has forbidden Buddha worship on pain of death. His father, Maharaja Bimbisara, having learnt from the Buddha, whose contemporary he was, the wisdom of renunciation and seeing his son ambitious of the throne, has voluntarily given up his kingdom to him and retired outside the city to spend his days in meditation and prayer. His younger son, Chitra, inspired by the same teaching, has embraced the Order and become a Bhikshu, a monk. The queen-mother, Lokeswari, once a devotee of the Buddha, turns bitter against a religion that has robbed her of her husband and her son.

The action of the play, which observes all the three classical unities, takes place on Vasanta Purnima, the full moon of spring, which is the birthday of the Buddha. Srimati, the dancing-girl, is

[13] English translation by Marjorie Sykes in *Three Plays: Rabindranath Tagore*, Oxford University Press.

chosen by the Order to offer worship at the shrine on this important day. The princess Ratnavali is highly incensed at the prospect of a low-born creature like the dancing-girl being honoured with this privilege in preference to a royal princess like her. In order to humiliate the Nati (dancing-girl) she gets an order from the King that the Nati, instead of offering worship, should dance before the altar so as to desecrate it. Srimati accepts the order and at the appointed hour of the evening appears on the scene dressed for the dance. She begins the dance which turns out to be one of religious devotion, in the course of which the dancer discards, one by one, all her gorgeous wrappings and her ornaments, throwing them before the altar as an offering, until she is left with only the ochre wrap of a Buddhist nun. As she kneels down and recites the verses of formal worship, her head is struck off by order of the King. The spectacle of this heroic devotion and sacrifice moves even the heart of Ratnavali who too kneels down to beg pardon of the dead Nati.

The Buddha had challenged the infallibility of the Vedas and the hierarchy of the Hindu caste. Worship of the Divine cannot be the monopoly of this caste or that, nor can its expression be for ever imprisoned in one particular Vedic pattern. True worship is the surrender or dedication of the best we have to the call of Truth. The sage dedicates his learning, the man of action his deeds, the poet his song, and the humble Nati her dance. Social institutions distort this fundamental equality of all human beings by their artificial standards and snobberies, exalting some and degrading others. But true religion ignores man-made prejudices and restores the basic evaluation by which all human beings must finally be measured and redeemed. Such, at any rate, is Tagore's interpretation of the spirit of Buddhism. And so the Nati by her sincerity and her devotion redeems the so-called degradation of her calling and vindicates by her death the innate majesty of her spirit.

Apart from the deep human appeal of the theme, the main interest of this play lies in the psychological tension in the character of the queen-mother Lokeswari. She is torn between her genuine devotion to the Buddha—having seen and worshipped him in person, how could she feel otherwise?—and her bitter wrath against a religion whose very humanity tramples under foot the claims of the human,

whose gospel of compassion and non-violence is a deadly, dis-
integrating poison wrecking the basic order of Hindu society,
turning the ruler into a monk, a warrior into a beggar. 'See what I
am today—widowed, though my husband lives; barren, having
borne a son; homeless, in the midst of a palace.' Religion should
uphold society and not break it, should provide divine sanction
for the exercise of human faculties instead of repudiating them.
Ahimsa (non-violence) may be good for the lower orders whose
duty it is to be servile, but it degrades the hero whose duty it is to
rule and to wield power. 'The mud has its uses, but the mountain
must be made of hard rock.' Her royal pride, stung to the quick
by an enforced frustration, makes her rebel against the extreme
individualism of a gospel which ignores the basic claims of flesh
and blood. 'Alas for flesh and blood! Alas for its unbearable hunger,
its intolerable pain! Is the *tapasya*, the struggle, of the flesh and
blood, any the less real than their quest for nothingness—their
sunya?'

On the other hand, her very Hinduism has developed in her a
spiritual sensibility which cannot but be moved by her vivid memory
of the serene and radiant presence of the Buddha, the Compassionate.
Having seen him once, she is for ever haunted by the deep spiritual
appeal of his personality which compels her reverence even when
she would fain rebel against it. In her character is symbolized the
great historical drama of the challenge of Buddhism to the traditional Hindu society. As Tagore used to say, Hinduism replaced
Buddhism only by absorbing it. Though formally dead, Buddhism
has never ceased to inspire the best minds of India. Tagore and
Gandhi are the two greatest, as they are the latest, witnesses to this
influence, conscious or unconscious. Again and again, Tagore has
invoked the spirit of the Buddha, in poem, song and drama. Here
are the opening lines of a song from this very drama; the anguished
appeal of its words is even more relevant today than at any time in
history:

> The world today is wild with the delirium of hatred,
> the conflicts are cruel and unceasing in anguish,
> crooked are its paths, tangled its bonds of greed.

All creatures are crying for a new birth of thine,
O thou of boundless life,
save them, raise thine eternal voice of hope,
let Love's lotus with its inexhaustible treasure of honey
open its petals in thy light.

O Serene, O Free,
in thine immeasurable mercy and goodness
wipe away all dark stains from the heart of this earth.[14]

One other point of interest to note about this play is that no male characters appear on the stage. The introduction of the Buddhist monk in the Prologue was a later addition to enable the author to satisfy the public clamour for his appearance on the stage. There was a deep-rooted prejudice in the Indian society, whether Hindu or Muslim, against the public appearance of women on the stage. With the staging of this play in Calcutta in January 1927, Tagore made a bold assault on this prejudice by recruiting the entire cast from girl students of his own university and ladies of good families, all of whom he himself trained and rehearsed. He also brought non-professional dancing on the stage. Since then not only has the old prejudice disappeared, but the pendulum has swung to the other side, filling the amateur Indian stage with society damsels who make some sort of rhythmic motions on the stage which they call Indian dancing.

[14] Tagore's own English rendering.

13

BETWEEN TWO WORLDS

Partly flattered by Mussolini's courtship and partly curious to see for himself this colourful personality, Tagore accepted an invitation from Italy and sailed for Naples on 15 May 1926 accompanied by his son and daughter-in-law.[1] As he himself put it, 'It is for me to study and not criticize from outside. I am glad of this opportunity to see for myself the work of one who is assuredly a great man and a movement that will certainly be remembered in history.' That Fascism will be remembered in history there is no doubt. That the Duce was 'a great man' was an illusion which Tagore temporarily shared with many shrewd and seasoned politicians of the time.

On arrival in Naples Tagore was received by the chief officials of the city with a message of welcome from Mussolini. Elmhirst had also come to meet him. 'But realizing that I was not at all approved of by the official Italian party of welcome, I explained to Tagore that it would be wiser for me to leave him free to pursue his own plans. He was very much upset by my suggestion, but I left the next day for home.' Tagore and his party were taken by special train to Rome where he met Mussolini. How impressionable the poet was can be seen from his following estimate after the meeting: 'His Excellency Mussolini seems modelled body and soul by the chisel of a Michael Angelo [sic], whose every action showed intelligence and force.' When he was asked to give a message in writing, he wrote, 'Let me dream that from the fire-bath the immortal soul of Italy will come out clothed in quenchless light.'

On 7 June the Governor of Rome held a public reception in the capital where he conveyed to the poet the greetings of the Eternal City. On the following day Tagore delivered his first public lecture,

[1] Later, Professor P. C. Mahalanobis and his wife joined the party in Rome.

328 RABINDRANATH TAGORE: A BIOGRAPHY

'The Meaning of Art', with Mussolini among the audience. He was also received by King Victor Emmanuel III and attended a performance of his play *Chitra* which was staged in Italian. But more than the King or the Duce, with whom he had another interview, Tagore was keen on meeting the philosopher Benedetto Croce who was at that time virtually home-interned in Naples. Some common friends, however, took the risk of bringing him over clandestinely to Rome where the two met on 15 June. On the same day Tagore left for Florence where the Leonardo da Vinci Society gave a public reception in his honour.

While he was being fêted in his almost royal tour of Italy, he did not realize that garbled and distorted versions of his speeches and interviews were being headlined by the Italian press to boost the Fascist régime. It was only when he crossed over to Switzerland to rest for a few days in Villeneuve[2] (from where Romain Rolland had sent him pressing invitations) that he came to know from the latter how the Italian propaganda machine had made a dupe of him, twisting and distorting his words to suit their end. He also met George Duhamel, J. G. Fraser, Forel, Bovet and others who all confirmed what Rolland had said. Tagore was shocked and found it difficult to reconcile what he now heard with what he had just seen. He resented taking his opinions from others and also knew that his own impressions had been based on what he had been shown and that he had no means of checking the facts for himself. He expressed this misgiving in a letter to Elmhirst:

'Of course my opinion is based upon inadequate data and my mind may still be obsessed with some bias in favour of Mussolini for what he has done for Visva-Bharati. Possibly some day I shall come to the conclusion that it was a sinister design on the part of my evil fate to have brought me into any relation with this man who may altogether be a fraud and no real personality. Somehow I have the unenviable knack of getting myself entangled in responsibilities that should have been avoided and I reget that I ever allowed myself to pay this last visit to Italy.

'Can you lend me an aeroplane if you have one at your disposal?

[2] In Villeneuve he stayed in Hotel Byrone in the very room in which Victor Hugo had lived for some time.

I want to fly back to Uttarayan[3] immediately, for the rain clouds of July have gathered about our Ashram and are wondering where the poet could have gone who was to greet them with his grateful songs in return for the music of rain.'

But the music of human adulation had become sweeter than 'the music of rain', for he continued his triumphant tour of Europe for five months more. From Villeneuve he proceeded to Zürich where he gave a public lecture and a recitation of his poems. Here he met Signora Salvadori who gave him a first-hand account of Fascist atrocities witnessed by herself. This was corroborated by Modigliani who met him in Vienna and gave him all the ghastly details of the murder of Matteoti, the anti-Fascist member of the Italian Chamber of Deputies. Profoundly shocked by all this unimpeachable evidence, Tagore wrote a letter to the *Manchester Guardian* explaining his visit to Italy and condemning Fascism in no uncertain terms. This exposed him to bitter revilement in the Italian press.

After a three-week stay in England he visited Oslo where he gave public lectures, was received by the King and made the acquaintance of Nansen, Bjørnson, Bojer and other distinguished writers. After a second visit to Stockholm where he met Sven Hedin again he went to Copenhagen and made the acquaintance of George Brandes and the philosopher Hoffding. The German tour was once again hectic and he received large ovations everywhere and was also received by President Hindenburg. His friendship with Albert Einstein began with this visit. After a week's stay in Prague where his play *The Post Office* was staged in Czech, he went via Vienna to Budapest where he was obliged to rest in a sanatorium on Lake Balaton, his health having broken down under the strain of the strenuous excitement of the tour. After crowded receptions and lecture engagements in Belgrade, Sofia, Bucharest and Athens where the Greek Government decorated him with the Order of the Redeemer, he visited Cairo where the Egyptian Parliament, then in session, was adjourned in his honour and King Fuad presented him with a set of Arabic books for Visva-Bharati. In December he returned to his own land.

[3] Name of his house in Santiniketan.

One would imagine that after this long and exciting tour during which his health had broken down more than once, the poet would have been content to enjoy the seclusion and peace of Santiniketan for which he had longed so much. In a charming poem of *Puravi*, called 'Asha' (Hope), he had expressed his wistful longing for a quiet nook in a secluded corner of the earth, with only one distraction, '. . . not wealth, not honour, only a little love'. But though one side of his genius throve 'under the shade of lazy hours', another constantly drove him to attempt 'laboriously built towers of my beneficent deeds'. Peace and glory are rarely found together and when they meet they soon part company. It is not without significance that his poetical and musical compositions of this period revolve round the conception of Nataraja, Shiva as the Divine Dancer holding the universe in the whirl of his cosmic dance. He embodied it in a song-and-dance sequence called *Nataraja Rituran-gasala* which was produced in Santiniketan in February. The previous month of January had been spent in the excitement of rehearsing the drama *Natir Puja* which was staged in Calcutta at the end of the month, the author himself appearing on the stage. In March he went on another tour of western India during which he presided over a Hindi Literary Conference held in the then princely state of Bharatpur.

He spent the summer in the pleasant hill-station of Shillong in Assam where he began his famous novel *Teen Purus* (Three Generations). He had planned it on an ambitious scale as the title indicates and he began it superbly, in the best traditional manner of story-telling, unburdened with sophistication or affectation. The poet, the story-teller and the social psychologist have reconciled their claims and achieved a balanced technique which makes some critics acclaim this novel as 'the most satisfying of all the novels Tagore has written'. But Tagore was no Tolstoy or Balzac and could not live for long at a stretch in a world peopled only by one set of characters, even though his own creations. The poet, the singer and the teacher constantly meddled with his mood and he could not concentrate for long on one plot or one set of characters. And so, having planned this saga as a trilogy, he gave it up after completing the story of one generation only and the novel was published two years later under the altered title *Yogayog* (Cross-Currents).[4]

The story relates the conflict between the values nurtured in an old and culture-conscious family of landed aristocrats which has lost its wealth but not its pride, and the aggressive claims of a self-made industrialist millionaire who thinks that money can buy anything. Kumudini, the lovely and gentle daughter of the former is married to Madhusudhan, the go-ahead millionaire, crude, vital and assertive, one of the few flesh-and-blood characters made by Tagore. Accustomed to imposing his will 'on his human and mechanical tools', he imagines he can possess Kumudini merely because she is his wife, but soon discovers that though he can possess her physically, the real she eludes his grasp. It is the tragedy of Soames Forsyte repeated in an Indian setting—with a difference. Soames is a respectable philistine, very correct and British, while Madhusudhan is vulgar, shameless and ruthless, very like the characters made familiar by American novels.

Nor is the lovely and seemingly fragile Kumudini a mere Indian counterpart of Irene. She wears a different spiritual armour. Brought up in the Hindu tradition she makes a conscious and determined effort to worship her husband as her lord and yields obediently to his embraces until repeated humiliations cause an inner revolt. The psychological interest of the novel lies in the gradual and almost imperceptible transformation in the husband's feelings towards her—at first brutal, violent and exultant, they are gradually inhibited by sudden spasms of tenderness and awe which he cannot understand, having never experienced them in any other sphere of life. The bullying, blustering boss loses his self-confidence and fumbles clumsily, reaching out for what his hands cannot grasp. The end of this fascinating drama is, unfortunately, weak and vague—a failing which many other novels of Tagore share.

Even as he was writing this novel depicting the spiritual weakness of mere success, he was himself restless for fresh fields to conquer. The missionary zeal once again proved stronger than the creative, and in July 1927 he set out on his ninth foreign tour, this time to the neighbouring lands of South-east Asia. After visiting Singapore,

[4] This novel, unfortunately, has not been translated into English.

Malacca, Kuala Lumpur, Ipoh, Taiping and Penang, attracting crowds and receiving ovations everywhere, he sailed for Indonesia, composing on the way a beautiful, long poem on Java which he read out (in English rendering) at a banquet given in his honour in Jakarta. In Java he met, among others, Achmed Soekarno, then a comparatively unknown revolutionary youth. In Java and Bali Tagore was deeply impressed by their dance-dramas and cultural traditions and noted with interest their affinity with the traditions in his own country.

His visit was fruitful in restoring a cultural link that had been snapped for centuries and since then many students have been exchanged between the two countries. The Javanese art of wax-painting-and-dyeing known as *batik* was first introduced in Santini-ketan from where it has since spread to other parts of India. The profound impression made on his mind by the monumental Borobudur was recorded by the poet in a well-known poem. Altogether, the visit to the picturesque islands of Indonesia had moved him deeply, as much because of the natural beauty of the country and the charm of the people as on account of the joy of recognizing an ancient kinship in culture. Soon after leaving the islands he wrote another beautiful poem on his visit, named 'Sagarika' (Sea-girt). After a short visit to Thailand where he was warmly received and where he delivered a lecture on Education at the University in Bangkok, he returned to India in December, in time to preside over the annual celebrations at Santiniketan.

In January 1928 V. Lesny arrived from Prague as visiting Professor to Visva-Bharati. Perhaps no other foreign scholar took such pains to study Tagore's writings in original Bengali and succeeded so well in entering in their spirit as this distinguished Czech Indologist. Soon after, Dame Clara Butt, the celebrated English singer, came to visit Tagore at Santiniketan and gave two recitals for him. Recalling the visit in her autobiography, *My Life of Song*, she wrote: 'In India I met three of the most wonderful personalities of that wonderful country, Mrs. Annie Besant, Gandhi and Sir Rabindranath Tagore. The last named lent me his villa, where he wrote many of those wonderful poems which rank among the great classics of all literature.

'I have heard that he sometimes sang and once when he was complimenting me after hearing me sing, I said, "But you too are a singer; I should so much like to hear you." He made excuses, deprecating any claim to having a voice, but said at last, "I have had such pleasure from listening to your wonderful voice that, since you wish it, I will sing to you."

'With me alone for an audience, and without accompaniment of any kind, he then sang two or three songs of his own composition. Rarely have I been so moved by anybody's singing as by that of the stately and venerable Poet; he sang with exquisite feeling, and his voice, though quite untrained, had a natural silvery sweetness.'[5]

Once again he prepared to leave for abroad on receipt of an invitation from Oxford University to deliver the Hibbert lectures, but the voyage had to be abandoned as he fell ill on arrival in Madras. After a week's rest at Adyar as the guest of Annie Besant and a few more days in the pleasant climate of Coonoor, he sailed for Ceylon hoping to recoup his health sufficiently there to take a boat to England. On the way he landed at Pondicherry to visit the philosopher-yogi Aurobindo Ghosh whom he had known well in his earlier days of revolutionary political activity. Recording the impression the poet wrote as he resumed his voyage on the French boat s.s. *Chantilly*: 'Years ago I saw Aurobindo in the heroism of his early political struggle and I said, Aurobindo, accept the salutation of Rabindra. Today I saw him again seated in the poise of calm wisdom, and I repeated in silence, Aurobindo, accept the salutation of Rabindra.'

He stayed in Colombo for ten days, but as there was no visible improvement in health, he gave up all hope of sailing for England and returned to the mainland, resting for three weeks in Bangalore as the guest of his old friend, the learned philosopher Sir Brajendranath Seal, then Vice-Chancellor of Mysore University. Having given up the voyage, he was no longer restless and fretful. The old poise returned and with it the creative mood. During this brief stay in Bangalore he not only completed the novel *Yogayog*, discussed earlier, but also finished another which he had begun during his

---

[5] Quoted in *Rabindra Jivani*, Vol. III, by Prabhat Mukherji.

recent voyage to Colombo, *Sesher Kavita* ('Last Poem').[6] This novel, which is almost half poetry, is very popular among Bengali readers and stands in a class by itself. Its modern setting, its playful mocking tone, its challenging style, the author's trick of introducing himself as the butt of the hero's merciless criticism, the scintillating wit of the dialogue and the final tragic note voiced in the beautiful poem at the end which gives the book its title—all these won for the novel an immediate popularity with the young readers. As a specimen of its style the following diatribe against himself which the author puts into the mouth of his hero who is addressing a literary gathering may be quoted:

'The strongest objection against Rabindranath Tagore is that this gentleman, imitating Wordsworth, insists most perversely on continuing. Many a time the messenger of death has called to switch off the light, but even as the old man rises from his throne, he still clings to its arms. If he doesn't quit of his own accord, it becomes our duty to quit his court in a body. The one who succeeds him will also enter in triumph, thundering and bragging that there shall be no end to his rule, that the very heavens shall be chained to his mortal abode. For a time his devotees will feed him and fête him and adore him, until the auspicious hour of the sacrifice arrives, when the devotees will clamour for liberation from the bondage of devotion. Such is the way the four-footed god is worshipped in Africa. Such is also the way the two-footed, three-footed, four-footed and fourteen-footed gods of metre may be worshipped. No desecration can compare with the profanation of dragging out devotion till it is hackneyed . . . The cult of literary dictatorship is fast becoming obsolete. My second contention against Rabindranath Tagore is that his literary creations are rounded or wave-like, like his handwriting, reminding one of roses and moons and female faces. Primitive, so to copy nature's hand. From the new dictator we expect creations straight and sharp like thorns, like arrows, like spear-heads. Not like flowers, but like a flash of lightning, like the pain of neuralgia . . . Poets who are not ashamed to stick on for sixty or seventy years cheapen themselves and must suffer the

---

[6] English translation by the present writer: *Farewell My Friend*. Jaico Publishing House, Bombay.

consequences. In the end they are ringed round by their imitators who make faces at them. Their writings lose all character and, pilfering from their own past, they degenerate into mere receivers of stolen property . . .'

Not only is the novel popular among young readers but it has won generous praise from mature and discriminating critics. 'Sesher Kavita,' says Professor S. K. Banerjee, 'is a novel written in a more consistent poetic strain and on a more purely poetic theme than perhaps any other novel in the world's history.' Dr Sukumar Sen describes it as 'a love story written as if to end all love stories', and Bhabani Bhattacharya, himself a novelist, has testified: 'Its beauty of feeling is as indescribable as its beauty of language—every passage is a unique and startling prose poem—and the astounding fact is that such freshness, such youthfulness, could come from a writer in his seventieth year. Somewhere in him Tagore was reborn, as it were, over and again so that the rich exuberance of the young in spirit along with the depth of understanding of the true seer made a perfect amalgam for his creative genius.' Indeed, the fact becomes even more astounding if we recall that he completed this and the other novel, Yogayog, almost simultaneously—and no two novels could be more dissimilar, whether in theme, style, treatment or language.

The story is very simple—the last word, as Bhabani Bhattacharya has put it, in love's asceticism. And yet this asceticism which gives seriousness and dignity to the theme is set in a background of frivolous affectation, giving the novel its unique quality. The hero is an amusing specimen of an ultra-modern Bengali intellectual whose Oxford education has not only given him a superiority complex but induced in him a craze for conscious originality which results in a deliberate and frivolous contrariness to all accepted opinion and convention. His aggressive self-complacence, however, receives a shock when he accidentally encounters and falls in love with a quite different product of modern education—a highly intelligent girl of fine sensibility and deep feelings. This experience is so utterly different from his previous excursions in flirting that it comes as a shock, releasing his submerged depth of sincerity which he finds hard to adjust to the habits of sophistry and pose practised so long. In the process he manages to strike a new romantic attitude.

The struggle makes of him a curiously pathetic figure—one who is being worked against his grain. The idol-breaker has become a worshipper so ardent that the girl understands that what he is in love with is not herself but an idealized image of her to which she can never correspond. Sensing the tragedy, she releases him from his troth and disappears from his life. The last poem in which she takes her farewell of her lover is her testament of the depth of feeling of which she was capable.

> No loss is yours in losing me,
> an image of clay.
> If of that mortal dust
> you have fashioned a goddess,
> let the goddess remain for you to adore
> with the evening star.
> No gross touch of the actual me
> shall disturb the play of your worship,
> no hot breath of ardour passion-lit
> sully its flowers, sacred, fragile . . .
> What I gave to you
> is yours by right everlasting.
> What others receive
> are the daily driblets the heart yields
> to tender importunity.
> O my princely, my peerless friend,
> what I gave to you was your own gift—
> fuller your acceptance, deeper my debt,
> my friend, farewell!

More than the theme about which there is nothing extraordinary —love is the most hackneyed of all themes in fiction as in poetry, though no one seems to tire of it—it is the form of its presentation, the artistry of the style, the exquisite poetry interwoven with sophisticated prose sparkling with wit, the half-lyrical, half-mocking tone of the narrative which startle the reader and give the novel its peculiar distinction. But however brilliant and entertaining, to call it a great novel or to regard it as better than *Gora* or *The Home and the World* is to prefer cleverness to genius.

The ageing poet was re-living in imagination his romantic youth. The embers were burning out and needed artificial blowing to work them into a flame. His younger contemporaries, charmed by his latest novel, begged him to make an anthology of his love poems and add a few new ones. The suggestion was enough to stimulate a mind that needed no more than a prod. As he himself put it lightly, he was like an automobile engine which kept on running, once the self-starter was pulled. So instead of compiling a selection he wrote a completely new volume of verses, mostly love poems, which he named *Mahua*, after the strong-scented Indian flower which yields a native heady wine. The title was appropriate, for these poems, some of them very tender and exquisite, were not born of the anguish of a living experience but were induced by an artificial stimulus, as by intoxication. Not quite artificial, for the poet was always in love with love, an impersonal love. As he had put it in an earlier verse:

When death comes and whispers to me:
'Thy days are ended,'
Let me say to him, 'I have lived in love,
And not in mere time.'
He will ask: 'Will thy songs remain?'
I shall say 'I know not, but this I know
That often when I sang I found my eternity.'

It was during the rainy season of this year, 1928, that Tagore introduced two new seasonal festivals, Vriksha-Ropana (Tree-planting) and Hala-Karshana (Ploughing), at Santiniketan and Sriniketan respectively. These picturesque festivals with their simple and artistic ceremonials accompanied by music, dance and Vedic chants, invoking nature's fertility and symbolizing its ever-recurring youth, are still celebrated annually and attract crowds of visitors from the neighbouring countryside and from Calcutta. Tagore, the lover of forests, whose favourite reading was Hudson's *Green Mansions*, and who had long bewailed the ruthless deforestation of the countryside, wanted to introduce a practice which would catch the popular imagination and make people plant trees for the love of them. He succeeded. Not only is Santiniketan, which was once a wasteland of corroded soil, now a miniature garden town, but the tree-planting ceremony initiated by him is now an all-India festival actively sponsored by the central and state governments.

One of his most characteristic volumes of verse is named *Vanavani*[7] (Voice of the Forest), a collection of poems on trees, shrubs and flowers and on the various seasons with which their life is linked. The entire book is a hymn to the green earth and is appropriately dedicated to his friend, the plant-physiologist J. C. Bose, who demonstrated that plants have almost the same life-reactions as we. It is difficult to say whether Tagore loved nature most or man or God. All the three were linked in his consciousness as aspects of the same reality and while man must at times have repelled him—who has not at times shrunk from his own kind?—and God must occasionally at least have seemed a mere abstraction, the earth was always concrete, dear and lovely. In one of his letters written as a young man when he was living in a boat on the river Padma, he refers movingly to the strange kinship he feels with the earth, an almost concrete awareness that not only in this life but through the various stages of evolution he had been part of it, its memory stored in the subconscious. 'I feel as if dim, distant memories come to me of the time when I was one with the rest of the earth; when on me grew the green grass, and on me fell the autumn light; when a warm scent of youth would rise from every pore of my vast, soft, green body at the touch of the rays of the mellow sun, and a fresh life, a sweet joy, would be half-consciously secreted and inarticulately poured forth from all the immensity of my being, as it lay dumbly stretched, with its varied countries and seas and mountains, under the bright blue sky.'[8]

Nineteen-twenty-eight was indeed a fruitful year, thanks partly to the fact that his health obliged him to stick to his own soil. It was in this year too that he began his experiments in an entirely new and unforeseen medium of creative expression, namely, painting. He had always been drawn to this art and had occasionally cast furtive and longing glances at it, ever since as a young boy he had seen his elder and versatile brother Jyotirindranath draw. He has re-

[7] Published in 1931. Not translated into English.
[8] *Chhinna Patra.*

called this early longing in his Reminiscences. 'I remember how I would lie on the covered floor in the afternoon, with a sketch-book in hand trying to draw—more like toying with picture-making than an exercise in the fine arts. The most important part of this play was what remained in the mind and of which no trace was left on paper.'

Later, when his nephews Abanindranath and Gaganendranath discovered their talents for painting he encouraged them in their pursuit and helped in founding what came to be known as the modern movement in Indian art. He himself hardly ever took the brush in hand. Writing to his niece Indira Devi in 1893, he confessed: 'To tell you the truth, I do not quite know what my real vocation is or should be. I am very much in the position of a young woman who, in the pride of her youth, is unwilling to part with any of her suitors . . . If I were to confess without fear or shame, I may as well tell you that very often I cast looks of longing, after the fashion of a disappointed lover, towards the muse of Fine Art.' But though he did not wield a brush, he doodled freely with his pen. His manuscripts bear ample and fascinating testimony to these playful exercises interwoven with his verses.

Most of these exercises were induced by what he has called 'casualties in my manuscripts', deletions and erasures which he hated to leave alone as desultory scratches on his page. They seemed to him like 'widowed gypsies' in frantic search of mates, calling to him piteously to rescue them from their irrelevance as outcasts; and so he would work on them with the selfsame pen and connect these various 'solitary incongruities' into some kind of rhythmic pattern, fanciful or grotesque.

From now on he painted not to provide rhythmic patterns to the erasures in his writing, but as he liked. He let himself go, delighted with his new plaything like a child with a new-found toy. Fortunately, he had had no training and no reputation at stake as a painter, and so he painted without inhibition, without affectation. The only unfortunate part was that, not taking his art seriously, he drew on whatever paper was at hand and with any instruments and colours, with the result that the preservation of these paintings, many of which are of extraordinary quality, is presenting a serious problem.

He painted fast and with a sure hand, in between the intervals of his literary activity, finishing each picture at one sitting, and has left behind nearly 2,500 paintings and drawings, all done during the last thirteen years of his life—a no mean achievement, considering that during the same period he also published more than sixty volumes of new literary writing, poetry and prose.

He himself described his paintings as 'my versification in lines' and confessed in a letter that he was '. . . hopelessly entangled in the spell that the lines have cast all around me'. There is no doubt that many of these drawings are marked by a strong feeling for rhythm, but apart from this affinity there is little in common between his poetry and his painting. In fact, it would seem that some other self of his, if not deeper, at any rate more hidden, were seeking expression through this new medium. In his literary writings Tagore is a conscious artist, a finished craftsman with perfect control over his tools and his medium, so that he is able to say what he wants to say and in a manner which he approves. What he says is therefore necessarily selective—as in all great art—and always beautiful, sometimes so beautiful that one wonders how far it is Rabindranath the individual of flesh and blood who is saying it and how far it is the spirit of India that is using his voice as its own. He writes as a spirit consciously dedicated to a higher purpose. But when he paints, it is rather like a somnambulist walking, sure of his step without seeing, driven by an urge of which the direction is outside his control. The grotesque, the bizarre, the cruel, the sardonic, all that he scrupulously kept out of his writings peeps out of his drawings. Not only Ariel but Puck and Caliban too have their full play on his canvas.

As he wrote in one of his letters, 'It is impossible to give names to my pictures, because they represent no preconceived subject. Accidentally, some form of whose genealogy I am totally unaware takes shape from the tip of my moving pen and stands out as an individual.' This outburst of creative frenzy drawing on submerged levels of consciousness was as much a wonder to him as to others. 'What is the meaning of all this?' he wrote. 'When all the different chapters of the book of my life were about to close, the presiding deity of my life has felt pleased to provide me this unprecedented opportunity and the wherewithal for composing its epilogue.'

'The pictures of Tagore,' wrote the Comtesse de Noailles in 1930 when they were exhibited in Galerie Pigalle in Paris, 'which begin like the entry of the spirit into sleep by dreamy and vague spirals, define themselves in the course of their remarkable execution, and one is stupefied before this masterly creativeness which reveals itself as much in the trifling as in the vast ... Why has Tagore, the great mystic, suddenly, without knowing, set at liberty that which in him scoffs, banters and perhaps despises?

'—I love you and have more admiration for you, Tagore, since when you made to us such rich and sometimes such cruel confidences; but would I ever find again the great ingenuous angel that you were, when your silent feet, on the garden gravel, made me think of my sins, imaginary perhaps, and of your sublime innocence?'

Less charmingly put but more illuminating is the comment of the distinguished art-philosopher Ananda Coomaraswamy made in the same year. 'An exhibition of drawings by Rabindranath Tagore is of particular interest because it puts before us, almost for the first time, genuine examples of modern primitive art. One may well wonder how those artists and critics who have so long striven for and praised the more calculated primitivisms, archaisms, and pseudo-barbarisms of European origin will respond; will they admire the real thing? ... This is a genuinely original, genuinely naïve expression; extraordinary evidence of eternal youth persistent in a hoary and venerable personage ...

'The poet gives no descriptive title to his pictures—how could he? They are not pictures about things, but pictures about himself. In this sense they are probably much nearer to his music than to his poetry. In the poetry, so far at least as the content is concerned, he is not primarily an inventor, but rather the sensitive exponent of a racial or national tradition, and therefore his words are more profoundly sanctioned and more significant than those of any private genius could be, all India speaks and understands the same language. The poetry reveals nothing of the poet's personality, though it establishes his status. But the painting is an intimacy comparable to the publication of private correspondence. What a varied and colourful person is revealed! ... The manner is as varied as the theme ... The means are always adequate to the end in view; this end is not Art with a capital A, on the one hand—nor, on the other, a merely pathological self-expression; not art intended to improve our minds, nor to provide for the artist himself an "escape", but without ulterior motives, truly innocent, like the creation of a universe.'

On 1 March 1929 Tagore sailed for Canada at the invitation of the National Council of Education of that country. Stopping for a few days in Japan on the way, he landed in Canada in April and gave two lectures, 'The Philosophy of Leisure' and 'The Principles of Literature', the former in Victoria, the latter in Vancouver, attracting packed audiences in both places. 'More than any other delegate to this conference,' reported the *Vancouver Sun*, 'he seized their imagination. They paid him the respect due to intellect.' Clifford Dowling wrote in the *Vancouver Star*, 'I believe Tagore is the first poet I have seen who combined completely the reality with the appearance.'[9]

Invitations had been received from several universities in the States, among them California, Harvard and Columbia, and so from Canada the poet sailed for Los Angeles. On arrival in Los Angeles his passport was unfortunately lost and he felt irritated by the formalities to which he was subjected by the Immigration Officers, some of which he considered humiliating. He therefore cancelled his engagements in the States and sailed for Japan. This was not the first occasion when an accident intervened to mar his understanding of the United States. On a previous visit too he had been rubbed the wrong way. It was unfortunate indeed that his high expectations received repeated rebuffs in a country that is known for its hospitality. He had, of course, as Elmhirst has pointed out, '. . . an immense respect and deep affection for certain individual Americans who remained his friends to the last. Mrs. William Vaughan Moody was probably, of all these, the most intimate with him and the one with whom he took refuge in Chicago on each of his visits, but America in general offended him in two directions. In the feeling of what I would call his higher consciousness, it was the maelstrom, the bustle, and the ugliness that combined to offend his spiritual approach to life. He found meditation difficult in that atmosphere, and never, to my knowledge, settled down happily anywhere. He never got

[9] Quoted in *Rabindra Jivani* by Prabhat Mukherji.

over what he felt was the gross insult of having to be finger-printed on his arrival in California. There was a time, of course, when we Britishers also had to be finger-printed, but I think he felt this privilege was confined by the Americans to criminals and people of colour from Asia and Africa. He could be entirely unreasonable on occasion when he allowed his emotions to spill over about certain aspects of American life, but there is no doubt that many of his criticisms were well justified.'

Unfortunately, it was about the same time that Miss Katherine Mayo's book, *Mother India*, was published—a book hardly likely to endear the author and her countrymen to Indians, who failed to understand why a country so big, prosperous and progressive like the United States should play a subservient role to the British game in India. Gandhi had likened its author's mentality to that of 'a drain-inspectress'. Tagore, when interviewed in Honolulu on his way to Japan observed, 'I do not feel any enthusiasm in contradicting this book, knowing that most of her readers are not interested in truth but a piece of sensationalism that has the savour of rotten flesh. Now that this woman has discovered a mine of wealth in an unholy business of killing reputation, no appeal to truth will prevent her plying a practised hand in wielding her assassin's knife, carefully choosing for her victims those who are already down.'[10]

He spent nearly a month in Japan. He loved this country and its brave and disciplined people and was filled with unhappiness as he watched their minds being steadily warped by a deliberately engineered hysteria of imperial ambition. With his usual courage he warned them in a public address against 'the ghosts of ideals which no longer have a living reality', which merely serve to alienate nations from one another. True education, he pointed out, had only one object, freedom—'freedom from ignorance of the laws of universe and freedom from passion and prejudice in our communication with the human world.'

After a pleasant halt in Saigon, then French Indo-China, where he was very warmly received, Tagore returned to India in July—in time to welcome with songs, as he used to say, the rain-laden clouds over the Santiniketan sky. But this time he was weary in spirit and

[10] *Ibid.*

body, and even the songs refused to gush forth as of old. Almost every foreign visit, with the sole exception of his sojourn in Buenos Aires, was a setback rather than a stimulus to his creative activity. The poet and the prophet went ill together. Fortunately, he commanded so many media that if one did not respond he had recourse to another. In his harem of muses there was always some mistress ready to oblige. So he contented himself with painting, with critical exposition of principles of literature which he gave as lectures in Calcutta and in recasting for the stage his old drama in blank verse, *Raja O Rani* (The King and the Queen). He rewrote the drama in prose and named it *Tapati*. It was successfully staged in Calcutta, the author appearing in the role of the King. One of the world's most prolific writers, Tagore was also one of the most economical in the use of his themes. He often recast the same theme in a different form, whether because of a natural poverty in inventing new plots, or whether because, like a good cook, he enjoyed serving old dishes with new dressing or because old familiar characters cried out to him for better justice than he had done them, it is difficult to say.

In January 1930 Tagore visited western India and gave lectures in Baroda, *Man the Artist*, returning to Santiniketan in early February to receive the Governor of Bengal, Sir Stanley Jackson, who had come to inaugurate a conference of Co-operative Workers at Sriniketan. Tagore was criticized by his countrymen for receiving a representative of the British régime at a time when Mahatma Gandhi was contemplating another mass struggle against the régime. But he never professed faith in non-co-operation as an infallible code of national virtue and was content to be misunderstood. Though he stood his ground and was not afraid of facing criticism, he loved his people and respected Mahatma Gandhi far too well to feel comfortable when he was at odds with them. It was painful to watch a struggle in which he could not actively participate.

He therefore welcomed the opportunity of sailing for Europe in early March, to keep his engagement for the Hibbert Lectures at Oxford which ill-health had prevented him from keeping earlier. Lecture engagements were a convenient excuse; the compelling reason was his own restlessness, this time made more imperious by the prospect of his paintings being exhibited in Paris. His charming Argentinian hostess had come all the way to Paris to organize the exhibition which opened at Galerie Pigalle in early May.

Landing in Marseilles, Tagore rested for a few days at Cap Martin as the guest of M. Kahn. Here he met President Masaryk of Czechoslovakia. The paintings were well received by Paris critics. 'Only those,' wrote Henry Bidou, 'who have never recognized those mysterious currents of thought and feeling, the outcome of the age itself, which penetrate all souls as by osmosis, and give its direction to a whole epoch, will be surprised that this pure painting, absolutely sincere and wholly uninfluenced by our studio customs, should resemble now and then the most recent researches of the painters of the west. There can be no question of imitation, but the convergence of spirit is remarkable.' For some reason Romain Rolland did not take kindly to this new and unexpected aspect of Tagore's genius, and noted in his diary that the end of the poet's life was sad and that he had taken to painting as a pastime. He also noted with regret that Tagore sought and accepted invitations in Paris from certain society people 'so little worthy of him'.

Commenting on this, Victoria Ocampo pertinently observes: 'The fact is that I was with Tagore in Paris at the time to which Romain Rolland alludes. His stay there was a brief one (on his reurn from Cap Martin). I looked after him in Paris as I had done in San Isidro and my dear, faithful Fani—of whom Tagore was very fond —kept all his belongings in order. I therefore know whom Tagore did and whom he did not see in Paris in 1930. He met Gide, his translator, for the first time. I was present at this encounter to which Gide came alone. Tagore received also the visit of Paul Valéry, Jean Cassou, and Georges Henri Rivière (of the Musée de l'Homme) who, at my request, organized a show of the poet's paintings. He had lunch with Abbé Brémond, the Abbé Mugnier and Comtesse Mathieu de Noailles. These seven people, of whom four at least bear illustrious names in French letters, cannot be described as particularly worldly-minded. To be sure, Madame de Noailles was high-born and Paul Valéry had friends in "Society". I fail to see that there was anything in this "unworthy" of Tagore.'

Arriving in England on 11 May, Tagore spent the first few days

at the Quaker Settlement at Woodbrooke, near Birmingham. Here
he was shocked to receive news of the painful happenings in India
since his departure, the arrest and internment of Mahatma Gandhi,
Jawaharlal Nehru and other Congress leaders, the martial law at
Sholapur, indiscriminate shootings and mass arrests all over the land.
'Though much suppressed,' he told a representative of the *Manchester Guardian*, 'news is trickling through travellers from India
telling how cruel and arbitrary punishments are meted out to entirely
inoffensive persons. Though such actions were called by the high-
sounding names of law and order, they are themselves the worst
breaches of the law of humanity which I feel is greater than any
other law.' The Hibbert Lectures delivered in Oxford later in the
month were published in the following year by Allen & Unwin,
London, as *The Religion of Man*—dedicated to Dorothy Elmhirst.

Dorothy and Leonard Elmhirst had purchased some years earlier
a medieval manor house in the picturesque county of Devonshire
known as Dartington Hall and had tried to establish there '. . . a
variety of enterprises, educational, research and commercial, not
unlike a mingling of the activities of Santi- and Sri-niketan'. Here
Tagore rested for a few days in summer, looked after by those
whose friendship had been England and America's joint gift to
him. 'One day,' recalls Elmhirst, 'he asked for bottles of coloured
ink and, when these arrived, there began to emerge a series of ink
paintings and sketches. "I can't tell you whence in my nature this
inspiration comes. Certainly my hand is not guided by any conscious control that I exert. Who are these strange beings that
emerge? Where do they come from? I don't know." '

After an exhibition of his paintings in Birmingham and London,
Tagore left for Berlin in July, accompanied by Amiya Chakravarty
and Aryanayakam. The visit to Germany was exciting as had been
the previous visits to that country. Whatever interpretations critics
may choose to put on the popular enthusiasm with which Tagore
was received in pre-Nazi Germany, the fact remains that Tagore
himself retained to the end of his life warm memories of his sojourns
in that country[11] and a warm affection for the people even during

[11] It is not without some significance that Germany was one of the few countries
outside his homeland where the fountain of his creative composition was to some

the years of his uncompromising hatred of Nazism. He never made the mistake of identifying the people with the State, and was thus able to admire the British people even while he opposed their odious role in India and to retain his affection for the Germans and the Japanese when the British and American war propaganda was painting them as inhuman monsters. This visit deepened his affection and regard for Einstein, with whom he had long discussions, the gist of which is recorded in an appendix to *The Religion of Man*. His pictures were exhibited at the Moller Gallery in Berlin and a civic reception was accorded to him in the ancient Town Hall of Munich. He visited many places in Germany, including Oberammergau where he witnessed the Passion Play. 'How like our Prophet!' whispered the audience as they saw the Indian poet.

That the Passion Play must have left a deep impression on his mind can be guessed from the theme of his poem *The Child*, which he wrote soon after, while still in Germany. This long poem which he wrote in the course of one night is the only poem he ever wrote directly in English.[12] This beautiful work, a product of Biblical inspiration and Hindu imagination has, strangely enough, received very little attention in the West. Tagore's interpretation of the theme has invested it with a significance which is universal and independent of any religious or political affiliations. Its relevance is even more striking to the present fear-torn age than to any other in history, as the following excerpts may illustrate:

> The Man of faith moves on along pitiless paths
> strewn with flints, over scorching sands . . .
> They follow him, the strong and the weak,
> the aged and young . . .
> Some grow weary and footsore, some angry
> and suspicious,
> they ask at every dragging step,
> How much farther is the end? . . .
> It is night.

extent released. During his previous visit to Germany, Austria and Hungary in 1926, he wrote (words and music) of seventeen beautiful songs.

[12] Published under the same title by Allen & Unwin, London, 1931. The Bengali version, *Sisu-tirtha*, was written after the English.

The travellers spread their mats on the ground . . .
A gust of wind blows out the lamp
and the darkness deepens like a sleep into a swoon.
Someone from the crowd suddenly stands up
and pointing to the leader with merciless finger
breaks out:
False prophet, thou hast deceived us!
Others take up the cry one by one,
women hiss their hatred and men growl.
At last one bolder than others suddenly deals him
a blow.
They cannot see his face, but fall upon him
in a fury of destruction . . .
Suddenly they become still and gasp for breath
as they gaze at the figure lying dead.
The women sob out aloud and men hide their faces
in their hands.
A few try to slink away unnoticed,
but their crime keeps them chained
to their victim.
They ask each other in bewilderment,
Who will show us the path?
The old man from the East bends his head and says:
The Victim . . .
And they all stand up and mingle their voices and sing,
Victory to the Victim!

After nearly a month's rest in Geneva, Tagore left for Moscow, at the invitation of the Soviet Government, accompanied by Amiya Chakravarty, Aryanayakam, Soumyendranath Tagore (his talented grand-nephew) and Miss Einstein. Fortunately, he kept a full record of his visit and impressions in a series of letters he wrote home, which were later published as *Rashiar Chithi* (Letters from Russia). These letters testify to one of the most significant qualities of the ageing poet, namely, that as he grew older in years, he became younger in spirit. He was far less conservative and more tolerant in his old age than during his manhood. Strange as it may sound, he even looked more handsome in old age than as a young man— this is borne out, not only by his photographs but by those contemporaries who had seen him at both the ages. He mellowed rather than grew old. Like Gandhi he discovered with the years that truth was higher than any religion and human welfare more important than any philosophy.

Were it not so the author of *Gitanjali* and the great exponent of India's spiritual heritage could hardly have looked upon his visit to the Soviet land as a pilgrimage. 'If I had not come to Russia,' he wrote, 'life's pilgrimage would have remained incomplete. Before judging the good and bad of their activities here, the first thing that strikes me is: What incredible courage! What is called tradition clings to man in a thousand different ways; its numerous apartments, its innumerable doors are guarded by sentries whose number is legion; its treasury rises mountain high, filled with taxes gathered over the centuries. Here in Russia they have torn it up by its roots; there is no fear, no hesitation in their minds . . . The cry of the Russian Revolution is also the cry of the world. At least this nation, of all the others in the world today, is thinking of the interest of the whole of humanity, over and above the national interest.'

Whether Stalin's Russia deserved this compliment or not, the fact remains that the poet, accepting the Communist claim at its face value, was able to overcome many a hurdle of lifelong beliefs. Instead of being squeamish at the violent and ruthless uprooting of traditional values, he was overjoyed, as he had once been overjoyed by a terrific storm at Santiniketan, hailing it as the *Rudra*, the terrific aspect of the divine, in one of his most magnificent poems. So, too, the internationalist in him was now thrilled to see the curtain go up on the stage of world history. 'It would have been unpardonable,' he wrote, 'not to see the light of the greatest sacrificial fire known in history.' Once he had been much moved by the words of a Korean youth that 'the strength of Korea was the strength of her sorrow'. It was this great miracle of sorrow's strength that drew him to Russia.

He had heard many contradictory reports about this country and had been told of the pitiless violence of the Bolshevik régime. Many friends had tried to discourage his visit by painting lurid pictures of the lack of civilized comforts and amenities in that land, had warned him of the coarse food and the crude ways of the people and had added that in any case whatever he would be shown would be mere window-dressing. But '. . . the words of the Korean youth were ringing in my ears. I was thinking within myself that in the very courtyard of Western civilization, so triumphant in the power of wealth, Russia has raised the seat of power of the dispossessed, totally ignoring the frowns and curses of the entire Western World. If I do not go to see such a sight, who will? They are striving to destroy the power of the powerful and the wealth of the wealthy. Why should we be afraid of that? And why should we be angry? We have neither power nor wealth. We belong to the hungry and the helpless underdog class of the world.'

This poet whom the 'superior' English-speaking critics had come to regard as 'medieval' and as 'goody-goody' was far more robust and virile than many of his younger contemporaries who thought of virility only in terms of sex. Gandhi who differed from him in so many public issues understood him intuitively when he described him as the Great Sentinel of the rights of man who upheld the right of every individual, white, brown or black, to a full development of his personality. If any social or political system, however sacrosanct, stood in the way of its development he had no hesitation in saying, *Écrasez l'infame!* And so when he went to Russia he could not but admire the great accomplishment of the Revolution in raising the underdogs to the status of human beings.

'Wherever I look,' he wrote, 'I see no one but workers . . . The question to ask here is: Where are the so-called gentlemen? The masses of Russia live no more in the dark shadows of the so-called gentlemen. Those that were hidden behind the curtain are now fully in the forefront of society . . . In the course of a few short years the ignorant masses have become full-fledged human beings. I cannot help thinking of the farmers and workers of my country. It seems as if the magicians of the Arabian Nights have been at work in Russia. Only a decade ago the masses here were as illiterate, helpless and hungry as our own masses; equally blindly religious, equally stupidly superstitious. In sorrow and in danger they were wont to supplicate before their saints in the churches; in fear of the other world their mind was mortgaged to the priests, and in fear of this world to their rulers, money-lenders and their landlords. Their duty was to polish the very boots with which they were kicked by their masters. They knew no change in their way of life for a thousand years. They had the same old carts, the same old spinning wheels, the same old oil presses. Any suggestion of change provoked them to revolt. As in the case of our three hundred millions, the ghost of time sat on their backs and blindfolded them from behind. Who could be more astonished than an unfortunate Indian like myself to see how in these few years they had removed the mountain of ignorance and helplessness?'

He knew and had seen with his own eyes that the vast majority in his country, as in many other countries, are the beasts of burden who have no time to become men. They grow up on the leavings of society's wealth, with the least food, least clothing and least education. They who toil most receive in return the largest measure of in-dignity—deprived of almost everything that gives worth to life. They are, as he put it, the lamp-stand bearing the lamp of civilization on their heads; people above receive the light while their own backs are smeared with the trickling oil. He had often thought of them, worked for them, and had felt ashamed of his own more fortunate lot. He had been forced to the conclusion that poverty and in-equality were perhaps the inevitable concomitants of a progressive society. 'Thus I thought within myself: It is necessary that a section of our society should remain on the top; and how could they remain on the top if there were no one at the bottom? . . . Civilization begins only when man extends his vision beyond the bounds of mere livelihood. The finest fruits of civilization have grown on the fields of leisure. The progress of civilization demands leisure.'

He had therefore at one time believed that it was divinely ordained that the majority should toil so that the privileged minority might bloom like lilies of the field. The most that the fortunate upper classes can do is to consider themselves, as advised by Gandhi, trustees for the welfare of the dispossessed and try to ameliorate their misery. 'But the trouble is,' he wrote, 'that we cannot do anything of a permanent nature as a matter of charity. If we seek to do good to anyone from the outside, that goodness becomes distorted in a number of ways. Real helpfulness emanates from a perfect sense of equality. Whatever it may be, I could not satisfactorily solve this complex problem for myself. And yet I felt ashamed of myself to be forced to the conclusion that the pyramid of civilization could only be built on the subjection and dehumanization of the vast majority in human society—the workers of the world.'

He was not misled by the obvious lack of the so-called civilized comforts that were paraded in the cities of Europe and America. On the contrary he was pleased that the '. . . polish of luxury is altogether absent from Moscow . . . The thing I like best in Russia is the complete banishment of this barbarity of the pride of wealth.' Nor was the author of *Gitanjali* scandalized by the professedly godless nature of the Soviet State. 'For many centuries,' he commented, 'the old philosophy of theology and the old philosophy of politics overpowered the intelligence of the Russian people and almost their very life itself. The Soviet revolutionists have now killed these two evils to their very roots. My heart leaps with joy to see such a painfully enslaved nation attain such a great liberation in so short a time. For the religion that destroys the freedom of the mind of man by keeping him ignorant is a worse enemy than the worst of monarchs; for the monarch crushes the spirit of his subjects only from the outside . . . Let the theologians of other countries condemn Soviet Russia all they want; but I cannot condemn her, and I do not. Atheism is much better than superstition in religion and the tyranny of the Czar, which were like heavy loads of stone on the breast of Russia.' Indeed, he goes on to say that it was only in Soviet Russia that he fully realized the meaning of the famous words of the *Upanishads: ma gridah*—Do not covet.

Tagore was anything but a believer in Communist ideology. Marxism or the philosophy of dialectic materialism was alien to his mental make-up which sought for harmony and co-operation rather than contradiction and conflict in the process of history. His faith in the validity of individual conscience and in the 'infinite personality of man' biased him against any technique of political action aimed at the wholesale and violent suppression of opposition. He had a horror of the machine dominating the man, and knew that the party machine did it more effectively than any other kind. He believed that inhumane means were capable of

perverting the most humane ends. He was by no means a blind
admirer of whatever he saw in the Soviet Union. He was aware of
the ruthless nature of the party dictatorship and of the many moral
limitations of the Soviet experiment. But these limitations did not
make him lose his perspective and miss the wood for the trees.

He knew that a certain element of barbarism was inevitable in a
revolution, as in a war, but he trusted the great creative urge behind
the Russian upheaval as evidenced in their enthusiasm for educating
the masses. 'I admit that dictatorship is a great nuisance,' he wrote,
'and I also believe that in its name many persecutions take place in
Russia. Its negative aspect is compulsion which is sin. But I have
also seen its positive aspect, and that is education, the very reverse
of force . . . To the zealots of authority the only means of obtaining
their ends is to keep everybody else's mind paralysed by ignorance.
In the reign of the Czars people's minds deprived of education were
under a spell and round them, like a boa-constrictor, coiled religious
superstition . . . In recent years Russia has witnessed the vigorous
rule of the dictator. But to perpetuate itself it has not chosen the
path of the Czars, namely, the subduing of the people's mind by
ignorance and superstition, the impairing of their manliness by the
lash of the Cossacks. I do not say that the punitive rod is inactive
in the present Russian régime, but at the same time education
expands with extraordinary vigour . . . Nobody can definitely say
what final shape the Bolshevik economic philosophy will take as it
passes through one experiment after another. But this much is
certain, that the education which at long last the Russian masses
are so freely and abundantly enjoying, has improved and brought
honour to their humanity for all time.'

One of Tagore's most interesting visits in Moscow was to a
commune of orphaned children known as 'Alice Kingina Commune
of Young Pioneers'. One of the young orphans who welcomed him
there was Alexander Filatov, now a well-known poet in his country.
Recalling this early impression, Filatov writes: 'Having shown the
guest round, the children seated him in an armchair in the Pioneers'
Hall. They surrounded him in a circle and a hearty talk began. Now
we had a chance to have a good look at the poet. We were charmed
with his appearance. His high, clear forehead, expressive eyes,

handsome face without a single wrinkle—all bespoke his wisdom, his great thoughts and deeds. He must have realized our curiosity, for touching his beard and whiskers he said: "This is only a mask, my heart is young and warm," and added with a smile "a heart of a pioneer" . . . We showed him our amateur production, *The Five-Year Plan*, performed an original comic sketch about the usefulness of crèches. Then we invited the poet to our dining-room and treated him to our supper. The poet was deeply touched by our reception and before taking his leave he wrote down his impressions in our guest book: "I will remember for ever the charming evening I spent with these pioneers. I learned many things from them which would be of great use to my people in India, and I am grateful to them. I sympathize with all my heart with these young builders of the destiny of their people and wish them all success." [13]

He had a crowded programme in Russia and visited many institutions and met many celebrities. An exhibition of his paintings was also held in Moscow. But no event left a deeper impression on his mind than his meeting with the orphans whose little faces glowed with hope and confidence. How different from the orphans in his own land! The poet loved children and it was impossible for him not to admire a land where children were so well looked after.

Returning to Germany, Tagore left for the United States, his last visit to the rival wonderland of modern civilization, where on 25 November a public banquet was given in his honour at the Biltmore Hotel by 400 leading citizens of New York. A reception was also organized for him at Carnegie Hall where he spoke on education. Ruth St. Denis gave dance-recitals to raise funds for his school, but as her own country had been recently hard hit by an economic crisis, the poet handed over the proceeds for the benefit of the unemployed in New York. An exhibition of his paintings was held in New York and Boston and in Washington the poet was received by President Hoover. This was a far cry from the days when President Wilson had not even deigned to acknowledge his cable from India. He was also happy to meet Will Durant whose book, *The Case for India*, had been banned by the British Government in Bengal. Inscribing

[13] *Soviet Land*, July 1960.

the book to Tagore, Will Durant had written, 'You alone are sufficient reason why India should be free.'

In January 1931 Tagore returned to India via London where he had a long talk with Bernard Shaw at a luncheon which the *Spectator* gave for him at the Hyde Park Hotel. It had been a long and tiring tour but rich and fruitful in experience. He had seen the Western world in its different phases and had left behind a trail of glory which, though it soon faded as all glory must, was not easily forgotten. He did not know then that this was his last visit to the West, that his sun in the Western sky had set.

14

A LONE VOICE

The Russian experiment had deeply impressed the poet. The spectacle of a whole nation, awakened from its stupor and trying to rebuild its life anew, had seemed to him truly magnificent and creative. In one of his early patriotic songs he had exhorted his countrymen to set fire, not to foreign cloth, but to the inertia of the centuries, the accumulated rubbish which the human spirit collects in its march through history. Had he lived a century and a half earlier, he would, with equal fervour, have welcomed the American and the French revolutions. At his very first public engagement after his return from abroad, when he presided over the annual celebrations of the Institute of Rural Reconstruction at Sriniketan, he talked of the Soviet experiment in co-operation and education.

One might ask why he who welcomed, despite his repugnance to violence, the violent upheaval in Russia did not show the same enthusiasm for the non-violent mass movement which the Mahatma was leading nearer home. As a matter of fact, he keenly sympathized with the political and social upsurge in his own country—had he not partly inspired it himself?—and held the Mahatma in higher esteem than he did any other leader or personality, Indian or foreign. On the other hand, he recoiled from what he felt was a medieval and reactionary element in the Mahatma's mental make-up and social ideology which he feared would be misused by his followers. The Mahatma could rise above the limitations of his own thinking, but would his followers do so? How far his misgivings were justified, history alone will show.

He himself had passed, at the turn of the century, through a phase of patriotic conservatism when he had harped on the glory of India's heritage and had imagined the mannerisms of her social tradition to be the language of her spirit. He soon learnt to distinguish the mask from the face and came to realize that India, for all her uniqueness, was but a part of humanity like any other part and must march with the rest. The spirit of the age was a better guide than the ghost of the past and love of truth and reverence for life the true religion of Man. Gandhi made the same discovery when he said, 'If it is possible for the human tongue to give the fullest description of God, I have come to the conclusion that God is Truth. Two years ago I went a step further and said that Truth is God.'

In his beautiful poem on Shah Jehan, Tagore had said that even greater than his achievement in building the Taj Mahal was its builder's triumph in leaving it behind. India too can surpass her past by leaving it behind and not by getting buried in it as in a mausoleum. The humblest cradle holding a new-born babe is a greater glory to man than the noblest mausoleum brooding over the dead. In his paintings Tagore had completely turned his back on tradition. In his poetry and prose he went on steadily discarding the very perfection he had himself achieved. In his themes he continually harped on the new, as he grew older. His very first production after his long foreign tour was a music-and-dance sequence called *Navin* (The New). This was produced in Santiniketan in March 1931 and later staged in Calcutta at the Empire Theatre.

In May the seventieth anniversary of his birth was celebrated in Santiniketan and in many cities and towns all over India. In Calcutta a public committee representing all communities and sections was set up to organize a festival at the end of the year to honour the occasion. The *Golden Book of Tagore*, edited by the veteran journalist Ramananda Chatterjee, and containing messages and tributes received from all over the world was presented to the poet during the festival. 'Rabindranath Tagore ne comptait encore,' wrote André Gide, 'en Angleterre même, que de très rares lecteurs, lorsque en 1912, je traduisis son *Gitanjali*. L'incomparable pureté poétique de ce petit livre rayonnait à mes yeux d'un tel éclat que je tien à honneur d'en apporter un reflet à la France. À travers la guerre, au dessus de toutes nos dissensions politiques ou confessionelles cette étoile fixe a continué de luire et de verser sur le monde une tranquille lumière d'amour, de confiance et de paix. Je suis heureux d'apporter aujourd'hui mon tribut d'hommage et de reconnaissance à la grande figure que vous vous proposez d'honorer.'[1]

Bertrand Russell wrote: 'He has contributed as much as any man living to the most important work of our time, namely, the promotion of understanding between different races. Of what he has done for India it is not for me to speak, but of what he has done for Europe and America in the way of softening of prejudices and the removal of misconceptions I can speak, and I know that on this account he is worthy of the highest honour.' Yeats wrote to him a personal letter assuring him that 'I am still your most loyal student and admirer. Your poems, as you know, came to me as a great excitement; and of recent years I have found wisdom and beauty, or both, in your prose—*The Home and the World*, your short stories and your *Reminiscences* . . . What an excitement it was, the first reading of your poems, which seemed to come out of the fields and the rivers and have their changelessness!' Will Durant, who had met him a few months earlier, wrote: 'We feel that we have been cleansed and ennobled by meeting you; it gives us a new faith to see that a man may still live a life true to all the highest ideals of our youth. We were cynics before you came; we thought that all ideals were false, and all hopes vain; but one look at you and we know that we were wrong, that the battle between Right and Might is not yet lost, and that life may still have a meaning for us that will not be frustrated by our deaths. Something of the ancient idealism of the East has been poured into our blood by the wine and music of your verse, by the example and majesty of your life.'

The Mahatma was, as usual, simple and brief. 'In common with thousands of his countrymen,' he wrote, 'I owe much to one who by his poetic genius and singular purity of life has raised India in the

---

[1] I am indebted to *Alliance Française* for the following rendering: 'The readers of Rabindranath Tagore numbered, even in England, still very few when in 1912 I was translating his *Gitanjali*. The incomparable poetical purity of this small book has been shining in my eyes so brightly that I consider it an honour to bring to France an image of it. Through the war and beyond all our political and confessional dissensions, this fixed star has continued to shine and pour on the world a tranquil light of love, confidence and peace. I am glad to bring today my tribute of homage and gratitude to this great figure whom you are proposing to honour.'

estimation of the world. But I owe also more. Did he not harbour in Santiniketan the inmates of my Ashram who had preceded me from South Africa? The other ties and memories are too sacred to bear mention in a public tribute.'

Albert Einstein's message is characteristic of a scientist who was also a thinker, a modern seer in the truest sense of the word, who having explored the farthest reach of knowledge was humble with doubt. Like the sage of *Rig-Veda* who wondered whence and how this creation arose, when there was neither not-being nor being in the primeval nothingness—'Wherefrom this creation has issued, whether He has made it or whether He has not, He who is the Overseer of this world in the highest heaven, He alone knows, or perhaps, even He does not know'—the modern sage also wonders how far any man, however great, can claim credit for his greatness:

'If the moon, in the act of completing its eternal way round the earth, were gifted with self-consciousness, it would feel thoroughly convinced that it would travel its way of its own accord on the strength of a resolution taken once for all.

'So would a Being, endowed with higher insight and more perfect intelligence, watching man and his doings, smile about the illusion of his, that he was acting according to his own free will.

'This is my conviction, although I know well that it is not fully demonstrable. If one thinks out to the very last consequence what one exactly knows and understands, there would hardly be any human being who would be impervious to this view, provided his self-love did not ruffle up against it. Man defends himself from being regarded as an impotent object in the course of the Universe. But should the lawfulness of happenings, such as unveils itself more or less clearly in inorganic nature, cease to function in front of the activities in our brain?

'Leaving aside the inconsistency of such a view, the influence of alcohol and other sharply controllable factors on our thoughts, feelings and activities should show very distinctly that determinism does not stop before the majesty of our human will.

'May be, that we and the human society require the illusion of the freedom of human activities!

'The conviction about the law of necessity in human activities introduces into our conception of man and life a mildness, a reverence, and an excellence such as would be unattainable without this conviction.'

Tagore would have wholeheartedly agreed with this thesis. At any rate in his most intuitive and exalted moments he had felt that he was nothing more than a mere note in a cosmic symphony, without beginning and without end. His whole conception of *Jivan-devata* was based on this intuitive experience that a power greater than himself—not a mere blind instinct—was using him as an instrument for a purpose beyond his comprehension. And yet even a mere instrument becomes sacred when it has served a noble purpose. And so Einstein, having stated his faith in the impersonal and the immutable, goes on to address Tagore personally:

'Thou sawest the fierce strife of creatures, a strife that wells forth from need and dark desire. Thou sawest the escape in calm meditation and in creations of beauty. Cherishing these thou hast served mankind all through a long and fruitful life, spreading everywhere a gentle and a free thought in a manner such as the Seers of thy people have proclaimed as the ideal.'

In the meanwhile India was passing through difficult times. Hundreds of brave Bengali youths, the flower of the people, were languishing in concentration camps on the mere suspicion of their sympathies with the revolutionary underground movement for freedom. In one of such camps at Hijli two youths were murdered in cold blood by the guards. When the news of this outrage leaked out, Tagore was greatly perturbed and excited and gave vent to his feelings at a mammoth public meeting held in Calcutta. Earlier he had sent a message of greetings in a poem to the prisoners in another concentration camp at Buxa. To the callousness of the rulers were added the ravages of nature caused by floods in North Bengal. In aid of the flood-stricken victims he staged in Calcutta a dramatized version in Bengali of the long poem *The Child*, which he had written in English the previous year in Germany. Two other productions were staged in Calcutta at the end of the year, *Natir Puja* (Worship of the Dancing-girl), discussed earlier, and a new musical drama, *Shapmochan* (Release from Curse), dealing with a mythological theme, the misadventure of Urvasi, the eternal feminine and celestial dancer at the court of Indra, the Indian Jupiter.

The Rabindra Jayanti or Tagore Festival which had been organized by the citizens of Calcutta at the end of the year was suddenly cut short on 4 January 1932 when the news was received of the arrest of Mahatma Gandhi within a week of his return to India from London where he had been invited to participate in a Round Table Conference.[2] The poet who had still considerable faith left in the British professions of justice and fair play, sent a cable to the British Prime Minister, Mr. Ramsay Macdonald, protesting against 'the policy of indiscriminate repression . . . causing permanent alienation of our people from yours'. On 26 January he issued a statement which the government censorship of press did not allow to be fully published. The poet, hurt and mortified, expressed his feelings in a poem, called 'Prashna' (The Question), in which he asks God:

'You have sent your messengers from time to time who have preached forgiveness and love of all mankind. They were noble souls and worthy of our reverence, and yet today their message seems a mockery and I want to ask you, "Are you yourself, O Lord, able to forgive and to love these creatures of yours who have poisoned your air and darkened your light?"'

The dejected poet sought retreat for a few days in a quiet villa on the Ganges at Khardah where he composed a number of poems directly inspired by paintings, some of his own and some those of other Indian artists. These were later published as *Vichitrita* (Variegated) and dedicated to the famous artist Nandalal Bose. In February an exhibition of his paintings was held at the Government Art School in Calcutta.

Age and the claims of a strenuous life were telling on Tagore's health and his straight back and stately shoulders were getting bent. Just as he had come to the regretful conclusion that he would no longer be able to undertake another foreign tour, there came an invitation from the King of Iran, Reza Shah Pehlavi, to visit his

[2] On the previous day, 3 January, Gandhiji wrote to Tagore from Bombay: 'As I try to steal a wink of sleep I think of you. I want you to give your best to the sacrificial fire that is being lighted.'

country. 'It would hardly do to refuse' an invitation from the august head of a neighbouring and friendly nation, he noted in his diary. And so on 11 April 1932 he left for Persia, accompanied by his daughter-in-law Pratima Devi, who looked after him in old age with the devotion of a loving daughter, and his literary secretary Amiya Chakravarty. To avoid the strain of a long and arduous journey they travelled by the Royal Dutch Airlines. This was his second experience of travel by air, the earlier one having been a short hop from London to Paris.

Air travel was neither common nor very comfortable in those days and the poet who was excited by the adventure of being suspended from the air has recorded his impressions in detail in the diary he kept of the journey.

'Men, beasts and birds were all out of sight. No sound, no movement, no sign of vitality—a world seemingly deserted by Life lay before us, swathed in a patchwork shroud. As we rose higher, even this little remnant of variety was reduced to a pattern of scratchy lines, as though some extinct country, of forgotten name, had recorded its annals on a hard, drab surface in unknown characters that could not be deciphered . . . As the plane rises higher and higher, it reduces the play of our senses to that of one alone—of sight—and even that is not left in fullness. All the signs for which we believe the earth to be obviously and variously real, are gradually wiped out, resolving its three-dimensional picture into lines of one dimension only. Thus deprived of its substantiality, its hold on our mind and heart is loosened. And it is borne in on me how terrible such aloofness can become, once it is found expedient to rain destruction on the vagueness below. Who is the slayer, who the slain? Who is kin, who is stranger? It is a travesty of this teaching of the Gita that the flying machine inculcates.'[3]

He could hardly have anticipated then that within a few years far more deadly machines carrying hydrogen bombs would encircle the earth, round the clock, ready to release the trigger at a wireless command from their governments.

---

[3] English translation by Surendranath Tagore, the *Visva-Bharati Quarterly*, February 1937.

His first halt was in Bushire where he was received with such genuine popular affection, apart from elaborate official honours, that he was deeply touched. 'Who or what am I to these Bushire crowds? Whether in my work, or thought, or everyday life, I am for them far distant, entirely out of their ken. When I had been to Europe, the people there knew something of me as a poet, and so could judge me on materials before them. These people also believe me to be a poet, but solely by force of imagination. To them I am a poet, not of this or that kind, but in the abstract; so that nothing stands in the way of their clothing me with their own idea of what a poet should be.

'In thus feeling me to be their own, they have made no mistake, for I too feel quite close to them—so easy and natural has been our meeting. No reserve have I come up against to make me conscious of belonging to a different nation or different religion.'

From Bushire he travelled by road to Shiraz, the land of Hafiz and Sa'adi, where Tagore was happy to pay his respects at the graves of the two celebrated poets whose names were as much a legend in India as in the country of their birth. After a brief halt at Ispahan, the party reached Teheran on 29 April where the Indian poet was overwhelmed with honour, both official and popular, the newspapers hailing him as 'the greatest star shining in the eastern sky'. His birthday was celebrated, on 6 May while he was still in Teheran, with great éclat and the poet was deeply moved by the affection and honour showered on him with oriental lavishness, both by the Shah and by the people, and expressed his feelings in his farewell speech. On his way back to India Tagore broke his journey at Baghdad where he was received by King Feisal of Iraq. While there he had the opportunity of spending a day in a Bedouin camp —a long-cherished desire since the days of his youth. 'Oh that I were a Bedouin!' he had written in one of his early poems.

Tragic news awaited him on his return from the land of roses and nightingales. His only grandson, Nitindra, a delicate, sensitive youth of much promise, whom he had sent to Germany for training in book-printing, was seriously ill with galloping phthisis. Nitindra died on 7 August. Many of the poems Tagore wrote during this period of anxiety bear evidence of his inner struggle with sorrow.

You seemed from afar
titanic in your mysterious majesty of terror.
With palpitating heart I stood before your presence,
your knitted brows boded ill
and sudden came down the blow
with a growl and a crash.
My bones cracked,
with bowed head I waited
for the final fury to come.
It came.
And I wondered, could this be all of the menace?
With your weapon held high in suspense,
you looked mightily big.
To strike me you came down
to where I crouched low on the ground.
You suddenly became small
And I stood up.
From thence there was only pain for me
but no fear.
Great you are as death itself
but your victim is greater than death.[4]

Tagore was never morbid. He considered morbidity as a disease of the mind worse than any disease of the body. Sorrow and defeat were part of life and must be accepted with manly dignity. The cult of whining like a beaten cur in which some poets have sought their solace was repugnant to his robust nature. Such sentimentalism as he sometimes indulged in was provoked by his pity for others, pity for life, but never by self-pity. His most dominant feeling was his love of life, and the sheer joy of living and of exercising his sensibilities was to him a gift divinely dispensed for which he never ceased to be grateful. Even while he was grappling with his private sorrow he wrote:

Once again I wake up when the night has waned,
when the world opens all its petals once more,
and this is an endless wonder.

[4] The poet's own English rendering, published in *Poems*, Rabindranath Tagore, Visva-Bharati, Calcutta, 1942. Edited by the present writer.

Vast islands have sunk in the abyss unnamed,
stars have been beggared of the last flicker of their light,
countless epochs have lost all their ladings,
world-conquerors have vanished into the shadow of a name
behind dim legends,
great nations raised their towers of triumph
as a mere offering to the unappeasable hunger of the dust.
Among this dissolving crowd of the discarded
my forehead receives the consecration of light,
and this is an endless wonder.[5]

These and many other poems, written on a variety of subjects
and all instinct with mellowed wisdom that comes of conquered
sorrow, were published as *Parisesh* (The End). He thought this was
the end of his creative career, but it was not. In fact, he was seized
with an urge to experiment—to strike music out of prose, to exploit
the rhythmic possibilities of this pedestrian medium. The success of
his English renderings in *Gitanjali* had encouraged this idea which
he had used with consummate skill in the exquisite sketches
published in 1922 as *Lipika*. But these had been printed in the run-on
style of prose and no attempt had been made to break the lines so as
to emphasize the rhythmic pattern. He now did that with the new
poems that he wrote, published as *Punascha* (Postscript), and dedicated to 'Nitu', his grandson whose recent premature death had
moved him deeply.

The poet has recovered his normal spiritual poise and his eyes
watch with gentle sympathy whatever passes before them, coaxing
the commonplace to reveal their modest beauty. One of the longest
and most beautiful of these poems is on the tiny river Kopai that
humbly winds its way, not far from Santiniketan. Once the poet
had lived on the bank of the mighty Padma, majestic in its calm and
destructive when it overflowed—like an arrogant queen. But Kopai
is different, like a simple village maiden. 'Slender is her body that
glides in curves across shadows and lights, clapping hands in a
tripping measure. In the rains her limbs become wild like those of
the village girls drunk with the *mahua* wine, yet she never in her
wantonness breaks or drowns her neighbouring land; only with a

[5] *Ibid.*

jesting whirl of her skirt sweeps the banks while she runs laughing loud.'

The ageing poet is once again keenly observant of his immediate rustic surroundings. No object is too humble or insignificant for his attention. The artist's eye watches the momentary, the passing, as the philosopher's mind broods on the eternal.

> An oldish upcountry man, tall and lean,
> with shaven, shrunken cheeks like wilted fruits,
> jogging along the road to the market town
> in his patched-up pair of countrymade shoes
> and a short tunic made of printed chintz,
> a frayed umbrella tilted over his head,
> a bamboo stick under his armpit.

> I imagine he has his cow in his stall,
> a parrot in the cage,
> his wife with bangles round her arms
> grinding wheat,
> the washerman for his neighbour,
> the grocer's shop across the lane,
> a harassing debt to the man from Peshawar,
> and somewhere my own indistinct self
> only as a passing person.[6]

One of the pieces in this book, *Punascha*, is the author's excellent translation of T. S. Eliot's *The Journey of the Magi*, under the Bengali title *Tirtha Yatri* (The Pilgrim).

On 20 September 1932 the whole nation was stunned by the news of Mahatma Gandhi in jail resorting to a fast 'unto death' as a protest against the British Prime Minister's decision known as the Communal Award, causing a permanent vivisection of the Hindu community by giving to the so-called 'untouchables' an independent status in the Constitution as a separate community with its own electorate. At 3 a.m. of the day on which he was to begin the fast he wrote to Tagore: 'Dear Gurudev, This is early morning 3 o'clock

---

[6] The poet's own rendering published in *Poems*, Rabindranath Tagore, Visva-Bharati, Calcutta, 1942. Edited by the present writer.

of Tuesday. I enter the fiery gate at noon. If you can bless the effort, I want it. You have been to me a true friend because you have been a candid friend often speaking your thoughts aloud. I had looked forward to a firm opinion from you one way or the other. But you have refused to criticize. Though it can now only be during my fast, I will yet prize your criticism, if your heart condemns my action. I am not too proud to make an open confession of my blunder, whatever the cost of the confession, if I find myself in error. If your heart approves of the action I want your blessing. It will sustain me. I hope I have made myself clear.' At 10 a.m. he added a postscript to the above: 'Just as I was handing this to the Superintendent, I got your loving and magnificent wire. It will sustain me in the midst of the storm I am about to enter. I am sending you a wire. Thank you.'

The wire referred to was sent by Tagore the previous day, immediately on receipt of the news of the Mahatma's intention to fast congratulating him on his heroic stand: 'It is well worth sacrificing precious life for the sake of India's unity and her social integrity. Though we cannot anticipate what effect it may have upon our rulers who may not understand its immense importance for our people, we feel certain that the supreme appeal of such self-offering to the conscience of our own countrymen will not callously allow such national tragedy to reach its extreme length. Our sorrowing hearts will follow your sublime penance with reverence and love.'[7] He also appealed to the people to support the Mahatma's challenge by removing from their society all traces of caste prejudice and social discrimination. 'Whoever fails,' he warned, 'would be held responsible for one of the saddest tragedies.'

On 24 September Tagore, unable to keep himself away, left for Poona to visit the Mahatma in Yeravda Jail. The British Government having conceded the main demand and accepted the compromise formula proposed by all the political parties and communities in the country, the Mahatma broke his fast on the 26th, Tagore being

---

[7] The Mahatma wired back: 'Have always experienced God's mercy. Very early this morning I wrote seeking your blessing if you could approve action, and behold I have it in abundance in your message just received. Thank you.'

present by his bedside in jail. 'The fast taken in the name of God,' said the Mahatma in a public statement, 'was broken in His name in the presence of Gurudev . . . The breaking was preceded by the poet singing one of his Bengali hymns.' The hymn sung was the original of the *Gitanjali* poem: 'When the heart is hard and parched up, come upon me with a shower of mercy. When grace is lost from life, come with a burst of song . . .' (How insipid the English version reads when one recalls the haunting melody and the exquisite imagery of the original!)

It so happened that the following day was the sixty-fourth birthday of Gandhi by the Indian calendar. Addressing a public meeting in Poona on that day Tagore said: 'Mahatmaji's birthday appears today before us in an awful majesty of death which has just left him victorious. It is our great good fortune today that such a man has come to us, and what is still rarer, that we have not repudiated him, as we have so often done with the messengers of freedom and truth. His inspiration is actively at work all through India and beyond its boundaries. It has awakened our consciousness to a truth which goes far beyond the limits of our self-interest. His life is a constant call to us to emancipation in service and self-dedication.' Later in the year Tagore published a booklet written during the Mahatma's fast, entitled *Mahatmaji and the Depressed Humanity*, which he dedicated to the eminent scientist Sir P. C. Ray, who was a devoted admirer of Gandhi.

In the meantime Tagore had been persuaded by the University of Calcutta to accept the university chair of Bengali, in which capacity he delivered a series of lectures. He also planned a project, under his direct personal supervision, for compiling a glossary of technical and scientific terms in Bengali, a subject in which he had shown interest more than half a century ago when he was in his youth. In January 1933 the Shah of Persia, in appreciation of the Indian poet's visit to his country, sent the distinguished scholar and savant Professor Poure Davoud as a visiting professor to Visva-Bharati. Welcoming him to Santiniketan, the poet recalled the ancient ties between the two peoples and said, 'The memory of that ancient union still runs in our blood, and in this great age of Asia's awakening we are once more discovering our affinities, we are rescuing from the debris of vanished ages the undying memorials of our co-operation.'

In the same month Bernard Shaw who was on a cruise round the world touched Bombay and in answer to Tagore's telegram of welcome, wrote back:

My dear Rabindranath Tagore,

Unfortunately I am not really visiting India; but the ship in which I am going round the world to get a little rest and do a little work has to put in at Bombay and Colombo to replenish her tanks; and on such occasions I step ashore for a few hours and wander about the streets and such temples as are open to European untouchables.

The organizers of the tour urge me to see India by spending five days and nights in a crowded railway carriage and being let out for a few minutes occasionally to lunch at a hotel and see Taj Mahal; but I am too old a traveller to be taken by such baits, and too old a man ($76\frac{1}{2}$) to endure such hardships without expiring.

My only regret is that I shall be unable to visit you. My consolation is that the present situation in India will not bear being talked about. I understand it only too well.

In the midst of his multifarious public activities which included several important lectures, two of them on Raja Rammohun Roy, the great Indian reformer whom Tagore fervently admired, he wrote two new plays, *Tasher Desh* (The Kingdom of Cards), a delightful satire based on an earlier short story, and *Chandalika* (The Untouchable Girl), a short drama with only two characters on the stage, based on the following Buddhist legend: Ananda, the favourite disciple of the Buddha, was one day returning from a visit when he felt thirsty. Noticing a well on the wayside and a girl lifting water, he asked her to give him some to drink. The girl, who belonged to the lowest caste of untouchables known as chandals, gave him water to drink and seeing his handsome appearance fell in love with him. Unable to forget the handsome monk she made her mother, who knew black magic, work a spell on him. The spell proved stronger than Ananda's will and the spell-bound monk presented himself at their cottage at night, but as he saw the girl spread the couch for him, he was overcome with shame and remorse and prayed to his master to save him. The Buddha heard the prayer and broke the magic spell and Ananda went back, undefiled.

This crude plot of the popular legend, showing how the psychic power of the Buddha saved his devotee from the lust of a chandal girl, has been transformed by Tagore into a psychological drama of intense spiritual conflict. It is no longer the story of a wanton female wanting to seduce a holy man, but of a very sensitive and proud girl, condemned by birth to a despised status, who is suddenly awakened to a consciousness of her rights as a human being. When Ananda asks for water from her hand, she hesitates, knowing that her touch pollutes the high-born. But Ananda assures her that she is as good as any other human being and teaches her to judge herself, not by the arbitrary values that society attaches to the accident of birth, but by her capacity for love and sacrifice. 'If the black clouds of July are dubbed chandals, what of it? It doesn't change their nature or make their gift of water any the less blessed.'

This is a revelation to her which she calls a new birth, for she is washed clean of the degradation with which society had wrapped her from birth, and rises up clean, a woman like any other, with her right to love and to give. To love and to give, Ananda had taught her, were the supreme virtues. But what has she to give better than herself and who is more worthy of her love than the noble monk who has redeemed her, or as she puts it, re-created her? So she yearns to give herself to him. But Ananda, detached from all earthly cares and immersed in himself, knows nothing of all this and does not even recognize her when he accidentally happens to pass by her cottage. Humiliated and wounded in her deepest sensibility, and wild with frustrated desire and pride, she determines to drag the monk down from his pride of renunciation to the abjectness of desire for her. She has lost all religious scruple or social fear, for she owed nothing to religion and society save her humiliation. A religion that degrades is no religion, she says, and forces her mother to exercise her art of magic on Ananda. She refers to it as the primeval spell, the spell of the earth, which is far more potent than the spiritual self-hypnotism of the monks, 'immature, of this day'. (The author has appropriately named her Prakriti which means Nature.)

The 'spell of the earth' proves its strength and soon Ananda is dragged to their door, his face distorted with the agony of desire and shame. Seeing her redeemer, so noble and resplendent before, thus cruelly transformed and degraded, she is horrified at the selfish and destructive nature of her desire. The hero to whom she longed to give herself was not this creature blinded with lust and darkened by desire, but Ananda of the radiant form who had given her the gift of a new birth and had revealed her own true humanity. In remorse she curses herself and falls at his feet, begging forgiveness. The mother, touched by her grief, revokes the spell. The chandalika is thus redeemed for the second time, purged of the pride and egoism that had made her forget that love does not bind but frees.

Chandalika is a tragedy of self-consciousness overreaching itself. Self-consciousness, up to a point, is necessary to self-development, for, without an awareness of one's own worth, one cannot give one's best to the world. Without rights there can be no obligations, and service and virtue when forced become marks of slavery. But self-consciousness, like good wine, intoxicates, and it is not always easy to control the dose and have just enough of it. Vanity and pride get the upper hand and he who clings to his rights very often trespasses on those of others. This is what happened to the heroine. Prakriti, in her eagerness to give, overlooked that Ananda need not take; wanting to surrender she had first to possess. Nor is it surprising that it should be so. A new-born consciousness of strength after ages of suppression is overpowering and one learns restraint and wisdom only with suffering. Hence the tragedy. The good mother, who so unwillingly worked the spell to please her importunate daughter, and who so willingly revoked it to save Ananda, dies in the process. The daughter, though chastened and made wise by suffering, has paid a heavy price, for wisdom is not happiness and renunciation is not fulfilment.

Both these plays, *Tasher Desh* and *Chandalika*, were staged in Calcutta in September.[8] Soon after the performances which were followed by a lecture on *Chhanda* (Prosody) at the Calcutta University Tagore left for Bombay with a party of Santiniketan students and

[8] *Chandalika* was later turned by the author into a ballet for which he composed music. Both the ballets are still very popular and have since been repeatedly staged in many parts of India.

artists to participate in a Tagore Week organized there by his admirers led by the Indian poetess Sarojini Naidu. During the week two of his plays, *Tasher Desh* and *Shapmochan*, were staged by the students of Santiniketan, an exhibition of paintings, both his and of Santiniketan artists, was held and two public lectures (in English) were delivered by the poet, 'The Challenge of Judgement' and 'The Price of Freedom'. From Bombay he went to the pleasant university town by the sea, Waltair, where he gave a series of lectures at the Andhra University, later published as *Man*. After a visit to Hyderabad where he was warmly received by the Nizam who had earlier given a handsome donation to Visva-Bharati for a Chair of Islamic Studies, Tagore returned to Calcutta at the end of December to deliver his famous address at the Senate Hall on *Bharat-Pathik Rammohun* (Rammohun the Indian Pilgrim). Before the year was over two new novels and a drama in prose were published, *Dui Bon* (Two Sisters), *Malancha* (The Garden) and *Bansari* (after the name of the main heroine in the play). It was indeed a fruitful year in literary activity, despite the many distractions of public engagements and political happenings.

Dui Bon[9] is a short novel, mainly psychological in interest, dealing with the usual triangle, in this case two sisters in love with the same man. It is as if the author is trying to show that a man seeks in woman both mother and sweetheart. Lucky the man who can find both in one. 'Women are of two kinds,' thus begins the novel, 'mother-kind and the beloved-kind—so I have heard some learned men say. If a comparison may be drawn with the seasons, the mother is the rainy season. She brings the gift of water and fruit, tempers the heat and dissolving from the heights drives away the drought. She fills with plenty. The beloved, on the other hand, is the spring. Deep its mystery, sweet its enchantment.' In other words, the one sustains, the other inspires. Human nature and society being what they are, a man cannot always have both and love is at best only a partial fulfilment. A heart that is alive cannot escape frustration. The situation in this novel is further complicated by the two rivals being sisters, each of them equally admirable, in her fashion. The author

[9] English translation by the present writer, *Two Sisters*, published by Visva-Bharati, Calcutta, 1945.

has tried to face boldly the psychological tangle caused by a conflict of loyalties, loyalty to married love and loyalty to love, free and unfettered—without sentimentalizing and without moralizing. In fact, the only unpleasant character in the novel is a moral prig.

Malancha is shorter in length but more dramatic in situation. It is mostly in dialogue and one wonders why the author did not write it as a play. The theme is similar to that of *Dui Bon*, two women and a man, though the rival in this case is not the wife's sister, but the husband's cousin. The psychological interest of this novel is, however, of a different nature. Niraja was happily married to a florist who was passionately devoted to his nursery garden. She grew to share this devotion—in the usual feminine way, for only by sharing his interests could she possess her husband fully. The husband doted on her and their happiness was the envy of friends. Because she was happy she was generous. But the fates were jealous and after ten years of unblemished happiness, she suddenly became a bed-ridden invalid with no hope of sharing her husband's work in the garden. She could only watch from a window by her bed the scene of her past happiness. Even this consolation turned into a source of bitterness when her husband sent for his young cousin Sarala to help in the garden. Seeing another woman, younger and healthy, take her place by her husband's side in the garden, Niraja assumed the worst and was wild with jealousy. Her very suspicions, which she took no care to hide, provoked fate and brought about what she most feared.

More tragic than her physical misfortune was its effect in warping her mind. She who was generous when happy became unjust and vindictive. Aware of this self-degradation she tried to fight it but was helpless. No tragedy is greater than the poverty of spirit which paralyses our capacity to love and to forgive.

Bansari is a witty play, sparkling with brilliant dialogue, depicting the sophistications of high society in Calcutta with their high-brow pretensions and snobberies. The capacity for love is dissipated in intellectual flirtations resulting in a tragedy presented as a comedy. The play was never staged by the author, though he once planned its production—probably because the play lacks in real dramatic

interest. The author's acquaintance with the life and type of characters he was depicting was remote, largely derived from hearsay
and gossip. Tagore was too old and famous to mix freely with the
new social types that were emerging and had no opportunities of
observing them, himself unobserved. His treatment of love was
becoming more and more intellectualized, bolder in thought but
less effective in conveying its feeling. Not only the flesh and blood
but even the heart was getting cold, only the mind was active and
in full armour.

Returning to Santiniketan at the beginning of January 1934,
Tagore received, a fortnight later, Jawaharlal Nehru and his wife,
Kamala.[10] The poet who admired Jawaharlal Nehru for his passionate sincerity and intellectual integrity, his rational outlook and
international sympathies, held a public reception to welcome him
and his wife.[11] In the meantime, on 15 January, north India was
rocked by an earthquake of great severity, causing untold damage
to life and property in several towns of Bihar. Gandhi, who was
at that time touring south India in a campaign against untouchability,
said in a public statement that this calamity was a divine chastisement for the sin of untouchability. 'A man like me cannot but
believe that this earthquake is a divine chastisement sent by God for
our sins . . . For me there is a vital connexion between the Bihar
calamity and the untouchability campaign.'[12]

Tagore was shocked to see the Mahatma resort to such characteristically priestly tactics of exploiting the conception of sin to din
fear in the minds of the people and said in a public statement: 'It
has caused me a painful surprise to find Mahatma Gandhi accusing
those who blindly follow their own social custom of untouchability
of having brought down God's vengeance upon certain parts of
Bihar, evidently specially selected for His desolating displeasure. It

[10] 'From Calcutta,' writes Jawaharlal Nehru in his *Autobiography*, 'we went to
Santiniketan to pay a visit to the poet Rabindra Nath Tagore. It was always a joy
to meet him and, having come so near, we did not wish to miss him. I had been to
Santiniketan twice before. It was Kamala's first visit, and she had come especially to
see the place as we were thinking of sending our daughter there.'

[11] Two years later, during a commemoration service held to mourn the death of
Kamala Nehru, Tagore referred to Jawaharlal Nehru as 'the leader of a new era'.

[12] *Mahatma*, Vol. 3, D. G. Tendulkar.

is all the more unfortunate because this kind of unscientific view of phenomenon is too readily accepted by a large section of our countrymen . . . If we associate ethical principles with the cosmic phenomena, we shall have to admit that human nature is morally much superior to Providence that preaches its lessons in good behaviour in orgies of the worst behaviour possible. For we can never imagine any civilized ruler of men making indiscriminate examples of casual victims, including children and the members of the untouchable community, in order to impress others dwelling at a safe distance, who possibly deserve more severe condemnation . . . What is truly tragic about it is the fact that the kind of argument that Mahatmaji used by exploiting an event of cosmic disturbance far better suits the psychology of his opponents than his own, and it would not have surprised me if they had taken this opportunity of holding him and his followers responsible for the visitation of divine anger . . . '

Gandhi, however, reiterated his faith in an article in his English weekly, *Harijan*, under the caption 'Bihar and Untouchability'. (He could be very obstinate at times and was capable of indulging in casuistries that take one's breath away.) 'To me the earthquake was no caprice of God, nor a result of a meeting of blind forces,' he wrote. 'We do not know the laws of God nor their working. Knowledge of the tallest scientist or the spiritualist is like a particle of dust . . . With me the connexion between cosmic phenomena and human behaviour is a living faith that draws me nearer to God, humbles me and makes me readier for facing Him.'

Jawaharlal Nehru's comment on this controversy is worth recalling: 'During my tour in the earthquake areas, or just before going there, I read with a great shock Gandhiji's statement to the effect that the earthquake had been a punishment for the sin of untouchability. This was a staggering remark and I welcomed and wholly agreed with Rabindra Nath Tagore's answer to it. Anything more opposed to the scientific outlook it would be difficult to imagine . . . The idea of sin and divine wrath and man's relative importance in the affairs of the universe—they take us back a few hundred years when the Inquisition flourished in Europe and burned Giordano Bruno for his scientific heresy and sent many a witch to the stake! Even in the eighteenth century in America leading Boston divines attributed earthquakes in Massachusetts to the impiety of lightning rods.'[13]

The poet was restless—athirst, as ever, for the far-away. That he still hoped to go once more to the West is obvious from the following letter written on 8 April 1934 to a Czech writer, Arnost Czech-Czecherherz, thanking him for a book: 'Your book through its unknown language speaks to me of those days which I spent in your land when hospitality was lavished upon me which made me feel that you had accepted me as your own. To feel that you have discovered in me a spirit that is not alien to you is a rare good fortune for a poet who has been allowed to transcend his geographical limits and send his voice to the heart of a distant land. I still hope, though I have grown old, to visit once again your country and meet you in your own home.'

More serious than the problem of age was that of money. Though coming from a family that was once very wealthy, Tagore himself had been brought up in comparative austerity and when he grew up his own share in what had remained of the family estates was by no means large. While it might have been adequate for his personal and family needs—since he lived simply and despised ostentation or luxury—it could hardly suffice to meet the expenses of his school as well. The royalties from his Bengali publications were meagre—poetry is rarely a profitable vocation and the buying capacity of the very limited reading public of his country was pitiful. In any case a major portion of these royalties had already been given by him to his university, Visva-Bharati. For a few years after the Nobel Prize the income from his English and other foreign-language publications was a very welcome windfall, but much of it was spent on his many foreign tours and in Germany, where his books had sold most, the phenomenal inflation reduced the value of his royalties to almost nothing. By 1934 Tagore had become more a memory in the West than a living voice and his royalties had considerably dwindled.

[13] Jawaharlal Nehru: *An Autobiography.* John Lane, The Bodley Head, London, 1936.

In the meantime his university at Santiniketan had grown so indiscriminately that it threatened to become a white elephant which everyone was willing to admire but no one ready to pay for. The poet who had given to his people greater and more lasting riches than any other man was reduced to the pitiful position of begging for doles to keep his university from starving. His pet child had become a prodigal, a source of constant headache and humiliation in the last years of a life otherwise free and glorious. Begging was a humiliation to this aristocratic mind; nor was it of much avail. In India the moneyed classes pour offerings either in the lap of priests or in the pockets of politicians. Tagore was neither and he often said with a rueful smile, 'If only I could put on an ochre wrap or a loin-cloth and hold a rosary in hand, money would pour in!' Had he offered to build a temple or even a sectarian institution instead of a house of knowledge open to all, he would have been in no want of funds. Indeed, on one occasion a Hindu millionaire offered a lavish amount for a girls' hostel in Santiniketan, provided it would be reserved for Hindu girls only. The poet declined the offer.

The only way left to the ageing poet was to earn money by making the school itself productive. This he could do by training troupes of actors and dancers who would stage his plays and ballets in different towns and help to raise money. This was not, of course, the only reason, perhaps not even the main reason. The artist in him itched to see his own creations on the stage. Unlike his other written works, the songs had to be sung to be enjoyed, the ballets staged to be appreciated. Moreover, these two aspects of his creative activity, along with his paintings, were the only ones which all his countrymen, even those who did not know Bengali—and they were the vast majority—could appreciate and enjoy. And so the country was regaled with the unusual spectacle of the venerable poet and seer escorting a band of performing artists, singers and dancers all over the country. Whatever this man did became somehow creative and educative, and these tours, apart from their other aspects, became a mission of considerable educative importance, creating a taste in the public for aspects of Indian culture hitherto ignored or despised, and freeing their minds from prejudices that looked askance at the professional stage and, in particular, dancing as vocations of disrepute.

The first of these cultural tours, apart from the earlier one to Bombay, was in Ceylon, for which charming island Tagore had always had a warm corner in his heart. The visit which took place in May–June 1934 left a deep impress on the minds of those who watched the performance of the dance-drama, *Shapmochan*, or saw the exhibition of paintings or listened to the poet's speeches.

It was during his stay in Ceylon that Tagore completed what was to be his last novel, *Char Adhyay* (Four Chapters).[14] In this short but powerful novel he returns to the theme he had discussed earlier, in a different setting, in his novel *The Home and the World*—human values and political ideals. The setting is the underground revolutionary movement in Bengal; against its heroism and its terrorism is depicted the frustration of love and the gradual debasement of human values. The author's analysis of the motives that inspire and condition political heroism is marked by deep insight in the psychology of the characters in this tragic drama of frustrated idealism and is expressed in language of great vigour and beauty. It is a novel that Turgenev might have written. The novel aroused a storm of controversy in Bengal and the author was mercilessly reviled. He had uttered too many home truths.

In August of the same year the British savant and humanist Gilbert Murray addressed an open letter to Tagore inviting his co-operation in promoting a better understanding between the intelligentsia of the East and the West. No subject was nearer the poet's heart. In his reply he assessed the values of civilizations in the two hemispheres and while he expressed his admiration for the West's contribution in the field of scientific thinking, he gave vent to his misgivings about the West's misuse of the machine. He, however, felt assured that 'the brighter spirits of young Europe are now alive to the challenge of the times'. Tagore was an incorrigible optimist and he added, 'I feel proud that I have been born in this great age.' These open letters exchanged between two leading humanists were published in 1935 under the auspices of the International Institute of Intellectual Co-operation, Paris.

[14] English translation by Surendranath Tagore, published by Visva-Bharati, Calcutta.

Two new books of poems, *Sesh Saptak* (Last Octave) and *Bithika* (Avenue), both remarkable for their experiments in free rhythm and diction, mark his main poetic achievement in 1935. The memory of an old love, once taken for granted, haunts the ageing poet, but passion has lost its edge and remorse is tempered with gratitude, for sorrow has transmuted all losses into gain.

Unable to travel about freely, the poet took to changing his dwelling place, from house to house. He now took it into his head that he must live in a mud cottage. So a mud hut had to be built, next to the house he was then occupying. Day after day he watched the walls of the new hut being raised by the nimble hands of Santal women.[16]

I sit on my terrace watching the young woman toiling at her task hour after hour. My heart is touched with shame when I feel that the woman's service sacredly ordained for her loved ones, should have been robbed by me with the help of a few pieces of copper, its dignity soiled by the market price.[16]

The mud cottage was soon ready to receive him and he moved into it on his birthday, 7 May, naming the cottage Syamali, meaning 'the dark one'. Later he gave this name to a book of poems written during his stay there. Before the year was over two of his plays were staged, *Saradotsav* (Autumn Festival) in Santiniketan, and *Arupratan* (Invisible Jewel), a modified version of *The King of the Dark Chamber*, in Calcutta, the poet appearing in both of them. It was not only that the public clamoured for his appearance on the stage; he also loved to act.

Two interesting visitors who came to see him about this time were Margaret Sanger, the American specialist on Birth Control, and Yeats-Brown, the noted author of *Bengal Lancer*. Having failed to persuade Mahatma Gandhi that birth control was not a sin, Margaret Sanger appealed to Tagore for support. Tagore needed

[15] Santals are an aboriginal tribe some of whom are settled in the vicinity of Santiniketan and provide better and cheaper labour than the Bengali villagers. Their women are healthy and attractive.

[16] *Bithika*. For the full text of the author's English rendering, see *Poems*, Visva-Bharati, Calcutta.

no persuasion. 'In a hunger-stricken country like India,' he wrote, 'it is a cruel crime thoughtlessly to bring more children into existence than could properly be taken care of, causing endless suffering to them and imposing a degrading condition upon the whole family.' The Mahatma too would have echoed the same sentiment but the solution, according to him, lay in moral control or self-control, and not in birth control, which was sin. And so Tagore went on to add that '. . . to wait till the moral sense of man becomes a great deal more powerful than it is now and till then to allow countless generations of children to suffer privations and untimely death for no fault of their own, is a great social injustice which should not be tolerated'.

Yeats-Brown, who visited Santiniketan in January 1936, described it as 'one of the most spiritually stimulating places in the world', adding shrewdly, 'Tagore remains in my mind as a beautiful but somewhat tragic figure . . . behind Santiniketan there is not yet the driving force of a great popular movement, but only a great man: a man who makes the arc of the sky seem bigger after one has met him.'[17]

After delivering three lectures in Calcutta in February 1936 (*Ideals of Education*, *Place of Music in Education* and *Education Naturalized*), the poet was absorbed in preparing a musical version of his early drama *Chitrangada* (Eng. *Chitra*), himself conducting rehearsals of the ballet. His talented daughter-in-law, Pratima Devi, a sweet and gracious lady, was his chief collaborator in the preparation of his ballets. This is perhaps the most popular of all his ballets or dance-dramas (*Nritya-natya*), as the author described them. It was success-fully staged in Calcutta, winning high praise, and was then taken by the poet on a tour of north India. After earning more applause than money in several big towns, including Lahore (which is now in Pakistan), the ballet was staged in Delhi in the last week of March. Gandhiji, who happened to be in Delhi, was much perturbed that the aged poet in failing health should be obliged, for want of funds for his university, to undertake such arduous tours; and immediately sent him a letter enclosing a bank draft for Rs.60,000 (about 12,000

---

[17] Quoted in *Rabindra-Jivani*, Vol. IV, by Prabhat Mukherjee, Visva-Bharati, Calcutta.

dollars) as an offering from 'your humble countrymen'. 'Now,' wrote the Mahatma, 'you will relieve the public mind by announcing cancellation of the rest of the programme.' Tagore was deeply touched and grateful, though at the back of his mind was a passing regret that he would miss the excitement of taking his troupe around, for there is no doubt that he thoroughly enjoyed putting his creations on the stage, himself seated in a corner, like a silent and motionless conductor, or, as a critic once put it, like an authentic signature to his own work.

Nor, indeed, did he sit back and relax, as Gandhiji would have wished him to do. He continued to preside over public meetings in Calcutta—a much greater strain than watching his own dramas. After paying a fervent tribute to the Mahatma at a special service held in the Santiniketan Mandir (temple) on the occasion of the Mahatma's birthday on 2 October, he set to work on a new dance-drama based on an earlier poem, *Parishodh* (Retribution), which he renamed *Syama* (after the name of the heroine). This was staged in Calcutta later in the month, the author as usual present on the stage.

The theme is the tragedy of love's blind egoism which does not scruple to sacrifice every other happiness to its own, only to find that it has thereby lost its right to happiness. Syama, the beautiful courtesan, is in love with Vajrasen, a handsome foreigner, who is falsely arrested for a crime he did not commit and is sentenced to death. Syama saves his life by persuading one of her many admirers to sacrifice himself in Vajrasen's place. The grateful foreigner easily turns Syama's lover, but when he comes to know of her inhuman conduct by which she procured his freedom, he is filled with disgust and shame and leaves her. The moral law working through him brings Nemesis, the inevitable retribution, to the unfortunate Syama, so devoted to her lover, so guilty to humanity. The theme is taken from an old Buddhist legend of Nepal, where it is given as 'the reason why Buddha abandoned his faithful wife Yasodhara . . . Buddha was that Vajrasena, and Syama Yashodhara'.[18]

In February 1937, Tagore delivered the Convocation address of the Calcutta University, a landmark in the history of that university, for it was the first occasion in the eighty years of its history when a

[18] *Sanskrit Buddhist Literature of Nepal*, Rajendralal Mitra.

private citizen was offered this privilege hitherto reserved for the British Viceroy or the Governor. It was also the first occasion when the address was delivered in Bengali, and not in English. Tagore used the occasion for a magnificent plea for the use of the mother-tongue as the medium of education.

After two more public addresses of importance, one to the Bengali Literary Conference in the French settlement of Chandernagore, the other to the Parliament of Religions held in Calcutta to mark the centenary of the birth of the great Indian saint Ramakrishna Paramahamsa, Tagore inaugurated at Santiniketan the Cheena-Bhavana (Department of Sino-Indian Studies), the first of its kind in India and still a leading centre of Chinese studies in the country. The summer was spent in the pleasant Himalayan resort Almora, where he wrote *Visva-parichaya*, an introduction to modern science for Bengali readers. He spent his birthday in comparative quiet, gazing at the distant snow peaks of the Himalayas.

He must have been reminded of his early boyhood when he had accompanied his father to the Himalayas and had freely roamed in the shadows of the deodars, for the poem he wrote on the occasion is wistful with longing for that period which he calls 'that holiday' of his life, when his name, then unknown, 'received its infinite worth from a sweet voice'—he never forgot his sister-in-law, his first love and guardian angel. Later, when he lived on the banks of the Padma he watched 'the morning star through the intervals of bamboo leaves on her bank', and his eyes 'followed the track of noisy girls to the river along the shady village lane'. He had looked at it all and said, 'I love it.' But now, alas, the man of fame is 'entangled in the meshes woven by countless gazing eyes . . . and lives in a solitary cell among the crowd, with a chain of honour ever jangling round his limbs'.[19]

In the meantime Mussolini's unwarranted attack on Ethiopia had considerably upset the poet whose sympathies were always with the underdog. The 'dark continent' had stirred his imagination and in February of the year he wrote a beautiful poem[20] addressed to

[19] Included in the book of poems *Senjuti* (Evening Light), published in 1938. For the full text of the English rendering (author's own), see *Poems*, Visva-Bharati, Calcutta.

[20] Included in the second edition of his book of poems *Patraput* (A Cup of Leaves),

Africa which he translated into English at the suggestion of Amiya
Chakravarty.

> You donned the disguise of deformity
> > to mock the terrible,
> and in a mimicry of a sublime ferocity
> made yourself fearful to conquer fear.
> You are hidden, alas, under a black veil,
> which obscures your human dignity
> to the darkened vision of contempt.
> With man traps stole upon you those hunters
> whose fierceness was keener than the fangs of your wolves,
> whose pride was blinder than your blighted forests.
> The savage greed of the civilized stripped naked
> > its unashamed inhumanity.
> You wept and your cry was smothered,
> your forest trails became muddy with tears and blood,
> while the nailed boots of the robbers
> left their indelible prints
> along the history of your indignity.
> And all the time across the sea,
> church bells were ringing in their towns and villages,
> the children were lulled in their mothers' arms,
> and poets sang to Beauty.

In August the poet addressed a public meeting in Calcutta to
voice the nation's protest against circumstances leading to the
hunger-strike of political prisoners in the Andamans, the islands in
the Bay of Bengal used by the British as a vast concentration camp.
In September the song-dance sequence known as *Varsha-Mangal*
(Festival of the Rains) was staged in Calcutta, with him on the stage.
Returning to Santiniketan the poet suddenly fell ill on 10 September,
with total loss of consciousness, the comatose state lasting for nearly
forty-eight hours. The cause of illness was later diagnosed as
erysipelas, a virulent infection located behind one of the ears.[21] His

---

originally published a year earlier. The English translation is included in *Poems*,
Visva-Bharati.

[21] This is now an easily controlled infection, thanks to the discovery of anti-
biotics during the war.

friend, the eminent physician Sir Nilratan Sircar, assisted by a team of specialists from Calcutta, was by his bedside for several days until his recovery. On the morning of the fifth day when he had recovered his consciousness and was propped up on pillows in his bed, almost the first thing he did was to ask for colours and brush and, noticing a rectangular piece of plywood in the room, painted on it a landscape of a dark forest with streaks of faint yellow light struggling to find their way through its thickness, a beautiful painting and obviously symbolic.[22] He also described the experience of suspended consciousness and its recovery in a poem written almost immediately after the recovery which, along with other poems written during the period, was published in a book entitled *Prantik* (The Borderland), 1938.

> This body of mine—
> the carrier of the burden of a past—
> seemed to me like an exhausted cloud
> slipping off from the listless arm
> of the morning.
> I felt freed from its clasp
> in the heart of an incorporeal light
> at the farthest shore
> of evanescent things.[23]

To the Mahatma who had made anxious inquiries during the critical stage of the illness, he wrote: 'The first thing which welcomed me into the world of life after the period of stupor I passed through was your affectionate anxiety and it was fully worth the cost of sufferings which were unremitting in their long persistence.'

All through the period of convalescence and after, the poet was greatly perturbed at Japan's ruthless aggression in China. He had

[22] The original, which is in the Tagore Museum, Santiniketan, is almost totally faded and destroyed—plywood is hardly a medium for painting, especially in the Indian climate where it makes excellent food for white ants. Fortunately, the painting was reproduced in an issue of the *Visva-Bharati Quarterly* (Nov. 1937, frontispiece) where it can still be seen. Had not the poet himself written: 'The worm finds it foolish that man does not eat his books!'

[23] For the full text of the author's English rendering see *Poems*, Visva-Bharati.

loved Japan very much and it was for him a source of deep anguish and humiliation that a nation which he had hailed as the new sunrise in Asia should prove itself a scourge of the East. When the Japanese poet Yone Noguchi, who had earlier visited Santiniketan and had been warmly welcomed by Tagore, wrote to him a long letter trying to justify Japan's 'mission' in China, the poet could contain himself no longer and spoke out his thoughts loudly.

'You are building your conception of an Asia,' he wrote in reply to Noguchi, 'which would be raised on a tower of skulls. I have, as you rightly point out, believed in the message of Asia, but I never dreamt that this message could be identified with deeds which brought exaltation to the heart of Tamerlane at his terrible efficiency in manslaughter. When I protested against "Westernization" in my lectures in Japan, I contrasted the rapacious Imperialism which some of the nations of Europe were cultivating with the ideal of perfection preached by Buddha and Christ, with the great heritages of culture and good neighbourliness that went to the making of Asiatic and other civilizations. I felt it my duty to warn the land of Bushido, of great art and traditions of noble heroism, that this phase of scientific savagery which victimized Western humanity and had led their helpless masses to a moral cannibalism was never to be imitated by a virile people who had entered upon a glorious renascence and had every promise of a creative future before them.

'The doctrine of "Asia for Asia" which you enunciate in your letter, as an instrument of political blackmail, has all the virtues of the lesser Europe which I repudiate and nothing of the larger humanity that makes us one across the barriers of political labels and divisions. I was amused to read the recent statement of a Tokyo politician that the military alliance of Japan with Italy and Germany was made for "highly spiritual and moral reasons" and "had no materialistic considerations behind them". Quite so. What is not amusing is that artists and thinkers should echo such remarkable sentiments that translate military swagger into spiritual bravado. In the West, even in the critical days of war-madness, there is never any dearth of great spirits who can raise their voice above the din of battle, and defy their own war-mongers in the name of humanity. Such men have suffered, but never betrayed the conscience of their

people which they represented. Asia will not be westernized if she
can learn from such men . . .

'You must forgive me if my words sound bitter. Believe me, it is
sorrow and shame, not anger, that prompt me to write to you. I
suffer intensely not only because the reports of Chinese suffering
batter against my heart, but because I can no longer point out with
pride the example of a great Japan. It is true that there are no better
standards prevalent anywhere else and that the so-called civilized
peoples of the West are proving equally barbarous and even less
"worthy of trust". If you refer me to them, I have nothing to say.
What I would have liked is to be able to refer them to you. I shall
say nothing of my own people, for it is vain to boast until one has
succeeded in sustaining one's principles to the end . . . Wishing your
people whom I love, not success, but remorse, Yours sincerely,
Rabindranath Tagore.'

Earlier he had written a poem in which his anguish found vent in
bitter words:

> The war drums are sounded.
> Men force their features into frightfulness
>   and gnash their teeth;
> and before they rush out to gather
> raw human flesh for death's larder,
> they march to the temple of Buddha,
>   the Compassionate,
> to claim his blessings,
> while loud beats the drum rat-a-tat
> and earth trembles.[24]

If Japan's bravado was a mockery of the Buddha, no less were
Hitler's maniac ambition and Chamberlain's pusillanimous con-
doning of it a mockery of Christ. When Hitler's hordes overran
Czechoslovakia, Tagore wrote to Professor Lesny, 'My words have
no power to stay the onslaught of the maniacs, nor the power to
arrest the desertion of those who erstwhile pretended to be saviours
of humanity . . . I feel so humiliated . . . so helpless.' He also wrote a
long poem which he sent to Lesny in Prague and which was later

[24] The poet's own rendering. For full text see *Poems*, Visva-Bharati, Calcutta.

included in his book of poems *Navajatak* (The New-born), published in 1940. On the Christmas day of 1939 he expressed his agony
in a poem:

> Those who struck Him once
> in the name of their rulers
> are born again in the present age.
> They gather in their prayer-halls
> in a pious garb,
> they call their soldiers,
> 'Kill, Kill,' they shout;
> in their roaring mingles
> the music of their hymns,
> while the Son of Man
> in His agony prays,
> 'O God, fling, fling far away
> this cup filled with the bitterest of poisons.'

Apart from the volumes of verses referred to in the above para-
graphs, Tagore's other major literary publications during the years
1937-39 were *Khapchhada* (The Odd), humorous poems in the
nursery rhyme manner illustrated by his own drawings, *Shey* (That
One), fantasies in prose, also illustrated by his drawings, *Visva-
Parichaya* (Introducing the Universe), a primer on modern science,
Bangla Bhasha Parichay, a treatise on Bengali language, *Kalantar*
(Changing Age), socio-political essays, *Chhadar Chhabi* (Rhymes and
Pictures), *Prahasini* (The Farcical), books of light, humorous poems,
and *Akash-pradip* (Sky-lamp), also a volume of poems.

In February 1940 Mahatma Gandhi and his wife Kasturba visited
the poet at Santiniketan—the last meeting of the saint and the poet.
Tagore held a public reception in their honour in the picturesque
mango-grove of Santiniketan and paid, in an address, his homage to
one whom he had earlier described as 'this great soul in a beggar's
garb', assuring him, 'We accept you as our own, as one belonging
to all humanity.' 'Even though,' replied the Mahatma, 'I call this
visit a pilgrimage . . . I am no stranger here. I feel as if I have come
to my home . . . I have received Gurudev's blessings and my heart
is full to the brim with joy.' Before Gandhi left, Tagore put a letter

in his hands in which he requested him, 'Accept this institution under your protection, giving it an assurance of permanence if you consider it to be a national asset. Visva-Bharati is like a vessel which is carrying the cargo of my life's best treasure, and I hope it may claim special care from my countrymen for its preservation.'

The Mahatma's reply was characteristic—modest and noble. 'Who am I to take this institution under my protection?' he wrote. 'It carries God's protection, because it is the creation of an earnest soul. It is not a show-thing. Gurudev himself is international because he is truly national. Therefore, all his creation is international, and Visva-Bharati is the best of all. I have no doubt whatsoever that Gurudev deserves to be relieved of all anxiety about its future so far as the financial part is concerned. In my reply to his touching appeal I have promised all the assistance I am capable of rendering. This note is the beginning of the effort.' Needless to say, the Mahatma kept his word. After his death the National Government of free India assumed full financial responsibility for the continuance of Visva-Bharati as a nationally recognized university. Very fittingly its present Chancellor is Jawaharlal Nehru who in a way represents in his personality some qualities of both these great men.

On 5 April the poet suffered the last great bereavement of his life in the death of his devoted friend C. F. Andrews. At a special memorial service in the Santiniketan Mandir Tagore said, 'In no man have I seen such a triumph of Christianity.' Earlier he had said that he could not harbour an ill-feeling against the British people, if for no other reason than that Andrews was one of them. 'Charlie Andrews,' wrote Gandhiji, 'was one of the greatest and best Englishmen. And because he was a good son of England, he became also a son of India.' Andrews himself, in a letter to Tagore dated as early as 5 October 1913, had written: 'I am, and shall always be, an Englishman, through and through; but I am sure we must pass these boundary lines of nationality where truth stares us in the face, which is universal and greater even than country.'

This genial and kindly spirit had an abundant sense of humour— a true English trait, as may be seen from this excerpt from a letter written by him to Tagore during one of his sea voyages when he had many Australian co-passengers on board: 'The passengers are all thoroughgoing Australians with a strong cockney accent and White Australia in their brain. One poor lady next to me at table looked so shocked when I told her we lived with Indians. We were evidently queer, uncanny creatures—neither fish, flesh, fowl, nor good red herring. Indeed we are not quite safe and scarcely respectable ... Our Bengali slippers are looked upon with grave suspicion as showing our un-English tendencies. In one of our joint efforts to be conversational we were explaining that India differed from Central Africa, and announced that you had won the Nobel Prize, stating its terms in cash. One of them said, "My! think of that!" Another said, "Did he go on the bust?" And a third said, "You don't mean to tell me that he's a full-blooded native?" We assured him gravely that you were and he answered, "My! you don't say so. Think of that now!" ...'

On 7 August 1940 the University of Oxford held a special Convocation at Santiniketan for the purpose of conferring on Tagore its Doctorate (*honoris causa*). The citation referred to Tagore as 'Most dear to all the Muses'. Sir Maurice Gwyer, then Chief Justice of India, Dr. Sarvepalli Radhakrishnan and Mr. Justice Hendersen of the Calcutta High Court represented Oxford University. 'The university whose representative I am,' said Sir Maurice Gwyer, 'has, in honouring you, done honour to itself.'

Before the year ended three short stories—his last contribution to this form—were published in a volume entitled *Teen Sangi* (The Trio). These stories, *Ravivar* (On a Sunday), *Sesh Katha* (Last Word) and *Laboretori* (The Laboratory), are as different from his earlier ones as Aldous Huxley is from Chekhov. The poet has hardened into an intellectual, the superb story-teller has turned into a commentator, the Himalayas have shrunk into a table-land of skyscrapers. Tagore the perfectionist was never content with perfection if it became static, for then, according to him, it ceased to be perfection. Having scaled the highest peak he left it behind for other heights which though lesser had the merit of being fresher.

15

LAST JOURNEY

In September while Tagore was in Kalimpong in the eastern
Himalayas he was again suddenly taken ill, this time with
enlarged prostate.[1] He was brought down to Calcutta and,
after about two months of medical attention when the ailment had
been seemingly brought under control, he was allowed to return to
Santiniketan. From now on he was no longer able to move about
freely and was more or less confined to his room. But his pen was
as active as ever and, before the year was over, four new volumes
were published, three of poems, *Navajatak*, referred to earlier,
Sanai (The Flute), *Rogasajyay* (From Sick-bed) and one of prose,
Chhele-bela (Boyhood Days), reminiscences of early years written
in a delightful, racy style.

Lying in his sick-bed and watching, like his beloved Amal in
The Post Office, the humdrum, placid life of Santiniketan, the poet
brooded on the past and wondered whether he had been able to
repay the world for the great gift of life. He had done his best to
understand and interpret what he had seen and experienced of this
world—but how little, it seemed to him, he had seen and understood! He expressed this mood in a poem which he wrote in
January 1941.[2]

> How little I know of this mighty world!
> Myriad deeds of men, cities, countries . . .
> have remained beyond my awareness.
> Great is life in this wide Earth
> and small the corner where my mind dwells.

[1] An affliction not uncommon in advanced age. His friend Andrews had died of
the same. Pending the arrival of doctors from Calcutta, the British Civil Surgeon
was called from Darjeeling. Failing to elicit a response from the patient who was
unconscious, he asked gruffly, 'Does he understand English?'

[2] Published in *Janmadine* (On the Birthday), 1941. The English rendering by
Amiya Chakravarty and Kshitis Roy was first published in the *Visva-Bharati Quarterly*,
February 1942.

What he could not see or know for himself, he tried to read about and fill the void.

> As I have listened to the one vast song of Nature
> with which poets of all ages and lands
> have mingled their rhymes,
> I have become one with the great symphony
> sharing the eternal joy of being
> and the meed of universal kinship.

But though he could share and lose himself in all the varied moods and aspects of Nature, he could not say the same of Man. His contacts with and understanding of his fellow men was limited and conditioned by his birth, his upbringing and circumstances which he could not always control.

> Not everywhere have I won access,
> my ways of life have intervened
> and kept me outside.
> The tiller at the plough
> the weaver at the loom
> the fisherman plying his net,
> these and the rest toil and sustain the world
> with their world-wide varied labour.
> I have known them from a corner
> banished to a high pedestal of society
> reared by renown.
> Only the outer fringe have I approached
> not being able to enter
> the intimate precincts.

In a mood chastened by humility such as only the truly great have felt, he hails the poet of the new age who will achieve what he failed to achieve and extend the limits of human sympathy and understanding to their farthest ends, and 'restore life and joy and song to this dry and desolate land bereft of music'. He will wait for the message of that poet 'whose words and deeds have achieved true concurrence'.

May his words reveal kinship,
may he conceal not, nor hoodwink,
nor his verse tempt the eye alone.
May he give what I lack.
May he save himself from luxury
of mimic sympathy for the labouring people,
which professes what is not its own
trying to achieve that
whose price is dearly paid.
Come, Poet of the unknown multitudes . . .
Resuscitate the dormant springs
where they lie hidden
deep in the heart of our humanity.

Deeply and passionately as he loved and felt for his own people, his love and interest were not confined to them. He brooded over the outcome of the war, then in its full savage fury, with Hitler's armies advancing in Russia, and worried over the fate of the innocent millions of all nations who had been dragged into the war as its victims, through no fault of their own. In particular, his sympathies went out to the Chinese and the Russians. He had hopes that the great social experiments of the latter would one day change the face of civilization all over the earth. Though he rejected much that he found crude in Marxian philosophy, he was greatly impressed by the spectacle of a civilization where the benefits of the highest education could be freely enjoyed by all its people. He wished the Russians well in the war and was depressed whenever he read in the papers of reverses on their front. Nor, despite his sympathies with the Allies, did he ever think of the Germans and the Japanese as the sole and unmitigated villains in the drama. The world—he had not tired of repeating—was caught in a trap of its own making, where religion, nationalism and all other 'isms' merely served to tighten its stranglehold, where the greedy merchant, the crafty priest and the wily politician exploited the heroism and sacrifice of the common people to serve their own ends.

To this anguish of watching the world in holocaust was added the almost constant physical agony of the ailment that had taken a turn for the worse and which the doctors were unable to control.

Even more agonizing than the pain was the sense of helplessness that he could not move, could not even sit up in bed without the help of his devoted nurses. Unable to write with his hand, he was obliged to dictate his poems, a process which he resented as a humiliation, as an intrusion on the privacy of his communion with his Muse. But there was no way. Poems overflowed[3] and he was obliged to utter them aloud for others to take down. One such poem, in Amiya Chakravarty's English rendering, is quoted in part as a specimen:[4]

> In this Great Universe
> the giant wheel of pain revolves;
> stars and planets split up;
> sparks of fiery dust, far-flung,
> scatter at terrific speed
> enveloping in network primordial
> the anguish of existence.
> In the armoury of pain
> spreading on the stretches of consciousness, aglow,
> clang the instruments of torture;
> bleeding wounds gape open.
> Small is man's body,
> how immense his strength of suffering!
> At the concourse of creation and chaos
> to what end does he hold up his cup of fiery drink
> in the weird festival of the gods
> drunk in their titanic power—O why
> filling his body of clay
> sweeps the red delirious tide of tears?

On 14 April 1941, which was the day of the Bengali New Year, his last public utterance, his testament of faith, was read at Santiniketan and published as *Sabhyatar Sankat* (Crisis in Civilization). In

---

[3] Despite his illness his literary output during the last six months of his life was amazing, not only considerable in quantity but of a new and rare richness of feeling and compactness of expression: three volumes of verse, *Janmadine*, referred to earlier, *Arogya* (Convalescence), *Sesh Lekha* (Last Words) which was published after his death, and one in prose, *Sabhyatar Sankat* (Crisis in Civilization).

[4] See *Poems*, Visva-Bharati, Calcutta.

this he traced the beginnings of his faith in modern civilization through his admiration of the humanistic tradition of English literature. He recalled how as a young student in London he had listened with rapt attention to the speeches of John Bright in the British Parliament. 'The large-hearted, radical liberalism of those speeches, overflowing all narrow national bounds, made so deep an impression on my mind that something of it lingers even today, even in these days of graceless disillusionment.' He described how this 'graceless disillusionment' had been almost forced on the Indian mind by the cynical disregard by the British rulers in India of the very values which were the pride of western civilization. 'The wheels of Fate will some day compel the British to give up their Indian Empire. But what kind of India will they leave behind, what stark misery? When the stream of their two centuries' administration runs dry at last, what a waste of mud and filth they will leave behind them!' Nevertheless, he refused to give up his faith in Man. 'As I look around I see the crumbling ruins of a proud civilization strewn like a vast heap of futility. And yet I shall not commit the grievous sin of losing faith in Man. I would rather look forward to the opening of a new chapter in his history after the cataclysm is over and the atmosphere rendered clean with the spirit of service and sacrifice.' He did not live to see the opening of this new chapter.

All his life he had lived by his faith in life, in humanity, in God. What else was there to live by? He was too sensitive not to feel suffering, whether his own or others', and too intelligent not to see through illusions.

One of his last poems has the boldness and austerity of a hymn from the *Rig-Veda*.

> The first day's Sun
> asked
> at the new manifestation of being—
> Who are you?
> No answer came.
> Year after year went by,
> the last Sun of the day
> the last question utters
> on the western seashore,

in the silent evening—
Who are you?
He gets no answer.[5]

In the midst of his suffering and his literary preoccupations, he
constantly thought of his beloved Santiniketan and its little school
for children. The school was his first love which he had rather
neglected when the glamorous Visva-Bharati came on the scene.
Now the old solicitude returned. 'Who is teaching Bengali in the
school these days?' he suddenly inquired. 'I hope someone who
loves literature and has a feeling for the language—and not a mere
erudite pundit. The children must catch the feeling of the sound
from the voice of the teacher.' He went on to recall how he used to
lose himself in joy when teaching little children. His voice was
thick as he added, 'But I can no longer teach them myself, nor
supervise.' Immediately he was annoyed with himself and murmured, 'I don't know how I have become so weak that I can hardly
talk without my voice betraying me.'

He saw to it that jars of lozenges or boxes of chocolates were
always kept in his room, at hand for little boys and girls who never
went to his room without coming out with something in their hand
or mouth. Not even pariah dogs were excluded from his affection.
One of them managed to make itself an honoured inmate of
Uttarayana[6] by the simple process of seeking shelter under his
reclining chair. Each morning it would come and obstinately stand
near him until the poet touched its head with his hand, when it
would sit down near his chair, moving to a farther corner if visitors
turned up. Nor did the poet fail to immortalize the dog in one of his
poems.

His sense of kindly and gentle humour never deserted him. His
nurses and attendants will treasure as their greatest reward the
witticisms and pleasantries he constantly exchanged with them. He
could not get over his amusement at being fed on Glaxo and would
refer to himself as a 'Glaxo baby'. As he could take nourishment in

[5] *Sesh Lekha.* Amiya Chakravarty's English rendering. See *Poems*, Visva-
Bharati, Calcutta.

[6] Name of the house in Santiniketan where he had once stayed and where he
again spent his last days.

very small quantities only, which would be gradually increased, he was greatly amused when he was told one day that the dose he was being given was the same as for a two-month-old baby. After that, each time Glaxo was served, he would inquire, 'How many months old am I today?'

The trees were his oldest love. As a little boy he had watched from a window the ancient banyan tree on the edge of the pond in the grounds of his family residence at Jorasanko; immobilized again in old age, he watched the graceful *shimool* tree outside his cottage in Santiniketan. During the summer drought he was much distressed at the fate of the trees in the asrama. The trees must be saved at all cost. 'Have you a *mahua* tree in your grounds?' he would suddenly inquire. 'If not, then you must plant one. When it grows, you will see how Santal women always gather under them.' He who was reluctant to taste the most carefully prepared delicacies would eagerly and excitedly, like a child, nibble at a wild *jambu* when a bunch of them was brought to him 'from my own tree at the back of Syamali!' He kept the bunch near his bed and would tempt others. 'Just try one and see how sweet my *jambus* are!'

And so the days passed. His fever rose higher each evening and the nights were less and less restful. The doctors decided that he must be removed to Calcutta for an operation. The decision upset him. 'Why can't I be allowed to die in peace? Haven't I lived enough?' When it was explained to him that modern surgery had made it easy to control this disease, he grudgingly submitted, murmuring, 'Perhaps I shall not see these trees again.'

On 25 July he was taken to Calcutta where the operation was performed on the morning of 30 July. In the early hours of the morning, before he was taken to the operation table, he dictated his last poem:

> Your creation's path you have covered
> with a varied net of wiles,
> Thou Guileful One.
> False belief's snare you have
> laid with skilful hands
> in simple lives.
> With this deceit have you left a mark

on Greatness;
for him kept no secret night . . .
He who has easefully borne your wile
gets from your hands
the unwasting right to peace.[7]

He did not have a chance to read what he had dictated or to revise the text. His condition steadily deteriorated after the operation and he gradually lost consciousness, never to recover it again. On 7 August at midday he breathed his last.[8]

He had earlier composed a song which he had desired should be sung at his death. It was and is still sung at each anniversary of his death.

> In front lies the ocean of peace,
> launch the boat, Helmsman,
> you will be the comrade ever . . .
> May the mortal bonds perish,
> may the vast universe take him in its arms,
> and may he know in his fearless heart
> the Great Unknown.

At last the restless pilgrim, 'athirst for the far-away', took his seat in the Golden Boat, with his Beloved whom he had sought in all the loves on this earth, at the helm, and set sail towards the Great Unknown which he had ever sought in the known.

With him, it seemed, died an age; an epoch which, despite the fact that India was in subjection to a foreign rule, will nevertheless be remembered as a golden age in Indian history, for it not only laid the foundations of India's freedom and of her future but gave to her and the world two of its greatest men. One of them did not live to see his country free, the other was murdered by an ungrateful countryman. But they cannot die whose deeds made them immortal.

[7] *Poems.* Visva-Bharati, Calcutta.

[8] It was an auspicious day in the Hindu calendar, the day of the full moon of *Sravana* (July-August), the month of the rainy season so well celebrated in his songs and poems. It was also a date of some coincidences of significance in his life: on this date a year ago the Oxford University had held a special Convocation in Santiniketan in his honour and on the same date nine years before his only grandson Nitu had died in Germany.

The Mahatma who described him as the greatest poet of the age wrote: 'There was hardly any public activity on which he has not left the impress of his powerful personality.' 'He was the greatest figure of the modern Indian Renaissance,' said Dr. S. Radhakrishnan. 'A poet of his qualities we have not had for some generations. He was in the grand line from Valmiki and Kalidasa.' Sarojini Naidu, the Indian poetess, wrote: 'By his genius, his beauty, his wisdom and wit, the charm and prestige of his gracious personality, he was in his lifetime a unique and fascinating figure of romance. Now that he has gone he will become an exquisite legend, a fairy tale for all time. But his song, however, will remain, generation after generation, as fresh as the first flowers of the springtime and as enchanting as the music of moonlit streams.' Jawaharlal Nehru who was in jail wrote to the present writer, then editor of the *Visva-Bharati Quarterly*, the following letter which is worth quoting in full, since it sums up the story of a great life more fittingly than any other words could:[9]

From
Jawaharlal Nehru,
District Jail,
Dehra Dun.

August 27, 1941.

To
Krishna Kripalani,
Santiniketan, Bengal.

My dear Krishna,

Just a month ago you wrote to me and soon after I received the Tagore Birthday Number of the Visva-Bharati Quarterly. I liked this Birthday Number very much and some of the pictures and articles were good.

How long ago it all seems! People must die some time or other and Gurudeva could not have lived much longer. And yet his death came as a grievous shock to me and the thought that I would never see his beautiful face and hear his gentle voice again oppressed me terribly. Ever since I came to prison this thought had haunted me. I wanted to see him once again so much. Not that I had anything special to say to him, and certainly

[9] The letter was published in the *Visva-Bharati Quarterly*, Vol. VII, Part III, New Series.

I had no desire to trouble him in any way. Perhaps the premonition that I was not fated to see him again itself added to this yearning.

However, all that is over and, instead of sorrow, let us rather congratulate ourselves that we were privileged to come in contact with this great and magnificent person. Perhaps it is as well that he died when he was still pouring out song and poem and poetry—what amazing creative vitality he had! I would have hated to see him fade away gradually. He died, as he should, in the fullness of his glory.

I have met many big people in various parts of the world. But I have no doubt in my mind that the two biggest I have had the privilege of meeting have been Gandhi and Tagore. I think they have been the two outstanding personalities in the world during the last quarter of a century. As time goes by, I am sure this will be recognized, when all the generals and field marshals and dictators and shouting politicians are long dead and largely forgotten.

It amazes me that India in spite of her present condition (or is it because of it?) should produce these two mighty men in the course of one generation. And that also convinces me of the deep vitality of India and I am filled with hope, and the petty troubles and conflicts of the day seem very trivial and unimportant before this astonishing fact—the continuity of the idea that is India from long ages past to the present day. China affects me in the same way. India and China; how can they perish?

There is another aspect which continually surprises me. Both Gurudeva and Gandhiji took much from the West and from other countries, especially Gurudeva. Neither was narrowly national. Their message was for the world. And yet both were one hundred per cent India's children, and the inheritors, representatives and expositors of her age-long culture. How intensely Indian both have been, in spite of all their wide knowledge and culture! The surprising thing is that both of these men with so much in common and drawing inspiration from the same wells of wisdom and thought and culture, should differ from each other so greatly! No two persons could probably differ so much as Gandhi and Tagore!

Again I think of the richness of India's age-long cultural genius which can throw up in the same generation two such master-types, typical of her in every way, yet representing different aspects of her many-sided personality.

My love to you and Nandita,

Yours affectionately,

Jawaharlal Nehru.

2 A

BIBLIOGRAPHY

A list of works by Rabindranath Tagore published in English

Gitanjali (Song Offerings). London, The India Society, 1912. Poems. (Prose translations by the author of a selection of poems from *Gitanjali, Naivedya, Kheya, Gitimalya,* etc.)

Glimpses of Bengal Life. Madras, G. A. Natesan, 1913. Stories. (Translated by Rajani Ranjan Sen.)

The Gardener. London, Macmillan & Co., [October] 1913. Poems. (Prose translations by the author of a selection of poems from *Kshanika, Kalpana, Sonar Tari,* etc.)

Sadhana. London, Macmillan & Co., [October] 1913. Essays and lectures, delivered in the United States.

The Crescent Moon. London, Macmillan & Co., 1913. Child-poems. (Translations by the author of poems mostly from *Sisu.*)

Chitra. London. The India Society, 1913. Drama. (A translation by the author of *Chitrangada.*)

The King of the Dark Chamber. London, Macmillan & Co., 1914. Drama. (A translation by K. C. Sen of *Raja.* The translation is erroneously attributed to the author in the title-page.)

One Hundred Poems of Kabir. London, The India Society, 1914. (Translated by Rabindranath Tagore.)

The Post Office, Dublin, The Cuala Press, [July] 1914. Drama. (A translation by Devabrata Mukhopadhyaya of *Dak Ghar.*)

Fruit-Gathering. London, Macmillan & Co., October 1916. Poems. (Translations of a selection of poems from *Gitimalya, Gitali, Balaka,* etc. *Fruit-Gathering* was issued together with *Gitanjali* under the title *Gitanjali and Fruit-Gathering* by Macmillan, New York, in September 1918, with illustrations by Nandalal Bose, Surendranath Kar, Abanindranath Tagore and Nabendranath Tagore.)

The Hungry Stones and Other Stories. London, Macmillan & Co., 1916. Stories.

Stray Birds. New York, Macmillan, 1916. Epigrams.

My Reminiscences. London, Macmillan & Co., 1917. Autobiography. (A translation of *Jivansmriti* by Surendranath Tagore.)

Sacrifice and Other Plays. London, Macmillan & Co., 1917.

The Cycle of Spring. London, Macmillan & Co., 1917. Drama. (A translation of *Phalguni*.)

Nationalism. London, Macmillan & Co., 1917. (Lectures delivered in Japan and the United States, followed by 'The Sunset of the Century', a poem adapted from some poems of *Naivedya*.)

Personality. London, Macmillan & Co., 1917. Lectures delivered in the United States.

Lover's Gift and Crossing. London, Macmillan & Co., 1918. Poems and Songs. (Translations of a selection of poems and songs from *Balaka, Kshanika, Kheya*, etc.)

Mashi and Other Stories. London, Macmillan & Co., 1918. Stories.

Stories from Tagore. Calcutta, Macmillan & Co., 1918 (?).

The Parrot's Training. Calcutta, Thacker Spink, 1918. Allegorical Satire. (A translation of *Tota-Kahini, Lipika*, by the author. A new edition of the book issued under the title *The Parrot's Training and Other Stories*, Visva-Bharati, October 1944, includes some other satires and fantasies.)

The Home and the World. London, Macmillan & Co., 1919. Novel. (A translation by Surendranath Tagore of *Ghare Baire*.)

The Fugitive. Santiniketan, Santiniketan Press, 1919 (?). Poems. (A selection of poems from various books. This is not identical with *The Fugitive*, 1921, and was for private circulation.)

Greater India. Madras, S. Ganesan, 1921. Essays.

The Wreck. London, Macmillan & Co., 1921. Novel. (A translation of *Nauka-Dubi*.)

Glimpses of Bengal. London, Macmillan & Co., 1921. Letters. (Translation by Surendranath Tagore of a selection from *Chhinnapatra*.)

The Fugitive. London, Macmillan & Co., 1921. Poems and Songs. (Translations of poems and songs from *Manasi, Sonar Tari, Gitimalya*, etc., and sketches from *Lipika*. It also includes translations of several dramatic pieces.)

Thought Relics. New York, Macmillan, March 1921. (Translation by the author of select prose pieces from his Bengali writings. A new and enlarged edition of the book, edited by C. F. Andrews, was published by Macmillan & Co., London, in 1929, under the title *Thoughts from Tagore*.)

Creative Unity. London, Macmillan & Co., 1922. Essays and Lectures.

Poems from Tagore. Calcutta, Macmillan & Co., 1922 (?). An anthology with an introduction by C. F. Andrews.

Letters from Abroad. Madras, S. Ganesan, 1924. Letters. (Letters to C. F. Andrews, May 1920–July 1921.)

The Visvabharati. By Rabindranath and C. F. Andrews. Madras, Natesan, April 1923. Essays.

Gora. London, Macmillan & Co., 1924. Novel. (A translation by W. W. Pearson of *Gora*.)

The Curse at Farewell. London, G. Harrap, 1924. Drama. (A translation by Edward Thompson of *Viday-Abhisap*.)

The Augustan Books of Modern Poetry: Rabindranath Tagore. London, Ernest Benn, 1925. (Translation by Edward Thompson of 21 poems and 12 epigrams.)

Talks in China. Calcutta, February, 1925. Lectures.

Red Oleanders. London, Macmillan & Co., 1925. Drama. (A translation of *Rakta-Karabi*.)

Broken Ties and Other Stories. London, Macmillan & Co., 1925.

Lectures and Addresses. London, Macmillan & Co., 1928. (Compiled by Anthony X. Soares.)

Fireflies. New York, Macmillan, 1928. Epigrams.

Letters to a Friend. London, Allen & Unwin, 1928. (Letters to C. F. Andrews, 1913–22).

The Tagore Birthday Book. London, Macmillan & Co., 1928. (Edited by C. F. Andrews.)

Fifteen Poems of Rabindranath Tagore. Bombay, K. C. Sen [1928]. (Translations, in verse, by Kshitischandra Sen, of 15 poems from *Balaka*. For private circulation.)

Sheaves. Allahabad, Indian Press, 1929. Poems and Songs. (Selected and translated by Nagendranath Gupta.)

The Child. London, Allen & Unwin, 1931. Poem. (This long poem was originally written in English. The Bengali version, *Sisutirtha*, *Punascha*, was written later.)

The Religion of Man. London, Allen & Unwin, 1931. Lectures. (The Appendices include a conversation between Tagore and Einstein on the 'Nature of Reality'.)

The Golden Boat. London, Allen & Unwin, 1932. (Contains translations by Bhabani Bhattacharya of pieces from *Lipika*, and of a selection of poems.)

Mahatmaji and the Depressed Humanity. Calcutta, Visva-Bharati, December, 1932. Lectures.

East and West. Paris, International Institute of Intellectual Co-operation, League of Nations, 1935. Two open letters exchanged between Gilbert Murray and Rabindranath Tagore.

Collected Poems and Plays of Rabindranath Tagore. London, Macmillan & Co., 1936.

Man. Waltair, Andhra University, 1937. Lectures delivered at the Andhra University.

My Boyhood Days. Santiniketan, Visva-Bharati, 1940. Autobiography. (A translation by Marjorie Sykes of *Chhelebela*.)

Crisis in Civilisation. Santiniketan, Visva-Bharati, 1941. (A translation of *Sabhyatar Sankat*, an Address delivered on completing his eighty years. Translated by Kshitis Roy and revised by Krishna Kripalani and the author.)

Poems. Calcutta, Visva-Bharati, 1942. (Translations are by the author, with the exception of the last nine poems, which are translated by Amiya Chakravarty. The poems cover all major divisions in the poet's writings, 1886–1941. References to the original Bengali composition are given in Notes at the end. Edited by Krishna Kripalani in collaboration with Amiya Chakravarty, Nirmalchandra Chattopadhyaya, and Pulinbihari Sen.)

Two Sisters. Calcutta, Visva-Bharati. 1945. Novel. (A translation by Krishna Kripalani of *Dui Bon*.)

Farewell, My Friend. London. The New India Publishing Company [1946]. Novel. (A translation of *Sesher Kavita* by Krishna Kripalani. A new edition of the book, issued under the title *Farewell My Friend and The Garden*, Bombay, Jaico Publishing House, August

1956, includes a translation of the novel *Malancha* (The Garden), also by Krishna Kripalani.)

Three Plays. Bombay, Oxford University Press, 1950. (*Muktadhara, Natir Puja*, and *Chandalika*. Translated by Marjorie Sykes.)

Four Chapters. Calcutta, Visva-Bharati, September 1950. Novel. (A translation by Surendranath Tagore of *Char Adhyaya*.)

A Tagore Testament. London, Meridian Books, 1953. Autobiographical Essays. (Translations by Indu Dutt of essays included in *Atmaparichay*, together with some poems selected by the translator to introduce the essays.)

A Flight of Swans. London, John Murray, 1955. Poems. (Translation by Aurobindo Bose of poems from *Balaka* and one poem from *Gitanjali*.)

Syamali. Calcutta, Visva-Bharati, September 1955. Poems. (A translation of *Syamali*. Translations are by Sheila Chatterji, with the exception of 'The Eternal March', translated by the author.)

The Herald of Spring. London, John Murray, 1957. Poems. (Translations by Aurobindo Bose of poems from *Mahua*.)

Our Universe. London, Meridian Books, 1958. A Science Primer. (A translation by Indu Dutt of *Visva-Parichaya*, with some poems included by the translator to introduce the chapters.)

Binodini. New Delhi, Sahitya Akademi, March 1959. Novel. (A translation by Krishna Kripalani of *Chokher Bali*.)

The Runaway and Other Stories. Calcutta, Visva-Bharati, 1959.

Wings of Death. London, John Murray, 1960. Poems (Translations by Aurobindo Bose of poems from *Prantik, Rogasajyay, Arogya* and *Sesh Lekha*.)

Poems from Puravi. Santiniketan, Uma Roy, 8 May 1960. (Translations by Kshitis Roy of six poems from *Puravi* and a poem from *Sesh Lekha*. For private circulation.)

Letters from Russia. Calcutta, Visva-Bharati, September 1960. (A translation by Sasadhar Sinha of *Rashiar Chithi*.)

A Tagore Reader. New York, Macmillan, 1961. (An anthology, edited by Amiya Chakravarty, published in observance of the centennial of Tagore's birthday.)

A Visit to Japan. New York, East West Institute. May 1961. Travel. (A translation by Shakuntala Rao Sastri of *Japan-Yatri*.)

Devouring Love. New York, East West Institute, May 1961. Drama. (A translation by Shakuntala Rao Sastri of *Raja O Rani.*)

Towards Universal Man. Bombay, Asia Publishing House, 7 May 1969. Essays. (A selection of essays on social, economic, political and educational topics to indicate Tagore's contributions in those fields, prepared by the Tagore Commemorative Volume Society, New Delhi, on the occasion of the centenary of Tagore's birth. Translated by various writers and edited by Bhabani Bhattacharya, with annotations by Kshitis Roy. Introduction by Humayun Kabir.)

Rabindranath Tagore, Pioneer in Education. London, John Murray, 1961. Essays and exchanges between Rabindranath Tagore and L. K. Elmhirst.

INDEX